MathTensor™

A
System
for Doing
Tensor Analysis
by
Computer

Leonard Parker

University of Wisconsin at Milwaukee
and MathSolutions, Inc.

Steven M. Christensen

University of North Carolina at Chapel Hill
and MathSolutions, Inc.

ADDISON-WESLEY PUBLISHING COMPANY

Reading, Massachusetts • Menlo Park, California • New York
Don Mills, Ontario • Wokingham, England • Amsterdam • Bonn
Sydney • Singapore • Tokyo • Madrid • San Juan • Milan • Paris

Many of the designations used by the manufacturers and sellers to distinguish their products are claimed as trademarks. Where those designations appear in this book, and Addison-Wesley was aware of a trademark claim, the designations have been printed in initial caps or all caps.

The procedures and applications presented in this book have been included for their instructional value. They have been tested with care but are not guaranteed for any particular purpose. The publisher does not offer any warranties or representations, nor does it accept any liabilities with respect to the programs or applications.

Library of Congress Cataloging-in-Publication Data

Parker, Leonard.
    MathTensor : a system for doing tensor analysis by computer / Leonard Parker, Steven M. Christensen.
        p.   cm
    Includes bibliographical references and index.
    ISBN 0-201-56990-6
    1. MathTensor. 2. Calculus of tensors—Data processing.
    I. Christensen, Steven M.   II. Title.
    QA433.P37   1994
    515' .63—dc20   93–51092
                                                                        CIP

Reproduced by Addison-Wesley Publishing Company, Inc. from camera-ready copy supplied by the authors.

1 2 3 4 5 6 7 8 9 10–MA–97969594

Preface

This book should be of interest to practitioners, researchers, and students in the sciences, engineering, and mathematics who wish to make efficient and accurate use of tensors and differential forms in solving problems. *MathTensor* is a computer program that works with *Mathematica* by extending its capabilities to include tensor analysis and differential forms. These pages are intended to serve, first of all, as a comprehensive introduction to all aspects of *MathTensor*. In addition, they contain pedagogical introductions to tensors and differential forms. The mathematical techniques for dealing with tensors have been developed by mathematicians and scientists over many years. Tensors are applied, among other things, to describe electromagnetic fields, energy and momentum, elementary particles, gravitational fields and spacetime, elastic stresses and strains in deformed bodies, fluid dynamics, the geometry of curved surfaces and spaces, and the curvature of the cornea of the eye. These applications range from physics, elasticity, and differential geometry to aerodynamics, meteorology, and medicine. Whether you are doing extensive tensor analysis or are only starting to learn about tensors and differential forms, you will find this book worth reading. Pedagogical introductions to tensors and differential forms make this book an excellent learning tool, suitable for self-study or as a textbook in a computer-based college or introductory graduate level course.

Following a brief chapter of short examples showing what you can do with *MathTensor*, the book is divided into three main parts. The first part begins with a chapter giving a pedagogical introduction to tensors. This introduction to tensors is followed by two comprehensive chapters discussing the *MathTensor* commands for dealing with tensors carrying symbolic or concrete indices. Included are short examples from physics, engineering, and mathematics.

The second part consists of two chapters on differential forms. The first chapter introduces differential forms and describes and illustrates the various differential form operations in *MathTensor*. The second chapter shows examples of how you may work with differential forms (as well as tensor-valued differential forms) in *MathTensor*. The examples include calculations involving explicit functions in a coordinate basis, as well as the Cartan structure equations with torsion in an arbitrary basis.

The third part gives longer examples and applications of *MathTensor*, including chapters on electromagnetism and special relativity, nonlinear elasticity in engineering mechanics, and general relativity, including variational methods. You are not expected to know all these areas, but you will nevertheless find in these chapters helpful techniques for using *MathTensor*. There is also an Appendix summarizing the usage of the various *MathTensor* commands and objects and a detailed index.

Chapter 1 through Chapter 8, except for Section 3.6, were written by Leonard Parker. Chapter 9 and Section 3.6 were written by Steven M. Christensen.

Reading this book will benefit anyone who is using or planning to use techniques of tensor analysis and differential forms. Even if you do not yet use *Mathematica* or *MathTensor*, you will gain an understanding of how they can be of help to you. The intended audience includes not only researchers and practitioners, but also students. *MathTensor* can be a great help in learning about tensors and subjects involving tensors. If you are already using *Mathematica*, this book will introduce you to new and powerful methods by means of which you can explore new areas. If you are using or expecting to use *MathTensor*, this book is essential reading.

Depending on your background, you will want to study some chapters more thoroughly than others. All readers will want to read the chapters in Part A because they serve as an introduction to tensor analysis and to *MathTensor*. If you are already familiar with tensors, you can skim through the introduction to tensors, but you should carefully read the chapter on how to use *MathTensor*.

Part B should be read if you wish to learn about or use differential forms. Differential forms are elegant objects related to antisymmetric tensors. Reading Part B of this book in conjunction with one of the many textbooks on differential forms is an effective way to teach yourself the subject. *MathTensor* will also help you carry out complicated differential form computations in your research and development work.

The chapters of Part C are independent of one another. You do not have to be a specialist in the subject of each chapter to find useful techniques that you may be able to apply to your own problems. Thus if you have the time you should look through all chapters of Part C. Engineers should certainly read the chapter on applications of *MathTensor* to nonlinear elasticity in engineering mechanics. This chapter includes an introduction to nonlinear elasticity, as well as detailed examples. The chapter on electromagnetism and special relativity should be read by anyone interested in this fundamental subject, which forms the basis for much of twentieth-century physics. The chapter on general relativity is worth reading if you are interested in gravitation or other areas involving the curvature of surfaces or spaces. The part of this chapter that uses variational techniques will be of interest to many physicists and mathematicians. Most of the basic equations of physics can be obtained through variation of a suitable integral called the action. Such variational methods occur in optics, gravitation, mechanics, electromagnetism, and many other areas.

The convention for numbering equations is illustrated by the following example.

Equation 10 of Chapter 2 is referenced as Eq. (10) in Chapter 2 and as Eq. (2.10) in other chapters.

The definitive reference on *Mathematica* is Stephen Wolfram, *Mathematica, A System for Doing Mathematica by Computer* (Addison-Wesley, 1991). You can find discussions of *MathTensor* and some of its applications in Richard Crandall, *Mathematica for the Sciences* (Addison-Wesley, 1991), and Thomas B. Bahder, *Mathematica for Scientists and Engineers* (Addison-Wesley, 1994).

MathTensor is in use at leading universities, governmental laboratories, research institutes, and corporations both here and abroad. *MathTensor* will run on any microcomputer, workstation, server, or mainframe that can run *Mathematica*. You can obtain more information about *MathTensor*, or order it, by contacting MathSolutions, Inc., 3049 N. Lake Drive, Milwaukee, WI 53211, USA, or MathSolutions, Inc., P.O. Box 16175, Chapel Hill, NC 27516, USA
Telephone numbers: (414) 964-6284 and (919) 967-9853
Fax numbers: (414) 964-6284 and (919) 967-9853
Electronic mail address: mathtensor@wri.com
An information request form is included on the last page of this volume.

The authors thank Stephen Wolfram, Roman Maeder, Kevin McIsaac, Paul Abbott, Jamie Petersen, Tom Sherlock, Ben Friedman, Joe Kaiping, Maury Kendell, and the entire staff of Wolfram Research, Inc., for their extremely valuable assistance over the past several years.

We are also grateful to Sun Microsystems for the donation of three workstations early in this project.

We thank numerous colleagues for helpful suggestions. These include Stephen Fulling, David Boulware, Ben Chow, Gautam Dasgupta, Timothy Gallivan, David Hobill, Richard Isaacson, Yefim Ivshin, Thomas Pence, Ulrich Jentschura, and all of the beta testers and users from many institutions.

Leonard Parker and Steven M. Christensen

Contents

PART B.   DIFFERENTIAL FORMS IN *MATHTENSOR*   201

PART C.   APPLICATIONS OF *MATHTENSOR*   243

Chapter 1
A Brief Look at *MathTensor*

The examples here are intended to give you an impression of how *MathTensor* works and what you can do with it. These examples are brief. If you do not know much about tensors, you may read Chapter 2, which is an introduction to tensor analysis, and then return to this part. Detailed instructions on using *MathTensor* start in Chapter 3.

■ 1.1 Creating Tensors with Symmetries

Many tensors of interest have special symmetries under interchange of indices.

This defines a symmetric second-rank tensor s. You can also define tensors of higher rank with more complicated symmetry properties.

```
In[1]:= DefineTensor[s,{{2,1},1}]
 PermWeight::sym: Symmetries of s assigned
 PermWeight::def: Object s defined
```

The indices are reordered in accordance with the symmetry. The l in la you type indicates a lower or covariant index, as you can see in the output.

```
In[2]:= s[la,lb] + s[lb,la]
Out[2]= 2 s
           ab
```

The u in ua indicates an upper or contravariant index. The summation convention is understood for a repeated index.

```
In[3]:= s[la,ua]
             a
Out[3]= s
             a
```

MathTensor knows that the Maxwell electromagnetic field tensor is antisymmetric. It also knows the properties of the Riemann curvature tensor, as well as of other tensors.

```
In[4]:=  {MaxwellF[lb,la], RiemannR[uc,ud,lb,la]}
                                    cd
Out[4]= {-F  ,  -R   }
            ab      ab
```

1

■ 1.2 Simplification

In many computations involving tensors, expressions having many terms arise. They can often be simplified by making use of the special symmetries of the tensors involved. This is generally a tedious process, prone to error when done by hand.

The Ricci tensor is symmetric. This expression can be simplified further.

$In[1]:=$ `RicciR[la,uc] RicciR[lc,lb] +`
`        RicciR[le,la] RicciR[lb,ue]`

$Out[1]= R_a{}^c R_{bc} + R_{ae} R_b{}^e$

One of the simplification functions in *MathTensor* is `Tsimplify`.

$In[2]:=$ `Tsimplify[%]`

$Out[2]= 2 R_a{}^c R_{bc}$

`MaxwellF` is antisymmetric.

$In[3]:=$ `Expand[(RicciR[la,lb] + MaxwellF[la,lb])*`
`        (RicciR[ua,ub] + MaxwellF[ua,ub])]`

$Out[3]= F_{ab} F^{ab} + F^{ab} R_{ab} + F_{ab} R^{ab} + R_{ab} R^{ab}$

MathTensor carries out the simplification.

$In[4]:=$ `Tsimplify[%]`

$Out[4]= F_{ab} F^{ab} + R_{ab} R^{ab}$

Here is a somewhat more advanced example.

$In[5]:=$ `RiemannR[la,lb,ld,le] RicciR[ua,ue] +`
`        RiemannR[lb,le,lc,ld] RicciR[ue,uc]`

$Out[5]= R^{ae}{}_{abde} R + R^{ce} R_{becd}$

The symmetries of the Riemann tensor reveal that the two terms are equal.

$In[6]:=$ `Tsimplify[%]`

$Out[6]= 2 R^{ae} R_{abde}$

■ 1.3 Derivatives

Here is the second covariant derivative of the electromagnetic field tensor, summed over all indices. The semicolon denotes the covariant derivative in the output line.

$In[1]:=$ CD[MaxwellF[ua,ub],la,lb]

$Out[1]=$ $F^{ab}{}_{;ab}$

Applying CDtoOD twice replaces both covariant derivatives by ordinary partial derivatives, denoted by commas, and affine connections, denoted by G in the output.

$In[2]:=$ CDtoOD[CDtoOD[%]]

$Out[2]=$ $-(G^{p}{}_{pq}\,G^{r}{}_{rs}\,F^{qs}) - G^{p}{}_{pq}\,G^{q}{}_{rs}\,F^{rs} + F^{pq}\,G^{r}{}_{pq,r} +$

$>$ $F^{pq}\,G^{r}{}_{pr,q} - G^{p}{}_{qr}\,F^{qr}{}_{,p} + F^{pq}{}_{,pq}$

MathTensor simplifies this using the various symmetry properties of the objects involved. *MathTensor* has similar commands for dealing with Lie derivatives.

$In[3]:=$ Tsimplify[%]

$Out[3]=$ $F^{pq}\,G^{r}{}_{pr,q}$

If the affine connection depends on a metric, then further simplification is possible.

$In[4]:=$ AffineToMetric[%]

$Out[4]=$ $\dfrac{F^{pq}\,g_{rs,p}\,g^{rs}{}_{,q}}{2} - \dfrac{F^{pq}\,g^{rs}\,g_{pr,qs}}{2} +$

$>$ $\dfrac{F^{pq}\,g^{rs}\,g_{ps,qr}}{2} + \dfrac{F^{pq}\,g^{rs}\,g_{rs,pq}}{2}$

This vanishes as a result of the symmetries.

$In[5]:=$ Tsimplify[%]

$Out[5]=$ 0

■ 1.4 Differential Forms

This defines a 2-form f.

```
In[1]:= DefineForm[f,2]
PermWeight::sym: Symmetries of f assigned
PermWeight::def: Object f defined
```

Let the dimension of the space be 4.

```
In[2]:= Dimension = 4;
```

Here is the exterior product of f.

```
In[3]:= xpf = XP[f,f]
Out[3]= f ∧ f
```

You can take its components using FtoC ("form to components"). You specify in the list the indices to use.

```
In[4]:= FtoC[%, {1a,1b,1c,1d}]
Out[4]= 2 f   f   - 2 f   f   + 2 f   f
           ad bc        ac bd        ab cd
```

The exterior derivative XD of $f \wedge f$ is 0 because it is a 5-form in 4 dimensions.

```
In[5]:= XD[xpf]
Out[5]= 0
```

Here is the exterior derivative XD of f.

```
In[6]:= XD[f]
Out[6]= df
```

If f were the electromagnetic field, then one of Maxwell's equations states that this is 0.

```
In[7]:= FtoC[%, {1a,1b,1c}]
Out[7]= f     - f     + f
         ab;c    ac;b    bc;a
```

Here is the codifferential of f.

```
In[8]:= CoXD[f]
Out[8]= delta(f)
```

The other Maxwell equation states that this is proportional to the current-density 4-vector. You can do much more with differential forms in *MathTensor*.

```
In[9]:= FtoC[%, {1a}]
              p
Out[9]= -f
           pa;
```

■ 1.5 Calculating Curvature

Here is the line element of a curved 3-dimensional space:

$$ds^2 = b^2[(1 - r^2)^{-1}dr^2 + r^2 d\theta^2 + r^2 sin(\theta)^2 d\phi^2].$$

You can put the components of this metric into a file; let us call it `metricIn.m`. You can then use a *MathTensor* function called `Components` to calculate the curvature tensors of this space. You must start a new *Mathematica* session and then load the *MathTensor* file `Components.m`.

`Components.m` contains the definition of the function `Components`.

```
In[1]:= << Components.m

=============================================================
MathTensor (TM) 2.2 (UNIX (R)) (January 6, 1994)
            Components Package
by Leonard Parker and Steven M. Christensen
Copyright (c) 1991-1994 MathSolutions, Inc.
Runs with Mathematica (R) Versions 1.2 and 2.X.
Licensed to machine gravity.
=============================================================
```

This step calculates the curvature tensors using the input file you prepare, `metricIn.m`, and puts the results in a file, `metricOut.m`, which you can load into a later *MathTensor* session, as well as a file, `metricOut.out`, which you can edit, read, and print.

```
In[2]:= Components["metricIn.m", "metricOut.m",
"metricOut.out"]
```

```
The following tensors have been calculated and stored

in the file metricOut.m in InputForm and

in the file metricOut.out in OutputForm:

Metricg
MatrixMetricgLower
MatrixMetricgUpper
Detg
AffineG[ua,lb,lc]
RicciR[la,lb]
ScalarR

RiemannR[la,lb,lc,ld]

WeylC[la,lb,lc,ld]

You can edit metricOut.out

>     to print a record of the results.
```

Here are the nonzero covariant components of the metric tensor. Negative integers represent covariant indices and positive integers contravariant indices.

```
In[3]:= Table[Metricg[-i,-i],{i,3}]
```

$$Out[3] = \{\frac{b^2}{1 - r^2}, b^2 r^2, b^2 r^2 Sin[theta]^2\}$$

Notice that the nonzero components of the Ricci tensor are proportional to those of the metric tensor. This space is highly symmetric.

```
In[4]:= Simplify[Table[RicciR[-i,-i],{i,3}] ]

             2
Out[4]= {---------, 2 r , 2 r  Sin[theta] }
              2
          1 - r
```

Here are some mixed components of the Riemann tensor.

```
In[5]:= Simplify[Table[RiemannR[-i,3,-i,3],{i,2}] ]

            Csc[theta]      Csc[theta]
Out[5]= {----------------, ------------}
          2  2        2         2
          b  r  (1 - r )        b
```

The scalar curvature is independent of the coordinates. This is a space of constant positive curvature: a 3-dimensional sphere. Its radius is b.

```
In[6]:= ScalarR

          6
Out[6]= ---
          2
         b
```

■ 1.6 Calculating Invariants

The scalar curvature R is an invariant because it does not change value under coordinate transformations. You can calculate other invariants of this space, such as $R_{ab}R^{ab}$, $R_{abcd}R^{abcd}$, and $R_{ac}R_{bd}R^{abcd}$. First you Quit and then start a new *Mathematica* and *MathTensor* session.

Then load the file metricOut.m, which you saved in the previous *Mathematica* session with Components.

```
In[1]:= << metricOut.m

 MetricgFlag has been turned off.
```

These sums over repeated indices are carried out using the values of the components that were previously calculated.

```
In[2]:= MakeSum[RicciR[la,lb] RicciR[ua,ub] ]

                    2    2
                   2    2 r
                2 (-- - ----)
                    4    4          2    2
          4      b    b        4 (r  - r  Cos[2 theta])
Out[2]= --- - ------------- - -------------------------
         4             2          4  2
        b          -1 + r       b  r  (-1 + Cos[2 theta])
```

This simplifies to a single term.

```
In[3]:= Simplify[%]

         12
Out[3]= ---
         4
        b
```

This shows that $R_{abcd}R^{abcd}$ has the same value as $R_{ab}R^{ab}$ for this spherical space.

```
In[4]:= Simplify[MakeSum[RiemannR[la,lb,lc,ld]
RiemannR[ua,ub,uc,ud] ] ]

Out[4]= 12
        --
         4
        b
```

This cubic invariant $R_{ac}R_{bd}R^{abcd}$ gives a result proportional to b^{-6}. The invariants of this maximally symmetric space are all proportional to a power of the radius b of the space.

```
In[5]:= Simplify[MakeSum[RicciR[la,lc]*
RicciR[lb,ld] RiemannR[ua,ub,uc,ud] ] ]

Out[5]= 24
        --
         6
        b
```

■ 1.7 Multiple Types of Indices

Regular indices in *MathTensor* are typed in as la,lb,...,lo. The command AddIndexTypes adds three more types of indices to *MathTensor*.

```
In[1]:= AddIndexTypes
```

Type-a indices begin with a, as in ala,alb, and appear in the output lines with a single prime. Type-b indices appear with two primes and type-c with three primes. The l means "lower" so that the index appears as a subscript.

```
In[2]:= {ld, ald, bld, cld}
Out[2]= {  ,   ,    ,     }
         d  d'  d''  d'''
```

This defines two vectors u and v.

```
In[3]:= DefineTensor[{u,v},{{1},1}]
PermWeight::def: Object u defined
PermWeight::def: Object v defined
```

Here is the scalar or dot product of u and v. Suppose regular indices, like la, range from 1 to 3, and type-a indices, like ala, range from 1 to 2, as on a surface.

```
In[4]:= dotProduct = u[la] v[ua]
                        a
Out[4]= u  v
         a
```

MakeSumRange here specifies the explicit ranges of the summation indices, here la and ua in the dot product. This is a simple illustration of dealing with a subspace. More complicated applications of multiple index types occur in Kaluza-Klein and gauge theories.

```
In[5]:= MakeSumRange[dotProduct, {la,ala,-3}]
           3       a'
Out[5]= u  v  + u   v
         3       a'
```

This defines a tensor rot[la,lb] with no symmetries.

```
In[6]:= DefineTensor[rot,{{1,2},1}]
PermWeight::def: Object rot defined
```

This expression is summed on index *b*. Suppose again that regular indices like 1b and ub range from 1 to 3, and type-a indices range from 1 to 2.

```
In[7]:= expr = rot[la,ub] rot[lc,lb]
```

$$Out[7]= rot_a{}^b\ rot_{cb}$$

This separates the terms in the sum with index 3. The list 1b,alb,-3 tells *MathTensor* to sum the covariant index 1b over the values alb and −3 and the paired dummy index ub over the corresponding contravariant values. The index −3 is a concrete covariant index, and 3 is the corresponding contravariant index.

```
In[8]:= MakeSumRange[expr,{lb,alb,-3}]
```

$$Out[8]= rot_a{}^3\ rot_{c3} + rot_a{}^{b'}\ rot_{cb'}$$

■ 1.8 Rules with Dummy Indices

Define a tensor "rot[la,lb]" with no symmetries.

```
In[1]:= DefineTensor[rot,{{1,2},1}]
PermWeight::def: Object rot defined
```

This sets up a rule that triggers when the patterns b_ and d_ match a pair of dummy indices. Kdelta is the Kronecker delta, which is 1 if the indices agree and 0 otherwise.

```
In[2]:= rotRule1 :=
rot[a_,b_] rot[c_,d_]/;PairQ[b,d] :>
  Kdelta[a,c]
```

Apply the rule to this.

```
In[3]:= rot[la,uc] rot[lb,lc]
```

$$Out[3]= rot_a{}^c\ rot_{bc}$$

If you wanted to take account of all possible positions of dummy indices, you would write several additional similar rules.

```
In[4]:= % /. rotRule1
Out[4]= Kdelta_{ab}
```

When dummy indices appear on the right-hand side of a rule, you use the *MathTensor* function RuleUnique to construct the rule. This creates a rule, called sRule, which replaces s by rot[la,ua].

```
In[5]:= RuleUnique[sRule, s, rot[la,ua] ]
```

When you apply sRule using the *MathTensor* command ApplyRules, notice that a new pair of dummy indices is created for each appearance of s.

```
In[6]:= ApplyRules[s^3, sRule]
```

$$Out[6]= rot_p{}^p\ rot_q{}^q\ rot_r{}^r$$

■ 1.9 Coordinate Transformations

In the theory of nonlinear elasticity, the simple shear of a rectangular solid can be described by giving the metric tensor of a body-fixed set of axes. Before deformation, the body-fixed axes are rectangular; but after deformation, they are deformed with the solid into an oblique system of axes.

```
In[1]:= Dimension = 3
Out[1]= 3
```

You can find the metric tensor `ga[1a,1b]` in the oblique coordinate system by transforming the metric tensor `Kdelta[1a,1b]` of the initial rectangular coordinate system to oblique coordinates. Here, `{x,y,z}` are the oblique coordinates of a point in the body, and `Kdelta[1a,1b]` is the Kronecker delta, δ_{ab}, which is 1 if $a = b$ and 0 otherwise.

```
In[2]:= coords = {x,y,z}
Out[2]= {x, y, z}
```

The rectangular coordinates, x', y', z', of the same point in the body are related to the oblique coordinates by $x' = x + Ky$, $y' = y$, $z' = z$, where K is a constant. The list `trans` consists of the right-hand sides of these equations.

```
In[3]:= trans = {x + K y, y, z}
Out[3]= {x + K y, y, z}
```

This defines the symmetric metric tensor `ga[1a,1b]`, the components of which you wish to calculate.

```
In[4]:= DefineTensor[ga,{{2,1},1}]
   PermWeight::sym: Symmetries of ga assigned
   PermWeight::def: Object ga defined
```

The *MathTensor* function `Ttransform` calculates the metric `ga[1a,1b]` in oblique coordinates in terms of the known components `Kdelta[1a,1b]` of the metric in rectangular coordinates.

```
In[5]:= Ttransform[ga,Kdelta[1a,1b],coords,trans,-1]
   Components assigned to ga
```

These are the components of the metric in the body-fixed oblique axes. These components characterize the strain.

```
In[6]:= MatrixForm[Table[ga[-i,-j],{i,3},{j,3}] ]
Out[6]//MatrixForm=
          1          K          0

          K        1 + K^2      0

          0          0          1
```

  These brief examples have demonstrated only a fraction of the things that you can do with *MathTensor*. In the remainder of this book you will find pedagogical introductions to tensors and differential forms, detailed explanations of the *MathTensor* commands for dealing with them, and applications of *MathTensor* to problems in physics, mathematics, and engineering.

Part A
Tensor Analysis in *MathTensor*

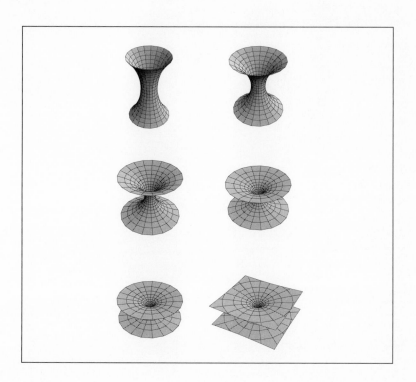

Chapter 2

An Introduction to Tensors and Differential Forms

This chapter is a pedagogical introduction to tensors. It includes a brief introduction to differential forms (which is continued in Chapter 6). It is intended for readers who are not already familiar with tensors or wish to refresh their memories. It is not about *MathTensor*. A detailed introduction to *MathTensor* will be deferred until the next chapter.

After reading the present chapter, you should have sufficient knowledge of tensors to follow most of this book. You may also find it convenient, as you read the later chapters, to refer back to this chapter.

The order of topics in this chapter is logical in the sense that structures that are introduced at a given stage do not depend on later structures. For example, the Lie derivative does not depend on the affine connection, and the affine connection or parallel transport can be defined in spaces without a metric.

You can find more on the topics discussed here in textbooks that discuss tensors, such as A. Einstein, *The Meaning of Relativity*; A. E. Green and W. Zerna, *Theoretical Elasticity*; C. W. Misner, K. S. Thorne, and J. A. Wheeler, *Gravitation*; E. Schrödinger, *Space-Time Structure*; R. Wald, *Gravity*; and S. Weinberg, *Gravitation and Cosmology*.

■ 2.1 Tensors of Rank 1: Vectors

A convenient starting point for introducing the concept of a tensor is the differential of a function along a curve. This approach will make it clear why tensors transform as they do from one coordinate system to another and that they represent objects that have a simple geometrical, coordinate-independent, meaning.

■ 2.1.1 Covariant Vectors

A curve C on a surface is characterized by a continuous differentiable function from the real numbers λ to points $p(\lambda)$ on the surface. If x^a are coordinates on the surface, with the index a ranging from 1 to the dimension d of the surface, then the curve C is characterized by the functions $x^a(\lambda)$, which give the points $p(\lambda)$ along the curve. Only a finite region of the surface need be considered here so the coordinate system is not required to cover the entire surface. You can think of a 2-dimensional surface when picturing things, but the value of the dimension d can be larger.

Let f be a real continuous differentiable function defined along the curve C. That is, $f = f(x^1(\lambda), x^2(\lambda), \ldots)$. The differential of f is

$$df = (\partial f/\partial x^a)dx^a. \tag{2.1}$$

Here, the repeated index a is summed from 1 to the dimension d of the surface. The implied summation over repeated indices is a convenient notational device known as the Einstein summation convention. The repeated index, a in this case, is called a dummy index because the particular letter used for it is immaterial. It is summed over the same set of numerical values regardless of whether the repeated index is called a or b. A restriction on naming a dummy index is that its name should appear exactly twice. The dx^a are differentials along the curve, that is, $dx^a = (\partial x^a(\lambda)/\partial\lambda)d\lambda$.

Because the differential df in Eq. (1) represents the change in the function f between two points along the curve C separated by parameter interval $d\lambda$, it is clear that df is independent of the particular coordinate system used to label points on the surface. The differential df is one way of representing a covariant tensor of rank one, also known as a covariant vector. Any covariant vector at a point p can be represented as a differential df of a function along a curve through p.

The components of the vector represented by df are the coefficients of dx^a in Eq. (1): $(\partial f/\partial x^a)$. The components depend on the coordinate system. New coordinates x'^a on the surface can be defined as continuous differentiable functions of the original coordinates x^a. (The transformation functions x'^a must be invertible functions of the x^a in the region or patch of the surface under consideration.) The differential df is not changed by the coordinate transformation because the parameter interval $d\lambda$ is not affected. In terms of the new coordinates, $df = (\partial f/\partial x'^b)dx'^b$. Comparing this expression with Eq. (1) and writing $dx^a = (\partial x^a/\partial x'^b)dx'^b$, you see that the components of the vector represented by df in each coordinate system are related by

$$(\partial f/\partial x'^b) = (\partial x^a/\partial x'^b)(\partial f/\partial x^a). \tag{2.2}$$

A covariant tensor of the first rank, or covariant vector v, is often defined as an object represented by components that transform in the same way as the components of df,

$$v'_b = (\partial x^a/\partial x'^b)v_a. \tag{2.3}$$

Here, v_a are the components of v in the unprimed coordinates and v'_b are the components of v in the primed coordinates. It is clear from the discussion of df that objects with components transforming in this way are well suited to describe geometrical or physical quantities having a simple meaning, independent of any particular coordinate system.

In fact, any given set of components v_a of a vector at a point p can be represented as partial derivatives of some function f along some curve through point p. Therefore a convenient way of representing a vector v is as $v \equiv v_a dx^a$. This is analogous to the familiar representation of a vector in terms of basis vectors along the coordinate directions, in which case the dx^a in the previous formula are replaced by basis vectors.

The common feature of all these ways of representing v is that v has components v_a that transform by Eq. (3). An object having components that transform by Eq. (3) is referred to as a *covariant* vector, or *covariant* tensor of the first rank.

You can think of v_a either as referring to the specific components of the vector v in one particular coordinate system, or alternatively, as a symbol for the vector, without reference to any particular coordinate system. In the abstract index notation (see e.g., Wald), Latin letters like a are used for the index when v_a is to refer to no particular coordinate system, and Greek letters like μ are used when v_μ is to refer to the components of v_a in some particular coordinate system. For notational convenience, Latin indices will be used throughout this book and the symbol v_a will sometimes refer to a vector without reference to any particular coordinate system and sometimes to its components in a particular coordinate system.

$$
\begin{array}{ll}
v_a & \text{covariant vector} \\[2mm]
v'_a = \frac{\partial x^b}{\partial x'^a} v_b & \text{transforming components} \\[2mm]
v_a dx^a & \text{another way of representing the vector}
\end{array}
$$

Covariant vectors and their transformation.

■ 2.1.2 Contravariant Vectors

Given a covariant vector v_a, the quantity $v_a u^a$ will have the same value in any coordinate system if the components of u^a transform as

$$u'^b = (\partial x'^b / \partial x^a) u^a. \tag{2.4}$$

The components u^a represent a *contravariant* vector, or *contravariant* tensor, u, of rank one. The invariant quantity $v_a u^a$ is the scalar, or dot, product of the vectors v and u. The index on a contravariant vector is represented as a superscript, and the index on a covariant vector as a subscript, by convention.

The summation convention requires that one of the repeated dummy indices is a covariant index and the other is a contravariant index. Whenever a covariant index is summed with a contravariant index, the transformations associated with the members of the dummy pair of indices cancel one another.

One example of a contravariant vector is the coordinate separation dx^a between two infinitesimally separated points. It transforms as in Eq. (4), $dx'^b = (\partial x'^b / \partial x^a) dx^a$. In general, the coordinate x^a itself does not transform in this way because $(\partial x'^b / \partial x^a)$ depends on position. (Only if you restrict the transformations under consideration to be linear, as in special relativity with rectangular coordinates, can you regard x^a as a contravariant vector.)

$$
\begin{array}{ll}
u^a & \text{contravariant vector} \\[2mm]
u'^a = \dfrac{\partial x'^a}{\partial x^b} u^b & \text{transforming components}
\end{array}
$$

Contravariant vectors and their transformation.

■ 2.2 Tensors of Higher Rank

The rank of a tensor is the number of indices required to specify its components. The tensor product $v \otimes w$ of two covariant vectors is a tensor of rank two, having components $v_a w_b$. It is clear that its components transform as $v'_a w'_b = \frac{\partial x^c}{\partial x'^a} \frac{\partial x^d}{\partial x'^b} v_c w_d$. A general second-rank tensor covariant tensor t has components t_{ab} that transform in the same way as a tensor product of two covariant vectors. Thus

$$t'_{ab} = \frac{\partial x^c}{\partial x'^a} \frac{\partial x^d}{\partial x'^b} t_{cd}. \tag{2.5}$$

Similarly, a contravariant tensor q of rank two has components q^{ab} that transform like the tensor product of two contravariant vectors:

$$q'^{ab} = \frac{\partial x'^a}{\partial x^c} \frac{\partial x'^b}{\partial x^d} q^{cd}. \tag{2.6}$$

A mixed tensor r of second rank with components $r^a{}_b$ transforms like a tensor product $u^a v_b$: $r'^a{}_b = \frac{\partial x'^a}{\partial x^c} \frac{\partial x^d}{\partial x'^b} r^c{}_d$. Thus each index transforms contravariantly or covariantly according to its position. A tensor of any rank is defined in the same way, with the positions of the indices on its components determining its transformation properties.

The symmetry properties of the components of a tensor under interchange of indices are preserved under transformation from one coordinate system to another.

For example, if $t_{ab} = -t_{ba}$, then it is easy to show that also $t'_{ab} = -t'_{ba}$. A tensor with this property is said to be antisymmetric. An example of a well-known antisymmetric tensor is the electromagnetic field tensor F_{ab}. An example of a tensor that is symmetric under interchange of indices is the stress tensor $T_{ab} = T_{ba}$.

When you write an equation that is a sum of terms involving tensors and products of tensors, you must be careful that in each term the free or unsummed indices are exactly the same, both in name and position. Although the names of dummy pairs of indices are not important, you must be careful not to repeat the same pair of dummy indices more than once in the same term. You will see that these rules are obeyed by the tensor equations in the sections below.

A very important property of equations that are written in terms of tensors is that the equations have the same form when the tensors are transformed to a new coordinate system. The equations are said to be covariant. The unprimed tensors in the original coordinate system are simply replaced by the corresponding primed tensors in the new coordinate system.

$$t^a{}_{bc} \qquad \text{a tensor of rank three}$$

$$t'^a{}_{bc} = \frac{\partial x'^a}{\partial x^d} \frac{\partial x^e}{\partial x'^b} \frac{\partial x^f}{\partial x'^c} t^d{}_{ef} \qquad \text{its transformation}$$

A tensor of rank three.

■ 2.3 Exterior Differential Forms

By introducing a product called the exterior, or wedge, product, denoted by $\wedge$, you can set up a correspondence between antisymmetric tensors and objects called exterior differential forms, which carry no indices. An exterior product of differentials dx^a is antisymmetric under interchange of any pair of differentials. For example,

$$dx^a \wedge dx^b \wedge dx^c = -dx^b \wedge dx^a \wedge dx^c = -dx^c \wedge dx^b \wedge dx^a. \qquad (2.7)$$

The exterior product is distributive and linear in each argument, just as for an ordinary product. Thus, if g and h are ordinary numbers or functions, then $dx^a \wedge (gdx^b + hdx^c) = gdx^a \wedge dx^b + hdx^a \wedge dx^c$.

The independent exterior products of three differentials, $dx^a \wedge dx^b \wedge dx^c$, form a basis for the space of 3-forms, which is the space of linear combinations of the independent basis 3-forms. For example, if w is a 3-form, it can be written as

$$w = (1/3!)w_{abc}dx^a \wedge dx^b \wedge dx^c, \qquad (2.8)$$

where the summations are over all values of the dummy indices a, b, and c, and the w_{abc} are ordinary functions or numbers, called the components of the differential form w. The components w_{abc} are taken to be totally antisymmetric in the indices (any symmetric part would not contribute to w). The 3-form w is independent of the coordinate system, so that the w_{abc} transform as do the components of a totally antisymmetric tensor. Thus each differential form corresponds to an antisymmetric tensor.

The factor of $(1/3!)$ in the above expression for w occurs because the indices are summed over all values of the indices. However, the independent components w_{abc} of the form are defined as the coefficients of the *independent* basis forms $dx^a \wedge dx^b \wedge dx^c$. You can, for example, take the independent basis forms to be the set of exterior products $dx^a \wedge dx^b \wedge dx^c$ with indices such that $a < b < c$. Then it is clear that each independent basis form appears 3! times in w, so that w can be written as

$$w = \sum (w_{abc} dx^a \wedge dx^b \wedge dx^c)_{a<b<c}, \qquad (2.9)$$

where the sum now includes only independent basis forms. For example, in three dimensions, there is only one independent $dx^a \wedge dx^b \wedge dx^c$, which you can take to be $dx^1 \wedge dx^2 \wedge dx^3$. In that case, $w = w_{123} dx^1 \wedge dx^2 \wedge dx^3$.

Similarly, a 2-form, f, can be written as

$$f = (1/2) f_{ab} dx^a \wedge dx^b, \qquad (2.10)$$

where f_{ab} is antisymmetric. In three dimensions, this can be expanded in terms of independent basis forms as

$$f = f_{12} dx^1 \wedge dx^2 + f_{13} dx^1 \wedge dx^3 + f_{23} dx^2 \wedge dx^3. \qquad (2.11)$$

A 1-form v can be written as

$$v = v_a dx^a \qquad (2.12)$$

and corresponds to a covariant vector. A 0-form is simply a scalar function. In general, a p-form can be expanded in terms of basis forms consisting of exterior products of p differentials. The integer p is the *degree* of the form. (It is equal to the rank of the corresponding antisymmetric tensor).

In the exterior differential calculus, there are many operations that take one form into another form. You can thus manipulate differential forms without using indices. The methods of exterior calculus are often simpler than working with indices and have given rise to penetrating theorems. This brief introductory discussion of differential forms is continued in Chapter 6, which describes in detail the implementation of the various differential form operations in *MathTensor*. In addition, in Chapter 3, you will find a relatively brief section illustrating and summarizing many of the differential form operations in *MathTensor*. The remainder of the present chapter is devoted to tensors in general, including how they are used to characterize curvature.

■ 2.4 The Lie Derivative

A tensor field is a tensor whose components are defined at all points of a region and are continuous differentiable functions of the coordinates. Let $v_a(x)$ be a vector field, where x in the argument is an abbreviation for the set of coordinates of a point. The vector field $v_a(x)$ can be used to generate an infinitesimal coordinate transformation at each point,

$$x'^a = x^a - \epsilon v^a. \tag{2.13}$$

We will work to first order in the infinitesimal quantity ϵ. Under this transformation, a tensor field $t_{ab}(x)$ will be transformed into $t'_{ab}(x')$, where x' and x label the same point p in the new and old coordinates, respectively. You can express the components of $t'^{ab}(x')$ in terms of those of $t^{ab}(x)$ by using the general transformation equation, together with the specific form of this infinitesimal transformation given in Eq. (13). Furthermore, you can write x' in the argument of $t'^{ab}(x')$ in terms of x and expand about x to first order in ϵ. The result of all this is

$$t'^{ab}(x) = t^{ab}(x) + \epsilon(-v^a{}_{,p}t^{pb} - v^b{}_{,p}t^{ap} + t^{ab}{}_{,p}v^p). \tag{2.14}$$

You can regard $t'^{ab}(x)$ as a new tensor field in the original coordinate system. Under transformation to a new coordinate system x'', $t'^{ab}(x)$ transforms at x in the same way as does $t^{ab}(x)$. The difference of two tensors at the same point is a tensor. (This is not generally true for the difference of two tensors at different points because under a nonlinear coordinate transformation, the transformation coefficients are different at each point.) Thus you can define a new tensor, $\mathrm{LieD}_v(t^{ab})$, called the Lie derivative of t^{ab} along the v-direction, by

$$\mathrm{LieD}_v(t^{ab}) = \lim_{\epsilon \to 0} \frac{t'^{ab}(x) - t^{ab}(x)}{\epsilon}. \tag{2.15}$$

With the previous expression for $t'^{ab}(x)$, you obtain

$$\mathrm{LieD}_v(t^{ab}) = -v^a{}_{,p}t^{pb} - v^b{}_{,p}t^{ap} + t^{ab}{}_{,p}v^p. \tag{2.16}$$

By carrying out the analogous calculation with t_{ab}, you find

$$\mathrm{LieD}_v(t_{ab}) = v^p{}_{,a}t_{pb} + v^p{}_{,b}t_{ap} + t_{ab,p}v^p. \tag{2.17}$$

Similarly, for a mixed tensor $t^a{}_b$,

$$\mathrm{LieD}_v(t^a{}_b) = -v^a{}_{,p}t^p{}_b + v^p{}_{,b}t^a{}_p + t^a{}_{b,p}v^p. \tag{2.18}$$

The pattern is clear. The Lie derivative along the v direction of any tensor t is a new tensor having the same indices as t. In the Lie derivative of t, each contravariant index of t is summed with a derivative index on $-v$, with v carrying the contravariant index that was replaced by a summation index on t. Each covariant index on t is summed with a contravariant index of v, and v acquires a derivative index that is the same as the covariant index of t that was replaced by the summation index. Finally, there is a term consisting of t with a derivative index that is summed with a contravariant index on v. The tensor t can have any number of indices. For a scalar, which has no indices, only the final term appears.

It follows easily from the definition of `LieD`, Eq. (15), that `LieD` behaves as a derivative when applied to a product. To show this from the definition, you need only use the fact that the primed tensor differs from the unprimed tensor by terms of order ϵ. An example of the action of `LieD` on a product is

$$\mathrm{LieD}_v(t^{ab}u_c) = u_c\mathrm{LieD}_v(t^{ab}) + t^{ab}\mathrm{LieD}_v(u_c). \tag{2.19}$$

$$\mathrm{LieD}_v(t^a{}_b) = -v^a{}_{,p}t^p{}_b + v^p{}_{,b}t^a{}_p + t^a{}_{b,p}v^p$$
$$\text{Lie derivative of } t^a{}_b$$

An example of a Lie derivative.

■ 2.5 Affine Connection, Covariant Derivative, Torsion

The Lie derivative compares a tensor and its coordinate transform at the same values of the coordinates. It takes one tensor to another tensor. The ordinary partial derivative of a tensor, such as $t^{ab}{}_{,c}$, does not give a tensor because it is defined in terms of the difference of t at two points, and under a general coordinate transformation, tensors at different points behave differently.

It is desirable to define a generalized derivative analogous to the ordinary partial derivative, which compares a single tensor field at two nearby points but which yields a new tensor. A derivative of this type, which yields a new tensor, will be called a *covariant* derivative.

You will recall that the ordinary partial derivative of a tensor t (suppressing all indices for brevity) is defined as

$$\partial t / \partial x = \lim_{\Delta x \to 0} \frac{(t(x + \Delta x) - t(x))}{\Delta x}, \tag{2.20}$$

In order to define a covariant derivative that will transform as a tensor, we define
an operation of parallel transport of a tensor, and parallel transport $t(x + \Delta x)$ from
point $x + \Delta x$ to point x, before taking the difference to form a derivative. Then we
will be taking the difference of two tensors at the same point x, and that difference
is also a tensor at x.

First, consider parallel transport of a vector v^a *from* point $x + \Delta x$ *to* point x. The
components of the vector will undergo a change which must vanish as Δx vanishes,
so it is reasonable to assume that to first order in Δx, the parallel transported
vector has the form

$$v^a{}_{par}(x) = v^a(x + \Delta x) + \Gamma^a{}_{bc}(x) v^b(x) \Delta x^c, \tag{2.21}$$

where the quantities $\Gamma^a{}_{bc}(x)$ are called affine connections and are defined to transform under coordinate transformations in such a way that $v^a{}_{par}(x)$ is a vector at
x (thus the affine connection does not transform as a tensor). Once the affine connections are given at each point, the process of parallel transport is well defined.
Specifying the affine connection on a space gives it sufficient structure to permit a
covariant derivative to be defined.

Then simply replace $v^a(x + \Delta x)$ by $v^a{}_{par}(x)$ in the definition of the derivative,
thus defining the covariant derivative of v^a with respect to x^c as

$$v^a{}_{;c} = \lim_{\Delta x^c \to 0} \frac{(v^a{}_{par}(x) - v^a(x))}{\Delta x^c}. \tag{2.22}$$

This gives

$$v^a{}_{;c} = v^a{}_{,c} + \Gamma^a{}_{bc} v^b. \tag{2.23}$$

The covariant derivative $v^a{}_{;c}$ is a second-rank tensor with the derivative index acting
as a covariant tensor index.

The covariant derivative is required to behave as a derivative when acting on
a product of tensors, with or without dummy indices present. For example, we
require that

$$(v^a u_b)_{;c} = v^a{}_{;c} u_b + v^a u_{b;c}. \tag{2.24}$$

The covariant derivative of a scalar s is the same as the ordinary partial deriva-
tive, $s_{;a} = s_{,a}$. For the scalar $v^a u_a$, this implies that $(v^a u_a)_{;c} = (v^a u_a)_{,c}$. For this to

be consistent with the previous equation for the covariant derivative of a product (with index b replaced by a), it is necessary that

$$u_{a;c} = u_{a,c} - \Gamma^{b}{}_{ac} u_{b}. \tag{2.25}$$

By similar arguments involving products of vectors, you can show, for example, that

$$t^{a}{}_{b;c} = t^{a}{}_{b,c} + \Gamma^{a}{}_{dc} t^{d}{}_{b} - \Gamma^{d}{}_{bc} t^{a}{}_{d}. \tag{2.26}$$

The general rule is that when taking the covariant derivative of a tensor, each contravariant index of the tensor gives rise to a term with $+\Gamma$, and each covariant index gives rise to a term with $-\Gamma$, as in the previous example.

The quantity

$$T^{a}{}_{bc} \equiv \Gamma^{a}{}_{bc} - \Gamma^{a}{}_{cb} \tag{2.27}$$

is called the torsion. You can show by looking at the detailed nontensorial transformation properties of the affine connections that the torsion does transform as a tensor. You will find further discussion of torsion in the chapters on differential forms. In the present context, the torsion tensor $T^{a}{}_{bc}$ will be taken to be zero, so that the affine connections, $\Gamma^{a}{}_{bc}$, are symmetric in the lower indices.

$$\boxed{\; t^{a}{}_{b;c} = t^{a}{}_{b,c} + \Gamma^{a}{}_{dc} t^{d}{}_{b} - \Gamma^{d}{}_{bc} t^{a}{}_{d} \qquad \text{a covariant derivative} \;}$$

An example of a covariant derivative.

The Lie derivative is independent of the affine structure of a space, as is clear from its definition in the previous section. You can in fact replace the ordinary partial derivatives appearing in the expressions for the Lie derivative by covariant derivatives. The affine connections will drop out when the covariant derivative are written out in terms of derivatives and affine connections. Here is a *MathTensor* session that demonstrates this.

This defines a tensor t of rank two having no symmetries.

```
In[1]:= DefineTensor[t,{{1,2},1}]
PermWeight::def: Object t defined
```

This defines a vector v.

```
In[2]:= DefineTensor[v,{{1},1}]
PermWeight::def: Object v defined
```

Here is the Lie derivative of t^{ab} along the v direction. A u in front of an index means it is an "upper" or raised index, as is evident from the output line.

```
In[3]:= LieD[t[ua,ub],v]

                    ab
Out[3]= LieD (t  )
           v
```

The command `LieDtoCD` expands out the previous Lie derivative expression using covariant derivatives.

$$In[4]:= \text{LieDtoCD[\%]}$$

$$Out[4]= -(v^a{}_{;p}\ t^{pb}) - v^b{}_{;p}\ t^{ap} + t^{ab}\ v^p{}_{;p}$$

The command `CDtoOD` expands out the covariant derivatives in terms of ordinary derivatives and affine connections. The latter appear as $G^a{}_{bc}$ in the output line.

$$In[5]:= \text{CDtoOD[\%]}$$

$$Out[5]= -(v^a{}_{,p}\ t^{pb}) - v^b{}_{,p}\ t^{ap} + t^{ab}\ v^p{}_{,p} - G^a{}_{pq}\ t^{qb}\ v^p -$$

$$> \quad G^b{}_{pq}\ t^{aq}\ v^p + G^a{}_{pq}\ t^{pb}\ v^q + G^b{}_{pq}\ t^{ap}\ v^q$$

`Tsimplify` makes use of the symmetry properties to simplify the previous expression. You will see that the affine connection terms have dropped out, as was to be shown.

$$In[6]:= \text{Tsimplify[\%]}$$

$$Out[6]= -(v^a{}_{,p}\ t^{pb}) - v^b{}_{,p}\ t^{ap} + t^{ab}\ v^p{}_{,p}$$

Next look at the Lie derivative of t_{ab} with two covariant indices. The 1 in front of an index indicates a "lower" index.

$$In[7]:= \text{LieD[t[1a,1b],v]}$$

$$Out[7]= \text{LieD}_v\ (t_{ab})$$

Write this once again in terms of CD.

$$In[8]:= \text{LieDtoCD[\%]}$$

$$Out[8]= v^p{}_{;a}\ t_{pb} + v^p{}_{;b}\ t_{ap} + t_{ab;p}\ v^p$$

This time the affine connection terms drop out without further simplification.

$$In[9]:= \text{CDtoOD[\%]}$$

$$Out[9]= v^p{}_{,a}\ t_{pb} + v^p{}_{,b}\ t_{ap} + t_{ab,p}\ v^p$$

Now there is one contravariant and one covariant index.

$$In[10]:= \text{LieD[t[ua,1b],v]}$$

$$Out[10]= \text{LieD}_v\ (t^a{}_b)$$

Convert to CD.

$$In[11]:= \text{LieDtoCD[\%]}$$

$$Out[11]= -(v^a{}_{;p}\ t^p{}_b) + v^p{}_{;b}\ t^a{}_p + t^a{}_{b;p}\ v^p$$

The affine connections have not cancelled without further simplification.

$In[12] :=$ **CDtoOD[%]**

$$Out[12] = -(v^a{}_{,p}\,t^p{}_b) + v^p{}_{,b}\,t^a{}_p + t^a{}_{b,p}\,v^p -$$

$$> \quad G^a{}_{pq}\,t^q{}_b\,v^p + G^p{}_{pq}\,t^a{}_b\,v^q$$

But after simplification they do.

$In[13] :=$ **Tsimplify[%]**

$$Out[13] = -(v^a{}_{,p}\,t^p{}_b) + v^p{}_{,b}\,t^a{}_p + t^a{}_{b,p}\,v^p$$

■ 2.6 The Metric Tensor

In order to talk about the invariant length of a vector, it is necessary to introduce the metric tensor, g_{ab}. The length squared of a contravariant vector v^a is defined as $g_{ab}v^a v^b$. It is a scalar, having no free (i.e., unsummed) indices. The metric tensor g_{ab} is generally a function of position and is taken to be symmetric, $g_{ab} = g_{ba}$. For the vector dx^a, the coordinate interval between two nearby points, the square of the invariant length is

$$ds^2 = g_{ab}dx^a dx^b. \tag{2.28}$$

It is always possible to find a coordinate transformation at a given point such that in the new coordinate system, the off-diagonal components of the transformed metric tensor are zero and the diagonal components are each of magnitude 1. The number of these $+1$ and -1 diagonal components is unique for a given space and is known as the signature of the metric. In a space of Riemannian signature, the components are all $+1$, and in a space (or spacetime) of Lorentzian signature, all but one of the components have the same sign. On a flat 2-dimensional plane in rectangular coordinates (x^1, x^2), the distance ds between two points satisfies $ds^2 = (dx^1)^2 + (dx^2)^2$, so that the metric tensor on the plane in these coordinates is $g_{ab} = \delta_{ab}$, where δ_{ab} is the Kronecker delta, defined by $\delta_{ab} = 1$ if $a = b$ and 0 otherwise. In polar coordinates, related to x^1 and x^2 by $x^1 = r\cos(\theta)$ and $x^2 = r\sin(\theta)$, the metric has non-zero components, $g_{rr} = 1$ and $g_{\theta\theta} = r^2$. On a curved 2-dimensional surface, such as part of a sphere, the metric at any single point can be reduced by a coordinate transformation to δ_{ab}, but there is no single coordinate system in which the metric is δ_{ab} everywhere on the surface. If the metric at a given point reduces to δ_{ab} and in addition all first derivatives of the metric are zero at the point, then the coordinate system is said to be *normal* at the point.

In special relativity theory, the points have coordinates x^1, x^2, x^3, and x^4 (or x^0), where x^4 is the time measured by a set of properly synchronized clocks. Each point has a position in space and time and is known as an *event*. The invariant interval between two nearby events, in a frame of reference based on rectangular spatial coordinates and properly synchronized clocks, is

$$ds^2 = (dx^1)^2 + (dx^2)^2 + (dx^3)^2 - (dx^4)^2. \qquad (2.29)$$

(The opposite signs of the metric components are sometimes used, which does not alter the physical content of the theory.) Such a frame of reference is called an inertial frame. The metric in these coordinates is often denoted by η_{ab}, where the indices take values from 1 to 4. A spacetime in which the metric can be transformed to η_{ab} everywhere is said to be flat.

In general relativity, the presence of a gravitational field curves the spacetime. Nevertheless, it is always possible, at any particular spacetime point, to find a coordinate system such that at the given point the first derivatives of the metric are all zero and the metric at the point reduces to η_{ab}. Such a coordinate system is referred to as *normal*, or *locally inertial*, at the given spacetime point or event. Near that event, the metric of spacetime is like that of special relativity, in which the spacetime is flat and there is no gravitational field. Thus a normal or locally inertial coordinate system corresponds to a reference frame that is freely falling at the given event. The assumed existence of a freely falling frame at any given point in a gravitational field is one form of Einstein's principle of equivalence.

■ 2.6.1 Affine Connection and the Metric

In a space with a metric g_{ab}, there is a relation between the affine connection $\Gamma^a{}_{bc}$ and g_{ab}. This relation is obtained by requiring that the length of a vector not change if the vector is carried by parallel transport along a curve. In Eq. (21), the vector $v^a{}_{par}(x)$ is obtained from $v^a(x + \Delta x)$ by parallel transport from point $x + \Delta x$ to x. To say that the vector is parallel transported along a curve means that if $x + \Delta x$ and x are nearby points that lie along the curve, then $v^a(x) = v^a{}_{par}(x)$. But then you can see from Eq. (22) that $v^a{}_{;c}dx^c$ of a parallel transported vector is zero, where $dx^c = (\partial x^c / \partial \lambda)d\lambda$ is the coordinate separation of the two points, which are taken to have a parameter separation of $d\lambda$ along the curve. The length of the vector, $g_{ab}v^a v^b$, must not change as the vector undergoes parallel transport. Hence, with dx^c taken along the curve,

$$0 = (g_{ab}v^a v^b)_{,c}dx^c. \qquad (2.30)$$

But the ordinary derivative of the square of the length, which is a scalar, is the same as the covariant derivative. Then using the rule for the covariant derivative of a product of tensors, one finds for this parallelly transported vector that

$$0 = g_{ab;c}v^a v^b dx^c. \qquad (2.31)$$

The only way that this relation can hold for parallel transport of an arbitrary vector v^a along any curve is if

$$g_{ab;c} = 0. \tag{2.32}$$

This vanishing of the covariant derivative is a fundamental property of the metric tensor. It determines the affine connection in terms of the metric and its derivatives. By writing out the relation $g_{ab;c} + g_{ca;b} - g_{bc;a} = 0$ in terms of ordinary partial derivatives and affine connections, you will find that you can solve the resulting equation for $g_{ad}\Gamma^d{}_{bc}$. Then by using the inverse of the metric tensor, which is a contravariant tensor denoted by g^{ab} and satisfies $g^{ab}g_{bc} = \delta^a{}_c$, you will arrive at

$$\Gamma^a{}_{bc} = \frac{1}{2}g^{ad}(g_{db,c} + g_{dc,b} - g_{bc,d}). \tag{2.33}$$

Thus, in a space with a metric tensor, the affine connection is determined.

■ 2.6.2 Geodesics

A geodesic curve $x^a(\lambda)$ is one for which the tangent vector, $u^a \equiv dx^a/d\lambda$, is proportional at each point of the curve to the vector obtained by parallel transport of u^a from a given reference point along the curve. The parameter λ can always be chosen in such a way that the proportionality constant is 1 at every point of the curve. In that case, the parameter is called an *affine parameter*. With λ chosen to be affine, the tangent vector u^a undergoes parallel transport along the geodesic. The condition that it undergo parallel transport is (as was derived above for a parallelly transported vector v^a),

$$u^a{}_{;c}(dx^c/d\lambda) = 0. \tag{2.34}$$

(The quantity on the left-hand side is sometimes written as $Du^a/d\lambda$ or $Du^a/D\lambda$.) With the help of Eq. (23), you can write this as

$$\frac{d^2x^a}{d\lambda^2} + \Gamma^a{}_{bc}\frac{dx^b}{d\lambda}\frac{dx^c}{d\lambda} = 0. \tag{2.35}$$

This differential equation determines the geodesics.

$\Gamma^a{}_{bc} = \frac{1}{2}g^{ad}(g_{db,c} + g_{dc,b} - g_{bc,d})$ affine connection and metric

$\frac{d^2x^a}{d\lambda^2} + \Gamma^a{}_{bc}\frac{dx^b}{d\lambda}\frac{dx^c}{d\lambda} = 0$ geodesic equation

---

Affine connection and geodesics.

In a normal coordinate system at the point where the first derivatives of g_{ab} are zero, it follows from Eq. (33) that the affine connection $\Gamma^a{}_{bc}$ is zero. Then the geodesic equation implies that an arbitrary geodesic curve $x^a(\lambda)$ is linear in λ, at least in an infinitesimal neighborhood of the point. Thus any geodesic appears locally as a straight line in coordinates that are normal at a point. In general relativity, this implies that in coordinates that are normal at a given event, a particle acted on only by gravitation moves on a straight line at constant velocity in a spacetime neighborhood of the event. Such a frame is called locally inertial because the particle obeys the law of inertia in an infinitesimal spacetime neighborhood of an event. In the gravitational field of Earth, the reference frame of a freely falling elevator is an example of a locally inertial frame.

■ 2.6.3 Lowering and Raising Indices

If v^a is a contravariant vector, then $g_{ab}v^b$ is a covariant vector. By convention, it is denoted by the same symbol v, but with a covariant index. Thus

$$v_a \equiv g_{ab}v^b. \tag{2.36}$$

The same convention is used to lower contravariant indices on any tensor. Thus, for example, $T^a{}_b \equiv g_{bc}T^{ac}$. We have already defined the inverse metric g^{ab} such that $g^{ab}g_{bc} = \delta^a{}_c$. It is easy to see that the notation is consistent, in the sense that $g_{ab} = g_{ac}g_{bd}g^{cd}$.

It follows from Eq. (36) that

$$v^a \equiv g^{ab}v_b. \tag{2.37}$$

Thus the metric tensor and its inverse lower and raise indices on tensors. If a tensor has an upper and a lower index, as in $A^a{}_{bc}$, then the tensor $A^a{}_{ba}$ (summed over a) is said to be the *contraction* of the first tensor over the first and third indices. The contraction can also be written as $A^a{}_{ba} = g^{ac}A_{abc}$.

$$
\begin{array}{ll}
v_a = g_{ab}v^b & \text{lowering an index} \\[2mm]
v^a = g^{ab}v_b & \text{raising an index} \\[2mm]
T_a{}^a = g^{ab}T_{ab} & \text{contracting indices}
\end{array}
$$

Raising, lowering, and contracting indices.

■ 2.7 The Riemann Curvature Tensor

In a flat space, you can choose a rectangular coordinate system in which the affine connections are zero everywhere. Then covariant derivatives reduce to ordinary derivatives. Therefore, if v^a is any vector field, one has in this coordinate system that

$$v^a{}_{;bc} - v^a{}_{;cb} = 0. \tag{2.38}$$

Since this equation is a tensor equation, it holds in any coordinate system in a flat space.

You can write the left-hand side in an arbitrary space by using the definition of the covariant derivative given earlier.

Define a vector v^a.

```
In[1]:= DefineTensor[v,{{1},1}]
PermWeight::def: Object v defined
```

Here is the commutator of covariant derivatives of v^a.

```
In[2]:= CD[v[ua],lb,lc] - CD[v[ua],lc,lb]
```

$$Out[2]= v^a{}_{;bc} - v^a{}_{;cb}$$

This replaces both covariant derivatives in each term by ordinary derivatives and affine connections. It also simplifies the result. In *MathTensor*, the input form of the affine connection Γ is **AffineG**, and this appears in the output as **G**.

```
In[3]:= CDtoOD[CDtoOD[%] ]
```

$$Out[3]= G^a{}_{pb,c}\, v^p - G^a{}_{pc,b}\, v^p - G^p{}_{qc}\, G^a{}_{pb}\, v^q +$$
$$> \quad G^p{}_{qb}\, G^a{}_{pc}\, v^q$$

The result can be written in the form,

$$v^a{}_{;bc} - v^a{}_{;cb} = -R^a{}_{pbc} v^p, \tag{2.39}$$

with

$$R^a{}_{pbc} \equiv \Gamma^a{}_{pc,b} - \Gamma^a{}_{pb,c} + \Gamma^q{}_{pc}\Gamma^a{}_{qb} - \Gamma^q{}_{pb}\Gamma^a{}_{qc}. \tag{2.40}$$

Because the covariant derivatives on the left-hand side of Eq. (39) are third-rank tensors and v^p on the right-hand side is a vector, it follows that $R^a{}_{pbc}$ must be a tensor of the fourth rank. It is called the Riemann tensor.

The overall sign in the definition of the Riemann tensor is conventional and is not fixed in the literature. The sign conventions in this chapter agree with those of Misner, Thorne, and Wheeler. In *MathTensor*, you can adopt your favorite convention by setting the values of certain quantities in a file called **Conventions.m**.

From Eq. (38), you see that a necessary condition for a space to be flat is that $R^a{}_{pbc} = 0$. Conversely, it can be shown that if $R^a{}_{pbc} = 0$ in a space, then the space is flat. Hence, the Riemann tensor characterizes the curvature of a space. In general relativity, a nonvanishing Riemann tensor at a point implies that there is a gravitational field in the neighborhood of the point.

From the definition of $R^a{}_{pbc}$, it is obvious that

$$R^a{}_{pcd} = -R^a{}_{pdc}. \tag{2.41}$$

The following symmetry properties, although less obvious, also follow from the definition:

$$R^a{}_{pcd} = -R_p{}^a{}_{cd}, \tag{2.42}$$

$$R^a{}_{pcd} = R_{cd}{}^a{}_p, \tag{2.43}$$

$$R^a{}_{pcd} + R^a{}_{dpc} + R^a{}_{cdp} = 0. \tag{2.44}$$

It is not difficult to see that Eq. (42) is a consequence of Eqs. (41) and (43).

Lowering the a index does not alter these symmetry properties. In summary, the Riemann tensor is antisymmetric under interchange of either the first or the last pair of indices and is symmetric when the first two indices are exchanged as a pair with the last two indices. In addition, the sum of terms obtained by cyclic interchange of the last three indices of the Riemann tensor is zero.

Another identity obeyed by the Riemann tensor, which you can verify by a tedious calculation, is known as the Bianchi identity. It is a differential identity involving cyclic interchange of three indices, one of which is a covariant derivative index:

$$R^a{}_{bcd;e} + R^a{}_{bec;d} + R^a{}_{bde;c} = 0. \tag{2.45}$$

Let us verify this identity by direct calculation using *MathTensor* (in a later chapter, we prove the same identity more elegantly with differential forms in *MathTensor*).

Here is the expression appearing on the left-hand side of the Bianchi identity. The indices are reordered in the output by *MathTensor* (to facilitate possible simplification).

```
In[4]:= exprBianchi =
    CD[RiemannR[ua,lb,lc,ld],le] +
      CD[RiemannR[ua,lb,le,lc],ld] +
        CD[RiemannR[ua,lb,ld,le],lc]

Out[4]= -R    a       + R    a       - R    a
          b cd;e        b ce;d        b de;c
```

This replaces covariant derivatives by ordinary derivatives and affine connections (which appear as G's).

```
In[5]:= CDtoOD[%]
```

$$Out[5]= -R^a{}_{b\,cd,e} + R^a{}_{b\,ce,d} - R^a{}_{b\,de,c} + G^a{}_{be}R^p{}_{p\,cd} -$$
$$> \quad G^p{}_{bd}R^a{}_{p\,ce} + G^p{}_{bc}R^a{}_{p\,de} - G^a{}_{pe}R^p{}_{b\,cd} + G^a{}_{pd}R^p{}_{b\,ce} -$$
$$> \quad G^a{}_{pc}R^p{}_{b\,de}$$

The Riemann tensors are replaced by their definition in terms of affine connections. The second and first derivative terms have cancelled out.

```
In[6]:= RiemannToAffine[%]
```

$$Out[6]= -(G^p{}_{qe}G^q{}_{bd}G^a{}_{pc}) + G^p{}_{qd}G^q{}_{be}G^a{}_{pc} +$$
$$> \quad G^p{}_{qe}G^q{}_{bc}G^a{}_{pd} - G^p{}_{qc}G^q{}_{be}G^a{}_{pd} - G^p{}_{qd}G^q{}_{bc}G^a{}_{pe} +$$
$$> \quad G^p{}_{qc}G^q{}_{bd}G^a{}_{pe} - G^p{}_{be}G^q{}_{pd}G^a{}_{qc} + G^p{}_{bd}G^q{}_{pe}G^a{}_{qc} +$$
$$> \quad G^p{}_{be}G^q{}_{pc}G^a{}_{qd} - G^p{}_{bc}G^q{}_{pe}G^a{}_{qd} - G^p{}_{bd}G^q{}_{pc}G^a{}_{qe} +$$
$$> \quad G^p{}_{bc}G^q{}_{pd}G^a{}_{qe}$$

The remaining terms cancel by symmetry, verifying the Bianchi identity.

```
In[7]:= Tsimplify[%]
Out[7]= 0
```

■ 2.7.1   The Ricci, Einstein, and Weyl Tensors

The second-rank tensor,

$$R^p{}_{apb} \equiv R_{ab}, \tag{2.46}$$

is known as the Ricci tensor. As a consequence of the symmetries of the Riemann tensor, the Ricci tensor is symmetric. One more contraction gives the scalar curvature

$$R^a{}_a \equiv R. \tag{2.47}$$

The combination,

$$R^{ab} - \frac{1}{2}g^{ab}R \equiv G^{ab}, \tag{2.48}$$

is known as the Einstein tensor. By contracting the Bianchi identity on the first index and on one of the last three indices, one finds that

$$G^{ab}{}_{;b} = 0. \tag{2.49}$$

The gravitational field equation postulated by Einstein is

$$G^{ab} = \kappa T^{ab}, \tag{2.50}$$

where the constant κ is inversely proportional to the Newtonian gravitational constant and T^{ab} is a tensor known as the energy-momentum tensor. It describes the matter present and satisfies the equation $T^{ab}{}_{;b} = 0$.

By subtracting from R_{abcd} appropriate terms formed from its contractions, you can construct a tensor that has no non-zero contractions. This tensor, known as the Weyl tensor, has the following form for spaces of dimension $d > 2$:

$$
\begin{aligned}
C_{abcd} \equiv{} & R_{abcd} \\
& - \frac{1}{(d-2)}(g_{ac}R_{bd} - g_{ad}R_{bc} \\
& - g_{bc}R_{ad} + g_{bd}R_{ac}) \\
& + \frac{1}{(d-1)(d-2)}R(g_{ac}g_{bd} - g_{ad}g_{bc}).
\end{aligned} \tag{2.51}
$$

It can be shown that the Weyl tensor is zero in 3 dimensions and that the vanishing of the Weyl tensor in any dimension occurs if and only if the metric can be expressed in the form $g_{ab} = f c_{ab}$, where f is a scalar function of position and c_{ab} is a constant diagonal tensor having diagonal components that are each ± 1.

As in Eq. (39), when covariant derivatives are commuted, terms involving the Riemann tensor appear. Here is an example involving a third-rank tensor.

This defines a third-rank tensor, s_{abc}, having no symmetries.

```
In[8]:= DefineTensor[s,{{1,2,3},1}]
PermWeight::def: Object s defined
```

Here is the second covariant derivative of $s^a{}_{bc}$.

```
In[9]:= CD[s[ua,lb,lc],le,ld]

         a
Out[9]= s
          bc;ed
```

The *MathTensor* function CommuteCD interchanges the order of the indicated covariant derivatives, replacing $s^a{}_{bc;ed}$ by an equal expression involving $s^a{}_{bc;de}$ and additional Riemann tensor terms. There is also a *MathTensor* function OrderCD, which puts terms having multiple covariant derivatives into a unique order.

```
In[10]:= CommuteCD[%,le,ld]

          a          a    p        a p          ap
Out[10]= s        - R    s      - R     s     - R     s
          bc;de      p de  bc      pcde  b       pbde  c
```

Further information on these and more advanced topics can be found in the books referred to in the first section of this chapter. You may wish to refer back to this introduction to tensors as you read the later chapters on how to use *Math Tensor*.

Chapter 3
Symmetries, Operations, and Rules

If you can work with tensors using paper and pencil, then you will have no difficulty learning *MathTensor*. You will have to learn the *MathTensor* symbols for covariant (lower) and contravariant (upper) indices, as well as the *MathTensor* names for the common operations of tensor analysis. Typing tensorial expressions in *MathTensor* is very similar to what you would do on paper. However, *MathTensor* will save you much of the labor involved in carrying out tensor operations and simplifying tensor expressions.

When doing tensor analysis, you carry around in your head such information as the symmetry properties of a tensor under interchanges of indices. *MathTensor* already knows the properties of many of the tensors that are commonly used in mathematics and physics. If you use other tensors with special symmetry properties, then you will have to tell *MathTensor* about those properties. There is a simple facility in *MathTensor* for doing that.

This chapter first describes these basic features. It tells you how to enter tensor expressions into *MathTensor* and how to enter the symmetries of special tensors that you use. It also discusses the metric tensor and the raising and lowering of indices. Since *MathTensor* is built on top of *Mathematica*, the standard *Mathematica* functions can be used to save definitions to a file and to get the file in another *MathTensor* session.

Further into the chapter, you will learn about many of the operations of *Math-Tensor*: How to simplify tensor expressions, work with differential forms, take covariant derivatives, commute covariant derivatives, take Lie derivatives, create your own functions and rules, manipulate the Riemann tensor with a built-in set of rules, and use **Contexts** with **MathTensor**. The rules *MathTensor* uses to manipulate expressions constructed from Riemann tensors and their contractions and derivatives are given in detail in Section 6 of this chapter. You may use this as guide and reference when manipulating expressions involving curvature tensors.

The remainder of Part A consists of Chapter 4. It explains how to assign values to and manipulate components of tensors, calculate and work with the components of curvature tensors if you are given the values of the components of the metric, transform components of tensors under coordinate transformations, and work with more than one type of index.

If some of the sections make use of tensors and concepts you are not yet familiar with, you should simply skip those sections. For example, someone in engineering may not have to know about Lie derivatives but will nevertheless find the other features of *MathTensor* quite useful. You may also find it helpful to refer back to Chapter 2, in which most of the tensors and operations appearing here were introduced and explained.

The examples given in these chapters are as short and simple as possible. Going over them should allow you to quickly learn to employ *MathTensor* to carry out many practical calculations, including ones that would otherwise be quite advanced or laborious.

MathTensor is not a substitute for human intelligence. However, it will carry out many of the tedious operations involved in simplifying and manipulating complicated tensor expressions, thus freeing you to concentrate on the larger picture and plan your strategy. In addition, *MathTensor* contains functions that should help you to create knowledge-base files aimed at dealing with specific problems and areas of interest to you.

There are a number of knowledge-base files already in *MathTensor*. For example, the properties of the Maxwell electromagnetic field tensor are known to *MathTensor*. For dealing with curved spaces and with gravitational fields in general relativity, the properties of the Riemann curvature tensor are also known to *MathTensor*.

MathTensor inherits the powerful pattern-matching facilities of *Mathematica* and also has its own special functions to help you in writing transformation rules and definitions that deal with tensor expressions. If you want to build your own knowledge base of rules special to your application, you will want to read the parts of this chapter that discuss the *MathTensor* commands for creating rules involving tensors and that describe the construction of files containing rules you create.

Some applications of *MathTensor*, such as one involving calculation of expressions made up of contractions and derivatives of Riemann curvature tensors, another involving conformal transformations, and another involving the Yang-Mills field, are discussed in this and the following chapter. A few applications of differential forms are given in this chapter. Further applications involving differential forms appear in Part B, which describes in more detail how to use differential forms in *MathTensor*. Numerous other examples of advanced applications of *MathTensor* appear in the chapters of Part C.

You will find the appendix containing short explanations of each *MathTensor* function and object very useful, once you have become acquainted with the basic workings of *MathTensor*. There is also an index to enable you to find particular subjects and commands quickly. In some cases, index page references may be to the beginning of a section in which an object is discussed rather than to the exact page on which the object appears.

MathTensor is an evolving project. It is our hope that as you develop knowledge-base files useful to others in your area of expertise, you will ask us to distribute them to all who are interested, with acknowledgment to you.

Finally, a word on the philosophy underlying *MathTensor*. The aim of *MathTensor* is to obtain results, making use of symmetries and rules that are built in or imposed by the user. You should not expect it to function like a typewriter, printing expressions in the precise way you wish. Once you have reached a satisfactory level of simplification, you may want to work with pencil and paper in order to write your result in the particular form you prefer. As with any symbolic manipulation system, you will find *MathTensor* easier to use and more satisfying if you remain flexible and are prepared to use human ingenuity to reach your goal. We hope that *MathTensor* will enable you to make unfettered use of your creativity and to have more fun in solving problems involving tensors.

■ Starting *MathTensor*

If you have *Mathematica* and *MathTensor* installed on your computer, then you should be able to start *MathTensor* by first beginning a *Mathematica* session and then getting *MathTensor* by typing `<< MathTensor.m`. It will take some time, depending on the computer you are using, for *MathTensor* to be loaded, after which you should see some messages and the *Mathematica* prompt `In[2]:=` waiting for you to type the next input. Installation of *MathTensor* is described in separate instructions for your particular computer. These instructions also describe several methods that can be used to speed-up the loading of *MathTensor*.

We assume that the reader has some knowledge of *Mathematica* and has read at least part of the book *Mathematica* by Stephen Wolfram. Following the usual procedure in *Mathematica*, you can obtain a description of a *MathTensor* object by typing ? followed by the name of the *MathTensor* object. If you do not remember the full name, type ? followed by the part of the object name that you remember, with a * replacing the rest, as in `*simp*` or `Ri*`. All names fitting the pattern will appear. Then you type ? followed by the full name of the object to get the complete usage information on that object.

You can use the standard *Mathematica* functions `Save`, `Put`, `PutAppend`, and `Definition` to write your *MathTensor* definitions or expressions to a file, which can later be loaded into a *Mathematica* or *MathTensor* session as usual with `<<` or `Get`. You end a *MathTensor* session just as you do any other *Mathematica* session, by typing `Quit` or `Exit` (you can optionally add square brackets, as in `Exit[ ]`). On systems like the Macintosh, you quit by using the appropriate menu.

The *MathTensor* dialogs shown in this book start with line number 1. If you are loading *MathTensor* into a *Mathematica* session, then your line numbers will start with 2. If you wish, you can make them begin with 1 by typing `$Line=0;` before starting the example. As you try out examples given in this book on your computer, you should remember to start a new *MathTensor* session whenever the input line number of the example starts with `In[1]:=`. If you do not, you may not always obtain the results shown.

`<< MathTensor.m`	start *MathTensor* within *Mathematica*
`Quit` or `Exit`	end your *MathTensor* session

Starting and exiting *MathTensor*.

You can add the following lines to your *init.m* file in order to record your *MathTensor* session in a file called *math.out*. The contents of *math.out* will be overwritten by the next *MathTensor* or *Mathematica* session. The contents of *math.out* can be preserved by copying *math.out* to another file.

```
mathoutstream = OpenWrite["math.out", FormatType -> OutputForm]
If[!(Head[$Output] === List), $Output = {$Output}]
If[!(Head[$Echo] === List), $Echo = {$Echo}]
PrependTo[$Output, mathoutstream ] (* records output *)
PrependTo[$Echo, mathoutstream ] (* records input *)
```

Add these lines to *init.m* to record your session.

■ 3.1 Tensors and Their Symmetries

■ 3.1.1 Indices

Tensors are mathematical objects that have meaning independent of the coordinate system that you choose to use. In any particular coordinate system, a tensor is represented by a set of components having symbolic or numerical values (vectors are one kind of tensor). The utility of tensors stems from the fact that fundamental physical laws and geometrical relations are independent of coordinates and are therefore often best stated in terms of tensors. In conventional tensor notation, the components of a tensor are labeled by indices that are written as superscripts or subscripts. An upper index is known as a contravariant index because it transforms contravariantly (like the coordinate differentials dx^a) under coordinate transformations. Similarly, a lower, or covariant, index transforms covariantly (like the gradient operator $\partial/\partial x^a$) under coordinate transformations. In general, a tensor can have more than one index, some indices being contravariant and others covariant. A vector is a tensor having one index.

When you start *MathTensor*, you will see messages that describe certain initial settings. One of these is "**TensorForm turned on**," which indicates that in the output lines tensors will be printed in standard notation, with indices appearing as superscripts and subscripts. In addition, tensor names that are known to the system will appear in output lines in standard form. For example, the Maxwell electromagnetic field tensor F_{ab} is known to the system.

This prints in the standard form for the Maxwell field tensor. You type the covariant indices a and b as 1a and 1b, where the leading 1 stands for "lower."	`In[1]:= MaxwellF[1a,1b]`
	
	`Out[1]= F`
	        `ab`

There are times when you will want to cause the output to be printed in the same form as the input, as when you wish to edit a line and use it as input at another time or when you wish to see the input form of a term that you want to redefine.

This causes the subsequent tensors and indices to print in input form.	`In[2]:= Off[TensorForm];`
Now the output is no longer printed in standard tensor form.	`In[3]:= MaxwellF[1a,1b]` `Out[3]= MaxwellF[1a, 1b]`

You can find the available set of symbolic coordinate indices by typing the name of the list containing them. This is the list of the possible covariant indices that are recognized by *MathTensor*. Each starts with 1 for lower.	`In[4]:= Downuserlist`
	`Out[4]= {1a, 1b, 1c, 1d, 1e, 1f, 1g, 1h, 1i, 1j, 1k, 1l,`
	`>    1m, 1n, 1o}`

This is the list of the possible contravariant indices that are recognized by *MathTensor*. Each starts with u for upper.	`In[5]:= Upuserlist`
	`Out[5]= {ua, ub, uc, ud, ue, uf, ug, uh, ui, uj, uk, ul,`
	`>    um, un, uo}`

This turns on **TensorForm** again.	`In[6]:= On[TensorForm];`

This is what covariant indices look like when `TensorForm` is on. The leading l has been stripped, and the index is lowered.

In[7]:= `MaxwellF[lc,ld]`

Out[7]= F$_{cd}$

Here are contravariant indices with `TensorForm` on. The leading u has been stripped, and the index is raised.

In[8]:= `MaxwellF[uc,ud]`

Out[8]= F^{cd}

There are also other types of indices available in *MathTensor*. These are useful when you want to have more than one type of index in the same expression. For example, you may want to have spinor and tensor indices on the same object. The use of multiple types of indices will be discussed later.

`la,lb,lc,ld,le,lf,lg,lh,li,lj,lk,lm,ln,lo`
                                  lower indices you type

`ua,ub,uc,ud,ue,uf,ug,uh,ui,uj,uk,um,un,uo`
                                  upper indices you type

            `Downuserlist`   list of covariant coordinate indices

              `Upuserlist`   list of contravariant coordinate indices

---

Symbolic coordinate indices the user can type in *MathTensor*.

■ 3.1.2 Some Common Tensors

In *MathTensor*, the names of tensors follow the same conventions as do the names of functions in *Mathematica*, as is clear from this list of some tensors known to the system.

MaxwellA[la]	electromagnetic vector potential, A_a
MaxwellF[la,lb]	electromagnetic field tensor, F_{ab}
Maxwellj[la]	current density four-vector, j_a
MaxwellT[la,lb]	electromagnetic stress-energy tensor, T_{ab}
Metricg[la,lb]	metric tensor, g_{ab}
RiemannR[la,lb,lc,ld]	Riemann curvature tensor, R_{abcd}
RicciR[la,lb]	Ricci tensor, R_{ab}
ScalarR	scalar curvature, R

Some tensors known to *MathTensor*.

The first part of each name is descriptive and starts with a capital letter, while the second part is meant to denote the conventional symbol by which that tensor is known. Names are easier to remember if abbreviations are avoided. The index names are enclosed in square brackets, as for ordinary functions.

If necessary, you can use the *Mathematica* function $PreRead to reduce the necessary typing. The function $PreRead is applied to each input string before it is processed by *Mathematica*. For example,
$PreRead = {#, {"MaxF" -> "MaxwellF", "RieR" -> "RiemannR"}}& allows you to type MaxF[la,lb] for MaxwellF[la,lb] and RieR[la,lb,lc,ld] for RiemannR[la,lb,lc,ld]. (In *Mathematica* 1.2, the Alias command can be used for this purpose, as in MaxF :: MaxwellF.)

System tensors also have an associated print form called a TensorForm, which causes them to appear in the output line in standard tensor notation.

■ 3.1.3 Symmetries

Many tensors have special symmetries under permutations of their indices.

The electromagnetic field tensor is antisymmetric. In the output line, the known symmetry is used to reorder the indices in lexical order.

```
In[1]:= MaxwellF[lb,la]
Out[1]= -F
          ab
```

The Ricci tensor is symmetric.

```
In[2]:= RicciR[lb,la]
Out[2]= R
          ab
```

The symmetry property of `MaxwellF[1a,1b]` under reordering of indices can be described by the following list `{{2,1},-1}`. The first element of the list is the permutation `{2,1}`; the 2 in the first position means that the index in slot 2 of the tensor is put in slot 1, while the 1 in the second position means that the index in slot 1 of the tensor is put in slot 2. The −1 appearing as the second element of the list is the weight by which the tensor is to be multiplied when the associated permutation is made. The symmetry property of `RicciR[1a,1b]` is similarly described by the list `{{2,1},1}`, where now the weight is 1.

Some tensors have more complicated symmetries.

RiemannR is antisymmetric under interchange of the first pair of indices.	`In[3]:= RiemannR[1b,1a,1c,1d]`
	
	`Out[3]= -R`
	       `     abcd`

It is also antisymmetric under interchange of the second pair.	`In[4]:= RiemannR[1a,1b,1d,1c]`
	
	`Out[4]= -R`
	       `     abcd`

Under exchange of the first pair with the second pair of indices, it is symmetric.	`In[5]:= RiemannR[1c,1d,1a,1b]`
	
	`Out[5]= R`
	       `    abcd`

This set of symmetries of `RiemannR[1a,1b,1c,1d]` is described by the list `{ {2,1,3,4},-1, {1,2,4,3},-1, {3,4,1,2},1}`. This list consists of pairs of permutations and corresponding weights. Thus the permutation `{2,1,3,4}` means that the index in slot 2 goes to slot 1 and the index in slot 1 goes to slot 2, while the indices in slots 3 and 4 are not moved. Each permutation in the list must have a length equal to the number of indices of the tensor. Thus `{2,1,3,4}` is specified, despite the fact that the indices in slots 3 and 4 are not moved.

The function `Symmetries` returns a permutation-weight list describing the symmetries of a tensor.

The particular indices you type inside `Symmetries` do not matter, but they should already be ordered.	`In[6]:= Symmetries[MaxwellF[1a,1b] ]`
	
	`Out[6]= {{2, 1}, -1}`

This is what happens if you type the indices in such a way that they get reordered.	`In[7]:= Symmetries[MaxwellF[1b,1a] ]`
	
	`Out[7]= Symmetries[-F  ]`
	       `                ab`

One way to avoid reordering inside of **Symmetries** is to place in the index slots any unassigned symbols that are not standard indices.	*In[8]:=* **Symmetries[MaxwellF[yy,xx]]** *Out[8]=* **{{2, 1}, -1}**
Here are the symmetries of the Ricci tensor.	*In[9]:=* **Symmetries[RicciR[lc,ld]]** *Out[9]=* **{{2, 1}, 1}**
Here are those of the Riemann tensor.	*In[10]:=* **Symmetries[RiemannR[lc,ld,le,lf]]** *Out[10]=* **{{2, 1, 3, 4}, -1, {1, 2, 4, 3}, -1,** > **{3, 4, 1, 2}, 1}**

The list provided by **Symmetries** gives a small number of permutations that uniquely specify the properties of a tensor under permutations of indices. That list is not necessarily unique; it does not give the full set of permutations and weights describing every possible reordering of indices.

The full set of permutations and weights is given by the function **AllSymmetries**.	*In[11]:=* **AllSymmetries[MaxwellF[la,lb]]** *Out[11]=* **{{1, 2}, 1, {2, 1}, -1}**
The full set for **RiemannR** is quite long.	*In[12]:=* **AllSymmetries[RiemannR[la,lb,lc,ld]]** *Out[12]=* **{{1, 2, 3, 4}, 1, {2, 1, 3, 4}, -1,** > **{1, 2, 4, 3}, -1, {3, 4, 1, 2}, 1, {2, 1, 4, 3}, 1,** > **{4, 3, 1, 2}, -1, {3, 4, 2, 1}, -1, {4, 3, 2, 1}, 1}**

Symmetries[*tensor***[la,lb,..]]**	short permutation-weight list uniquely specifying symmetries of a tensor
AllSymmetries[*tensor***[la,lb,..]]**	complete permutation-weight list

---

Functions in *MathTensor* showing the symmetries of a tensor.

■ 3.1.4 Defining Your Own Tensors

You can define new tensors in *MathTensor* by using the function **DefineTensor**. Suppose that you want to define a rank two, or two index, tensor called anti with print symbol "a" and that you want it to be antisymmetric. Its symmetries will be described by the same permutation-weight list as for **MaxwellF**: **{{2,1},-1}**. Messages that appear from **DefineTensor** can be turned off if desired, for example, by entering **Off[PermWeight::sym]**.

This defines a tensor with the desired properties. It is important that the input name anti not be quoted, but the print symbol "a" should be quoted.

```
In[1]:= DefineTensor[anti,"a",{{2,1},-1}]
 PermWeight::sym: Symmetries of a assigned
 PermWeight::def: Object a defined
```

It is antisymmetric and has print symbol "a".

```
In[2]:= anti[lb,la]
Out[2]= -a
           ab
```

This appends the definition of anti to a file called **NewTensors.m**. You can collect the definitions of tensors you commonly use in such a file and load them into a future *MathTensor* session using Get. You do not have to put the definition into a file if you need it only for one session. You should use your editor to delete from **NewTensors.m** definitions pertaining to tensors you no longer require.

```
In[3]:= Definition[anti] >>> NewTensors.m
```

This recalls the permutation-weight list that you entered.

```
In[4]:= Symmetries[anti[la,lb] ]
Out[4]= {{2, 1}, -1}
```

Here is the complete list of permutations and weights.

```
In[5]:= AllSymmetries[anti[la,lb] ]
Out[5]= {{1, 2}, 1, {2, 1}, -1}
```

If you try to enter an inconsistent permutation-weight list, you will be told:

A nonzero tensor cannot be both symmetric and antisymmetric. This is a trivial example, but more subtle errors will also be caught.

```
In[6]:= DefineTensor[wrong, "w", {{2,1},1,{2,1},-1}]
 MakePermWeightGroup::inconsistent:
     Not consistent as a list of symmetries of a tensor.
 PermWeight::sym: Symmetries of w assigned
 PermWeight::def: Object w defined
```

If you make a mistake and wish to redefine a tensor such as anti[la,lb], you can start over by first clearing the definition with Clear[anti].

You can use the symmetries of existing tensors to save typing when defining new tensors having the same symmetries.

This defines a permutation-weight list. Note that *Mathematica* 2.X produces warning messages pointing to possible naming conflicts. In this instance, there is no problem.

```
In[7]:= permweights = Symmetries[RiemannR[la,lb,lc,ld] ]
Out[7]= {{2, 1, 3, 4}, -1, {1, 2, 4, 3}, -1,
>     {3, 4, 1, 2}, 1}
```

The tensor **newRiemannr** has the same symmetries as **RiemannR**.

In[8]:= **DefineTensor[newRiemannr, "r", permweights]**

PermWeight::sym: Symmetries of r assigned

PermWeight::def: Object r defined

The indices are reordered using the Riemann symmetries.

In[9]:= **newRiemannr[ld,lc,lb,la]**

Out[9]= r
    abcd

This defines a tensor of the second rank with no symmetries. In general, if there are no symmetries present, you enter **{{1,2,..,rank},1}** as the third argument of **DefineTensor**, where rank is the number of indices.

In[10]:= **DefineTensor[w,"w",{{1,2},1}]**

PermWeight::def: Object w defined

This defines a vector or tensor of the first rank.

In[11]:= **DefineTensor[v,"v",{{1},1}]**

PermWeight::def: Object v defined

No reordering of the indices of **w** occurs.

In[12]:= **{w[lb,la],w[uc,la],v[la],v[ub]}**

Out[12]= {w , w , v , v }
      ba a a

This is an abbreviated syntax that defines a second-rank symmetric tensor having input name q and having print symbol "q", the same as its input name.

In[13]:= **DefineTensor[q,{{2,1},1}]**

PermWeight::sym: Symmetries of q assigned

PermWeight::def: Object q defined

This abbreviated syntax defines two second rank antisymmetric tensors p and t having input names and print symbols the same.

In[14]:= **DefineTensor[{p,t},{{2,1},-1}]**

PermWeight::sym: Symmetries of p assigned

PermWeight::def: Object p defined

PermWeight::sym: Symmetries of t assigned

PermWeight::def: Object t defined

This shows the symmetries and print symbols.

In[15]:= **{q[lb,la], p[lb,la], t[lb,la]}**

Out[15]= {q , -p , -t }
     ab ab ab

DefineTensor[*name,string,permWeights*]

> defines tensor called *name* with print symbol *string*, where *string* is quoted, and with permutation-weight list *permWeights*

DefineTensor[*name,permWeights*]

> abbreviated syntax in which the print symbol is the same as the input name

DefineTensor[{*name1*,#*name2*,..},*permWeights*]

> extension of previous syntax in which several tensors are defined with the same symmetries

---

Basic function for defining a new tensor.

You can also define tensors with cyclic symmetry.

This gives left-handed cyclic permutations in which the index in slot 3 of cyc moves left to slot 1, with unit weight.	*In[16]:=* DefineTensor[cyc,"c",{{3,1,2},1}] PermWeight::sym: Symmetries of c assigned PermWeight::def: Object c defined
In this case, each term is put into a unique form by cyclic permutation so that simplification will occur.	*In[17]:=* cyc[1c,1a,1b] + cyc[1a,1b,1c] + cyc[1c,1b,1a] *Out[17]=* 2 c_{abc} + c_{acb}

The weights in the permutation-weight list are almost always 1 or -1, although there are cases in which other weights are consistent. For example, with cyclic symmetry of a third-rank tensor, you can consistently have weights given by any one of the three cube roots of 1. In this case, you must also create a rule to tell *Mathematica* how to simplify powers of the cube root you are using as a weight. The rest of this section is rather advanced and can be skipped on first reading. If you are using *Mathematica* 1.2, you will see somewhat different output from that shown in the rest of this section. The reason is that in *Mathematica* 2.X powers of the complex cube root of 1 are automatically simplified. The steps below involving the definition of powers of the complex exponential are required only in *Mathematica* 1.2 in order to bring about that simplification. If you are using *Mathematica* 1.2, then you will see Exp[(4 I/3) Pi] instead of the Exp[(-2 I/3) Pi] appearing below. The results are equivalent, corresponding to different branch cuts for the complex exponential.

This sets cr to one of the cube roots of 1.

```
In[18]:= cr = Exp[ (2 I/3) Pi]
            (2 I)/3 Pi
Out[18]= E
```

This is equal to Exp[(2 I/3) Pi]. The following rule will produce the necessary simplification. You can just copy the steps given if you are not familiar with creating such a rule.

```
In[19]:= cr^4
            (2 I)/3 Pi
Out[19]= E
```

First unprotect the *Mathematica* function Power.

```
In[20]:= Unprotect[Power];
```

This is the required rule. The left-hand side is based on the FullForm of the type of expressions to be matched. An example of such an expression is Exp[(8 I/3) Pi]. The right-hand side is based on the form to be output by the rule.

```
In[21]:= Power[E,Times[Complex[0, Rational[n_,3]],Pi]] :=
            Exp[(Mod[n,6] I)/3 Pi] /; n>6
```

Finally, protect Power again.

```
In[22]:= Protect[Power];
```

Now powers of the cube root simplify properly. Finally, you are ready to define a tensor with cyclic symmetry and a complex weight.

```
In[23]:= {cr^4,cr^8}
            (2 I)/3 Pi    (-2 I)/3 Pi
Out[23]= {E          , E          }
```

The weight is a cube root of unity.

```
In[24]:= DefineTensor[compcyc, "cc", {{3,1,2}, cr}]
 PermWeight::sym: Symmetries of cc assigned
 PermWeight::def: Object cc defined
```

These reorderings are unique and consistent.

```
In[25]:= compcyc[lc,la,lb] + compcyc[la,lb,lc] +
compcyc[lc,lb,la]
                  (-2 I)/3 Pi         (2 I)/3 Pi
Out[25]= cc    + E           cc    + E          cc
           abc                 abc               acb
```

Here is the full symmetry list of compcyc.

```
In[26]:= AllSymmetries[compcyc[xx,yy,zz] ]
                                    (-2 I)/3 Pi
Out[26]= {{1, 2, 3}, 1, {2, 3, 1}, E           ,
                         (2 I)/3 Pi
 >    {3, 1, 2}, E          }
```

■ 3.2 Contraction and the Metric Tensor

■ 3.2.1 Forming New Tensors by Contraction

If you set a contravariant index of one tensor equal to a covariant index of the same or another tensor and sum over all possible values of the index, as in $\sum_a v^a w_{ba}$, then you get a new tensor with transformation properties corresponding to the remaining unsummed indices. This process of forming a new tensor by summing over a repeated contravariant and covariant index is called *contraction*. It is conventional to assume that in an expression having repeated upper and lower indices, the repeated indices are summed over their possible values. According to this summation convention, the previous expression is written as $v^a w_{ba}$. This expression would be input to *MathTensor* as `v[ua] w[lb,la]`, assuming that tensors `v` and `w` have already been defined using `DefineTensor`. Note that indices `ua` and `la` form a pair that is contracted; one index must be contravariant and the other covariant. Because of the way that contravariant and covariant indices transform, a contracted pair of indices behaves like a scalar, undergoing no change under coordinate transformations. Summing over an identical pair of lower indices would not in general produce a new tensor, and it is illegal to repeat the same lower or upper index more than once in a product of tensors. The tensors `v[uc] w[lb,lc]` and `v[ua] w[lb,la]` are equal because the paired indices are contracted, or summed over their possible values. The contracted pair of indices is known as a dummy pair because the names of the indices are irrelevant. The only restriction on the naming of dummy indices is that the names should not conflict with those of uncontracted indices or other pairs of dummy indices. The names should of course be taken from the list of index names recognized by *MathTensor*, as discussed earlier.

In Section 3.1.4, you used `Definition` to record the definition of a second-rank antisymmetric tensor, `anti`, in the file `NewTensors.m`. This recovers that definition.

$$In[1]:= \text{<< NewTensors.m}$$

Here we contract on index a. The indices have been reordered so that the lower index comes before the upper. This is done in general by *MathTensor* when the symmetry permits.

$$In[2]:= \text{expr1 = anti[la,lb] anti[ua,lc]}$$

$$Out[2]= -(a_{ab} \, a^{\ a}_{\ c})$$

The two terms in this sum are equal because of the antisymmetry of `anti`. We will see later how to cause simplification of such expressions. In this case, simplification can be brought about simply by renaming the dummy indices.

```
In[3]:= % + anti[1b,1d] anti[1c,ud]
```

$$Out[3]= -(a_{ab}{}^{a}{}_{c}) + a_{bd}{}^{a}{}^{d}{}_{c}$$

A function that does this is `Dum`.

```
In[4]:= Dum[%]
```

$$Out[4]= -2\, a_{pb}{}^{p}\, a_{c}$$

The dummy index pair was renamed l1 and u1 by `Dum`. These are internally generated dummy index names.

```
In[5]:= Off[TensorForm]; %
Out[5]= -2*anti[11, 1b]*anti[1c, u1]
```

Here is the list of covariant dummy indices that *MathTensor* generates internally.

```
In[6]:= Downdummylist
Out[6]= {11, 12, 13, 14, 15, 16, 17, 18, 19, 110, 111,
>     112, 113, 114, 115}
```

These are the contravariant dummy indices that *MathTensor* generates internally.

```
In[7]:= Updummylist
Out[7]= {u1, u2, u3, u4, u5, u6, u7, u8, u9, u10, u11,
>     u12, u13, u14, u15}
```

`Dum` has a second argument that can be used to specify the number at which dummy index numbering in an expression should begin.

```
In[8]:= Dum[expr1, 2]
Out[8]= -(anti[12, 1b]*anti[1c, u2])
```

This has the same dummy index as `expr1`, but different free indices.

```
In[9]:= expr2 = anti[1a,1d] anti[ua,1e]
Out[9]= -(anti[1a, 1d]*anti[1e, ua])
```

The second argument of `Dum` can be used to prevent conflicting dummy index names from appearing when forming a product.

```
In[10]:= Dum[expr1, 1] Dum[expr2, 2]
Out[10]= anti[11, 1b]*anti[12, 1d]*anti[1c, u1]*
>     anti[1e, u2]
```

When more than one dummy pair is present, `Dum` will number them consecutively starting at the integer specified or at 1 if unspecified. The specified integer should be small enough so that the system will not run out of dummy indices. For calculations involving many dummy pairs, another method is available, which will be discussed later.

```
In[11]:= expr3 = Dum[%,3]
Out[11]= anti[13, 1b]*anti[14, 1d]*anti[1c, u3]*
>     anti[1e, u4]
```

By turning `TensorForm` on again, you can see how the internal dummy indices will be printed in standard tensor notation. These are the covariant ones. The last four dummy indices do not have special print forms because it is very unlikely that you will ever have more than 11 pairs of dummy indices in a single product of tensors. If you do, you can turn off `TensorForm` to see expressions in input form.

$In[12] :=$ `On[TensorForm]; Downdummylist`

$Out[12] = \{\, p,\, q,\, r,\, s,\, t,\, u,\, v,\, w,\, x,\, y,\, z,\, 112,\, 113,\, 114,$

$>\quad 115\}$

Here are the contravariant internal dummy indices.

$In[13] :=$ **Updummylist**

$Out[13] = \{\, p,\, q,\, r,\, s,\, t,\, u,\, v,\, w,\, x,\, y,\, z,\, u12,\, u13,\, u14,$

$>\quad u15\}$

Here is `expr3` with `TensorForm` on.

$In[14] :=$ **expr3**

$Out[14] = a_{rb}\, a_{sd}\, a_c{}^r\, a_e{}^s$

If you wish to make a substitution in an expression involving dummy indices, you can either remember the input form of the dummy indices or look at the expression in input form, as was already done a few steps before. Here, the standard *Mathematica* function `ReplaceAll` or `/.` is used.

$In[15] :=$ **expr3 /. anti[13,1b] -> MaxwellF[13,1b]**

$Out[15] = a_{sd}\, a_c{}^r\, a_e{}^s\, F_{rb}$

Dum[*expr*]	relabel dummy indices starting with the first pair of internal dummy indices
Dum[*expr*, *n*]	relabel dummy indices starting with the *n*th pair of internal dummy indices
Updummylist	list of internally generated contravariant dummy indices
Downdummylist	list of internally generated covariant dummy indices

A function and lists relevant to the renaming of contracted indices.

■ 3.2.2 Raising and Lowering Indices with the Metric Tensor

The distance ds between two nearby points on a surface (or hypersurface) is related to the coordinate separation dx^a between the points by a relation

$$ds^2 = g_{ab}\, dx^a\, dx^b.$$

The set of functions g_{ab} constitute a tensor known as the metric tensor, which is denoted in *MathTensor* by `Metricg[la,lb]`. If a contravariant tensor v^a is contracted with the metric tensor to form $g_{ab}v^b$, the new tensor transforms covariantly and is denoted by v_a. Similarly, $v^a = g^{ab}v_b$, where g^{ab} is defined as the inverse of g_{ab}, so that $g_{ab}g^{bc} = \delta_b{}^c$. Thus the metric tensor is used to raise and lower indices.

Automatic absorption of `Metricg` by raising or lowering indices whenever possible is controlled by a variable called a flag, which takes only the two values `True` or `False`. The flag variable, in this case, is called `MetricgFlag` and is `True` when *MathTensor* starts, meaning that automatic absorption will occur.

The metric tensor is used here to raise the first index on `anti[lb,lc]` to form, in input notation, `anti[ua,lc]`.

```
In[16]:= Metricg[ua,ub] anti[lb,lc]
                   a
Out[16]= -a
                 c
```

The metric tensor is symmetric, the indices being reordered alphabetically.

```
In[17]:= Metricg[lb,la]
Out[17]= g
             ab
```

`Metricg[la,ub]`, with one covariant and one contravariant index, acts as the Kronecker delta, $\delta_a{}^b$, which is 0 if the two indices have different values and 1 otherwise.

```
In[18]:= Metricg[la,ub] RicciR[lb,lc]
Out[18]= R
             ac
```

As noted earlier, lower indices will be ordered before upper ones if permitted by the symmetry, as in this result.

```
In[19]:= Metricg[ua,ub] Metricg[lb,lc]
                 a
Out[19]= g
             c
```

The metric tensor can be used to contract indices. This contraction of the Riemann tensor is equal to `RiemannR[ub,lc,lb,ld]`. It is called the Ricci tensor and would be input to *MathTensor* as `RicciR[lc,ld]`.

```
In[20]:= Metricg[ua,ub] RiemannR[la,lc,lb,ld]
Out[20]= R
             cd
```

The contraction of the Ricci tensor, `RicciR[ua,la]`, is called the scalar curvature and is denoted in input form by `ScalarR`.

```
In[21]:= Metricg[ua,ub] RicciR[la,lb]
Out[21]= R
```

Metricg[*la*,*lb*]	metric tensor g_{ab} lowers indices
Metricg[*la*,*ub*]	$g_a{}^b$ acts as Kronecker delta $\delta_a{}^b$
Metricg[*ua*,*ub*]	g^{ab} raises indices

The metric tensor raises and lowers indices.

■ 3.2.3 Preventing Automatic Absorption of the Metric

There are occasions when you may want to prevent automatic raising and lowering of indices through absorption of the metric. Automatic absorption of the metric is controlled by MetricgFlag.

This sets MetricgFlag to False and also invokes Update, which updates rules having conditions involving the changed flag variable.

In[22]:= **Off[MetricgFlag];**

Now the metric is not absorbed by raising an index.

In[23]:= **Metricg[ua,ub] anti[lb,lc]**

$Out[23]= a_{bc}{}^{ab}\, g^{ab}$

This causes automatic absorption to occur again.

In[24]:= **On[MetricgFlag];**

If you are carrying out a calculation in which you do not want automatic absorption of the metric to occur but you do want to absorb the metric in certain terms or expressions, you can use the function Absorbg.

Again prevents automatic absorption of the metric tensor.

In[25]:= **Off[MetricgFlag]**

Standard *Mathematica* functions can be used in a *MathTensor* session. Here, Expand is used to distribute the factor involving the metric.

In[26]:= **expr4 = Expand[Metricg[la,lb](RicciR[ub,uc] + anti[ub,uc])]**

$Out[26]= a_{ab}{}^{bc}\, g + g_{ab}\, R^{bc}$

The *MathTensor* function Absorbg will cause absorption of Metricg by lowering or raising indices when possible. In some complicated expressions, you may have to apply Absorbg more than once to raise or lower all possible indices.

In[27]:= **Absorbg[expr4]**

$Out[27]= a_a{}^c + R_a{}^c$

This applies `Absorbg` only to the first term of `expr4`. The second argument specifies the number of the term in a sum to which `Absorbg` is applied.

$In[28] := $ **`Absorbg[expr4, 1]`**

$$Out[28] = a\begin{smallmatrix}c\\a\end{smallmatrix} + g\begin{smallmatrix}bc\\ab\end{smallmatrix}R$$

The value of `expr4` has not been altered.

$In[29] := $ **`expr4`**

$$Out[29] = a\begin{smallmatrix}bc\\ \\ab\end{smallmatrix}g + g\begin{smallmatrix}bc\\ab\end{smallmatrix}R$$

Here is another way to apply `Absorbg` to the first term of `expr4`, but this time the value of `expr4` has been changed.

$In[30] := $ **`expr4[[1]] = Absorbg[expr4[[1]] ] ; expr4`**

$$Out[30] = a\begin{smallmatrix}c\\a\end{smallmatrix} + g\begin{smallmatrix}bc\\ab\end{smallmatrix}R$$

With `MetricgFlag` turned on, all factors of `Metricg` that can lower or raise an index will be automatically absorbed.

$In[31] := $ **`On[MetricgFlag]; expr4`**

$$Out[31] = a\begin{smallmatrix}c\\a\end{smallmatrix} + R\begin{smallmatrix}c\\a\end{smallmatrix}$$

`On[MetricgFlag]`	turn on automatic absorption of `Metricg`
`Off[MetricgFlag]`	prevent automatic absorption of `Metricg`
`Absorbg[`*expr*`]`	cause absorption when possible of `Metricg`
`Absorbg[`*expr,n*`]`	cause absorption in *n*th term of a sum

Controlling absorption of `Metricg`.

There are times when you may have more than one metric tensor present and may want to raise and lower indices, not with `Metricg`, but with another metric tensor. This is done with the *MathTensor* function `Absorb`.

`Absorb[`*expr, metric*`]`	cause absorption, when possible, of *metric*
`Absorbg[`*expr,metric,n*`]`	cause absorption in *n*th term of a sum

Raising and lowering indices with an arbitrary metric.

This defines a symmetric tensor called `Metricga`.

$In[32] := $ **`DefineTensor[Metricga,"ga",{{2,1},1}]`**

`PermWeight::sym: Symmetries of ga assigned`

`PermWeight::def: Object ga defined`

Its print symbol is ga.

$$In[33]:= \texttt{Metricga[li,lj]}$$
$$Out[33]= \texttt{ga}_{ij}$$

Suppose that you want to use `Metricga` to raise an index of `RicciR` in this expression.

$$In[34]:= \texttt{RicciR[li,lj] Metricga[ui,uj]}$$
$$Out[34]= \texttt{ga}^{ij}\ \texttt{R}_{ij}$$

`Absorb` does this.

$$In[35]:= \texttt{Absorb[\%, Metricga]}$$
$$Out[35]= \texttt{R}$$

■ 3.3 Simplification

■ 3.3.1 Methods of Simplifying Tensor Expressions

When you are dealing with tensors having components that are specified algebraic functions, simplification of each component is carried out as with any algebraic function in *Mathematica*. Tensors with given components will be discussed later. The tensors in this section contain symbolic indices that specify their rank and transformation properties, but that do not have any specific numerical values (i.e., the tensors are manipulated as single entities, like vectors in ordinary vector analysis). New commands are required to recognize when two terms are equal in a sum of products of tensors containing contracted indices. This recognition is not simple, particularly when the tensors involved have special symmetries. Here are some examples of expressions with terms that are equal.

These terms are equal because of the symmetries of the Ricci and Riemann tensors, which were discussed in Section 3.1.3.

```
In[1]:= expr1 =
RicciR[ua,ub] RiemannR[la,li,lb,lj] +
RicciR[ua,ub] RiemannR[la,lj,lb,li]
```

$$Out[1]= \texttt{R}^{ab}\ \texttt{R}_{aibj} + \texttt{R}^{ab}\ \texttt{R}_{ajbi}$$

Here is an example of two equal terms cubic in the Riemann tensor.

```
In[2]:= expr2 =
RiemannR[la,lb,lc,ld] RiemannR[ua,ub,ue,uf]*
RiemannR[uc,ud,le,lf] + RiemannR[lc,ld,ug,uh]*
RiemannR[le,lf,lg,lh] RiemannR[uc,ud,ue,uf]
```

$$Out[2]= \texttt{R}_{abcd}\ \texttt{R}^{abef}_{ef}\ \texttt{R}^{cd} + \texttt{R}^{gh}_{cd}\ \texttt{R}_{efgh}\ \texttt{R}^{cdef}$$

Here is one cubic in the Ricci tensor.

$In[3] :=$ **expr3 =**
RicciR[la,lc] RicciR[lb,uc] RicciR[ua,ub] +
RicciR[la,lb] RicciR[ua,lc] RicciR[ub,uc]

$$Out[3] = R_{ac} R^{c}_{b} R^{ab} + R_{ab} R^{a}_{c} R^{bc}$$

These are equal because the dummy
indices merely have different names.

$In[4] :=$ **expr4 =**
RiemannR[ua,ub,uc,ud] RiemannR[la,lb,lc,ld] +
RiemannR[ua,uc,ub,ud] RiemannR[la,lc,lb,ld]

$$Out[4] = R^{abcd} R_{abcd} + R^{acbd} R_{acbd}$$

More complicated examples can easily be constructed. There are two main
approaches that can be taken to simplify such expressions. One approach was
already illustrated by the command Dum and consists of relabeling dummy indices
in such a way that the terms become identical.

This is an example on which the approach
works.

$In[5] :=$ **Dum[expr4]**

$$Out[5] = 2 R^{pqrs} R_{pqrs}$$

The method fails to simplify this
expression, or the others above.

$In[6] :=$ **Dum[expr1]**

$$Out[6] = R^{pq} R_{piqj} + R^{pq} R_{pjqi}$$

We will use these definitions in several of
the next subsections, so we write them to
a file, which you can later delete.

$In[7] :=$ **Definition[expr1,expr2,expr3,expr4]>>**
Temporary.m

In Section 3.3.4, you will learn about commands that rename dummy indices
and attempt to order the indices in a unique canonical way so that terms that are
equal become identical. This approach is called *canonicalization*.

Another approach to simplification is pattern matching. Terms are combined
if they fit a common pattern, even if they are not strictly identical. This is closer
to the way in which the human mind works. The command Tsimplify performs
simplification through pattern matching and is the most powerful command you can
use to do simplification in *MathTensor*. If there is one command in *MathTensor*
that you should remember in connection with simplification, it is Tsimplify. It
will be described in the next several sections.

■ 3.3.2 Simplifying with Symmetries

In Section 3.1.3, you learned how to define new tensors. Here you will recall some previously saved definitions and will define some new tensors to help you learn about simplification with the *MathTensor* command `Tsimplify`.

This recalls the definition of `anti`.

$$In[1]:= \ll NewTensors.m$$

This recalls the definitions of the four expressions defined in Section 3.3.1. The last expression in the file is printed out.

$$In[2]:= \ll Temporary.m$$

$$Out[2]= R_{abcd}{}^{abcd} + R_{acbd}{}^{acbd}$$

This defines a symmetric second-rank tensor.

$$In[3]:= DefineTensor[sym,"s",\{\{2,1\},1\}]$$

PermWeight::sym: Symmetries of s assigned

PermWeight::def: Object s defined

This appends its definition to the file `NewTensors.m` for future use.

$$In[4]:= Definition[sym] \gg NewTensors.m$$

Here, an antisymmetric and a symmetric tensor are contracted.

$$In[5]:= anti[la,lb]\ sym[ua,ub]$$

$$Out[5]= a_{ab}\ s^{ab}$$

`Tsimplify`, when applied to a single term, tests whether it vanishes by symmetry. If it does not, it returns the term unchanged.

$$In[6]:= Tsimplify[\%]$$

$$Out[6]= 0$$

The contraction or trace of an antisymmetric tensor is 0.

$$In[7]:= Tsimplify[anti[la,ua]\ ]$$

$$Out[7]= 0$$

Here is an expression in which the two terms are equal because of the symmetries of the tensors involved.

$$In[8]:= anti[lb,ld]\ sym[lc,ub] - anti[ld,ub]\ sym[lb,lc]$$

$$Out[8]= -(a_{d}{}^{b}\ s_{bc}) + a_{bd}\ s^{b}{}_{c}$$

`Tsimplify` combines all terms in a sum that are equal by symmetry.

$$In[9]:= Tsimplify[\%]$$

$$Out[9]= -2\ a_{d}{}^{b}\ s_{bc}$$

Here are the same two terms with coefficients.

$In[10] := $ **m anti[lb,ld] sym[lc,ub] + n anti[ld,ub] sym[lb,lc]**

$Out[10] = n\, a^{b}{}_{d}\, s_{bc} + m\, a_{bd}\, s^{b}{}_{c}$

The terms are recognized as equal, and the factors are grouped as a single factor.

$In[11] := $ **Tsimplify[%]**

$Out[11] = (-m + n)\, a^{b}{}_{d}\, s_{bc}$

Here is a sum of four terms. You could use Tsimplify[expr] to simplify this. There are also optional integer arguments that control the action of Tsimplify.

$In[12] := $ **expr = expr3 + expr4**

$Out[12] = R_{ac}\, R^{c}{}_{b}\, R^{ab} + R_{ab}\, R^{a}{}_{c}\, R^{bc} + R_{abcd}\, R^{abcd} +$

$> \quad R_{acbd}\, R^{acbd}$

This compares the second term with every other term and attempts to simplify.

$In[13] := $ **Tsimplify[expr,2]**

$Out[13] = 2\, R_{ab}\, R^{a}{}_{c}\, R^{bc} + R_{abcd}\, R^{abcd} + R_{acbd}\, R^{acbd}$

This finds other terms that combine with the third term.

$In[14] := $ **Tsimplify[expr,3]**

$Out[14] = R_{ac}\, R^{c}{}_{b}\, R^{ab} + R_{ab}\, R^{a}{}_{c}\, R^{bc} + 2\, R_{abcd}\, R^{abcd}$

In this case, only terms 1 and 2 are compared to see if they will combine.

$In[15] := $ **Tsimplify[expr,1,2]**

$Out[15] = 2\, R_{ac}\, R^{c}{}_{b}\, R^{ab} + R_{abcd}\, R^{abcd} + R_{acbd}\, R^{acbd}$

The command TsimplifyAfter compares the indicated term (in this case term 3) to see if it combines with any terms *after* it.

$In[16] := $ **TsimplifyAfter[expr,3]**

$Out[16] = R_{ac}\, R^{c}{}_{b}\, R^{ab} + R_{ab}\, R^{a}{}_{c}\, R^{bc} + 2\, R_{abcd}\, R^{abcd}$

This is cubic in the Riemann tensor.

$In[17] := $ **expr2**

$Out[17] = R_{abcd}\, R^{cd}{}_{ef}\, R^{abef} + R_{cd}\, R^{gh}{}_{efgh}\, R^{cdef}$

This may take some time on your computer because of the complicated symmetries of the products of three Riemann tensors.

$In[18] := $ **Tsimplify[%]**

$Out[18] = 2\, R_{abcd}\, R^{cd}{}_{ef}\, R^{abef}$

TensorSimp is similar to Tsimplify but much less powerful. When you are dealing with very long expressions, you can occasionally save time by using TensorSimp to reduce the number of terms before applying Tsimplify. There is also a command TensorSimpAfter that works like TsimplifyAfter but is not as powerful.

$In[19] :=$ **TensorSimp[expr4]**

$Out[19] =$ $2\ R_{abcd}\ R^{abcd}$

Tsimplify[*expr*]	combine terms in a sum, taking account of symmetries; if *expr* is a single term, test if it is 0 by symmetry
Tsimplify[*expr*,*n*]	compare the *n*th term with all others and combine terms if possible
Tsimplify[*expr*,*n*,*m*]	compare term *n* with term *m* and combine them if possible
TsimplifyAfter[*expr*,*n*]	compare the *n*th term with all terms *after* it and combine terms if possible
TensorSimp[*expr*]	combine terms in a sum; less powerful but faster than Tsimplify
TensorSimpAfter[*expr*,*n*]	compare the *n*th term with all terms after it; less powerful than TsimplifyAfter

Commands that use pattern matching to simplify sums of tensors.

■ 3.3.3 Simplifying Traces and Contractions of Products

As is well known, the trace of a product of matrices or tensors can be cyclically permuted without changing its value.

This defines a second-rank tensor with no symmetries.

$In[1] :=$ **DefineTensor[nosym1,"ns1",{{1,2},1}]**
PermWeight::def: Object ns1 defined

This defines another.

$In[2] :=$ **DefineTensor[nosym2,"ns2",{{1,2},1}]**
PermWeight::def: Object ns2 defined

And here is a third.

$In[3] :=$ **DefineTensor[nosym3,"ns3",{{1,2},1}]**
PermWeight::def: Object ns3 defined

Each of these terms is a trace, with the second term being a cyclic permutation of the first. In the output line, the terms are already reordered so that the only difference is in the naming of dummy indices.

```
In[4]:= expr =
nosym1[la,ub] nosym2[lb,uc] nosym3[lc,ua] +
nosym3[la,ub] nosym1[lb,uc] nosym2[lc,ua]
```

$$Out[4] = ns1_b{}^c \, ns2_c{}^a \, ns3_a{}^b + ns1_a{}^b \, ns2_b{}^c \, ns3_c{}^a$$

The terms are combined by `Tsimplify`.

```
In[5]:= Tsimplify[expr]
```

$$Out[5] = 2 \, ns1_b{}^c \, ns2_c{}^a \, ns3_a{}^b$$

The command `TensorSimp` will also simplify this expression.

```
In[6]:= TensorSimp[expr]
```

$$Out[6] = 2 \, ns1_b{}^c \, ns2_c{}^a \, ns3_a{}^b$$

This defines a fourth-rank tensor having no symmetries.

```
In[7]:= DefineTensor[n,"n",{{1,2,3,4},1}]

PermWeight::def: Object n defined
```

This sum of two quadratic products has a more complicated interconnection among indices than a simple trace.

```
In[8]:= n[ua, ub, lc, ld] n[uc, ud, le, lh]*
n[ue, uf, lg, lf] n[ug, uh, la, lb] -
n[ua, ub, lc, ld] n[uc, ud, le, lf]*
n[ue, uf, lg, lb] n[ug, uh, la, lh]
```

$$Out[8] = n^{ab}{}_{cd} \, n^{cd}{}_{eh} \, n^{ef}{}_{gf} \, n^{gh}{}_{ab} - n^{ab}{}_{cd} \, n^{cd}{}_{ef} \, n^{ef}{}_{gb} \, n^{gh}{}_{ah}$$

It is rapidly simplified by the command `Tsimplify`.

```
In[9]:= Tsimplify[%]

Out[9] = 0
```

You will find that the command `Tsimplify[`*expr*`]` with no additional arguments is sufficient for simplification of essentially all tensor expressions. The additional arguments and functions are provided so that you will have the option of more control over which terms in an expression are combined. When you are dealing with very long expressions, it may save time to reduce the number of terms using weaker but faster commands before applying `Tsimplify`.

■ 3.3.4 Canonical Ordering of Indices

There are a number of commands in *MathTensor* that relabel dummy indices and attempt to select a unique canonical ordering for each term in a sum so that terms that are equal will combine. The command `Dum` was already discussed in Section 3.2.1.

Dum[*expr*]	insert system-generated dummy indices
Dum[*expr*, *n*]	insert system-generated dummy indices starting with the pair l*n*, u*n*
CanDum[*expr*]	insert system-generated dummy indices, ordering covariant before contravariant ones if possible
CanDum[*expr*, *n*]	insert system-generated dummy indices, starting with the pair l*n*, u*n*, and ordering covariant before contravariant ones if possible
CanAll[*expr*]	insert system-generated dummy indices and perform certain index permutations to find a lexically first canonical form
Canonicalize[*expr*]	like CanAll but will also work after a substitution rule has generated new pairs of dummy indices
CanNonInvert[*expr*]	attempt canonicalization but without raising or lowering dummy indices; use on expressions with noncovariant derivatives

Commands that canonicalize terms to simplify sums of tensors.

This loads the four expressions defined in Section 3.3.1. The last expression loaded is printed out.

$$In[1] := \texttt{<<Temporary.m}$$

$$Out[1] = R_{abcd}R^{abcd} + R_{acbd}R^{acbd}$$

This is cubic in the Riemann tensor.

$$In[2] := \texttt{expr2}$$

$$Out[2] = R_{abcd}R^{cd}_{ef}R^{abef} + R^{gh}_{cd}R_{efgh}R^{cdef}$$

The command CanDum combines terms through reordering and relabeling the dummy indices.

$$In[3] := \texttt{CanDum[expr2]}$$

$$Out[3] = 2\,R_{pqrs}R^{rs}_{tu}R^{pqtu}$$

This is cubic in the Ricci tensor.

$$In[4] := \texttt{expr3}$$

$$Out[4] = R_{ac}R^{c}_{b}R^{ab} + R_{ab}R^{a}_{c}R^{bc}$$

This time CanDum fails to combine terms.

But the more powerful command CanAll succeeds. CanAll decides whether to use CanDum or a more powerful version of it, called CannnDum, on an expression. Usually, CanDum will work on terms quadratic in the Riemann tensor and its contractions but not on terms cubic in the Riemann tensor.

$$In[5] := \text{CanDum[expr3]}$$

$$Out[5] = R_{pq}{}^{q}{}_{r} R^{pr} + R_{pq}{}^{p}{}_{r} R^{qr}$$

$$In[6] := \text{CanAll[expr3]}$$

$$Out[6] = 2 R_{pq}{}^{p}{}_{r} R^{qr}$$

There is also a command Canonicalize that works like CanAll. When you are dealing with noncovariant terms, as when noncovariant derivatives are present in an expression, you cannot freely raise and lower indices. In that case, only Dum and CanNonInvert may be applied in order to attempt canonicalization. Tsimplify will also work in such cases. The command CanNonInvert will be discussed when ordinary derivatives are introduced.

The commands Tsimplify and CanAll or Canonicalize provide two different approaches, pattern matching and canonicalization, to simplifying expressions. This allows one to check results by two independent methods.

■ 3.4 Operations on Tensors

■ 3.4.1 Symmetrization and Antisymmetrization

There are many operations defined on tensors. Among the most fundamental are symmetrization and antisymmetrization.

Symmetrize[*expr*,{la,lb,..}]   symmetrize *expr* with respect to the listed indices

Antisymmetrize[*expr*,{la,lb,..}]

antisymmetrize *expr* with respect to the listed indices

PairSymmetrize[*expr*,{{la,lb},{lc,ld},..}]

symmetrize *expr* under exchange among listed pairs

PairAntisymmetrize[*expr*,{{la,lb},{lc,ld},..}]

antisymmetrize *expr* under exchange among listed pairs

SetSymmetric[*tensor*]   redefine *tensor* so that it is totally symmetric

SetAntisymmetric[*tensor*]   redefine *tensor* so that it is totally antisymmetric

---

Commands that symmetrize and antisymmetrize tensor expressions.

This symmetrizes the Riemann tensor on the first and third indices. In the second term, *MathTensor* uses the known symmetries of the Riemann tensor to automatically switch the first and second pair of indices so that the index la is in the first slot and to reorder the second pair of indices so that lb comes before lc. The latter interchange is responsible for the final minus sign.

$$In[1]:= \texttt{Symmetrize[RiemannR[la,lb,lc,ld],\{la,lc\}]}$$

$$Out[1]= \frac{R_{abcd} - R_{adbc}}{2}$$

This antisymmetrizes on the first and third indices.

$$In[2]:= \texttt{Antisymmetrize[RiemannR[la,lb,lc,ld],\{la,lc\}]}$$

$$Out[2]= \frac{R_{abcd} + R_{adbc}}{2}$$

The Riemann tensor is antisymmetric under interchange of the first pair of indices, so the two terms produced by this symmetrization add up to zero.

$$In[3]:= \texttt{Symmetrize[RiemannR[la,lb,lc,ld],\{la,lb\}]}$$

$$Out[3]= 0$$

Similarly, the two terms produced by antisymmetrization with respect to the first two indices add up to the original tensor.

$$In[4]:= \texttt{Antisymmetrize[RiemannR[la,lb,lc,ld],\{la,lb\}]}$$

$$Out[4]= R_{abcd}$$

This antisymmetrizes the product of the antisymmetric tensor `MaxwellF[la,lb]` with the symmetric tensor `RicciR[lc,ld]` over the indices `la,lb,lc`.

$In[5] :=$ `Antisymmetrize[MaxwellF[la,lb]`
`RicciR[lc,ld],{la,lb,lc}]`

$$Out[5] = \frac{F_{bc}\ R_{ad}}{3} - \frac{F_{ac}\ R_{bd}}{3} + \frac{F_{ab}\ R_{cd}}{3}$$

Suppose that you want to symmetrize this expression over interchange of the pair of indices (a,c) with (b,e) or with (d,f), and of (b,e) with (d,f).

$In[6] :=$ `expr1 = MaxwellF[la,lb] RicciR[lc,ld]`
`RicciR[le,lf]`

$$Out[6] = F_{ab}\ R_{cd}\ R_{ef}$$

The resulting expression is symmetric under the desired exchanges of index pairs with one another.

$In[7] :=$ `PairSymmetrize[expr1,{{la,lc},{lb,le},{ld,lf}}]`

$$Out[7] = \frac{-(F_{bd}\ R_{af}\ R_{ce})}{6} - \frac{F_{ad}\ R_{bf}\ R_{ce}}{6} + \frac{F_{bd}\ R_{ae}\ R_{cf}}{6} -$$

$$> \quad \frac{F_{ab}\ R_{cf}\ R_{de}}{6} + \frac{F_{ad}\ R_{bc}\ R_{ef}}{6} + \frac{F_{ab}\ R_{cd}\ R_{ef}}{6}$$

This expression is antisymmetric under the same set of exchanges among index pairs.

$In[8] :=$
`PairAntisymmetrize[expr1,{{la,lc},{lb,le},{ld,lf}}]`

$$Out[8] = \frac{F_{bd}\ R_{af}\ R_{ce}}{6} - \frac{F_{ad}\ R_{bf}\ R_{ce}}{6} + \frac{F_{bd}\ R_{ae}\ R_{cf}}{6} +$$

$$> \quad \frac{F_{ab}\ R_{cf}\ R_{de}}{6} - \frac{F_{ad}\ R_{bc}\ R_{ef}}{6} + \frac{F_{ab}\ R_{cd}\ R_{ef}}{6}$$

Suppose you want to define a totally symmetric tensor, `tens` of rank 4. You can first define a fourth-rank tensor, `tens`, having no symmetries (this defines the desired input and output formatting).

$In[9] :=$ `DefineTensor[tens,{{1,2,3,4},1}]`

`PermWeight::def: Object tens defined`

The command `SetSymmetric` makes the tensor symmetric in all its indices. (The particular indices entered here do not matter.)

$In[10] :=$ `SetSymmetric[tens[la,lb,lc,ld] ]`

`PermWeight::sym: Symmetries of tens assigned`

Here is an example of the symmetry.

$In[11] :=$ `tens[ld,lc,lb,la]`

$$Out[11] = tens_{abcd}$$

Similarly, `SetAntisymmetric` makes the tensor antisymmetric in all its indices.

$In[12] :=$ `SetAntisymmetric[tens[la,lb,lc,ld] ]`

`PermWeight::sym: Symmetries of tens assigned`

This is reordered using the total
antisymmetry.

```
In[13]:= tens[1d,1b,1c,1a]
Out[13]= -tens
              abcd
```

■ 3.4.2 Differential Form Operations

You can also build operations on differential forms, regarded as antisymmetric tensors, using the command **Antisymmetrize**. However, *MathTensor* has built-in differential forms commands and operations by means of which you can define and deal with differential forms in the standard way without using indices. You can, at any stage of the calculation, give a command to rewrite the expression in terms of antisymmetric tensors with indices. There are two later chapters on differential forms, but this section gives a few simple examples to give a preview of using differential forms in *MathTensor*.

As explained in the section on exterior differential forms in Chapter 2, differential forms in a coordinate basis consisting of the exterior products of differentials, dx^i, correspond to totally antisymmetric covariant tensors. The formalism of differential forms takes advantage of the total antisymmetry to dispense with indices altogether. An example of a differential p-form is

$$\omega = (1/p!)A_{i_1,i_2,\ldots,i_p}dx^{i_1} \wedge dx^{i_2} \wedge \ldots \wedge dx^{i_p},$$

where the integer p is less than or equal to the dimension of the space. The components of ω are the totally antisymmetric covariant tensor $A_{i_1,i_2,\ldots,i_p}$. The factor of $(1/p!)$ is present in ω because the summations are over all values of the indices, but because of the antisymmetry of the exterior, or wedge, product, $\wedge$, each independent exterior product of p basis vectors appears in the sum $p!$ times. Thus the components are the coefficients of the *independent* exterior products of the basis vectors. One can also work with a noncoordinate basis, e^j, formed from independent linear combinations of coordinate basis vectors dx^i. That is, $e^j = b^j{}_i dx^i$ need not be the differential of any coordinate function. By substituting the inverse expressions for the dx^i in terms of the e^j into the above expansion of ω, you obtain the expansion of ω in terms of exterior products of the e^j, with antisymmetric components that are linear combinations of the $A_{i_1,i_2,\ldots,i_p}$.

The command **DefineForm** is used to define a differential form. You can use the command **FtoC** (form to components) to find the components of any differential form expression that you construct. The components need not necessarily be with respect to a coordinate basis. When naming differential forms, you should use a different name for each different form and you should not give the form a name that is the same as the names of free or dummy indices used in *MathTensor*.

The present section is a brief illustration of some differential form operations in *MathTensor*. If you are not familiar with differential forms, you may want to read one of the many textbooks available (for references, see Chapters 5 and 6 on differential forms). An efficient way to learn about differential forms is to use *MathTensor* in conjunction with a textbook on differential forms. You will also find introductory material in the two later chapters of this book devoted to differential forms. Here are some examples of differential form operations.

This defines a 2-form with the name w2.	```In[14]:= DefineForm[w2, 2]```
	```PermWeight::sym: Symmetries of w2 assigned```
	```PermWeight::def: Object w2 defined```

This is the exterior derivative of w2.

```
In[15]:= XD[w2]
Out[15]= dw2
```

The exterior derivative of w2 is a 3-form, so you must specify three indices in a list as shown in order to obtain the components using the FtoC (form to components) command. By default, covariant derivatives are used, although the result is independent of the metric structure, so that ordinary derivatives can also be used.

```
In[16]:= FtoC[%,{1a,1b,1c}]
Out[16]= w2      - w2      + w2
           ab;c       ac;b       bc;a
```

CDtoOD takes covariant derivatives to ordinary partial derivatives and affine connections. The affine connection terms drop out of this result.

```
In[17]:= CDtoOD[%]
Out[17]= w2      - w2      + w2
           ab,c       ac,b       bc,a
```

If you want to get ordinary derivatives immediately, you can turn off XDtoCDflag.

```
In[18]:= Off[XDtoCDflag]
```

The result now appears with ordinary derivatives.

```
In[19]:= FtoC[XD[w2],{1a,1b,1c}]
Out[19]= w2      - w2      + w2
           ab,c       ac,b       bc,a
```

This defines a 1-form w1 and a 3-form w3.

```
In[20]:= DefineForm[{w1,w3},{1,3}]
PermWeight::def: Object w1 defined
PermWeight::sym: Symmetries of w3 assigned
PermWeight::def: Object w3 defined
```

When the dimension of the space is 3, any forms of higher order than 3 are zero.

```
In[21]:= Dimension = 3
Out[21]= 3
```

This is zero because it is a 4-form in a 3-dimensional space.

```
In[22]:= XD[w3]
Out[22]= 0
```

The function XP is the exterior product. As explained after the next table, you can use the *Mathematica* command StringReplace and $PreRead to permit you to type the input XP[w1,w2] in the familiar infix form w1 ^ w2.

```
In[23]:= XP[w1,w2]
Out[23]= w1 ^ w2
```

The exterior derivative would give a 4-form, which is zero in 3 dimensions.

```
In[24]:= XD[%]
Out[24]= 0
```

Define another 1-form called s1.

```
In[25]:= DefineForm[s1,1]
 PermWeight::def: Object s1 defined
```

This gives the exterior derivative of the exterior product of s1 with w1.

```
In[26]:= XD[XP[s1,w1] ]
Out[26]= -s1 ^ dw1 + w1 ^ ds1
```

This is the Hodge star or dual of w1.

```
In[27]:= HodgeStar[w1]
Out[27]= *(w1)
```

The Hodge star of w1 is a 2-form in 3 dimensions, so two indices must be specified to obtain its components. Epsilon is the totally antisymmetric Levi-Civita tensor. It will be discussed in the next section.

```
In[28]:= FtoC[%,{1a,1b}]
                       p
Out[28]= Epsilon      w1
                ab     p
```

DefineForm[*name, p*]	define a *p*-form *name*, where *p* is an integer
DefineForm[{*name1,name2,..*}, {*p1,p2,..*}]	
	define forms of the specified names and degrees
XD[*expr*]	exterior derivative of a differential form expression
XP[*expr1,expr2*]	exterior product of two differential form expressions
HodgeStar[*expr*]	Hodge star or dual of a differential form expression
FtoC[*expr*, {*1a,1b,..*}]	the tensor components of a differential form expression; if the expression is a *p*-form, the *p*-indices of the tensor components must be specified in the list.
CoXD[*expr*]	codifferential of a differential form expression
GenLap[*expr*]	generalized or Hodge Laplacian
Lap[*expr*]	standard or Bochner Laplacian

Some differential form commands and operations.

The later chapters on differential forms contain more detailed discussions, including definitions and examples of the codifferential, CoXD; the Hodge Laplacian, GenLap; and the Bochner Laplacian, Lap. The interior product, IntP of a 1-form with a *p*-form is described below, as well as in the later chapters. The Lie derivative acting on forms is called LD. It is discussed in Chapters 5 and 6 on differential forms.

In order to use the standard infix symbol for inputting the exterior product, you can issue the *Mathematica* command

$PreRead = StringReplace[#, {" ^ " -> "~XP~"}]& .

Then you can type, for example, w1 ^ w2 instead of XP[w1,w2]. Notice that spaces have been included on each side of ^. That is done so that you can still access the infix operator for Power. Thus you can type x^2 with no spaces for the second power of x but w1 ^ w2 for the exterior product of two forms. You are free to employ this form of input if you wish, although in this book the functional form using XP will be shown in the input line. If you prefer the infix form of input, then you can put the above assignment for $PreRead in your init.m file. You can also change other input names by including the replacements you wish inside the list appearing as the second argument of StringReplace in the above assignment of $PreRead.

In the previous examples, a differential form was denoted by a string of symbols. The components of the form were found by applying FtoC to the string representing the form. In general, the basis 1-forms need not be a coordinate basis, consisting of the dx^i, but can be constructed from independent linear combinations of the dx^i.

Another way to proceed would be to represent a p-form in a coordinate representation as an explicit linear combination of independent basis wedge products, $dx^{i_1} \wedge dx^{i_2} \wedge \ldots \wedge dx^{i_p}$. The components of the p-form, which are the coefficients of the independent basis wedge products, appear explicitly in such a representation. Just as with the components of a tensor having concrete integer indices, these concrete components of a form can have values that are explicit functions of the coordinates.

In *MathTensor*, a p-form can be expanded as a linear combination of independent basis p-forms in a coordinate representation by using the command `CoordRep`. The value of `Dimension` must be an integer n, and by convention, the coordinates are $x[1]$, $x[2]$, ..., $x[n]$. You may give them names, as in $x[1]$ = r, etc.

Let the space be 3-dimensional.	`In[29]:= Dimension = 3;`
Consider spherical coordinates. Give them names: r, theta, phi.	`In[30]:= x[1]=r; x[2]=theta; x[3]=phi;`
This defines Cartesian coordinates f1, f2, f3. Each coordinate is a 0-form.	`In[31]:= f1 = r Sin[theta] Cos[phi]; f2 = r Sin[theta] Sin[phi]; f3 = r Cos[theta];`
This turns off XDtoCDFlag so that ordinary derivatives, rather than covariant derivatives, will be used when evaluating exterior derivatives in a coordinate basis.	`In[32]:= Off[XDtoCDFlag]`
Take the exterior derivative of each Cartesian coordinate.	`In[33]:= xdf1 = XD[f1]; xdf2 = XD[f2]; xdf3 = XD[f3];`

Here is `xdf1` represented in terms of spherical coordinates. The ordinary partial derivatives are not evaluated because `EvaluateODFlag` is False by default.

```
In[34]:= df1 = CoordRep[xdf1]
Out[34]= Cos[phi] Sin[theta] dr +

>      r Sin[theta] (Cos[phi]    dphi + Cos[phi]    dr +
                             ,3                  ,1

>           Cos[phi]    dtheta) +
                    ,2

>      r Cos[phi] (Sin[theta]    dphi + Sin[theta]    dr +
                            ,3                   ,1

>           Sin[theta]    dtheta)
                      ,2
```

This turns on the flag.	*In[35]:=* **On[EvaluateODFlag]**

Now the ordinary derivatives have been evaluated.

In[36]:= **df1**
Out[36]= -(r Sin[phi] Sin[theta] dphi) +
>   Cos[phi] Sin[theta] dr + r Cos[phi] Cos[theta] dtheta

Here is **xdf2** in spherical coordinates.

In[37]:= **df2 = CoordRep[xdf2]**
Out[37]= r Cos[phi] Sin[theta] dphi +
>   Sin[phi] Sin[theta] dr + r Cos[theta] Sin[phi] dtheta

Finally, here is **xdf3**.

In[38]:= **df3 = CoordRep[xdf3]**
Out[38]= Cos[theta] dr - r Sin[theta] dtheta

Here is the element of area on a surface perpendicular to the **f3** direction.

In[39]:= **dArea3 = Simplify[XP[df1,df2]]**
Out[39]= -(r Sin[theta]
>   (Sin[theta] dphi ^ dr + r Cos[theta] dphi ^ dtheta)
>   )

Here is the volume element before simplification.

In[40]:= **dVolume = XP[df1,df2,df3]**
Out[40]= r^2 $Cos[phi]^2$ $Cos[theta]^2$ Sin[theta]
>   dphi ^ dr ^ dtheta +
> r^2 $Cos[theta]^2$ $Sin[phi]^2$ Sin[theta]
>   dphi ^ dr ^ dtheta +
> r^2 $Cos[phi]^2$ $Sin[theta]^3$ dphi ^ dr ^ dtheta +
> r^2 $Sin[phi]^2$ $Sin[theta]^3$ dphi ^ dr ^ dtheta

Here is the familiar form of the volume element in spherical coordinates.

In[41]:= **dVolume = Simplify[%]**
Out[41]= r^2 Sin[theta] dphi ^ dr ^ dtheta

You can group terms in a differential form using the *MathTensor* command **CollectForm**. It groups terms according to independent coordinate basis exterior products having the same degree as the form. If you want to see the components of a form that has been expanded in terms of a coordinate basis, then **CollectForm** shows them in the simplest way. The command **FtoC**, as in **FtoC[df1,{la}]** or **FtoC[dArea3, {la,lb}]**, yields a single expression for the component with the specified indices, which can be interpreted as indices of an arbitrary coordinate or noncoordinate basis.

There is also an interior product that takes a 1-form, w1, and a *p*-form, wp, to a $(p-1)$-form. In *MathTensor*, this interior product is denoted by IntP[w1,wp]. It is the $(p-1)$-form having components w1[ua] wp[1a,12,13,...,1p] formed by contracting the index of the components of w1 with the first index of the components of wp. The first argument of IntP must be a 1-form.

This defines a 1-form w1 and a 2-form w2.	*In[42]:=* DefineForm[{w1,w2},{1,2}] PermWeight::def: Object w1 defined PermWeight::sym: Symmetries of w2 assigned PermWeight::def: Object w2 defined
Because no explicit coordinate dependence is included in the components of w1 and w2, you do not want derivatives evaluated.	*In[43]:=* Off[EvaluateODFlag]

Here is the coordinate representation of w2. The coefficients of the basis 2-forms are the components of w2.	*In[44]:=* CoordRep[w2]
	
	Out[44]= w2 dphi ∧ dr + w2 dphi ∧ dtheta −
	             31 32
	
	  > w2 dr ∧ dtheta
	             21

Here is the coordinate representation of the exterior derivative of w1.	*In[45]:=* CoordRep[XD[w1]]
	
	Out[45]= −(w1 dphi ∧ dr) + w1 dphi ∧ dr −
	              3,1 1,3
	
	  > w1 dphi ∧ dtheta + w1 dphi ∧ dtheta +
	              3,2 2,3
	
	  > w1 dr ∧ dtheta − w1 dr ∧ dtheta
	              2,1 1,2

The *MathTensor* function CollectForm groups terms according to the independent basis exterior products.	*In[46]:=* CollectForm[%]
	
	Out[46]= (−w1 + w1) dphi ∧ dr +
	               3,1 1,3
	
	  > (−w1 + w1) dphi ∧ dtheta +
	               3,2 2,3
	
	  > (w1 − w1) dr ∧ dtheta
	              2,1 1,2

Here is the interior product of w1 with the 2-form XD[w1].	*In[47]:=* IntP[w1,XD[w1]] *Out[47]=* IntP(w1, dw1)

Here are the components of IntP[w1, XD[w1]], with terms grouped according to the coordinate basis forms.

$In[48]:=$ `CollectForm[CoordRep[%] ]`

$Out[48]=$ $(w1_{3,1}\, w1^1 - w1_{1,3}\, w1^1 + w1_{3,2}\, w1^2 - w1_{2,3}\, w1^2)$

> $dphi + (-(w1_{2,1}\, w1^2) + w1_{1,2}\, w1^2 - w1_{3,1}\, w1^3 +$

> $w1_{1,3}\, w1^3)\, dr +$

> $(w1_{2,1}\, w1^1 - w1_{1,2}\, w1^1 - w1_{3,2}\, w1^3 + w1_{2,3}\, w1^3)$

> $dtheta$

Sometimes it is convenient to deal with matrices having elements that are differential forms [see for example, H. Flanders *Differential Forms* (Academic Press, New York, 1963), Chapter 4]. You can use the *MathTensor* operators `MatrixMap` and `MatrixXP` to deal with such matrices. The command `MatrixMap[op,matrix]` maps an operator, `op`, to each element of a matrix. The command `MatrixXP[matrix1, matrix2]` performs matrix multiplication of `matrix1` with `matrix2` but with their matrix elements multiplied using the exterior product, `XP`, instead of the ordinary product.

You will be dealing with explicit functions and will want to evaluate derivatives.

$In[49]:=$ `On[EvaluateODFlag]`

This matrix, `m`, takes a column matrix consisting of the Cartesian unit vectors into a column matrix consisting of the unit vectors in the r, theta, and phi directions in spherical coordinates. The matrix `m` is orthogonal; it is a rotation matrix.

$In[50]:=$ `m = {{Sin[theta] Cos[phi], Sin[theta] Sin[phi], Cos[theta]},`
`     {Cos[theta] Cos[phi], Cos[theta] Sin[phi], -Sin[theta]},`
`     {-Sin[phi], Cos[phi], 0} }`

$Out[50]=$ `{{Cos[phi] Sin[theta], Sin[phi] Sin[theta],`

> `Cos[theta]}, {Cos[phi] Cos[theta],`

> `Cos[theta] Sin[phi], -Sin[theta]},`

> `{-Sin[phi], Cos[phi], 0}}`

This maps the operator
`CoordRep[XD[#] ]&` to each element of the
matrix `m`. That operator is a pure function
that first applies `XD` and then `CoordRep`.

```
In[51]:= dm = MatrixMap[CoordRep[XD[#] ]&, m]
Out[51]= {{-(Sin[phi] Sin[theta] dphi) +
>        Cos[phi] Cos[theta] dtheta,
>      Cos[phi] Sin[theta] dphi +
>        Cos[theta] Sin[phi] dtheta, -(Sin[theta] dtheta)},
>    {-(Cos[theta] Sin[phi] dphi) -
>        Cos[phi] Sin[theta] dtheta,
>      Cos[phi] Cos[theta] dphi -
>        Sin[phi] Sin[theta] dtheta, -(Cos[theta] dtheta)},
>    {-(Cos[phi] dphi), -(Sin[phi] dphi), 0}}
```

Here is the matrix inverse of `m`.

```
In[52]:= mInverse = Simplify[Inverse[m] ]
Out[52]= {{Cos[phi] Sin[theta], Cos[phi] Cos[theta],
>      -Sin[phi]}, {Sin[phi] Sin[theta],
>      Cos[theta] Sin[phi], Cos[phi]},
>    {Cos[theta], -Sin[theta], 0}}
```

This takes the matrix exterior product of
`dm` with `mInverse`. It can be proved that
when `m` is a rotation matrix, then this
matrix exterior product must yield an
antisymmetric matrix.

```
In[53]:= Simplify[MatrixXP[dm, mInverse] ]
Out[53]= {{0, dtheta, Sin[theta] dphi},
>    {-dtheta, 0, Cos[theta] dphi},
>    {-(Sin[theta] dphi), -(Cos[theta] dphi), 0}}
```

`CoordRep[`*expr*`]`	represent a differential form expression in a coordinate basis
`CollectForm[`*expr*`]`	group *expr* in terms of the coordinate basis forms
`IntP[`*w1*, *wp*`]`	interior product of a 1-form with a *p*-form
`LD[`*wp*, *w1*`]`	Lie derivative of a *p*-form with respect to a 1-form
`LDtoXDrule`	rule replacing LD by XD and IntP
`LDtoXD[`*expr*`]`	replace LD by XD and IntP in *expr*
`MatrixXP[`*m1*,*m2*`]`	matrix exterior product of matrices *m1* and *m2* of forms
`MatrixMap[`*op*,*m*`]`	map the operator *op* to each element of the matrix *m*

Further differential form commands.

A tensor-valued differential form is a differential form containing explicit tensor indices. For example, let h^a be a tensor-valued differential form of degree 2. This means that each component of the 2-form h^a is a first-rank tensor (a is the tensor index). A component of the 2-form h^a is represented as $h^a{}_{bc}$, with antisymmetry under interchange of indices b and c. The notation alone does not tell you if h^a and $h^a{}_{bc}$ are tensor-valued forms or *components* of such forms. In *MathTensor*, the command FormComponentQ gives False when applied to a form or tensor-valued form, such as h^a above, and gives True when applied to a component of a form or tensor-valued form, such as $h^a{}_{bc}$ above.

There are also commands for determining the degree of a differential form expression, expr. The command DegreeForm[expr] gives the degree of expr, and ZeroDegreeQ[expr] gives True if expr is of degree 0 and False otherwise. These commands can also be applied to tensor-valued form expressions having tensor indices (tensor indices are ignored in determining the form degree). Another way to represent a tensor-valued differential form is as a matrix (with the tensor indices suppressed). You dealt with matrices of forms in the previous *MathTensor* dialogue. The commands DegreeForm, ZeroDegreeQ, and FormComponentQ should not be applied to matrices unless you are using MatrixMap to map the commands to the elements of the matrix.

The old commands RankForm and ZeroFormQ are retained for compatibility with old versions of *MathTensor*. However, those commands do not treat components of forms as being of degree 0. Therefore you will find DegreeForm preferable to RankForm and ZeroDegreeQ preferable to ZeroFormQ in most applications.

This defines a tensor-valued 2-form.	In[54]:= DefineForm[h[ua], 2]
	PermWeight::sym: Symmetries of h assigned
	PermWeight::def: Object h defined
The tensor index is explicit.	In[55]:= h[ua]
	Out[55]= h^a
DegreeForm gives the degree, and ZeroDegreeQ gives False.	In[56]:= {DegreeForm[h[ua]], ZeroDegreeQ[h[ua]]}
	Out[56]= {2, False}
FtoC gives a component of the form, where lb and lc are the specified form component indices.	In[57]:= FtoC[h[ua], {lb,lc}]
	Out[57]= $h^a{}_{bc}$

The degree of a component of a form or tensor-valued form is 0. The components are forms of 0-degree.

```
In[58]:=  {DegreeForm[h[ua,1b,1c] ],
ZeroDegreeQ[h[ua,1b,1c] ]}
Out[58]= {0, True}
```

This uses `Map` or `/@` to map `FormComponentQ` to list. The first element gives `False` because `h[ua]` is the 2-form itself and not a form component. The second gives `True` because `h[ua,1b,1c]` is a component of the 2-form. `FormComponentQ` should only be applied to a single form or tensor-valued form, not to expressions made from them.

```
In[59]:=  FormComponentQ /@ {h[ua], h[ua,1b,1c]}
Out[59]= {False, True}
```

The old function `RankForm` gives the degree of the form having the name or `Head` `h`. It thus does not recognize that the degree of a component of a form is 0. `RankForm` is retained for compatibility with older versions but is supplanted by `DegreeForm`.

```
In[60]:=  RankForm /@ {h[ua], h[ua,1b,1c]}
Out[60]= {2, 2}
```

Similarly, the old function `ZeroFormQ` does not recognize that a component of a form is a 0-form. You should use `ZeroDegreeQ` instead.

```
In[61]:=  ZeroFormQ /@ {h[ua], h[ua,1b,1c]}
Out[61]= {False, False}
```

`DefineForm[h[ua], 2]`	define tensor-valued 2-form h^a
`FtoC[h[ua], {1b,1c}]`	give component $h^a{}_{bc}$ of 2-form h^a
`DegreeForm[expr]`	give the form degree of *expr*
`ZeroDegreeQ[expr]`	test if *expr* is of 0 degree
`FormComponentQ[h[ua,1b,1c]]`	test if $h^a{}_{bc}$ is a *component* of a form or tensor-valued form

Tensor-valued forms and tests for degree and component.

■ 3.4.3 Levi-Civita Epsilon Tensor

A tensor of fundamental significance is the Levi-Civita tensor. This tensor, denoted by `Epsilon[1a,1b,..]` is totally antisymmetric and has the number of indices equal to the dimension.

The minus sign appears because the indices are reordered in accordance with the total antisymmetry of Epsilon.

```
In[1]:= Epsilon[lb,la,lc,ld]
Out[1]= -Epsilon
                abcd
```

After setting Dimension to a specific value, 4 in this case, the Epsilon tensor with the correct number of concrete indices will be evaluated. If you have already typed expressions involving Epsilon (with concrete integer indices) that you will want to evaluate, you should type Update[ ] after setting the value of Dimension.

```
In[2]:= Dimension = 4;
```

The Levi-Civita tensor is equal to the square root of the absolute value of the determinant of the metric tensor when the covariant indices are an even permutation of {-1,-2,-3,-4}. Recall that covariant concrete indices are typed in with minus signs, while contravariant indices are typed as integers without minus signs. The square root of Abs[Detg] is required if Epsilon is to transform as a tensor.

```
In[3]:= Epsilon[-1,-2,-3,-4]
Out[3]= Sqrt[Abs[g]]
```

The sign convention for Epsilon can be altered by changing the value of EpsilonSign. This variable normally has the value +1, which is set in the file Conventions.m. You can change the values in that file if you use different conventions.

```
In[4]:= EpsilonSign = -1;
```

Now the sign is different. EpsilonSign also controls the signs of the various antisymmetric tensor densities associated with the Levi-Civita tensor Epsilon.

```
In[5]:= Epsilon[-1,-2,-3,-4]
Out[5]= -Sqrt[Abs[g]]
```

This sets the sign back to its original value, which is the most commonly used convention.

```
In[6]:= EpsilonSign = 1;
```

The antisymmetric object that is 1 when the covariant indices are an even permutation of {-1,-2,-3,-4} is denoted by EpsDown. Because it is defined to have this value in any coordinate system, it transforms as a tensor density of weight −1 (i.e., with a factor of the inverse of the Jacobian determinant of the coordinate transformation).

```
In[7]:= EpsDown[-1,-2,-3,-4]
Out[7]= 1
```

Raising the indices on this object introduces a factor of 1/Detg.

$In[8]:=$ `EpsDown[1,2,3,4]`

$Out[8]= \dfrac{1}{g}$

There is a separate tensor density called `EpsUp` that has the value +1 when the contravariant indices are an even permutation of {1,2,3,4}. There are also rules for going between these various objects.

$In[9]:=$ `EpsUp[1,2,3,4]`

$Out[9]= 1$

This rule replaces the tensor density `EpsDown` by the equivalent expression involving the tensor `Epsilon`. The various rules are summarized in the next table.

$In[10]:=$ `EpsDown[1a,1b,1c,1d]/.EpsDownToEpsilonRule`

$Out[10]= \dfrac{\text{Epsilon}_{abcd}}{\text{Sqrt[Abs[g]]}}$

`Epsilon[1a,1b,..]`	antisymmetric Levi-Civita tensor having value $\lvert g \rvert^{1/2}$ when the concrete covariant indices are an even permutation of {-1,-2,-3,-4}
`EpsDown[1a,1b,..]`	antisymmetric Levi-Civita tensor density having value +1 when the concrete covariant indices are an even permutation of {-1,-2,-3,-4}
`EpsUp[ua,ub,..]`	antisymmetric Levi-Civita tensor density having value +1 when the concrete contravariant indices are an even permutation of {1,2,3,4}
`EpsilonSign`	if `EpsilonSign` is set to −1, the above signs of the Levi-Civita tensor and tensor densities are changed
`expr/. EpsDownToEpsilonRule`	replace `EpsDown` in *expr* by equivalent with `Epsilon`
`expr/. EpsUpToEpsilonRule`	replace `EpsUp` in *expr* by equivalent with `Epsilon`
`expr/. EpsUpToEpsDownRule`	replace `EpsUp` in *expr* by equivalent with `EpsDown`
`expr/. EpsDownToEpsUpRule`	replace `EpsDown` in *expr* by equivalent with `EpsUp`
`expr/. EpsilonToEpsUpRule`	replace `Epsilon` in *expr* by equivalent with `EpsUp`
`expr/. EpsilonToEpsDownRule`	replace `Epsilon` in *expr* by equivalent with `EpsDown`

Antisymmetric Levi-Civita symbols and associated rules.

The Levi-Civita tensor is used in forming the dual of an antisymmetric tensor. This consists of the contraction of the tensor with Epsilon, divided by $p!$, where p is the number of indices of the tensor. The function that forms the dual is called DualStar. Acting on a tensor or rank p, it forms a tensor of rank $(n - p)$, where n is the integer value of Dimension. DualStar is closely related to HodgeStar. The latter acts on a differential form (no indices) and represents a new differential form. If its components are taken with the command FtoC, then the result is the same as would be given by DualStar applied directly to the components of the original differential form. The use of DualStar is illustrated in the next dialogue. Recall that Dimension has been set to the value 4. This dialogue also demonstrates how to simplify products of Levi-Civita tensors or tensor densities.

This is the dual of the antisymmetric Maxwell tensor. The list of indices in the second argument of DualStar are the indices that will appear on Epsilon. The leading indices in this list must be contracted with indices of the tensor in the first argument until all the indices have been contracted.

$In[11]:=$ DualStar[MaxwellF[la,lb],{ua,ub,uc,ud}]

$$Out[11]= \frac{Epsilon^{abcd}\,F_{ab}}{2}$$

In order to define a new tensor based on this expression, first replace the dummy indices by system-generated dummy indices. This procedure will prevent later conflict of dummy index names with those you may type.

$In[12]:=$ rhs = Dum[%]

$$Out[12]= \frac{Epsilon^{pqcd}\,F_{pq}}{2}$$

You may want to see the input names of the indices so that you can use them in defining the pattern symbols that will appear on the left-hand side of your new definition. InputForm is convenient for that purpose.

$In[13]:=$ InputForm[rhs]

$Out[13]//InputForm=$
   (Epsilon[u1, u2, uc, ud]*MaxwellF[l1, l2])/2

This defines a new tensor, StarMaxwellF, which is the dual of the Maxwell tensor. The blank indices are chosen to match the names of the free indices on the right-hand side of the definition.

$In[14]:=$ StarMaxwellF[uc_,ud_] = rhs;

The tensor is defined for any index names.

$In[15]:=$ StarMaxwellF[ua,ub]

$$Out[15]= \frac{Epsilon^{pqab}\,F_{pq}}{2}$$

This applies `DualStar` to `StarMaxwellF`, thus taking the dual of the dual of the Maxwell tensor.

$$In[16]:= \text{DualStar[StarMaxwellF[la,lb],\{ua,ub,uc,ud\}]}$$

$$Out[16]= \frac{\text{Epsilon}^{pq}_{ab}\,\text{Epsilon}^{abcd}\,F_{pq}}{4}$$

Whenever a product of two Epsilon tensors or corresponding tensor densities appears in an expression, you can use `EpsilonProductTensorRule` to simplify the expression.

$$In[17]:= \text{\% /. EpsilonProductTensorRule}$$

$$Out[17]= \frac{F_{pq}\,(2\,g^{pd}\,g^{qc} - 2\,g^{pc}\,g^{qd})}{4}$$

The dual of the dual is the negative of the original tensor.

$$In[18]:= \text{Expand[\%]}$$

$$Out[18]= -F^{cd}$$

`DualStar[`*expr*`,`*list*`]`	give the dual of a tensor. Here, *expr* is an antisymmetric tensor and *list* is a list of *n* indices, where *n* is the dimension, and the leading indices in the list are contracted with those in the tensor. For example,

`DualStar[anti[la,lb,lc],{ua,ub,uc,ud}]`

give the result
`(1/3!) anti[la,lb,lc] Epsilon[ua,ub,uc,ud]`

expr `/. EpsilonProductTensorRule`

simplify products of Levi-Civita tensors or tensor densities

EpsilonProductTensorRule and DualStar.

You can use the Levi-Civita tensor to do ordinary 3-dimensional tensor analysis.

This makes the space 3-dimensional, sets to +1 the sign of the determinant of the metric tensor g, and sets g to 1, as in Euclidean 3-dimensional space with Cartesian coordinates.

$$In[19]:= \text{Dimension = 3; DetgSign = 1; Detg = 1;}$$

This defines a vector `s[ua]`.

$$In[20]:= \text{DefineTensor[s,"s",\{\{1\},1\}]}$$

This defines a second vector `v[ua]`.

$$In[21]:= \text{DefineTensor[v,"v",\{\{1\},1\}]}$$

This is a component of the vector product, $\vec{s} \times \vec{v}$.

$In[22]:= \texttt{sxv[ua\_] = Dum[Epsilon[ua,lb,lc] s[ub] v[uc]]}$

$Out[22]= \text{Epsilon}^{a}{}_{pq}\, s^{p}\, v^{q}$

Define a third vector, $\texttt{w[ua]}$.

$In[23]:= \texttt{DefineTensor[w,"w",\{\{1\},1\}]}$

$\texttt{PermWeight::def: Object w defined}$

This is the a component of $\vec{s} \times \vec{v} \times \vec{w}$.

$In[24]:= \texttt{Epsilon[ua,lb,lc] sxv[ub] w[uc]}$

$Out[24]= \text{Epsilon}^{b}{}_{pq}\, \text{Epsilon}^{a}{}_{bc}\, s^{p}\, v^{q}\, w^{c}$

This proves the identity,
$(\vec{s} \times \vec{v}) \times \vec{w} = (\vec{s} \cdot \vec{w})\vec{v} - (\vec{v} \cdot \vec{w})\vec{s}$.

$In[25]:= \texttt{Expand[\% /. EpsilonProductTensorRule]}$

$Out[25]= s^{p}\, v^{a}\, w_{p} - s^{a}\, v^{q}\, w_{q}$

■ 3.4.4   Derivative Operators

There are several types of derivative operators that are commonly used in tensor analysis. These are the ordinary derivative, the covariant derivative, and the Lie derivative. The following dialogues show you how to use those operators in *MathTensor*. The exterior derivative, which is used on differential forms, has already been introduced in Section 3.4.1.

In *Mathematica*, $\texttt{D[Sin[x] Cos[y], x]}$ takes the partial derivative of the function $\texttt{Sin[x] Cos[y]}$ with respect to $\texttt{x}$. In tensor analysis, the partial derivative of a tensor, T_{ab}, with respect to the coordinate x^c is often denoted by $T_{ab,c}$. To input such an ordinary partial derivative to *MathTensor*, you type $\texttt{OD[T[la,lb],lc]}$. In a later section, you will learn about tensors with concrete positive (contravariant) or negative (covariant) integer indices. You will then see how, when the components of the tensor have definite functional forms in terms of the coordinates, the *MathTensor* function $\texttt{OD}$ is converted into the *Mathematica* function $\texttt{D}$. The following dialogue illustrates the use of $\texttt{OD}$ on tensors with symbolic indices.

This is an expression built from the Ricci and Maxwell tensors.

$In[1]:= \texttt{expr = RicciR[la,lb] MaxwellF[ub,lc]}$
$\texttt{+RicciR[la,lc]}$

$Out[1]= -(F^{b}{}_{c}\, R_{ab}) + R_{ac}$

This is the partial derivative with respect to x^d.

$$In[2]:= \text{OD}[\%,1d]$$

$$Out[2]= -(F^{\ b}_{\ c}\ R_{ab,d}) + R_{ac,d} - F^{\ b}_{\ c\ ,d}\ R_{ab}$$

This is the second partial derivative with respect to x^d and then x^e.

$$In[3]:= \text{OD}[\text{expr},1d,1e]$$

$$Out[3]= -(F^{\ b}_{\ c\ ,e}\ R_{ab,d}) - F^{\ b}_{\ c\ ,d}\ R_{ab,e} - F^{\ b}_{\ c}\ R_{ab,de} +$$

$$>\quad R_{ac,de} - F^{\ b}_{\ c\ ,de}\ R_{ab}$$

Here is the second derivative of the Maxwell tensor. This can be simplified.

$$In[4]:= \text{OD}[\text{MaxwellF}[ua,ub],1a,1b]$$

$$Out[4]= F^{ab}_{\ \ ,ab}$$

This is zero because OD is symmetric with respect to the derivative indices, while MaxwellF is antisymmetric.

$$In[5]:= \text{Tsimplify}[\%]$$

$$Out[5]= 0$$

Ordinary derivatives of tensors do not in general transform as tensors. You cannot raise or lower indices of the ordinary partial derivative of a tensor using the metric because the derivatives of the metric tensor are generally nonzero. By contrast, the covariant derivative does produce a tensor. Furthermore, the covariant derivative of the metric tensor is zero. The covariant derivative with respect to x^c of a tensor T_{ab} is denoted by $T_{ab;c}$ and is input in *MathTensor* by typing CD[T[1a,1b],1c]. The next dialogue demonstrates the use of the covariant derivative as well as of the commands CDtoOD and CommuteCD.

As an illustration of the syntax of CommuteCD, the command CommuteCD[CD[RicciR[1a,1b],1c,1d,1e],1c,1d] will produce an equivalent expression in which CD[RicciR[1a,1b],1d,1c,1e] appears together with terms generated by commutation of the covariant derivatives. The covariant derivative indices to be commuted must be adjacent. In addition, if any integer indices appear in the expression acted on by CommuteCD, the expression will be returned unchanged.

This is the covariant derivative of expr with respect to x^d.

$$In[6]:= \text{CD}[\text{expr},1d]$$

$$Out[6]= R_{ac;d} - R_{ab;d}\ F^{\ b}_{\ c} - F^{\ b}_{\ c\ ;d}\ R_{ab}$$

The covariant derivative of the metric vanishes.

$$In[7]:= \text{CD}[\text{Metricg}[1a,1b],1c]$$

$$Out[7]= 0$$

MaxwellVectorPotentialRule converts MaxwellF to the equivalent expression involving the covariant derivatives of the vector potential, MaxwellA.

In[8]:= MaxwellF[la,lb] /. MaxwellVectorPotentialRule

$Out[8] = -A_{a;b} + A_{b;a}$

The command CDtoOD replaces covariant derivatives by ordinary derivatives OD and affine connections AffineG. The latter drop out in this case.

In[9]:= CDtoOD[%]

$Out[9] = -A_{a,b} + A_{b,a}$

Because the metric cannot raise or lower indices on a tensor appearing inside OD, MetricgFlag is set to False by CDtoOD when it is applied. When this flag is False, the metric will not automatically raise or lower indices. This turns MetricgFlag on again.

In[10]:= On[MetricgFlag]

This expression appears in the tensor form of Maxwell's equations.

In[11]:= CD[MaxwellF[ua,ub],lb]

$Out[11] = F^{ab}_{;b}$

Convert this to the equivalent expression involving the vector potential and call the result DivF.

In[12]:= DivF = % /. MaxwellVectorPotentialRule

$Out[12] = -A^{ab}_{;b} + A^{ba}_{;b}$

This commutes the order of covariant differentiation in the second term of DivF. This process generates a term involving the Ricci tensor.

In[13]:= CommuteCD[DivF,ua,lb,2]

$Out[13] = A^{pa}_{p;} - A^{ap}_{;p} + A^{pa} R_p$

This imposes the Lorentz gauge condition, that CD[MaxwellA[ua],la] is zero, thus causing the first term to vanish. The result shows that in curved spacetime, the electromagnetic wave equation for the vector potential will have a term involving the Ricci tensor.

In[14]:= % /. LorentzGaugeRule

$Out[14] = -A^{ap}_{;p} + A^{pa} R_p$

The command OrderCD orders covariant derivative indices into lexical order (the same order as Sort), generating terms involving Riemann tensors that arise when the covariant derivatives are commuted. Covariant derivatives in the generated terms are also ordered. Just as for CommuteCD, OrderCD acts only on expressions not having integer indices.

Suppose you want to order the covariant derivative indices in this expression.

$In[15] := \texttt{CD[MaxwellF[1a,1b],1e,1d,1c]}$

$Out[15] = F_{ab;edc}$

This does the job, ordering as well covariant derivatives in the Riemann tensor terms generated by commutation.

$In[16] := \texttt{OrderCD[\%]}$

$Out[16] = F_{ab;cde} - R_{pbcd;e} F^p_a - R_{pbde;c} F^p_a +$

$> \quad R_{pacd;e} F^p_b + R_{pade;c} F^p_b + F_{pb;e} R^p_{acd} +$

$> \quad F_{pb;d} R^p_{ace} + F_{pb;c} R^p_{ade} - F_{pa;e} R^p_{bcd} -$

$> \quad F_{pa;d} R^p_{bce} - F_{pa;c} R^p_{bde} + F_{ab;p} R^p_{ced}$

Another derivative operator that is often used in tensor analysis is the Lie derivative. The change in a tensor at a given *coordinate* point under an infinitesimal coordinate transformation is its Lie derivative. The Lie derivative operator acting on tensors with indices is called LieD and is illustrated below. There is also a Lie derivative operator, called LD, that acts on differential forms (it is discussed in Chapter 6).

This defines a vector, v[ua].

$In[17] := \texttt{DefineTensor[v,"v",\{\{1\},1\}]}$
PermWeight::def: Object v defined

Here is the Lie derivative of expr, defined above, with respect to the vector v. Note that the index of v is not typed inside LieD.

$In[18] := \texttt{Expand[LieD[expr,v]]}$

$Out[18] = LieD_v (R_{ac}) - LieD_v (R_{ab}) F^b_c - LieD_v (F_c{}^b) R_{ab}$

Using the command LieDtoCD, you can expand the Lie derivatives in the first two terms as covariant derivatives. Although the affine connections, AffineG, would drop out if the covariant derivatives were written in terms of ordinary derivatives and affine connections, it is often desirable to retain covariant derivatives, as here.

$In[19] := \texttt{LieDtoCD[\%[[1]] + \%[[2]]]}$

$Out[19] = -(v^p_{;a} F_c{}^q R_{pq}) + v^p_{;c} R_{pa} - v^p_{;q} F_c{}^q R_{pa} +$

$> \quad v^p_{;a} R_{pc} + R_{ac;p} v^p - R_{pa;q} F_c{}^p v^q$

Define a second-rank tensor q[1a,1b] with no symmetries.

$In[20] := \texttt{DefineTensor[q,"q",\{\{1,2\},1\}]}$
PermWeight::def: Object q defined

Take its Lie derivative.

$In[21] := $ **LieD[q[ua,lb],v]**

$$Out[21] = \mathtt{LieD}\ (q^{\ \ a}_{v\ \ b})$$

Convert to covariant derivatives.

$In[22] := $ **LieDtoCD[%]**

$$Out[22] = -(v^{\ \ \ a}_{\ ;p}\, q^{\ \ p}_{\ \ b}) + v^{\ \ p}_{\ ;b}\, q^{\ \ a}_{\ \ p} + q^{\ \ a}_{\ \ b;p}\, v^{\ \ p}$$

This converts the covariant derivatives to ordinary derivatives and affine connections.

$In[23] := $ **CDtoOD[%]**

$$Out[23] = -(v^{\ \ \ a}_{\ ,p}\, q^{\ \ p}_{\ \ b}) + v^{\ \ p}_{\ ,b}\, q^{\ \ a}_{\ \ p} + q^{\ \ a}_{\ \ b,p}\, v^{\ \ p} -$$

$$> \quad G^{\ \ a}_{pq}\, q^{\ \ q}_{\ \ b}\, v^{\ \ p} + G^{\ \ a}_{pq}\, q^{\ \ p}_{\ \ b}\, v^{\ \ q}$$

This shows that the affine connections drop out of the Lie derivative. The Lie derivative is independent of the metric structure.

$In[24] := $ **Tsimplify[%]**

$$Out[24] = -(v^{\ \ \ a}_{\ ,p}\, q^{\ \ p}_{\ \ b}) + v^{\ \ p}_{\ ,b}\, q^{\ \ a}_{\ \ p} + q^{\ \ a}_{\ \ b,p}\, v^{\ \ p}$$

OD[*expr*,*la*,*lb*,..]	ordinary partial derivative of *expr* with respect to coordinates x[ua], x[ub],...
CD[*expr*,*la*,*lb*,..]	covariant derivative of *expr* with respect to coordinates x[ua], x[ub],...
LieD[*expr*,*v*]	Lie derivative of a tensor expression, *expr*, with respect to a vector b[ua]
CDtoOD[*expr*]	express covariant derivatives in *expr* in terms of ordinary derivatives and affine connections
LieDtoCD[*expr*]	express Lie derivatives in *expr* in terms of covariant derivatives
LieDtoOD[*expr*]	express Lie derivatives in *expr* in terms of ordinary derivatives
CommuteCD[*expr*,*index1*,*index2*]	interchange indices in an expression involving second or higher covariant derivatives, generating terms containing the curvature tensor
CommuteCD[*expr*,*ind1*,*ind2*,*n*]	interchange indices only in term *n* of *expr*
OrderCD[*expr*]	order all covariant derivative indices in *expr*, generating terms containing the curvature tensor

Some derivative operators and related commands.

■ 3.5 Creating Rules and Definitions

You should already have at least a minimal knowledge of the facilities available in *Mathematica* for producing rules. Special problems arise when you attempt to write rules that involve tensors, particularly if the rules involve dummy (or summed) pairs of indices. *MathTensor* has its own powerful functions that you should use in creating transformation rules and definitions involving expressions with dummy indices. These functions, RuleUnique and DefUnique, are described after a preliminary discussion of rules and pitfalls. The new *MathTensor* functions make it easy to create transformation rules and definitions involving tensors and dummy indices. They are the key to creating your own specialized knowledge-base files.

■ 3.5.1 Simple Definitions and Rules

When there are no dummy indices involved, it is simple to make definitions or transformation rules involving tensors.

This creates a second-rank tensor with no symmetries.

$In[1]:=$ `DefineTensor[tx,"tx",{{1,2},1}]`
`PermWeight::def: Object tx defined`

This defines a first-rank tensor or vector.

$In[2]:=$ `DefineTensor[ty,"ty",{{1},1}]`
`PermWeight::def: Object ty defined`

This defines a rule that will take, for example, tx[1c,uc] to ty[1c] ty[uc]. PairQ[u,v] is True if u and v evaluate to be indices that are a dummy pair, such as 1c and uc. Note that on the left-hand side of the definition are patterns that can match any index names.

$In[3]:=$ `tx[la_,lb_] := ty[la] ty[lb] /; PairQ[la,lb]`

The condition PairQ[ud,ld] is True in this case.

$In[4]:=$ `tx[ud,ld]`

$Out[4]=$ $ty_d \; ty^d$

The condition PairQ[la,lb] is False, so no action is taken.

$In[5]:=$ `tx[la,lb]`

$Out[5]=$ tx_{ab}

It is often advantageous to use transformation rules rather than definitions. This removes all rules or definitions for tx.

$In[6]:=$ `Clear[tx]`

This time tx will be used in making a simple transformation rule.

$In[7]:=$ `DefineTensor[tx,"tx",{{1,2},1}]`
`PermWeight::def: Object tx defined`

This transformation rule will carry out the replacement that the previous definition did, but only on command rather than automatically.

$In[8]:=$ `txTotyRule := tx[la_,lb_] :> ty[la] ty[lb] /; PairQ[la,lb]`

The condition involving PairQ is satisfied.

$In[9]:=$ `tx[le,ue] /. txTotyRule`

$Out[9]=$ $ty_e \; ty^e$

The condition involving PairQ is not satisfied, so no transformation occurs.

$In[10]:=$ `tx[lb,uc] /. txTotyRule`

$Out[10]=$ $tx_b{}^c$

Substitution is carried out in the correct term.

$In[11]:=$ `tx[le,ue] tx[lb,uc] /. txTotyRule`

$Out[11]=$ $tx^c_b \; ty^e \; ty_e$

Now each term in the product is transformed. There is no duplication of dummy pairs of indices because the dummy pairs are present in the expression acted upon, but not in the transformation rule itself.

$In[12]:=$ `tx[le,ue] tx[lf,uf] /. txTotyRule`

$Out[12]=$ $ty \; ty_e \; ty^e \; ty^f_f$

■ 3.5.2 Pitfalls of Dummy Indices

When dummy indices are present in the transformation rules or definitions, things are not so simple.

Suppose you want to replace `tx` by a product of four `ty` vectors with one pair of vectors contracted. This rule contains a pair of dummy indices, `lc`, `uc`, that are specific, not representing patterns as do `la` and `lb`.

$In[13]:=$ `txTotyRule2 := tx[la_,lb_] :> ty[la] ty[lb] ty[lc] ty[uc] /;`
  `PairQ[la,lb]`

There is no problem here because only one substitution occurs.

$In[14]:=$ `tx[le,ue] /. txTotyRule2`

$Out[14]=$ $ty_c \; ty_e \; ty^c \; ty^e$

Something strange has occurred! If you look back at txTotyRule2, you will see that two substitutions have been made and hence that ty[lc] ty[uc] appears twice. This means that ty[lc] and ty[uc] each appear squared, and that is how they show up in the output.

$In[15]:=$ `tx[le,ue] tx[lf,uf] /. txTotyRule2`

$Out[15]=$ $ty_c^2 \; ty_e \; ty_f \; ty^{c2} \; ty^e \; ty^f$

You can use InputForm to see this expression as it would be typed as an input line. Clearly, the repeated dummy pair lc,uc is a syntax error when dealing with tensors.

$In[16]:=$ `InputForm[%]`

$Out[16]//InputForm=$
    `ty[lc]^2*ty[le]*ty[lf]*ty[uc]^2*ty[ue]*ty[uf]`

A rather awkward way to avoid repeating dummy index pairs in this situation is to apply the rule separately to each factor and to use Dum to relabel dummy indices differently in each factor. The second argument of Dum tells it where to start numbering dummy system-generated dummy index pairs. You will learn a better way to avoid repeating dummy indices later, using RuleUnique and DefUnique.

In[17]:= Dum[tx[le,ue]/.txTotyRule2, 1]
Dum[tx[le,ue]/.txTotyRule2, 3]

$$Out[17]= ty_p \; ty^p \; ty_q \; ty^q \; ty^r_r \; ty^r \; ty_s \; ty^s$$

You can look at the input form of this expression to remind yourself that the system-generated dummy index pairs are l1,u1,l2,..,l4,u4 in this case and appear as lower and upper p,..,s indices in the output line.

In[18]:= InputForm[%]
Out[18]//InputForm=
  ty[l1]*ty[l2]*ty[l3]*ty[l4]*ty[u1]*ty[u2]*ty[u3]*ty[u4]

When the print symbol is the same as the name of the tensor, you can omit the quoted print symbol in DefineTensor, as here. The second-rank tensor **tv** will be used to demonstrate another more subtle way in which repeating pairs of dummy indices may arise.

In[19]:= DefineTensor[tv,{{1,2},1}]
  PermWeight::def: Object tv defined

This defines a rule that converts the tensor **tv** to twice the tensor **tx**.

In[20]:= tvTotxRule := tv[la_,lb_] :> 2 tx[la,lb]

If you want to look at a rule, it is best to use InputForm, as otherwise index symbols will automatically appear formatted; for example, la will appear as a subscripted *a*.

In[21]:= tvTotxRule//InputForm
Out[21]//InputForm= tv[la_, lb_] :> 2*tx[la, lb]

This builds a compound rule consisting of the other two rules.

In[22]:= rule = {tvTotxRule, txTotyRule2};

With SyntaxCheck on, incorrect dummy indices will be detected and a warning message will be printed.

In[23]:= On[SyntaxCheck]
Out[23]= {SyntaxCheck}

The *MathTensor* function ReplaceRepeated, or //., applies the list of rules repeatedly until the expression stops changing.

In[24]:= tv[la,ua] //. rule

$$Out[24]= 2 \; ty_a \; ty^a \; ty_c \; ty^c$$

This causes repeating dummy pairs to occur. The cause is at the second level of replacement, when tx is replaced by products of ty's. It is clear that for you to construct sets of rules that are to be applied to complicated tensor expressions with confidence, you must have more sophisticated methods available in *MathTensor*.

```
In[25]:= tv[la,ua] tv[lb,ub] //. rule
 MathTensor Warning: Possible Bad or Unmatched Dummy Index
                         2   a   b   c2
Out[25]= 4 ty  ty  ty   ty  ty  ty
              a   b   c
```

Here is one last example.

```
In[26]:= ScalarRtotxRule := ScalarR :> tx[la,lb] tx[ua,ub]
```

Again the dummy indices are not properly paired. You could use the function Dum as before to avoid the repeating pairs, but there is a better way.

```
In[27]:= ScalarR^2 /. ScalarRtotxRule
 MathTensor Warning: Possible Bad or Unmatched Dummy Index
              2   ab2
Out[27]= tx   tx
           ab
```

■ 3.5.3 Making Rules and Definitions Containing Dummy Indices

MathTensor has functions that permit you to create transformation rules and definitions containing dummy indices. There are also functions that you can use to safely apply the rules to arbitrary expressions. The function $RuleUnique$ creates a rule that generates a unique new pair of dummy indices each time it is applied. It should be applied using the functions $ApplyRules$ or $ApplyRulesRepeated$. Finally, the function $DefUnique$ creates a definition that generates a unique new pair of dummy indices each time it is triggered. The following dialogue shows you how to use these functions.

This defines two second-rank tensors tx and ty having no symmetries.

```
In[1]:= DefineTensor[{tx,tv},{{1,2},1}]
 PermWeight::def: Object tx defined
 PermWeight::def: Object tv defined
```

This defines a vector ty.

```
In[2]:= DefineTensor[ty,{{1},1}]
 PermWeight::def: Object ty defined
```

This defines a rule equivalent to txTotyRule2 of the previous section, but with unique dummy indices. The first argument of $RuleUnique$ is the name of the rule, the second argument is the left-hand side of the rule, the third argument is the right-hand side, and the fourth argument, if present, is the condition.

```
In[3]:= RuleUnique[txTotyRule, tx[la_,lb_],
   ty[la] ty[lb] ty[lc] ty[uc], PairQ[la,lb] ]
```

In the previous section, `txTotyRule2` acting on this expression would give duplicated pairs of dummy indices.

$In[4] := $ `expr1 = tx[lb,ub] tx[lc,uc]`

$Out[4] = tx\begin{smallmatrix}b\\b\end{smallmatrix}\ tx\begin{smallmatrix}c\\c\end{smallmatrix}$

Now it gives the desired result, with properly matched dummy indices.

$In[5] := $ `ApplyRules[expr1, txTotyRule]`

$Out[5] = ty\begin{smallmatrix}p\\p\end{smallmatrix}\ ty\begin{smallmatrix}q\\q\end{smallmatrix}\ ty\begin{smallmatrix}r\\r\end{smallmatrix}\ ty\begin{smallmatrix}s\\s\end{smallmatrix}$

This defines the equivalent of `tvTotxRule` of the previous section. In this case, there are no dummy indices in the rule and there is no condition.

$In[6] := $ `RuleUnique[tvTotxRule, tv[la_,lb_], 2 tx[la,lb] ]`

This defines a set of rules, called `rule`. (Your version of *Mathematica* may warn you about the spelling of rule, but such a warning can be ignored.)

$In[7] := $ `rule := {txTotyRule, tvTotxRule}`

This applies `rule` once until the first rule that matches is found.

$In[8] := $ `ApplyRules[tv[la,ua] tv[lb,ub], rule]`

$Out[8] = 4\ tx\begin{smallmatrix}p\\p\end{smallmatrix}\ tx\begin{smallmatrix}q\\q\end{smallmatrix}$

This applies `rule` again. Note that dummies are properly paired.

$In[9] := $ `ApplyRules[%, rule]`

$Out[9] = 4\ ty\begin{smallmatrix}p\\p\end{smallmatrix}\ ty\begin{smallmatrix}q\\q\end{smallmatrix}\ ty\begin{smallmatrix}r\\r\end{smallmatrix}\ ty\begin{smallmatrix}s\\s\end{smallmatrix}$

`ApplyRulesRepeated` applies `rule` repeatedly until the expression stops changing.

$In[10] := $ `ApplyRulesRepeated[tv[la,ua] tv[lb,ub], rule]`

$Out[10] = 4\ ty\begin{smallmatrix}p\\p\end{smallmatrix}\ ty\begin{smallmatrix}q\\q\end{smallmatrix}\ ty\begin{smallmatrix}r\\r\end{smallmatrix}\ ty\begin{smallmatrix}s\\s\end{smallmatrix}$

This defines the equivalent of the rule having the same name in the previous section, but with unique dummy indices generated by the rule.

$In[11] := $ `RuleUnique[ScalarRtotxRule, ScalarR, tx[la,lb] tx[ua,ub] ]`

Now there is no duplication of dummy pairs.

$In[12] := $ `ApplyRules[ScalarR^2, ScalarRtotxRule]`

$Out[12] = tx\begin{smallmatrix}pq\\pq\end{smallmatrix}\ tx\begin{smallmatrix}rs\\rs\end{smallmatrix}$

The *MathTensor* function UpLo is used by RuleUnique to generate unique upper and lower dummy index pairs. Here a new contravariant (upper) index is assigned to the variable upind and the corresponding covariant (lower) index is assigned to loind.

```
In[13]:= UpLo[upind,loind]
```

The names of indices generated by UpLo are preceded by the symbol $.

```
In[14]:= {upind, loind}
            $11
Out[14]= {     ,    }
                 $11
```

Sets of matching unique pairs of contravariant and covariant indices are produced by using lists as arguments to UpLo.

```
In[15]:= UpLo[{upind1,upind2},{loind1,loind2}]
```

Here are the newly generated indices.

```
In[16]:= {upind1, upind2, loind1, loind2}
            $12   $13
Out[16]= {     ,      ,     ,     }
                      $12  $13
```

This is the InputForm of the new indices, which you would type in a substitution rule if, for example, you wanted to replace such an index by another symbol. When the indices are generated by UpLo, their names are recognized by the system as names of dummy index. You can also use Dum to replace such indices by the more familiar dummy index names.

```
In[17]:= InputForm[%]
Out[17]//InputForm= {uu12, uu13, ll12, ll13}
```

You can append your transformation rules or definitions to a knowledge-base file that you are constructing. The best way is to use Definition as here, since it prints only the definitions of the symbols you give it as arguments. If you look in the file MyRules.m that you just created, you will see how RuleUnique uses UpLo in the rules it produces.

```
In[18]:= Definition[txTotyRule, ScalarRtotxRule,
tvTotxRule, rule]>>>MyRules.m
```

You can also produce definitions that involve new dummy indices each time they are triggered. The first argument of DefUnique is the left-hand side of the definition, the second argument is the right-hand side, and the third argument, if present, is the condition that must be satisfied for the definition to trigger.

```
In[19]:= DefUnique[tx[la_, lb_],
ty[la]*ty[lb]*ty[lc]*ty[uc],
  PairQ[la, lb] ]
```

The definition or rule is now triggered automatically because paired indices occur in **tx**. The effect is as though **txTotyRule** had been applied. Using transformation rules rather than definitions is often preferable because it provides more control over expressions.

```
In[20]:= tx[la,ua]

                        a    $14
Out[20]= ty  ty     ty  ty
           a    $14
```

Dum replaces the two pairs of dummy indices in this expression by more standard system-generated pairs of dummy indices.

```
In[21]:= Dum[%]

                     p   q
Out[21]= ty  ty  ty  ty
           p   q
```

Here is a definition that will always be triggered when **tv** is typed with two arguments.

```
In[22]:= DefUnique[tv[la_,lb_], 2 tx[la,lb] ]
```

This is a simple example.

```
In[23]:= tv[la,lb]
Out[23]= 2 tx
            ab
```

In this case, the earlier definition involving **tx** with paired indices is also triggered, so **ty** finally appears.

```
In[24]:= tv[la,ua]

                          a    $15
Out[24]= 2 ty  ty     ty  ty
             a    $15
```

This example shows that there is no duplication of dummy pairs as definitions are triggered more than once.

```
In[25]:= tv[la,ua] tx[lb,ub]

                           a   b   $16   $17
Out[25]= 2 ty  ty  ty    ty   ty  ty  ty    ty
             a   b   $16   $17
```

This saves *all* definitions associated with **tx** and **ty** to a knowledge-base file. You don't have to use **DefineTensor** to set up these tensors if you **Get** the file **MyDefs.m** in a later *MathTensor* session.

```
In[26]:= Definition[tx,tv]>>>MyDefs.m
```

For a scalar like **ScalarR**, which has no indices, you should avoid using DefUnique as here.

```
In[27]:= DefUnique[ScalarR, tx[la, ua] tx[lb, ub] ]
```

Because the symbol `ScalarR` appears only once in powers like `ScalarR^2`, the definition is triggered only once, rather than twice as would be required to generate the correct pairs of unique dummy indices. When `RuleUnique` is used with `ApplyRules`, this problem is avoided.

```
In[28]:= ScalarR^2

                2      2      2      2    $202   $212   $222
Out[28]=   ty     ty     ty     ty     ty     ty     ty
             $20    $21    $22    $23

            $232
  >      ty
```

`RuleUnique[`*ruleName*`,`*lhs*`,`*rhs*`]`	create a transformation rule called *ruleName* that transforms *lhs* to *rhs*
`RuleUnique[`*ruleName*`,`*lhs*`,`*rhs*`,`*cond*`]`	
	create a transformation rule called *ruleName* that transforms *lhs* to *rhs* only when the condition *cond* holds
`DefUnique[`*lhs*`,`*rhs*`]`	create a definition or rule that automatically sets *lhs* to *rhs*
`DefUnique[`*lhs*`,`*rhs*`,`*cond*`]`	create a definition or rule that automatically sets *lhs* to *rhs* only when the condition *cond* holds
`Definition[`*rule1*`,`*rule2*`,`*tensor*`]>>>`*filename*	
	append transformation rules, *rule1*, *rule2*, and all definitions assigned to *tensor* to a file called *filename*

Commands that produce transformation rules and definitions having unique dummy indices.

■ 3.5.4 Building Your Own Knowledge-Base Files

Now that you know how to make transformation rules and definitions that contain dummy indices, you can create your own knowledge-base files. This will be illustrated here with a nontrivial example. Suppose that a metric g_{ab} is multiplied by a continuous real scalar function Ω^2. Such a transformation does not change the world lines of photons because the new line element, $ds^2 = \Omega^2 g_{ab} dx^a dx^b$, is zero along the same set of world lines (the paths of photons) as was the original line element, $ds^2 = g_{ab} dx^a dx^b$. A transformation taking g_{ab} to $\Omega^2 g_{ab}$ is called a *conformal* transformation of the metric because it preserves normalized scalar products (and hence angles) between vectors at any given point.

When a conformal transformation,

$$g_{ab} \rightarrow \Omega^2 g_{ab},$$

is performed on the metric, in a spacetime of any number of dimensions, it is easy to show that the affine connection $\Gamma^a{}_{bc}$, undergoes the following transformation:

$$\Gamma^a{}_{bc} \to \Gamma^a{}_{bc} + \Omega^{-1}(\delta^a{}_b \Omega_{,c} + \delta^a{}_c \Omega_{,b} - g_{bc} g^{ad} \Omega_{,d}).$$

Suppose that you want to put this into a knowledge-base file along with the conformal transformation undergone by the Ricci tensor. To do that, you can calculate the transformation of the Ricci tensor from that of the affine connections. The Ricci tensor is defined (in the convention with **Rmsign** and **Rcsign** equal to 1) by

$$R_{ab} = \frac{\partial \Gamma^c{}_{ab}}{\partial x^c} - \frac{\partial \Gamma^c{}_{ac}}{\partial x^b} + \Gamma^d{}_{ab} \Gamma^c{}_{cd} - \Gamma^d{}_{ac} \Gamma^c{}_{bd}.$$

There is a *MathTensor* command called **RicciToAffine** that already knows this expression for the Ricci tensor. Therefore you can start the knowledge-base file by recording rules for the conformal transformation of the metric and affine connection. Then you can calculate the conformal transformation of the Ricci tensor and record the rule that you discover. Let us start with the metric transformation rules, which do not involve dummy indices.

Although the first few rules entered below do not involve dummy indices, **RuleUnique** will be used to produce them. This is because **RuleUnique** is the same from one version of *Mathematica* to another, whereas the appearance of the explicit rule is different in different versions of *Mathematica*, such as versions 1.2 and 2.X. This insulates the user of *MathTensor* from changes in *Mathematica*. If you prefer, you can enter the rules using the syntax of *Mathematica* directly. However, the rule for the conformal transformation of **AffineG** does involve dummy indices on the right-hand side, so **RuleUnique** must be used.

This gives the conformal transformation of the covariant metric tensor. The first argument is the rule name, then comes the left-hand side of the rule, then the right-hand side, and finally the condition. **LowerIndexQ** tests if an index is a covariant index.

```
In[1]:= RuleUnique[MetricConfRule1, Metricg[a_,b_],
        om^2 Metricg[a,b], LowerIndexQ[a]&&LowerIndexQ[b] ]
```

This is the effect of the rule. Although here you can use **Replace** (i.e, /.) instead of **ApplyRules**, there are situations in which the latter is necessary, and it is best to use it consistently in tensor calculations.

```
In[2]:= ApplyRules[Metricg[la,lb], MetricConfRule1]

Out[2]= om  g
            ab
```

This appends the rule to your knowledge-base file.

```
In[3]:= Definition[MetricConfRule1] >>> MyCfRules.m
```

This is the transformation of the contravariant metric tensor, which gives the inverse of the transformed covariant metric tensor.

```
In[4]:= RuleUnique[MetricConfRule2, Metricg[a_,b_],
  om^(-2) Metricg[a,b], UpperIndexQ[a]&&UpperIndexQ[b] ]
```

This adds the next rule.

```
In[5]:= Definition[MetricConfRule2] >>> MyCfRules.m
```

This combines the rules into one rule, which can be applied to the metric having indices in any positions. The metric with one upper and one lower index is unchanged by conformal transformation.

```
In[6]:= MetricConfRule := {MetricConfRule1,
MetricConfRule2}
```

This writes the compound rule to the file.

```
In[7]:= Definition[MetricConfRule] >>> MyCfRules.m
```

Because you are working with ordinary derivatives and affine connections here, it is necessary to turn off automatic raising and lowering of indices by the metric.

```
In[8]:= Off[MetricgFlag]
```

This will be the right-hand side of the rule for conformal transformation of the affine connection, AffineG.

```
In[9]:= rhs = AffineG[ua,lb,lc] +
   om^(-1) Metricg[ua,lb] OD[om,lc] +
   om^(-1) Metricg[ua,lc] OD[om,lb] -
   om^(-1) Metricg[lb,lc] Metricg[ua,ud] OD[om,ld]
```

$$Out[9]= G^{a}_{bc} + \frac{g^{a}_{c}\ om_{,b}}{om} + \frac{g^{a}_{b}\ om_{,c}}{om} - \frac{g_{bc}\ g^{ad}\ om_{,d}}{om}$$

Notice that the patterns ua_,lb_,lc_, which appear in the argument corresponding to the left-hand side of the rule, correspond to the symbols that appear in rhs, just as when you explicitly write a rule in *Mathematica*. Although you do not have to use index names like ua for these symbols as long as they are the same on each side of the rule, when dummy indices appear on the right-hand side of a rule, you must use index names to denote them, such as ud,ld here. Otherwise RuleUnique will not recognize them.

```
In[10]:= RuleUnique[AffineConfRule,
   AffineG[ua_,lb_,lc_], rhs,
   UpperIndexQ[ua]&&LowerIndexQ[lb]&&LowerIndexQ[lc]]
```

This checks that the rule works.

$In[11]:= $ `ApplyRules[AffineG[ua,lb,lc], AffineConfRule]`

$$Out[11]= G^a_{bc} - \frac{g_{bc}\, g^{pa}\, om_{,p}}{om} + \frac{g^a_c\, om_{,b}}{om} + \frac{g^a_b\, om_{,c}}{om}$$

This saves the rule to the file of conformal transformation rules. Now you are ready to work out the transformation of the Ricci tensor.

$In[12]:= $ `Definition[AffineConfRule]>>>MyCfRules.m`

The transformation rule you are going to work out relates tensors at a point. It will make it much easier to recognize the form of the rule if you work in normal coordinates at the point. In such coordinates, the affine connection, but not its derivatives, vanish at the point under consideration. In addition, the first derivatives of the metric vanish at the point. After the rule has been written manifestly as a transformation between tensors, it will hold in any coordinate system. First you must make rules to cause the affine connections and the first derivatives of the metric to vanish.

This rule is written this way so that if `ApplyRules` or `Replace` (`/.`) is used, ordinary partial derivatives of `AffineG` will not be set to zero. `ApplyRules` and `Replace` stop acting on a given term after the first time one of the subrules inside the list of rules is applied.

$In[13]:= $ `AffineZeroRule :=`
`{OD[AffineG[a_,b_,c_],d_] -> OD[AffineG[a,b,c],d],`
`AffineG[a_,b_,c_] -> 0}`

The ordinary derivative of `AffineG` is not changed.

$In[14]:= $ `ApplyRules[OD[AffineG[ua,lb,lc],ld],`
`AffineZeroRule]`

$$Out[14]= G^a_{bc,d}$$

This rule will set first derivatives of the metric to zero.

$In[15]:= $ `MetricDerivZeroRule = OD[Metricg[a_,b_],c_] -> 0;`

`Flatten` is necessary here to combine the rules into a single list. To cast an expression into its form at the origin of normal coordinates, you can apply this rule. Now you are ready to find the conformal transformation of the Ricci tensor.

$In[16]:= $ `normalCoordRule := Flatten[{AffineZeroRule,`
`MetricDerivZeroRule}]`

This is the expression for `RicciR[1a,1b]` in terms of `AffineG`. If you had not already turned off `MetricgFlag`, there would be a message now telling you that it is turned off by `RicciToAffineRule`.

$$In[17] := \text{expr1} = \text{ApplyRules[RicciR[1a,1b],}$$
$$\text{RicciToAffineRule]}$$

$$Out[17] = G^{p}_{ab} G^{q}_{pq} - G^{p}_{qa} G^{q}_{pb} - G^{p}_{pa,b} + G^{p}_{ab,p}$$

Perform a conformal transformation on the affine connections. The command is ended with ";" to save the time required for formatted output to be printed. This step will take some time.

$$In[18] := \text{Expand[ApplyRules[expr1, AffineConfRule]];}$$

This removes first derivatives of the metric. It will take some time for formatted printing of these terms to occur. You are working in normal coordinates only after making the conformal transformation. Since the transformation changes geodesics, you cannot also assume that you had normal coordinates before the transformation.

$$In[19] := \text{expr2} = \text{ApplyRules[\%, normalCoordRule]}$$

$$Out[19] = \frac{2\, g_{ab}\, g^{pq}\, om_{,p}\, om_{,q}}{om^2} - \frac{g^{p}_{p}\, g_{ab}\, g^{qr}\, om_{,q}\, om_{,r}}{om^2} -$$

$$> \frac{g_{pb}\, g_{qa}\, g^{pr}\, g^{qs}\, om_{,r}\, om_{,s}}{om^2} +$$

$$> \frac{g_{pq}\, g_{ab}\, g^{pr}\, g^{qs}\, om_{,r}\, om_{,s}}{om^2} - \frac{g_{pa}\, g^{pq}\, om_{,q}\, om_{,b}}{om^2} -$$

$$> \frac{2\, om_{,a}\, om_{,b}}{om^2} + \frac{2\, g^{p}_{p}\, om_{,a}\, om_{,b}}{om^2} - G^{p}_{pa,b} + G^{p}_{ab,p} -$$

$$> \frac{g_{ab}\, g^{pq}\, om_{,pq}}{om} + \frac{g_{pa}\, g^{pq}\, om_{,qb}}{om} + \frac{om_{,ab}}{om} - \frac{g^{p}_{p}\, om_{,ab}}{om}$$

Pausing to contemplate this result, you see that the terms involving `AffineG` give back `RicciR[1a,1b]` of `expr1`, which is a tensor. To write the rest of this expression explicitly in tensor form, use the fact that because `om` is a scalar, so that its first and second derivatives at the origin of normal coordinates are the same as the first and second covariant derivatives, respectively. Therefore you can turn on `MetricgFlag`, it being understood that the commas will go over to covariant derivatives in general coordinates.

Now the metric will raise and lower indices. In addition, it will be recognized that $g^p{}_p$ is equal to the dimension of the spacetime.

In[20]:= `On[MetricgFlag]`

Some terms have been combined. The factor of d is the dimension of the spacetime, which is arbitrary. This is the desired form of the result in normal coordinates because it can immediately be rewritten in terms of tensors in a way that will be valid in any coordinate system.

In[21]:= `Dum[expr2]`

$$Out[21] = \frac{-4\, om_{,a}\, om_{,b}}{om^2} + \frac{2\, d\, om_{,a}\, om_{,b}}{om^2} + \frac{3\, g_{ab}\, om_{,p}\, om^{,p}}{om^2} -$$

$$> \frac{d\, g_{ab}\, om_{,p}\, om^{,p}}{om^2} - G^p{}_{pa,b} + G^p{}_{ab,p} - \frac{g_{ab}\, om^{,p}{}_{,p}}{om} +$$

$$> \frac{2\, om_{,ab}}{om} - \frac{d\, om_{,ab}}{om}$$

To write this explicitly in terms of tensors, first recognize that the terms involving **AffineG** give back the original **RicciR[1a,1b]** of **expr1**. Next, note that the second ordinary partial derivative of the scalar, **om**, is equal to the second covariant derivative of **om** in normal coordinates.

This replaces the affine connections terms by the Ricci tensor.

In[22]:= `expr3 = expr2 - expr2[[5]] - expr2[[6]] + RicciR[1a,1b]`

$$Out[22] = \frac{-4\, om_{,a}\, om_{,b}}{om^2} + \frac{2\, d\, om_{,a}\, om_{,b}}{om^2} + \frac{3\, g_{ab}\, om_{,p}\, om^{,p}}{om^2} -$$

$$> \frac{d\, g_{ab}\, om_{,q}\, om^{,q}}{om^2} - \frac{g_{ab}\, om^{,p}{}_{,p}}{om} + \frac{2\, om_{,ab}}{om} - \frac{d\, om_{,ab}}{om} + R_{ab}$$

This replaces the ordinary derivatives by covariant ones. Now this expression in normal coordinates is written manifestly in terms of tensors so that it is valid in any coordinate system. This is then the right-hand side of the rule for conformal transformation of the Ricci tensor. It is valid in any dimension.

```
In[23]:= expr4 = expr3 /. OD -> CD
```

$$Out[23]= \frac{-4\ om_{;a}\ om_{;b}}{om^2} + \frac{2\ d\ om_{;a}\ om_{;b}}{om^2} + \frac{2\ om_{;ab}}{om} -$$

$$> \frac{d\ om_{;ab}}{om} + \frac{3\ om_{;p}\ om_{;}{}^{p}\ g_{ab}}{om^2} - \frac{d\ om_{;q}\ om_{;}{}^{q}\ g_{ab}}{om^2} -$$

$$> \frac{om_{;p}{}^{p}\ g_{ab}}{om} + R_{ab}$$

This constructs the rule. The condition that the indices be covariant is required because if an index is raised on the left-hand side, the original metric g^{ab} is used, while if an index is raised on the right-hand side, the transformed metric $\Omega^{-2}g^{ab}$ is used. That would introduce a factor of `om^(-2)` on the right-hand side for each index that is raised. Thus the rules with one or two raised indices could be easily written down.

```
In[24]:= RuleUnique[RicciConfRule, RicciR[la_,lb_], expr4,
           LowerIndexQ[la]&&LowerIndexQ[lb] ]
```

It is a good idea to check that your rules work.

```
In[25]:= ApplyRules[RicciR[la,lb], RicciConfRule]
```

$$Out[25]= \frac{-4\ om_{;a}\ om_{;b}}{om^2} + \frac{2\ d\ om_{;a}\ om_{;b}}{om^2} + \frac{2\ om_{;ab}}{om} -$$

$$> \frac{d\ om_{;ab}}{om} + \frac{3\ om_{;p}\ om_{;}{}^{p}\ g_{ab}}{om^2} - \frac{d\ om_{;p}\ om_{;}{}^{p}\ g_{ab}}{om^2} -$$

$$> \frac{om_{;p}{}^{p}\ g_{ab}}{om} + R_{ab}$$

Finally, append the rule to your file of conformal transformation rules.

```
In[26]:= Definition[RicciConfRule]>>>MyCfRules.m
```

The `InputForm` of the symbol *d* appearing in the formatted form of the rule is `Dimension`. Here is the transform of R_{ab} in a 4-dimensional spacetime. The rules in your file are good in spaces of arbitrary dimension.

$$In[27]:= \text{\%\% /. Dimension -> 4}$$

$$Out[27]= \frac{4\ om_{;a}\ om_{;b}}{om^2} - \frac{2\ om_{;ab}}{om} - \frac{om_{;p}\ om_{;}\ g_{ab}}{om^2} -$$

$$> \frac{om_{;p}{}^{p}\ g_{ab}}{om} + R_{ab}$$

This example, although rather advanced, gives a realistic illustration of how you might go about setting up knowledge-base files for your own applications. If you wanted to distribute such knowledge-base files to others, you would probably want to introduce appropriate factors of `Rmsign` and `Rcsign` so that the formulas would be valid with any sign convention. It is usually not difficult to figure out these factors.

Setting up a knowledge-base file almost always requires some experimentation to derive the desired rules, and to make sure that the rules are working properly. You should not be discouraged if it takes some trial and error. A calm and determined approach will usually succeed.

■ 3.6 The Riemann and Related Rules

■ 3.6.1 Organization of Rules

There are many different ways to devise and apply rules to tensors. Because tensor expressions can become extremely complex, it is a good idea to organize rules in as logical a fashion as possible. In *MathTensor*, there are a number of ways that rules are presented. The largest sets of rules included with *MathTensor* are the rules related to the Riemann tensor and its contractions and covariant derivatives. There are over fifty such rules. In the next few sections, we will discuss two general types. The first are rules that *MathTensor* applies automatically; the second are rules that are used manually, either one by one or in groups.

The examples given here illustrate the use of `ApplyRules` and related functions as well as the rules for manipulating curvature tensors. You may find these sections to be a useful reference on the rules for manipulating curvature tensors.

■ 3.6.2 Automatic Riemann Rules

The first box lists the rules related to symmetries of the Riemann tensor. These are there so that the user does not have to use **DefineTensor** to define **RiemannR**. They express the standard antisymmetries of the first and last pairs of indices and the symmetry under interchange of the indices in pairs.

Automatic rules are ones that are used without user interaction. When the pattern on the left-hand side of the rule is generated by a computation, the right-hand side is substituted before the output is generated. In *MathTensor*, we keep this type of rule to the minimum because we consider that it is better for the user to control what rules are used when.

```
RiemannR[a_, b_, c_, d_] := -RiemannR[b, a, c, d] /;
IndicesAndNotOrderedQ[{a, b}]

RiemannR[a_, b_, c_, d_] := -RiemannR[a, b, d, c] /;
IndicesAndNotOrderedQ[{c, d}]

RiemannR[a_, b_, c_, d_] := RiemannR[c, d, a, b] /;
IndicesAndNotOrderedQ[{a, c}]
```

Automatic basic Riemann tensor symmetries.

The predicate **IndicesAndNotOrderedQ** in the rules returns **True** if its arguments are tensor indices and they are not in lexical order.

```
IndicesAndNotOrderedQ[{a, b, ...}] = True
                    when a, b, ..., are tensor indices and not in lexical order
```

The predicate **IndicesAndNotOrderedQ**.

In tensorial notation, this first set of rules might be written as

$$
\begin{aligned}
R_{bacd} &= -R_{abcd}, \\
R_{abdc} &= -R_{abcd}, \\
R_{cdab} &= +R_{abcd}
\end{aligned}
$$

on a Riemann tensor with all covariant indices.

Note that the names of the indices in these rules really represent the "a-blank", "b-blank", and so forth and need not be "a", "b", etc. Their exact positions depend on whether they are upper or lower indices.

At this point, we come across an important subtlety regarding tensor symmetries that you will need to consider in all computations. Given the symmetries above, what will *MathTensor* do to an object like `RiemannR[ua,lb,lc,ld]`? What will happen with `RiemannR[ua,ub,lc,ld]`?

Enter a Riemann tensor with an upper index in its first position. Due to the fact that ua comes after lb lexically, ua will be moved to the second index position and a minus sign introduced.	$In[1] :=$ `RiemannR[ua,lb,lc,ld]` $$Out[1] = -R^{a}_{bcd}$$
Similarly, upper indices in the first pair are moved to the second pair.	$In[2] :=$ `RiemannR[ua,ub,lc,ld]` $$Out[2] = R^{ab}_{cd}$$

This may appear to be a limitation. In fact, it is a time saver since only the following forms of the Riemann tensor appear in any rules:
`RiemannR[lower,lower,lower,lower]`, `RiemannR[lower,lower,lower,upper]`
`RiemannR[lower,upper,lower,lower]`, `RiemannR[lower,lower,upper,upper]`
`RiemannR[lower,upper,lower,upper]`, `RiemannR[lower,upper,upper,upper]`
`RiemannR[upper,upper,upper,upper]`

It is often the case in pattern matching rules that specific rule substitutions will be found and executed much faster than general rules will be. In the case of `RiemannR` rules, inserting multiple specific rules where needed will be faster than applying one more general rule that requires the program to work harder to pattern-match a given expression. If we want to define some function acting on `RiemannR`, we need to define it only for at most the six forms above and not for all possible positions of indices. This situation will appear later in the `Variation` function and in the `RiemannToAffine` function in this chapter. Some users may still want to be able to have upper indices in the first position of the Riemann tensor. One way to do this would be to define your own Riemann tensor with `DefineTensor` without symmetries and then put them in later. (In version 2.X of *Mathematica*, it is possible to force `ua` to appear before `lb` by modifying the `$StringOrder` list by adding a sublist like `{"la","ua","lb","ub"}` to it. This is **not** advisable, however, since it may disturb certain aspects of *MathTensor*.)

The next set of rules involve contractions on pairs of indices. Note again that there are five possible rules. Note also the use of `Rcsign`, which is ± 1 depending on the sign convention used. `Rcsign` is $+1$ if the Ricci tensor is obtained by contraction of the first and third indices of the Riemann tensor and -1 if the first and fourth indices are contracted to form the Ricci tensor. We typically use the $+1$ value. `Rcsign` is set in the file `Conventions.m`, which can be edited. The sign convention

of the Riemann tensor is determined by the variable **Rmsign**, which is also set in
the file **Conventions.m**.

```
RiemannR[a_,b_,c_,d_] := 0 /; (PairQ[a,b]) || (PairQ[c,d])

RiemannR[a_,b_,c_,d_] := Rcsign*RicciR[b,d] /; PairQ[a,c]

RiemannR[a_,b_,c_,d_] := -Rcsign*RicciR[b,c] /; PairQ[a,d]

RiemannR[a_,b_,c_,d_] := - Rcsign*RicciR[a,d] /; PairQ[b,c]

RiemannR[a_,b_,c_,d_] := Rcsign*RicciR[a,c] /; PairQ[b,d]
```

Automatic rules for contractions of **RiemannR**.

In tensor notation, with **Rcsign** set equal to one, the above rules are

$$
\begin{aligned}
R_a{}^a{}_{cd} &= 0, \\
R_{abc}{}^c &= 0, \\
R_{ab}{}^a{}_d &= R_{bd}, \\
R_{abc}{}^a &= -R_{bc}, \\
R_{ab}{}^b{}_d &= -R_{ad}, \\
R_{abc}{}^b &= R_{ac}
\end{aligned}
$$

when the free indices are all covariant.

There are two automatic rules related to the Ricci tensor, **RicciR**. The first
expresses the symmetry of its two indices and the second its contraction to become
the Riemann scalar, **ScalarR**.

```
RicciR[a_,b_] := RicciR[b,a] /; IndicesAndNotOrderedQ[{a,b}]

RicciR[a_,b_] := ScalarR /; PairQ[a,b]
```

Automatic rules for **RicciR**.

Again, in usual notation,

$$
\begin{aligned}
R_{ba} &= R_{ab}, \\
R_a{}^a &= R.
\end{aligned}
$$

The final automatic rule says that there is a symmetry on the first two covariant derivatives of the Riemann scalar, `ScalarR`.

```
CD[ScalarR,a_,b_,c__] := CD[ScalarR,b,a,c] /; IndicesAndNotOrderedQ[{a,b}]
```

Automatic rule for the symmetry of covariant derivatives on <code>ScalarR</code>.

In tensor language, this is

$$R_{;bac...} = R_{;abc...}.$$

■ 3.6.3 Riemann Rules Used with the ApplyRules Functions

MathTensor includes many built-in rules that may be applied individually, either in user-defined groups, or all at once. They are collected together in one big rule as the rule set, `RiemannRules`. Each rule has its own name that consists of the word `RiemannRule` with a number (and perhaps a letter also) after it, as in `RiemannRule1`, `RiemannRule2`, `RiemannRule9a`, and so forth. A complete list of all of the RiemannRules in their *MathTensor* forms would take up too many pages and will not be written here. Instead, several typical examples to illustrate rule construction will be given. Generally speaking, *MathTensor* users should use `RuleUnique` to create their own rules. Those user-defined rules can be combined with built-in rules to create customized rule lists. Here is a complete list of the `RiemannRules` in typeset form.

$$R_{a\ cd}^{\ a} = 0 \quad R_{abc}^{\quad c} = 0 \qquad\qquad RiemannRule1$$

$$R_{ab\ d}^{\ \ a} = R_{bd} \qquad\qquad RiemannRule2$$

$$R_{abc}^{\quad a} = -R_{bc} \qquad\qquad RiemannRule3$$

$$R_{ab\ d}^{\ \ b} = -R_{ad} \qquad\qquad RiemannRule4$$

$$R_{abc}^{\quad b} = R_{ac} \qquad\qquad RiemannRule5$$

$$R_{abcd}R^{ab} = 0 \quad R_{abcd}R^{cd} = 0 \qquad\qquad RiemannRule6$$

$$R_{abcd} R_e{}^{abc} = -\frac{1}{2} R_{pdqr} R_e{}^{pqr} \qquad\qquad Riemann\,Rule7$$

$$R_{abcd} R^{acbh} = \frac{1}{2} R_{pdqr} R^{phqr} \qquad\qquad Riemann\,Rule8$$

$$R_{abcd} R_e{}^a{}_g{}^b = \frac{1}{2} R_{pqcd} R_{eg}{}^{pq} \qquad\qquad Riemann\,Rule9a$$

$$R_{abcd} R^{eabh} = -\frac{1}{2} R_{pqcd} R^{ehpq} \qquad\qquad Riemann\,Rule9b$$

$$R_{abcd} R^{afbh} = \frac{1}{2} R_{pqcd} R^{pqfh} \qquad\qquad Riemann\,Rule9c$$

$$R_{abcd} R^{afgb} = -\frac{1}{2} R_{pqcd} R^{pqfg} \qquad\qquad Riemann\,Rule9d$$

$$R_{ab} R_{cde}{}^a R^{bcde} = -\frac{1}{2} R_{pq} R_{rst}{}^p R^{qtrs} \qquad\qquad Riemann\,Rule10$$

$$R_{abcd} R_{ef}{}^{ab} R^{cedf} = \frac{1}{2} R_{pqrs} R_{tu}{}^{pq} R^{rstu} \qquad\qquad Riemann\,Rule11$$

$$R_{abcd} R_e{}^a{}_f{}^b R^{cedf} = \frac{1}{4} R_{pqrs} R_{tu}{}^{rs} R^{pqtu} \qquad\qquad Riemann\,Rule12$$

$$R_{abcd} R_e{}^a{}_g{}^b R^{cdeg} = \frac{1}{4} R_{pqrs} R_{tu}{}^{pq} R^{rstu} \qquad\qquad Riemann\,Rule13$$

$$R_{abcd} R_e{}^a{}_g{}^c R^{bdeg} = \frac{1}{4} R_{pqrs} R_{rs}{}^{tu} R_{tu}^{pq} \qquad\qquad Riemann\,Rule14$$

$$R_{abcd} R_e{}^a{}_g{}^c R^{bgde} = R_{pqrs} R_t{}^p{}_u{}^r R^{qtsu} - \frac{1}{4} R_{pqrs} R_{tu}{}^{pq} R^{rstu} \qquad\qquad Riemann\,Rule15$$

$$R_{ab;}{}^b = \frac{1}{2} R_{;a} \qquad\qquad Riemann\,Rule16$$

$$R_{ab;}{}^a = \frac{1}{2}R_{;b} \qquad\qquad RiemannRule17$$

$$R_{ab;c}{}^b = \frac{1}{2}R_{;ac} + R_{pa}R_c{}^p - R_{pd}R_a{}^q{}_c{}^p \qquad\qquad RiemannRule18$$

$$R_{ab;c}{}^a = \frac{1}{2}R_{;bc} + R0_{pb}R_c{}^p - R_{pq}R_b{}^q{}_c{}^p \qquad\qquad RiemannRule19$$

$$R_{abcd;}{}^a = -R_{bc;d} + R_{bd;c} \qquad\qquad RiemannRule20$$

$$R_{abcd;}{}^b = R_{ac;d} - R_{ad;c} \qquad\qquad RiemannRule21$$

$$R_{abcd;}{}^c = -R_{ad;b} + R_{bd;a} \qquad\qquad RiemannRule22$$

$$R_{abcd;}{}^d = R_{ac;b} - R_{bc;a} \qquad\qquad RiemannRule23$$

$$R_{;ab}{}^{ab} = \frac{1}{2}R_{;p}R_{;}{}^p + R_{;p}{}^p{}_q{}^q + R_{;pq}R^{pq} \qquad\qquad RiemannRule24$$

$$R_{ab;c}{}^{cab} = \frac{1}{2}R_{;p}R_{;}{}^p - 3R_{pq;r}R^{pq}{}_{;}{}^r + 4R_{pq;r}R^{pr}{}_{;}{}^q + \frac{1}{2}R_{;p}{}^p{}_q{}^q +$$

$$2R_{;pq}R^{pq} - R_{pq;}{}^r R^{pq} + 2R_{pq}R_r{}^p R^{qr} - 2R_{pq;rs}R^{prqs} - 2R_{pq}R_{rs}R^{prqs}$$

$$RiemannRule25$$

$$R_{abcd;e}{}^e = R_{ac;db} - R_{ad;cb} - R_{bc;da} + R_{bd;ca} - R_{pqcd}R_a{}^p{}_b{}^q + R_{pb}R_a{}^p{}_{cd} - R_{pbqd}R_a{}^p{}_c{}^q +$$

$$R_{pbqc}R_a{}^p{}_d{}^q - R_{pa}R_b{}^p{}_{cd} + R_{paqd}R_b{}^p{}_c{}^q - R_{paqc}R_b{}^p{}_d{}^q - R_{paqb}R_{cd}{}^{pq}$$

$$RiemannRule26$$

$$R_{abcd;e}{}^{a} = -R_{bc;de} + R_{bd;ce} - R_{pe}R_{b}{}^{p}{}_{cd} + R_{pqcd}R_{b}{}^{p}{}_{e}{}^{q} - R_{pbqd}R_{c}{}^{q}{}_{e}{}^{p} + R_{pbqc}R_{d}{}^{q}{}_{e}{}^{p}$$

$$RiemannRule27$$

$$R_{abcd;e}{}^{b} = R_{ac;de} - R_{ad;ce} + R_{pe}R_{a}{}^{p}{}_{cd} - R_{pqcd}R_{a}{}^{p}{}_{e}{}^{q} + R_{paqd}R_{c}{}^{q}{}_{e}{}^{p} - R_{paqc}R_{d}{}^{q}{}_{e}{}^{p}$$

$$RiemannRule28$$

$$R_{abcd;e}{}^{c} = -R_{ad;be} + R_{bd;ae} - R_{pe}R_{abd}{}^{p} - R_{pbqd}R_{a}{}^{p}{}_{e}{}^{q} + R_{paqd}R_{b}{}^{p}{}_{e}{}^{q} + R_{pqab}R_{d}{}^{p}{}_{e}{}^{q}$$

$$RiemannRule29$$

$$R_{abcd;e}{}^{d} = R_{ac;be} - R_{bc;ae} + R_{pe}R_{abc}{}^{p} + R_{pbqc}R_{a}{}^{p}{}_{e}{}^{q} - R_{paqc}R_{b}{}^{p}{}_{e}{}^{q} - R_{pqab}R_{c}{}^{p}{}_{e}{}^{q}$$

$$RiemannRule30$$

$$R_{abcd;e}R^{ab} = 0 \qquad R_{abcd;e}R^{cd} = 0 \qquad\qquad RiemannRule31$$

$$R_{abcd;e}R^{ab}{}_{;f} = 0 \qquad R_{abcd;e}R^{cd}{}_{;f} = 0 \qquad\qquad RiemannRule32$$

$$R_{ab;c}R^{abde} = 0 \qquad R_{ab;c}R^{deab} = 0 \qquad\qquad RiemannRule33$$

$$R^{afbc}{}_{;e}R_{abcd} = -\frac{1}{2}R^{pfqr}{}_{;e}R_{pdqr} \qquad\qquad RiemannRule34$$

$$R_{abcd;e}R^{agbc}{}_{;j} = -\frac{1}{2}R_{pdqr;e}R^{pgqr}{}_{;j} \qquad\qquad RiemannRule35$$

$$R^{acbh}{}_{;i}R_{abcd} = \frac{1}{2}R^{bhqr}{}_{;i}R_{pdqr} \qquad\qquad RiemannRule36$$

$$R_{abcd;j}R^{acbh}{}_{;i} = \frac{1}{2}R_{pdqr;j}R^{phqr}{}_{;i} \qquad\qquad RiemannRule37$$

$$R_{abcd;i}R^{cedf}{}_{;}{}^{i} = \frac{1}{2}R_{pqab;r}R^{pqce}{}_{;}{}^{r} \qquad\qquad RiemannRule38$$

$$R^{adbc}{}_{;j}R_{ab;cd} = R^{pqrs}{}_{;j}R_{pr;qs} \qquad\qquad RiemannRule39$$

$$R_{ab;cd}R^{adbc} = R_{pq;rs}R^{prqs} \qquad\qquad RiemannRule40$$

Note that, for completeness, some of the automatic rules also appear in the numbered Riemann rules. Rules 1–5 are automatic rules and do not have to be used with **ApplyRules**. If the user creates an object like the Riemann tensor but does not want the symmetry and other automatic rules, analogs to Rules 1–5 might be included in a new set of rules for the new object. Each rule prints out a message when it is used. To see the detailed form of each rule, a command like **??RiemannRule1** will show it. (Some indices may contain information on the *MathTensor* context, which can be ignored.)

The *MathTensor* form for the rules stated here were first constructed for *Mathematica* version 1.2. They use the **Block** construction. These will also work in later *Mathematica* versions. The **Module** structure created by **RuleUnique** is the preferred form for *Mathematica* versions 2.X.

In the rules listed above, we have left out any references to the **Rmsign** and **Rcsign** objects that appear in the actual *MathTensor* rules. If the user wishes to make very general rules, then it will be necessary to save the rule to a file and then edit in **Rmsign** and **Rcsign** and other conventions carefully.

The first rule we look at is the same as one of the automatic Riemann rules already presented. We see the basic rule structure. We start with a **Rule::Applied** message that tells us the message the rule will print out if it is used. We then give the rule name and the structure of the left-hand side of the rule. Then inside the **Block** (or **Module** if we like), we first print out the message and give the right-hand side of the equation — in this case, zero. Finally, we provide the tests that must be done before the rule is applied. In this case, the tests use the `PairQ` function to test if index pairs are summed in a particular way before the rule is applied.

```
RiemannRule1::Applied := "RiemannRule1 has been used."

RiemannRule1 := RiemannR[a_,b_,c_,d_] :>
Block[{},
Message[RiemannRule1::Applied];
0] /;
(PairQ[a,b]) || (PairQ[c,d])
```

RiemannRule1, one of the automatic rules.

The first Riemann rule that is not one of the automatic rules is the sixth one. This one merely states that when the symmetric Ricci tensor has its pair of indices summed on one of the antisymmetric pairs on the Riemann tensor, the result must be zero. This rule was created before the development of the powerful `Tsimplify` function, which notices this kind of structure for any tensor combination. It remains in the Riemann rules so that this rule can be applied without using `Tsimplify`.

```
RiemannRule6::Applied := "RiemannRule6 has been used."

RiemannRule6 := RiemannR[a_,b_,c_,d_] RicciR[e_,f_] :>
Block[{},
Message[RiemannRule6::Applied];
0] /;
(PairQ[a,e] && PairQ[b,f]) || (PairQ[c,e] && PairQ[d,f])
```

RiemannRule6.

The symmetric indices of the Ricci tensor are summed on the antisymmetric first pair of indices on the Riemann tensor.

$In[3]:=$ `RiemannR[la,lb,lc,ld] RicciR[ua,ub]`

$Out[3]= R^{ab} R_{abcd}$

The Riemann rules are applied and we get the zero result we expect using rule 6.

$In[4]:=$ `ApplyRules[%,RiemannRules]`

  RiemannRule6::Applied: RiemannRule6 has been used.

$Out[4]= 0$

Similarly, `Tsimplify` gives the same result.

$In[5]:=$ `Tsimplify[%%]`

$Out[5]= 0$

The new rules that follow `RiemannRule6` are designed to take certain Riemann tensor constructs and put them into a form we have chosen as "standard." Unfortunately, there is no absolute standard for such constructs. As the number of Riemann tensors in a term grows and as the number of derivatives grows, the number of possible terms that can be formed grows dramatically. Mathematicians are hard at work trying to define linearly independent sets of terms that can be used to reduce the number of terms to a minimum number. The goal of a set of Riemann tensor rules is to be able to write any term generated by a calculation as a linear combination of some convenient independent set. The Riemann rules currently programmed into *MathTensor* will not do this yet. In some future version of *MathTensor*, we hope to present at least a partial solution to this problem. For now, we give the rules we have found useful.

One of the key structures in most of the rules is the use of the `UpLo` function to generate new dummy index pairs. In many cases, this might not be necessary, since index conflicts might not appear. But the consistent use of `UpLo` gives the canonicalization and simplification functions a better chance of reducing the size of expression because all rules are applied consistently.

The most common rearrangement of indices we apply in the rules below is represented in Rule 7, for example. We see that a "cross sum" is converted to an index pair to index pair sum, as in

$$R_{abcd} R^{cd}_{ef} \rightarrow \frac{1}{2} R_{abcd} R_{ef}^{cd}.$$

Many of the rules apply this conversion to various combinations of Riemann tensors and their derivatives.

```
RiemannRule7::Applied := "RiemannRule7 has been used."

RiemannRule7 := RiemannR[a_,b_,c_,d_]*RiemannR[e_,f_,g_,h_] :>
Block[{up1,up2,up3,lo1,lo2,lo3},
Message[RiemannRule7::Applied];
UpLo[{up1,up2,up3},{lo1,lo2,lo3}];
-(1/2)*RiemannR[lo1,lo2,lo3,d] RiemannR[e,up3,up1,up2]] /;
PairQ[a,f] && PairQ[b,g] && PairQ[c,h]
```

RiemannRule7.

A product of two Riemann tensors with three pairs of summed indices.

$In[6] := $ `RiemannR[la,lb,lc,ld] RiemannR[le,ua,ub,uc]`

$Out[6] = R_{abcd} R_e{}^{abc}$

Rule 7 is applied.

$In[7] := $ `ApplyRules[%,RiemannRules]`

RiemannRule7::Applied: RiemannRule7 has been used.

$$Out[7] = \frac{-(R_{pdqr} R_e{}^{pqr})}{2}$$

`RiemannRule16` represents one of the most common substitutions done involving covariant derivatives of the Ricci tensor.

RiemannRule16::Applied := "RiemannRule16 has been used."

RiemannRule16 :=
CD[RicciR[a_,b_],c_,d___] :>
Block[{},
Message[RiemannRule16::Applied];
(1/2)*CD[ScalarR,a,d]] /; PairQ[b,c]

RiemannRule16.

A simple contraction of a covariant derivative on a Ricci tensor index.

$In[8] := $ `CD[RicciR[la,lb],ub,ld]`

$Out[8] = R_{ab;d}{}^{b}$

Rule 16 uses the contracted Bianchi identity to simplify the expression.

$In[9] := $ `ApplyRules[%,RiemannRules]`

RiemannRule16::Applied: RiemannRule16 has been used.

$$Out[9] = \frac{R_{;ad}}{2}$$

Note that in Rule 16 and elsewhere, derivatives of the form d___ are often added. This will permit the rule to match more complicated structures with extra indices. We can see the need for this in the following example.

NewRule16 does not contain the extra derivatives.

$In[10] := $ `NewRule16 := CD[RicciR[a_,b_],c_] :>`
`(1/2)*CD[ScalarR,a] /; PairQ[b,c]`

We look at multiple derivatives of the Ricci tensor.

$$In[11]:= \text{CD[RicciR[la,lb],ub,ld]}$$

$$Out[11]= R^{b}_{ab;\,d}$$

The new rule without the d___ does not match this form and so is not applied like Rule 16 is.

$$In[12]:= \text{ApplyRules[\%,NewRule16]}$$

$$Out[12]= R^{p}_{pa;\,d}$$

Whenever possible on rules with derivatives like the one above, it is a wise idea to generalize the rule as much as possible so that it can be applied to more general terms. Of course, you may only want to match terms with no extra derivatives and would not want to add the extra d___.

Now consider `RiemannRule19`.

```
RiemannRule19::Applied := "RiemannRule19 has been used."

RiemannRule19 :=
CD[RicciR[a_,b_],c_,d_,e___] :>
Block[{up1,up2,lo1,lo2},
Message[RiemannRule19::Applied];
UpLo[{up1,up2},{lo1,lo2}];
(1/2)*CD[ScalarR,b,c,e] +
CD[RicciR[lo1,lo2]*Rmsign*RiemannR[b,up2,c,up1],e] +
CD[RicciR[lo1,b]*Rmsign*Rcsign*RicciR[c,up1],e]] /;
PairQ[a,d]
```

RiemannRule19.

The first Ricci index is summed on the second covariant derivative index.

$$In[13]:= \text{CD[RicciR[la,lb],lc,ua]}$$

$$Out[13]= R^{a}_{ab;c}$$

Rule 19 is used to create a new form, which can also be derived using `CommuteCD`.

$$In[14]:= \text{ApplyRules[\%,RiemannRules]}$$

RiemannRule19::Applied: RiemannRule19 has been used.

$$Out[14]= \frac{R_{;bc}}{2} + R_{pb}R^{p}_{c} - R^{q}_{pq}R^{p}_{bc}$$

One might ask why *MathTensor* does not automatically see that `CommuteCD` can be applied in any term in which the indices are not in alphabetical order and then find any rules, like `RiemannRule19`, no matter how complex. The reason for this is that there is no systematic algorithm for deciding which term is in its simplest form. An extra `CommuteCD` operation might actually produce many more total terms and make an expression much more complicated. Further, we do not assume that a *MathTensor* user will want to commute indices in every case. It is possible, of course, to devise functions and rules that will automatically commute indices or apply any other function or rule using the programming structure provided by *MathTensor* and *Mathematica*.

Riemann rules 20–23 are all similar and will be lumped together with one example of their use.

```
RiemannRule20::Applied := "RiemannRule20 has been used."

RiemannRule20 :=
CD[RiemannR[a_,b_,c_,d_],e_,f___] :>
Block[{},
Message[RiemannRule20::Applied];
- CD[Rcsign*RicciR[b,c],d,f] + CD[Rcsign*RicciR[b,d],c,f]] /; PairQ[a,e]
```

$$\text{RiemannRule20.}$$

The covariant derivative is summed on the first Riemann tensor index.

$$In[15]:= \texttt{CD[RiemannR[la,lb,lc,ld],ua]}$$

$$Out[15]= R^{a}{}_{abcd};$$

Rule 20 is used in this case. The other three rules behave the same way for each index of the Riemann tensor.

$$In[16]:= \texttt{ApplyRules[\%,RiemannRules]}$$

RiemannRule20::Applied: RiemannRule20 has been used.

$$Out[16]= -R_{bc;d} + R_{bd;c}$$

The final rule we present here is another important structure that appears in many curvature-related calculations.

```
RiemannRule26::Applied := "RiemannRule26 has been used."

RiemannRule26 :=
CD[RiemannR[a_,b_,c_,d_],e_,f_,g___] :>
Block[{up1,up2,lo1,lo2},
Message[RiemannRule26::Applied];
UpLo[{up1,up2},{lo1,lo2}];
CD[CD[Rcsign*RicciR[a, c], d, b] -
CD[Rcsign*RicciR[a, d], c, b] -
CD[Rcsign*RicciR[b, c], d, a] +
CD[Rcsign*RicciR[b, d], c, a] -
Rcsign*Rmsign*RicciR[lo1, b]*RiemannR[up1, a, c, d] -
Rmsign*RiemannR[lo1, lo2, c, d]*RiemannR[up1, a, up2, b] -
Rmsign*RiemannR[lo1, b, lo2, d]*RiemannR[up1, a, up2, c] +
Rmsign*RiemannR[lo1, b, lo2, c]*RiemannR[up1, a, up2, d] +
Rcsign*Rmsign*RicciR[lo1, a]*RiemannR[up1, b, c, d] +
Rmsign*RiemannR[lo1, a, lo2, d]*RiemannR[up1, b, up2, c] -
Rmsign*RiemannR[lo1, a, lo2, c]*RiemannR[up1, b, up2, d] -
Rmsign*RiemannR[lo1, a, lo2, b]*RiemannR[up1, up2, c, d],g] ] /; PairQ[e,f]
```

RiemannRule26.

The covariant d'Alembertian operator on the Riemann tensor.

In[17]:= `CD[RiemannR[la,lb,lc,ld],le,ue]`

$$Out[17]= R_{abcd;e}{}^{e}$$

Gives a new set of terms.

In[18]:= `ApplyRules[%,RiemannRules]`

RiemannRule26::Applied: RiemannRule26 has been used.

$$Out[18]= R_{ac;db} - R_{ad;cb} - R_{bc;da} + R_{bd;ca} -$$

$$> \quad R_{pqcd}R_{a}{}^{p}{}_{b}{}^{q} + R_{pb}R_{a}{}^{p}{}_{cd} - R_{pbqd}R_{a}{}^{p}{}_{c}{}^{q} +$$

$$> \quad R_{pbqc}R_{a}{}^{p}{}_{d}{}^{q} - R_{pa}R_{b}{}^{p}{}_{cd} + R_{paqd}R_{b}{}^{p}{}_{c}{}^{q} -$$

$$> \quad R_{paqc}R_{b}{}^{p}{}_{d}{}^{q} - R_{paqb}R_{cd}{}^{pq}$$

`Tsimplify` combines a few of the terms.

$$In[19] := \texttt{Tsimplify[\%]}$$

$$Out[19] = R_{ac;db} - R_{ad;cb} - R_{bc;da} + R_{bd;ca} -$$

$$> \quad 2 R_{pqcd} R^{pq}{}_{ab} + R_{pb} R^{p}{}_{a\,cd} - 2 R_{pbqd} R^{pq}{}_{ac} +$$

$$> \quad 2 R_{pbqc} R^{pq}{}_{ad} - R_{pa} R^{p}{}_{b\,cd}$$

Obviously, the 40 or so rules above do not exhaust the possible Riemann rules. They are common ones that appear in many calculations or were useful to the authors in various practical calculations. It will be standard practice for a user to take some of these rules and combine them with rules derived specifically for a given problem.

■ 3.6.4 Rules Used Individually

The next set of rules are used individually. They are not generally applied using any of the `ApplyRules` functions but are instead used with the *Mathematica* substitution function.

We first look at the familiar cyclic rules.

```
RiemannCyclicFirstThreeRule[a_,b_,c_,d_]
{RiemannR[a,b,c,d] :> -RiemannR[b,c,a,d] - RiemannR[c,a,b,d]}

RiemannCyclicSecondThreeRule[a_,b_,c_,d_] =
{RiemannR[a,b,c,d] :> -RiemannR[a,c,d,b] - RiemannR[a,d,b,c]}
```

The two cyclic rules, `RiemannCyclicFirstThreeRule` and `RiemannCyclicSecondThreeRule`.

We enter a Riemann tensor.

$$In[20] := \texttt{RiemannR[la,lb,lc,ld]}$$

$$Out[20] = R_{abcd}$$

This rule rotates the first three indices on the Riemann tensor.

$$In[21] := \texttt{\% /. RiemannCyclicFirstThreeRule[la,lb,lc,ld]}$$

$$Out[21] = R_{acbd} - R_{adbc}$$

This rule rotates the second three indices on the Riemann tensor.

$$In[22] := \texttt{\%\% /. RiemannCyclicSecondThreeRule[la,lb,lc,ld]}$$

$$Out[22] = R_{acbd} - R_{adbc}$$

We can now show how to derive one of the standard Riemann rules.

Here is a product of two Riemann tensors.

$In[23]:=$ **RiemannR[la,lb,lc,ld] RiemannR[ua,uc,ub,ud]**

$Out[23]=$ $R_{abcd} R^{acbd}$

Apply the cyclic rule on the last three indices.

$In[24]:=$ **% /. RiemannCyclicSecondThreeRule[ua,uc,ub,ud]**

$Out[24]=$ $R_{abcd} (R^{abcd} + R^{adbc})$

Expand the result.

$In[25]:=$ **Expand[%]**

$Out[25]=$ $R_{abcd} R^{abcd} + R_{abcd} R^{adbc}$

Set the original product equal to the expanded result.

$In[26]:=$ **%%% == %**

$Out[26]=$ $R_{abcd} R^{acbd} == R_{abcd} R^{abcd} + R_{abcd} R^{adbc}$

Canonicalize will run CanAll on an equation.

$In[27]:=$ **Canonicalize[%]**

$Out[27]=$ $R_{pqrs} R^{prqs} == R_{pqrs} R^{pqrs} - R_{pqrs} R^{prqs}$

The *MathTensor* EqSolve function will solve for a complicated structure. This is a standard identity already programmed into the RiemannRules.

$In[28]:=$ **EqSolve[%,%[[1]]]**

$Out[28]=$ $\{\{R_{pqrs} R^{prqs} \rightarrow \dfrac{R_{pqrs} R^{pqrs}}{2}\}\}$

The next set of rules provides one way to use the famous Bianchi identities.

```
BianchiFirstPairRule[a_,b_,c_,d_,e_] =
CD[RiemannR[a,b,c,d],e,f___] :> CD[RiemannR[a,e,c,d],b,f] -
CD[RiemannR[b,e,c,d],a,f]

BianchiSecondPairRule[a_,b_,c_,d_,e_] =
CD[RiemannR[a,b,c,d],e,f___] :> CD[RiemannR[a,b,c,e],d,f] -
CD[RiemannR[a,b,d,e],c,f]
```

The two Bianchi identity rules, BianchiFirstPairRule and BianchiSecondPairRule.

A simple derivative of a Riemann tensor.

$In[29] := $ `CD[RiemannR[la,lb,lc,ld],le]`

$Out[29] = $ $R_{abcd;e}$

The usual two terms are generated.

$In[30] := $ `% /. BianchiFirstPairRule[la,lb,lc,ld,le]`

$Out[30] = R_{aecd;b} - R_{becd;a}$

Now suppose we want to use these identities to derive one of our previous rules.

This the often called "Box" of the Riemann tensor.

$In[31] := $ `CD[RiemannR[la,lb,lc,ld],le,ue]`

$Out[31] = R_{abcd;e}{}^{e}$

We apply the first Bianchi rule to move the **le** index inside the Riemann tensor.

$In[32] := $ `% /. BianchiFirstPairRule[la,lb,lc,ld,le]`

$Out[32] = R_{aecd;b}{}^{e} - R_{becd;a}{}^{e}$

We commute the derivative indices on the first term so that the summed upper index is next to the Riemann tensor.

$In[33] := $ `CommuteCD[%,lb,ue]`

$Out[33] = -R_{pacd;}{}^{p}{}_{b} + R_{pbcd;a}{}^{p} - R_{pqcd}{}^{p}{}_{a}{}^{q}{}_{b} + R_{pb}{}^{p}{}_{a}{}^{q}{}_{cd} +$

$> \quad R_{paqd}{}^{p}R{}^{q}{}_{b}{}_{c} - R_{paqc}{}^{p}R{}^{q}{}_{b}{}_{d}$

Next, we commute the indices on the second term. **u1** corresponds to the p upper summed index.

$In[34] := $ `CommuteCD[%,la,u1]`

$Out[34] = -R_{pacd;}{}^{p}{}_{b} + R_{pbcd;}{}^{p}{}_{a} - 2 R_{pqcd}{}^{p}{}_{a}{}^{q}{}_{b} +$

$> \quad R_{pb}{}^{p}R{}_{a}{}_{cd} - R_{pa}{}^{p}R{}_{b}{}_{cd} + 2 R_{paqd}{}^{p}R{}^{q}{}_{b}{}_{c} - 2 R_{paqc}{}^{p}R{}^{q}{}_{b}{}_{d}$

We use the second Bianchi rule to bring the upper summed index inside the Riemann tensor on the first term.

$In[35] := $ `% /. BianchiSecondPairRule[l1,la,lc,ld,u1]`

$Out[35] = R_{ac;db} - R_{ad;cb} + R_{pbcd;}{}^{p}{}_{a} - 2 R_{pqcd}{}^{p}{}_{a}{}^{q}{}_{b} +$

$> \quad R_{pb}{}^{p}R{}_{a}{}_{cd} - R_{pa}{}^{p}R{}_{b}{}_{cd} + 2 R_{paqd}{}^{p}R{}^{q}{}_{b}{}_{c} - 2 R_{paqc}{}^{p}R{}^{q}{}_{b}{}_{d}$

The second Bianchi rule is used on the third term next.

$In[36]:= \% /. \text{BianchiSecondPairRule}[11,1b,1c,1d,u1]$

$$Out[36]= R_{ac;db} - R_{ad;cb} - R_{bc;da} + R_{bd;ca} -$$

$$> \quad 2 R_{pqcd} R_{ab}{}^{pq} + R_{pb} R_{acd}{}^{p} - R_{pa} R_{bcd}{}^{p} +$$

$$> \quad 2 R_{paqd} R_{bc}{}^{pq} - 2 R_{paqc} R_{bd}{}^{pq}$$

We get the same result (modulo swapping a few up and down indices) as Rule 26 of the Riemann rules.

$In[37]:= \text{Expand}[\%]$

$$Out[37]= R_{ac;db} - R_{ad;cb} - R_{bc;da} + R_{bd;ca} -$$

$$> \quad 2 R_{pqcd} R_{ab}{}^{pq} + R_{pb} R_{acd}{}^{p} - R_{pa} R_{bcd}{}^{p} +$$

$$> \quad 2 R_{paqd} R_{bc}{}^{pq} - 2 R_{paqc} R_{bd}{}^{pq}$$

We have separated out some of the `RiemannRules` that are common and given them names and forms that do not use the `UpLo` construct, but we keep the original index names. `FirstQuadraticRiemannRule` is the inverse of `SecondQuadraticRiemannRule`.

```
FirstQuadraticRiemannRule =
RiemannR[a_,b_,c_,d_]*RiemannR[e_,f_,g_,h_]  :>
2*RiemannR[a,b,c,d]*RiemannR[e,g,f,h]  /;
PairQ[a,e] && PairQ[b,f] && PairQ[c,g] && PairQ[d,h]

SecondQuadraticRiemannRule =
RiemannR[a_,b_,c_,d_]*RiemannR[e_,g_,f_,h_]  :>
(1/2)*RiemannR[a,b,c,d]*RiemannR[e,f,g,h]  /;
PairQ[a,e] && PairQ[b,f] && PairQ[c,g] && PairQ[d,h]
```

FirstQuadraticRiemannRule and SecondQuadraticRiemannRule.

```
FirstCubicRiemannRule =
RiemannR[a_,b_,c_,d_]*RiemannR[e_,f_,g_,h_]*RiemannR[i_,j_,k_,l_] :>
(1/2)*RiemannR[a,b,c,d]*RiemannR[e,g,f,h]*RiemannR[i,j,k,l] /;
PairQ[a,f] && PairQ[b,h] && PairQ[c,j] && PairQ[d,l] &&
PairQ[e,i] && PairQ[g,k]
SecondCubicRiemannRule =
RiemannR[a_,b_,c_,d_]*RiemannR[e_,f_,g_,h_]*RiemannR[l_,j_,k_,l_] :>
(1/4)*RiemannR[a,b,c,d]*RiemannR[e,g,f,h]*RiemannR[i,k,j,l] /;
PairQ[a,f] && PairQ[b,h] && PairQ[c,j] && PairQ[d,l] &&
PairQ[e,i] && PairQ[g,k]
```

FirstCubicRiemannRule and SecondCubicRiemannRule.

A simple square of the Riemann tensor.

$In[38] := \texttt{RiemannR[la,lb,lc,ld] RiemannR[ua,ub,uc,ud]}$

$Out[38] = R_{abcd} R^{abcd}$

Gives us a cross sum form.

$In[39] := \texttt{\% /. FirstQuadraticRiemannRule}$

$Out[39] = 2 R_{abcd} R^{acbd}$

Reverses the effect of
FirstQuadraticRiemannRule

$In[40] := \texttt{\% /. SecondQuadraticRiemannRule}$

$Out[40] = R_{abcd} R^{abcd}$

A common product of three Riemann tensors.

$In[41] := \texttt{RiemannR[la,lb,lc,ld] RiemannR[le,ua,lf,ub] RiemannR[ue,uc,uf,ud]}$

$Out[41] = R_{abcd} R_{e\ f}^{a\ b} R^{cedf}$

FirstCubicRiemannRule converts one cross product into a pair-to-pair sum.

$In[42] := \texttt{\% /. FirstCubicRiemannRule}$

$Out[42] = \dfrac{R_{abcd} R_{ef}^{ab} R^{cedf}}{2}$

SecondCubicRiemannRule converts both cross products into pair-to-pair sums.

$In[43] := \texttt{\%\% /. SecondCubicRiemannRule}$

$Out[43] = \dfrac{R_{abcd} R_{ef}^{ab} R^{cdef}}{4}$

■ 3.6.5 Conversion Rules

It is often necessary to convert objects like the Riemann tensor or affine connection to another form in terms of more elementary building blocks. *MathTensor* contains a few functions for this purpose.

The first function is used to convert affine connections in an expression to derivatives of the metric. It is called **AffineToMetric**.

AffineToMetric[*expr*]   Converts AffineG's in *expr* to Metricg's

---

AffineToMetric uses AffineToMetricRule.

We look at a single connection term.

$$In[44] := \text{AffineG[ua,lb,lc]}$$

$$Out[44] = G^{a}_{\ bc}$$

We get one possible form for the connection in terms of derivatives of the metric. Note that to avoid the invalid absorption of the metric, MetricgFlag is set to False.

$$In[45] := \text{AffineToMetric[\%]}$$

MetricgFlag::off:
    MetricgFlag is turned off by this operation

$$Out[45] = \frac{g^{pa}g_{pb,c}}{2} + \frac{g^{pa}g_{pc,b}}{2} - \frac{g^{pa}g_{bc,p}}{2}$$

The **AffineToMetric** function uses the **CanNonInvert** function to canonicalize expressions, since they contain ordinary derivatives and nontensorial objects.

The next conversion function puts the appropriate affine connections in which a Riemann tensor is found in an expression.

RiemannToAffine[*expr*]   Converts RiemannR's in *expr* to AffineG's

---

Function for conversion of Riemann tensors to affine connections.

The function **RiemannToAffine** uses a set of seven rules called **RiemannToAffineRule0** through **RiemannToAffineRule6**. The rule for the case in which all indices are covariant is shown in the next box.

```
RiemannToAffineRule0 :=
RiemannR[a_,b_,c_,d_] :>
Block[{lo1,lo2,up1,up2},
MetricgFlagOffMessage;
MetricgFlagOff;
UpLo[{up1,up2},{lo1,lo2}];
Expand[
Metricg[b,lo2]*Rmsign*
(
-OD[AffineG[up2,a,d],c] + OD[AffineG[up2,a,c],d] -
AffineG[up2,lo1,c] AffineG[up1,a,d] +
AffineG[up2,lo1,d] AffineG[up1,a,c]
)
]] /; LowerIndexQ[a]&&LowerIndexQ[b]&&LowerIndexQ[c]&&LowerIndexQ[d]
```

An example of a `RiemannToAffineRule`.

Consider a Riemann tensor with all indices in covariant positions.

In[46]:= **RiemannR[1a,1b,1c,1d]**

Out[46]= R_{abcd}

`RiemannToAffine` gives us the form for the Riemann tensor in terms of the affine connection and its derivative.

In[47]:= **RiemannToAffine[%]**

Out[47]= $-(G^p{}_{ad} G^q{}_{pc} g_{qb}) + G^p{}_{ac} G^q{}_{pd} g_{qb} + g_{pb} G^p{}_{ac,d} -$

$> \quad g_{pb} G^p{}_{ad,c}$

Several other functions similar to `RiemannToAffine` are also available in *Math-Tensor*. They are `RicciToAffine` and `ScalarRtoAffine`.

`RicciToAffine[`*expr*`]`	convert `RicciR`'s in *expr* into terms involving `AffineG`'s
`ScalarRtoAffine[`*expr*`]`	convert `ScalarR`'s in *expr* into terms involving `AffineG`'s

More functions to convert curvature objects into affine connections.

We enter a Ricci tensor.

In[48]:= **RicciR[1a,1b]**

Out[48]= R_{ab}

The Ricci tensor is rewritten in terms of the affine connection.

$In[49]:=$ `RicciToAffine[%]`

$$Out[49]= G^{p}_{\ ab} G^{q}_{\ pq} - G^{p}_{\ qa} G^{q}_{\ pb} - G^{p}_{\ pa,b} + G^{p}_{\ ab,p}$$

Now we take the Riemann scalar.

$In[50]:=$ `ScalarR`

$Out[50]=$ R

And convert it into affine connection terms.

$In[51]:=$ `ScalarRtoAffine[%]`

$$Out[51]= G^{p}_{\ qr} G^{s}_{\ ps} g^{qr} - G^{p}_{\ qr} G^{q}_{\ ps} g^{rs} + g^{pq} G^{r}_{\ pq,r} -$$

$$> \quad g^{pq} G^{r}_{\ qr,p}$$

Finally, several sets of rules are included for completeness. These rules relate the Weyl tensor to the Riemann tensor and the so-called trace-free Ricci tensor to the Ricci tensor. These rules are written for arbitrary dimension.

WeylToRiemannRule	convert Weyl tensors to Riemann tensors
RiemannToWeylRule	convert Riemann tensors to Weyl tensors
TraceFreeRicciToRicciRule	convert trace-free Ricci tensors to Ricci tensors
RicciToTraceFreeRicciRule	convert Ricci tensors to trace-free Ricci tensors

Several rules that convert between the Weyl tensor and trace-free Ricci tensor and the Riemann and Ricci tensors.

Consider the Weyl tensor.

$In[52]:=$ `WeylC[la,lb,lc,ld]`

$Out[52]=$ C_{abcd}

The Weyl tensor is written in terms of the Riemann tensor, Ricci tensor, and Riemann scalar. It is given for dimension d.

$In[53]:=$ `% /. WeylToRiemannRule`

$$Out[53]= \frac{R \ (-(g_{ad} g_{bc}) + g_{ac} g_{bd})}{(-2 + d) \ (-1 + d)} -$$

$$> \quad \frac{g_{bd} R_{ac} - g_{bc} R_{ad} - g_{ad} R_{bc} + g_{ac} R_{bd}}{-2 + d} + R_{abcd}$$

The inverse rule gives back the Weyl tensor.

$In[54]:=$ `% /. RiemannToWeylRule`

$Out[54]=$ C_{abcd}

Consider the Ricci tensor. It has a trace, the Riemann scalar.

```
In[55]:= RicciR[1a,1b]
Out[55]= R
           ab
```

Separates out the trace term for dimension d and the trace-free Ricci tensor, which is written as TraceFreeRicciR or TFR.

```
In[56]:= % /. RicciToTraceFreeRicciRule

           R g
            ab
Out[56]= ------- + TFR
            d         ab
```

Reverses the effect of the first rule.

```
In[57]:= % /. TraceFreeRicciToRicciRule
Out[57]= R
           ab
```

```
WeylToRiemannRule = WeylC[a_,b_,c_,d_] :>
RiemannR[a,b,c,d] -
(1/(Dimension -2)) *
(RicciR[a,c] Metricg[b,d] - RicciR[a,d] Metricg[b,c] -
RicciR[b,c] Metricg[a,d] + RicciR[b,d] Metricg[a,c]) +
(1/(Dimension - 1))(1/(Dimension - 2)) *
ScalarR (Metricg[a,c] Metricg[b,d] - Metricg[b,c] Metricg[a,d])

RiemannToWeylRule = RiemannR[a_,b_,c_,d_] :>
WeylC[a,b,c,d] +
(1/(Dimension -2)) *
(RicciR[a,c] Metricg[b,d] - RicciR[a,d] Metricg[b,c] -
RicciR[b,c] Metricg[a,d] + RicciR[b,d] Metricg[a,c]) -
(1/((Dimension - 1)(Dimension - 2))) *
ScalarR (Metricg[a,c] Metricg[b,d] - Metricg[b,c] Metricg[a,d])

TraceFreeRicciToRicciRule =
TraceFreeRicciR[a_,b_] :> RicciR[a,b] - (1/Dimension) ScalarR Metricg[a,b]

RicciToTraceFreeRicciRule =
RicciR[a_,b_] :> TraceFreeRicciR[a,b] + (1/Dimension) ScalarR Metricg[a,b]
```

The form of the Weyl and TraceFreeRicci rules is very straightforward.

Another rule helps us to move from the Einstein tensor to the Ricci tensor.

EinsteinToRicciRule	give the Einstein tensor in terms of its 4-dimensional definition

The EinsteinToRicciRule.

Enter the Einstein tensor.

In[58]:= **EinsteinG[la,lb]**

$Out[58]= G_{ab}$

The 4-dimensional definition results.

In[59]:= **% /. EinsteinToRicciRule**

$$Out[59]= \frac{-(R\ g_{ab})}{2} + R_{ab}$$

One final rule that can prove useful in working with **AffineG** is the following.

AffineDrule	is a transformation rule that orders indices in expressions such as **OD[AffineG[ua,la,lc],lb]** and **OD[AffineG[ud,lb,ld],la]**

The **AffineDrule**.

Consider the ordinary derivative of **AffineG**.

In[60]:= **OD[AffineG[ua,la,lc],lb]**

$Out[60]= G^{a}_{\ ac,b}$

The indices are reversed.

In[61]:= **% /. AffineDrule**

$Out[61]= G^{a}_{\ ab,c}$

In *MathTensor*, it is straightforward to create all kinds of rules like the ones above. With a little practice and care, you can devise nearly any transformation rule to put tensor equations into a given form. The addition of torsion is one possible extension of the **RiemannRules**. This would require not only a new set of rules but also a new definition of a covariant derivative operator and its related functions.

■ 3.6.6 Other Rules Functions

In some very large or complicated calculations involving many rule sets, it may be that the basic **ApplyRules** and **ApplyRulesRepeated** functions will not find all the rules that can be applied or not give a result in its simplest form. In these very rare situations, the use of some more tenacious functions might be useful. *MathTensor* provides five more functions: **CanApplyRulesFast**, **CanApplyRules**, **CanApplyRulesRepeated**, **SuperApplyRules**, and **CanSuperApplyRules**. **CanApplyRulesFast** uses **ApplyRules** on an expression and then uses **CanAll**. **CanApplyRules** applies **CanAll**, **ApplyRules**, and finally **CanAll** again.

`CanApplyRulesRepeated` is the same as `CanApplyRules` except that `ApplyRulesRepeated` is used in place of `ApplyRules`.

The rules with `Super` in them have their own expression checking built in. `SuperApplyRules` applies `ApplyRules` to an expression and then checks to see if the result is different from the original expression. If it is, the result is returned. If it is not, `ApplyRules` is used again and again until no change occurs. `CanSuperApplyRules` does the same thing as `SuperApplyRules` except that it uses `CanApplyRules` rather than `ApplyRules`. Further technical discussion of these functions is beyond the scope of this book.

■ 3.7 Using Contexts with *MathTensor*

If you wish, you can put functions and rules that you create into a separate *Mathematica context*. This prevents the names of your functions and rules from being confused with others of the same name. The full name of a function of object in *Mathematica* has a prefix called the context. For example, in `Global`MySum` the context is `Global`` and the symbol is `MySum`. When you type a symbol such as `MySum`, *Mathematica* searches in order through a list of active contexts, called `$ContextPath`, looking for a name that begins with a prefix corresponding to one of the active contexts. It identifies `MySum` with the first active context in which such a name has been defined.

MathTensor has its own context, called `MathTensor``. Here is a file illustrating how you can use *MathTensor* objects to create new commands with a context name of your own choosing. It is conventional to make the file name the same as the context name, but with " ` " replaced by " .m ". Here, the name of the file is `mf.m` and the name of the context is `mf``. The command defined in the file is called `MakeFlat` or, with its context name included, `mf`MakeFlat`. It takes no arguments, and makes the metric into a flat Euclidean metric in Cartesian coordinates. (The existing *MathTensor* function called `MakeMetricFlat` takes one argument and can produce a Euclidean or a Minkowskian metric, depending on the argument specified.) The definition of `MakeFlat` uses various *MathTensor* functions, such as `Metricg`, `Kdelta`, and `AffineG`. In order to use these *MathTensor* functions, you must include `{"MathTensor`"}` as the second argument of `BeginPackage` in your file. The other *Mathematica* commands in this file relevant to contexts are `Begin`, `End`, and `EndPackage`.

```
BeginPackage["mf`", {"MathTensor`"}]

MakeFlat::usage =
" MakeFlat produces a flat metric with\n
diagonal values of 1, and off-diagonal values of 0. It\n
also sets MetricgSign, DetgSign, and  Detg to 1,\n
and the components of AffineG to 0. It requires that\n
the value of Dimension is already set to an integer."

MakeFlat::nodim = "Dimension should be set to an integer."
Euclid::usage = "Possible argument of the function MakeFlat."
Minkowski::usage = "Possible argument of the function MakeFlat."

(* The above messages must come before Begin["Private`"]
   to be able to access these objects in the mf` context. *)

Begin["Private`"]

Off[RuleDelayed::rhs]; (*prevents certain warnings*)

MakeFlat := (
        If[!IntegerQ[Dimension],
           Message[MakeFlat::nodim];
           Return[]
        ];
        Metricg[i1_Integer,j1_Integer] := Kdelta[i1,j1];
        MetricgSign = 1;
        Detg = 1;
        DetgSign = 1;
        AffineG[a_,b_,c_] = 0;
        CD[a_,b__] := OD[a,b] )

On[RuleDelayed::rhs]; (*turns back on the warnings*)

End[]
EndPackage[]
```

Defining MakeFlat in mf` context. File mf.m

Here is a brief *MathTensor* session in which this file is loaded.

The first context searched for names is "MathTensor`".	`In[1]:= $ContextPath` `Out[1]= {MathTensor`, Global`, System`}`
This loads the file **mf.m** shown above.	`In[2]:= << mf.m`

Now the first context searched is "mf`". Thus, even if MakeFlat had been defined in the "MathTensor`" context, the new definition of MakeFlat in the "mf`" context would be found first.

```
In[3]:= $ContextPath
Out[3]= {mf`, MathTensor`, Global`, System`}
```

The message reminds you to first set Dimension.

```
In[4]:= MakeFlat
 MakeFlat::nodim: Dimension should be set to an integer.
```

Set the dimension to 3.

```
In[5]:= Dimension = 3;
```

Now the command is executed.

```
In[6]:= MakeFlat
```

This displays the Euclidean metric.

```
In[7]:= Table[Metricg[-i,-j],{i,3},{j,3}]//MatrixForm
Out[7]//MatrixForm= 1   0   0
                    0   1   0
                    0   0   1
```

BeginPackage[*context*,{"MathTensor`"}]	
	make "MathTensor`" an available context as the functions in *context* are loaded
Begin["Private`"]	cause new names not having previous usage messages to be put in a private context
End[ ]	end the private context
EndPackage[ ]	end the package

Packaging commands making *MathTensor* objects available in a file.

The various names of *MathTensor* objects in the file **mf.m** were recognized because the second argument of **BeginPackage** put the context **"MathTensor`"** into the context path *during* the loading of the file. If you were to use no packaging commands in your file and were to load it in a *MathTensor* session, then *MathTensor* commands would of course also be recognized in the file. However, packaging commands protect you from accidentally using symbols that have already been defined and permit you to use the same name for symbols in different contexts.

Chapter 4

Components, Transformations, and Types of Indices

■ 4.1 Components and Their Values

The components of tensors often have specific values. For example, you may want to set $F^{14} = -e^1$, where F^{14} is a component of the Maxwell tensor and e^1 is the x^1 component of the electric field vector. Or you may want to assign a function such as a Sin[x] to the component F^{14} of the Maxwell tensor. In *MathTensor*, specific components of tensors are labeled by means of integer rather than symbolic indices. You can work with tensor expressions containing both integer and symbolic indices and evaluate them when the values of the components are known. You can also calculate the components of curvature tensors if the metric tensor is known. Given the curvature tensors, you can evaluate other tensor expressions such as the invariants of the space.

■ 4.1.1 Integers as Indices

As in standard tensor notation, you can specify particular components of a tensor such as F^{ab} by giving the indices integer values. The indices take values from 1 to the value of **Dimension**, where the latter variable is set to the number of dimensions of the space (or spacetime). Zero is not used in *MathTensor* as the value of an index.

For example, **MaxwellF[1,4]** denotes the contravariant (1,4) component of the Maxwell tensor.

```
In[1]:= MaxwellF[1,4]

Out[1]= F
         14
```

The indices are ordered lexically using the antisymmetry of the Maxwell tensor.

```
In[2]:= MaxwellF[4,1]

Out[2]= -F
          14
```

In *MathTensor*, covariant indices are entered as *negative* integers.

```
In[3]:= MaxwellF[-4,-1]

Out[3]= F
          41
```

125

The antisymmetry of `MaxwellF` is used to order the indices lexically. The present ordering results because −4 is less than −1.

In[4]:= `MaxwellF[-1,-4]`
Out[4]= -F$_{41}$

This sets the number of dimensions of the spacetime to 4.

In[5]:= `Dimension = 4;`

This defines a vector `e[ua]` denoting the electric field.

In[6]:= `DefineTensor[e,{{1},1}]`
 `PermWeight::def: Object e defined`

You can give components values in the usual manner.

In[7]:= `MaxwellF[1,4] = -e[1]; MaxwellF[2,4] = -e[2];`

Here, the fourth column of the Maxwell tensor has been set to the electric field components. The system knows that `MaxwellF[4,4]` is zero by antisymmetry of `MaxwellF`.

In[8]:= `MaxwellF[3,4] = -e[3];`

The symbols `x[1]`, `x[2]`, ..., conventionally denote the coordinates in *MathTensor*. In a curved space, these do not transform as a tensor, although the coordinate differentials do. `DefineTensor` was used here to set up the proper output form for the coordinate symbols.

In[9]:= `DefineTensor[x,{{1},1}]`
 `PermWeight::def: Object x defined`

You can give the coordinates symbolic values like x, y, z, t. Although `x[1]`, `x[2]`, ..., always denote the coordinates, the names you assign to those symbols, such as `x`, `y`, ..., are up to you. You can use `x` as the name of one of the coordinates without causing a problem.

In[10]:= `x[1]=x;x[2]=y;x[3]=z;x[4]=t;`

This specifies the x-component of the electric field to be proportional to $\sin(t - z)$, as in an electromagnetic wave moving in the z-direction.

In[11]:= `e[1] = a Sin[t-z]`
Out[11]= a Sin[t - z]

This is the ordinary partial derivative with respect to x^3. Note that the derivative index is a covariant index and is thus denoted by a negative integer. In the output, it appears as a subscript after a comma. Recall that `MaxwellF[1,4]` is −e[1], which is $a \sin(t - z)$.

In[12]:= `OD[MaxwellF[1,4],-3]`
Out[12]= -(a Sin[t - z]$_{,3}$) - a$_{,3}$ Sin[t - z]

This command turns on evaluation and updates previous expressions. `EvaluateODFlag` governs evaluation of OD. In *MathTensor*, the original value of `EvaluateODFlag` is `False`.

```
In[13]:= On[EvaluateODFlag]
```

The previous expression has now been evaluated, with a treated as a constant because it has no explicit z-dependence.

```
In[14]:= %%
Out[14]= a Cos[t - z]
```

When `EvaluateODFlag` is `True`, you must be careful. For example, this gives zero because no explicit z-dependence has been assigned to the (2,4) components of `MaxwellF`. To avoid mistakes, the user must turn on `EvaluateODFlag` explicitly after assigning functional dependencies to components of tensors.

```
In[15]:= OD[MaxwellF[2,4],-3]
Out[15]= 0
```

This turns off the flag to stop automatic evaluation of OD.

```
In[16]:= Off[EvaluateODFlag]
```

Now the derivative is not evaluated.

```
In[17]:= OD[MaxwellF[2,4],-3]
```
$$Out[17]= -e^2_{,3}$$

After we pause briefly to summarize what has been learned in this section, the present *MathTensor* session will continue.

`Dimension`	the number of dimensions of the space or spacetime
`1,2,...,Dimension`	the values of contravariant tensor indices
`-1,-2,...,-Dimension`	the values of covariant tensor indices
`x[1],x[2],...,x[Dimension]`	the coordinates
`x[1] = `*r*`; x[2] = `*theta*`;...`	assigning names to the coordinates
t`[1,2]`	the contravariant (1,2) component of tensor *t*
t`[-3,-1]`	the covariant (3,1) component of tensor *t*
`OD[`*t*`[1,3],-2]`	ordinary derivative of the (1,3) component of tensor *t* with respect to `x[2]`
`EvaluateODFlag`	governs evaluation of `OD` with covariant integer derivative index

Integer indices in components and derivatives of tensors.

■ 4.1.2 Using Integer and Symbolic Indices

Continuing the previous *MathTensor* session, you will see how to use mixed integer and symbolic indices in the same expression. You will also see how to evaluate the components of an expression having symbolic indices when the components of tensors appearing in the expression are known. The *MathTensor* functions `MakeSum`, `SetComponents`, and `MakeSumRange` enable you to perform summations over dummy indices in various ways.

This unsets the value of e[1].

In[18]:= `e[1]=.`

Gauss's law for the electric field in empty flat space takes this form. Note the mixing of integer and symbolic indices, and the use of the summation convention.

In[19]:= `GaussLaw = OD[MaxwellF[4,ua],la] == 0`

Out[19]= $F^{4a}{}_{,a} == 0$

The command `MakeSum` recognizes the summation convention and evaluates the sum using the assigned values of the components.

In[20]:= `MakeSum[GaussLaw]`

Out[20]= $e^{1}{}_{,1} + e^{2}{}_{,2} + e^{3}{}_{,3} == 0$

This defines a vector representing the magnetic field.

In[21]:= `DefineTensor[b,{{1},1}]`

`PermWeight::def: Object b defined`

This sets the appropriate components of the Maxwell tensor to the magnetic field vector.

```
In[22]:=
MaxwellF[1,2]=b[3];MaxwellF[1,3]=-b[2];MaxwellF[2,3]=b[1];
```

This sets the off-diagonal components of the metric tensor to zero. (The values are already known when the indices have opposite signs.)

```
In[23]:= Metricg[i_?IntegerQ,j_?IntegerQ] :=
   If[!(i===j), 0]
```

This sets the remaining contravariant components of the metric (in units with the speed of light equal to 1). These are the values of the metric tensor of special relativity.

```
In[24]:= Metricg[-1,-1]=1; Metricg[-2,-2]=
 1; Metricg[-3,-3]=1; Metricg[-4,-4]= -1;
```

Here are a few examples to check the definition. The value of `Metricg[3,-3]` is the same in any spacetime and is already known to the system.

```
In[25]:= {Metricg[-1,-4], Metricg[-3,-3], Metricg[-4,-4],
   Metricg[-4,-2], Metricg[3,-3]}
Out[25]= {0, 1, -1, 0, 1}
```

Turning off `MetricgFlag` prevents the metric from automatically lowering symbolic indices.

```
In[26]:= Off[MetricgFlag]
```

`SetComponents` sets all the indicated components of the tensor in the first argument to the values specified in the second argument. The summation convention is recognized. Here, all the covariant components of the Maxwell tensor are calculated. The set of components that will be calculated depends on the indices in the tensor appearing in the first argument of `SetComponents`.

```
In[27]:= SetComponents[MaxwellF[la,lb],
   Metricg[la,lc] Metricg[lb,ld] MaxwellF[uc,ud] ]
Components assigned to F
```

Here are a few of the values that were calculated by `SetComponents`.

```
In[28]:= {MaxwellF[-1,-4], MaxwellF[-2,-3],
MaxwellF[-1,-2]}
```
$$Out[28]= \{e^1, b^1, b^3\}$$

Define a second tensor, `MaxwellF2`, with the same symmetries as `MaxwellF`. You can assign values to its components in a different way.

```
In[29]:= DefineTensor[MaxwellF2,"F2",{{2,1},-1}]
PermWeight::sym: Symmetries of F2 assigned
PermWeight::def: Object F2 defined
```

You can set up a definition that will evaluate the components with appropriate indices when requested. `NegIntegerQ` and `PosIntegerQ` return `True` for negative or positive integers, respectively. The semicolon suppresses output of the long sum on the right-hand side of the definition.

```
In[30]:= MaxwellF2[la_?NegIntegerQ,lb_?NegIntegerQ] =
  MakeSum[Metricg[la,lc] Metricg[lb,ld] MaxwellF[uc,ud] ];
```

Here are the corresponding components of `MaxwellF2` to compare with those of `MaxwellF`. The components of `MaxwellF2` are computed at the time they are requested. If `SetComponents` takes too long to compute the components or if not all components are required, then this second method would be preferable.

```
In[31]:= {MaxwellF2[-1,-4], MaxwellF2[-2,-3],
MaxwellF2[-1,-2]}
```
$$Out[31]= \{e^1, b^1, b^3\}$$

If you wish to see the definitions associated with a symbol, such as `MaxwellF2`, you can type `Definition[MaxwellF2]`. This will list all components that have been specified, as well as any other definitions associated with the symbol. The output of this command can be appended to a file with `Definition[MaxwellF2] >>> filename`. Some symbols, such as `MaxwellF`, may have the attribute `ReadProtected`. If the attributes are not `Locked`, you can type `Attributes[MaxwellF] = {}`, followed by `Definition[MaxwellF]` to see the components and other definitions associated with the symbol. That is the procedure to use when you want to write the values of components you have defined for tensors like `MaxwellF`, `Metricg`, or `RicciR`.

Here is one set of Maxwell equations in empty flat spacetime written in a system of units in which the various constants are unity (rationalized Gaussian or Heaviside-Lorentz units). The condition `PairQ[ub,lb]` is true only if the indices matched by the patterns `ub_` and `lb_` are a valid pair of dummy indices.

```
In[32]:= eq1[ua_,ub_,lb_] :=
  OD[MaxwellF[ua,ub],lb] == 0 /;
    PairQ[ub,lb]
```

Here is the other set of Maxwell equations.

```
In[33]:= eq2[la_,lb_,lc_] = OD[MaxwellF[la,lb],lc] +
  OD[MaxwellF[lb,lc],la] + OD[MaxwellF[lc,la],lb] == 0
```
$$Out[33]= F_{ab,c} - F_{ac,b} + F_{bc,a} == 0$$

You can use `MakeSum` to write the first components of the equation in terms of the electric and magnetic fields.

```
In[34]:= MakeSum[eq1[1,ub,lb] ]
```
$$Out[34]= -b^2{}_{,3} + b^3{}_{,2} - e^1{}_{,4} == 0$$

Here is another component. These are components of Maxwell's generalization of Faraday's law, relating the curl of the magnetic field to the rate of change of the electric field in free space.

$$In[35]:= \texttt{MakeSum[eq1[2,ub,lb]]}$$

$$Out[35]= b^1_{\ ,3} - b^3_{\ ,1} - e^2_{\ ,4} == 0$$

This is Gauss's law, which you considered earlier.

$$In[36]:= \texttt{MakeSum[eq1[4,ub,lb]]}$$

$$Out[36]= e^1_{\ ,1} + e^2_{\ ,2} + e^3_{\ ,3} == 0$$

This states that the divergence of the magnetic field is zero.

$$In[37]:= \texttt{eq2[-1,-2,-3]}$$

$$Out[37]= b^1_{\ ,1} + b^2_{\ ,2} + b^3_{\ ,3} == 0$$

This is Maxwell's equation relating a component of the curl of the electric field to the rate of change of the magnetic field. The indices are covariant (that is, negative integers).

$$In[38]:= \texttt{eq2[-1,-2,-4]}$$

$$Out[38]= b^3_{\ ,4} - e^1_{\ ,2} + e^2_{\ ,1} == 0$$

After these examples, you should be able to employ the commands `MakeSum` and `SetComponents` to evaluate expressions when the components of tensors appearing in the expressions are known.

`MakeSum[`*expr*`]`	sum dummy indices in *expr* from 1 to `Dimension`
`SetComponents[`*tensor*,*expr*`]`	set the indicated components of *tensor* equal to *expr*
`MakeSumRange[`*expr*,*list*,..`]`	sum dummy indices in *expr* over ranges specified in a set of lists, which may contain symbolic and integer values

Commands that evaluate the components of tensor expressions.

The commands `MakeSum` and `SetComponents` require that `Dimension` be an integer and sum dummy indices over the integers from 1 to the value of `Dimension`. However, these commands will not sum dummy indices over a range that includes both integer and symbolic values. In addition, they work only with regular dummy indices, such as `la,ua`, but not with the additional types of indices that become available when the command `AddIndexTypes` is invoked (as described in a later section). In many cases, it may not be appropriate to sum the other types of indices over the range from 1 to `Dimension`. For example, those indices may be spinor or group indices, which have a different range. Therefore `MakeSum` and `SetComponents` sum only over regular dummy indices in an expression with more than one type of index.

A more versatile command for performing summations of dummy indices of all types over any specified ranges is MakeSumRange. As the name implies, in using MakeSumRange you explicitly specify the range for each *lower* member of a dummy index pair. (The value of Dimension need not be set for MakeSumRange to work.) The ranges may contain both integer and symbolic index values. For example, MakeSumRange[MaxwellF[la,lb] MaxwellF[ua,ub], {la,-4,li},{lb,-4,lj}] will sum index la over the values -4 and li and the complementary dummy index ua over the complementary values of 4 and ui. Similarly, lb will be summed over -4 and lj, and ub over 4 and uj. In special relativity, such sums arise when you are separating space and time index values, but you do not want to sum explicitly over the integer values of the spatial indices. In that case, certain index names, such as li and lj could be reserved for spatial indices, as in the above example. A more flexible way to treat this case would be to use AddIndexTypes to make available additional types of indices and to use them to represent spatial indices. That method will be illustrated when multiple types of indices are described. In Kaluza-Klein and related theories, the additional types of indices can be used to represent indices that correspond to different subspaces. Here is an example of the use of MakeSumRange in a situation in which only regular indices are involved.

This is an invariant formed from the electromagnetic field.

$In[39]:=$ MaxwellF[la,lb] MaxwellF[ua,ub]

$Out[39]=$ $F_{ab} F^{ab}$

This uses MakeSumRange to separate the sums over spatial indices, which are denoted here by li and lj. Suppose that after working with such split expressions, you want to perform the remaining sum over the spatial dummy indices.

$In[40]:=$ expr = MakeSumRange[%,{la,-4,li},{lb,-4,lj}]

$Out[40]=$ $F_{4i} F^{4i} + F_{4j} F^{4j} + F_{ij} F^{ij}$

You can use MakeSumRange again to do this. The second superscript 2 on each b^i is actually the power 2, not an additional index.

$In[41]:=$ MakeSumRange[%,{li,-1,-2,-3},{lj,-1,-2,-3}]

$Out[41]=$ $2 b^{12} + 2 b^{22} + 2 b^{32} - 2 e^{12} - 2 e^{22} - 2 e^{32}$

Or you can reset Dimension to the value 3 and then use MakeSum.

$In[42]:=$ Dimension = 3

$Out[42]=$ 3

Both methods give the same result: the well-known invariant proportional to $b \cdot b - e \cdot e$.

$In[43]:=$ MakeSum[expr]

$Out[43]=$ $2 b^{12} + 2 b^{22} + 2 b^{32} - 2 e^{12} - 2 e^{22} - 2 e^{32}$

The command `ClearComponents` clears all assigned values of components of the indicated tensor for positive and negative integer indices in the range `-Dimension` to `Dimension`. In this case, all covariant and contravariant components of `MaxwellF` are cleared.

In[44]:= `ClearComponents[MaxwellF[1a,1b] ]`

These components now have no assigned values.

In[45]:= `{MaxwellF[-2,-1], MaxwellF[1,3]}`

Out[45]= $\{F_{21}, \ F^{13}\}$

The symmetry properties of `MaxwellF` are not deleted by `ClearComponents`.

In[46]:= `{MaxwellF[-1,-1], MaxwellF[-1,-2]}`

Out[46]= $\{0, \ -F_{21}\}$

`ClearComponents[`*tensor*`[1a,1b,...]]`

> Clear assigned upper and lower components of *tensor* having the indicated number of indices. The value of `Dimension` must be an integer.

Clear assigned components of tensor expressions.

■ 4.1.3 Flat Metric in Cartesian Coordinates

Sometimes you will want to work in a flat space or spacetime in Cartesian coordinates. To do that, you have to set the values of the components of `Metricg` appropriately. For example, in special relativity the Minkowski metric corresponding to a flat 4-dimensional spacetime corresponds to the invariant line element

$$ds^2 = -dt^2 + dx^2 + dy^2 + dz^2. \tag{4.1}$$

Here, `Metricg[-1,-1]` is 1, corresponding to the convention in which `MetricgSign` is 1 (this convention is set in the file Conventions.m and can be changed). In addition, `Detg` is -1, as is `DetgSign`. With the same convention for `MetricgSign`, a Euclidean 3-dimensional space has line element in Cartesian coordinates given by

$$ds^2 = dx^2 + dy^2 + dz^2, \tag{4.2}$$

and `Detg` and `DetgSign` are each 1.

To save the tedium of typing in these flat metrics, there exists a function, `MakeMetricFlat`, that sets up the values of the components of `Metricg` consistent with the value of `MetricgSign` and also assigns values to `Detg` and `DetgSign`. It also sets the components of the affine connection, `AffineG` to 0, and makes the covariant derivative `CD` equivalent to the ordinary partial derivative `OD`, since the coordinates are assumed to be Cartesian.

There are two arguments that `MakeMetricFlat` can take, namely, `Euclid` and `Minkowski`. `MakeMetricFlat[Euclid]` produces a flat metric with diagonal values of 1 and off-diagonal values of 0. It also sets `MetricgSign` to 1, `DetgSign` to 1, and `Detg` to 1. It uses the value of `Dimension`, which should be an integer.

`MakeMetricFlat[Minkowski]` produces a Minkowski metric with the first (`Dimension - 1`) diagonal values equal to `MetricgSign` and the last diagonal value equal to (`-MetricgSign`). The off-diagonal values are 0. It also sets the value of `Detg` and `DetgSign` to `-(MetricgSign)^Dimension`.

The value of `MetricgSign` in the file `Conventions.m` is used in determining the sign of the Minkowski metric, while for the Euclidean metric the nonzero components are always taken as 1 and `MetricgSign` is set to 1 regardless of its value in `Conventions.m`. In each case, the components of `AffineG` are set to 0 and `CD` is made equivalent to `OD`.

When working with a Euclidean metric, you may find the command `SetEuclideanIndices` convenient for setting all the components of a tensor when only components with upper or lower indices have been previously assigned. For a general metric, the commands `SetAllIndices` and `SetMovedIndices` perform similar functions. See the the Appendix listing *MathTensor* objects for more information on these three commands.

Set the dimension to 4.	`In[1]:= Dimension = 4;`

This produces a Minkowskian metric.	`In[2]:= MakeMetricFlat[Minkowski]`

```
MakeMetricFlat::Mnkwski:
    Metricg is now Minkowskian with Metricg[-1,-1] = 1.
```

Here are its values. In this case, `MetricgSign` was set to 1 in the file `Conventions.m`.

```
In[3]:= Table[Metricg[-i,-j], {i,4},{j,4}]//MatrixForm
Out[3]//MatrixForm=
```

$$\begin{pmatrix} 1 & 0 & 0 & 0 \\ 0 & 1 & 0 & 0 \\ 0 & 0 & 1 & 0 \\ 0 & 0 & 0 & -c^2 \end{pmatrix}$$

Next construct a Euclidean metric in 3 dimensions.	$In[4] :=$ **Dimension = 3;**
This produces a Euclidean metric.	$In[5] :=$ **MakeMetricFlat[Euclid]** MakeMetricFlat::Ecld: Metricg is now Euclidean in Cartesian coordinates.

This displays its values.	$In[6] :=$ **Table[Metricg[-i,-j], {i,3},{j,3}]//MatrixForm**
	$Out[6]//MatrixForm=$ 1 0 0
	                                    0 1 0
	                                    0 0 1

By convention, OD uses **x[1]** through **x[Dimension]** as the coordinates when evaluating derivatives. Here, they are given the names **x**, **y**, and **z**.	$In[7] :=$ **x[1]=x; x[2]=y; x[3]=z;**
This causes ordinary derivatives OD to be evaluated.	$In[8] :=$ **On[EvaluateODFlag]**
Here, a *covariant* derivative CD was entered. Because the space is flat and the coordinate system is Cartesian, it was converted to ordinary partial derivatives.	$In[9] :=$ **CD[(x y z)^2, -1,-3]** $Out[9]= 4 \ x \ y^2 \ z$

MakeMetricFlat[Euclid]	make a Euclidean metric
MakeMetricFlat[Minkowski]	make a Minkowskian metric
SetEuclidianIndices[t[la,lb]]	assume the indicated class of components is known and set values for the others using a Euclidean metric
SetAllIndices[t[la,lb]]	acts like **SetEuclideanIndices** but uses assigned values of **Metricg**
SetMovedIndices[t[ua,ub], t[la,lb]]	assume all components of the second argument are known and use **Metricg** to set all components of the first argument

Producing a flat metric and finding components.

■ 4.1.4 Calculating the Components of Curvature Tensors

The situation often arises in which you are given the values of the metric tensor of a space (or spacetime) and want to calculate the curvature and other tensors characterizing the space. In *MathTensor*, you can use the command `Components` to calculate the affine connections and the Riemann, Ricci, Einstein, and Weyl tensors associated with the given metric.

`Components["`*inputfile*`","`*outputfile1*`","`*outputfile2*`"]`

            take the metric in *inputfile*, calculate the affine connections and curvature tensors and put their values in *outputfile1* in a form that can be read into a future session and in *outputfile2* in user readable form

---

Command for calculating components of curvature tensors.

The general method of using `Components` is as follows. First, you create with your preferred editor a file containing the components of the metric tensor for which you wish to compute the various curvature tensors. This file will serve as the input file for `Components`. Several model files containing metrics are provided. For example, the file `CompInSchw.m` contains the Schwarzschild metric together with many comments on the features of `Components`. You can copy it to a new file and modify it by putting in the coordinate names and components of the metric tensor of interest to you. There is also the sample file `CompInRW.m` containing the spatially flat Robertson-Walker metric. Additional sample metrics are provided in the METRICS subdirectory of your main *MathTensor* directory. After creating an input file, you start a fresh session of *Mathematica*. You can type the command `Share[ ]` in order to save memory. Do *not* load *MathTensor*. Instead load the file `Components.m`. Then type the command
`Components["input.m","output.m", "output.out"]`,
where `input.m` is the name of the input file that you prepared in advance. The second argument, `output.m`, is the name you designate for the file that `Components` will create, and that contains the values of the computed curvature tensor components in a form suitable for input into a future *MathTensor* session. The third argument, `output.out`, contains the calculated results in a form that you can edit and can more easily read and print. It is important that all three arguments be enclosed in quotes.

After `Components` has calculated the curvature tensors and has created the new files, you should exit from the *Mathematica* session. Then start an *entirely* new *Mathematica* session. This requires that you actually `Quit` *Mathematica* before starting the new session; it will not do to merely open a new window within the same

Mathematica session. Once in the new *Mathematica* session, you load *MathTensor* and then load the file output.m, which you designated above as the second argument of Components. That will read in all the calculated curvature components and the original metric. The curvature tensors can then be manipulated using the various functions of *MathTensor* and *Mathematica*.

The invariant interval of the Schwarzschild metric is

$$ds^2 = -(1 - 2GM/r)dt^2 + (1 - 2GM/r)^{-1}dr^2 + r^2d\theta^2 + r^2sin^2(\theta)d\phi^2.$$

This metric describes the gravitational field outside a spherical mass. Here is an input file for Components that will calculate the components of the affine connection, Ricci tensor, scalar curvature, and Einstein, Riemann, and Weyl tensors (the file CompInSchw.m contains many more comments, but this shows the required content).

```
Dimension = 4 (* dimension of the spacetime *)

x/: x[1] = r  (* assign the coordinate names *)
x/: x[2] = theta
x/: x[3] = phi
x/: x[4] = t

Metricg/: Metricg[-1, -1] = (1 - (2*G*M)/r)^(-1)  (* the metric *)
Metricg/: Metricg[-2, -1] = 0
Metricg/: Metricg[-3, -1] = 0
Metricg/: Metricg[-4, -1] = 0
Metricg/: Metricg[-2, -2] = r^2
Metricg/: Metricg[-3, -2] = 0
Metricg/: Metricg[-4, -2] = 0
Metricg/: Metricg[-3, -3] = r^2*Sin[theta]^2
Metricg/: Metricg[-4, -3] = 0
Metricg/: Metricg[-4, -4] = -(1 - (2*G*M)/r)

Rmsign = 1 (* sign convention for Riemann tensor *)
Rcsign = 1 (* sign convention for Ricci tensor *)

CalcEinstein = 1 (* If 1, calculate the Einstein tensor *)
CalcRiemann = 1 (* Calculate the Riemann tensor components *)
CalcWeyl = 1 (* Calculate the Weyl tensor components *)
```

Input file for Schwarzschild metric.

Only the independent covariant components of the metric are listed, with their indices in lexical order (for example, −3 before −1). The conventions for the sign of the Riemann tensor (Rmsign) and Ricci tensor (Rcsign) are also listed. If you alter these, be sure that they are also altered in the file Conventions.m so that they are consistent. There are also variables called `CalcEinstein`, `CalcRiemann`, and `CalcWeyl` in the input file that you can set to 1 or 0 to control which tensors will be calculated. Here is a session showing how you would calculate the curvature tensors associated with the Schwarzschild metric. It uses the sample file `CompInSchw.m` as the input file for `Components`. If you cannot access that sample file, copy the input file shown above and use the name of that file in place of `CompInSchw.m`. Start a fresh *Mathematica* session (not merely a new window) but do *not* load *MathTensor*. Instead, `Get` the file `Components.m`.

This gets the file containing the `Components` command.	`In[1]:= <<Components.m`

```
========================================================
MathTensor (TM) 2.2 (UNIX (R)) (January 6, 1994)
                 Components Package
by Leonard Parker and Steven M. Christensen
Copyright (c) 1991-1994 MathSolutions, Inc.
Runs with Mathematica (R) Versions 1.2 and 2.X.
Licensed to machine gravity.
========================================================
```

The command `Components` reads the metric from the first file and sends the output to the second file in a form that can be loaded into a later *MathTensor* session. It also sends the output in user-readable form to the third file, which you can edit to suit your requirements and then print. Note the quotes around the name of each file. It will take some time to calculate the various curvature tensors.

`In[2]:=`
`Components["CompInSchw.m","CompSchw.m","CompSchw.out"]`

```
The following tensors have been calculated and stored
in the file CompSchw.m in InputForm and
in the file CompSchw.out in OutputForm:
Metricg
MatrixMetricgLower
MatrixMetricgUpper
Detg
AffineG[ua,lb,lc]
RicciR[la,lb]
ScalarR

EinsteinG[la,lb,lc,ld]

RiemannR[la,lb,lc,ld]

WeylC[la,lb,lc,ld]

You can edit CompSchw.out
>       to print a record of the results.
```

This is the value of the determinant of the Schwarzschild metric tensor.

`In[3]:= Detg`

$$Out[3]= -(r^4 \, Sin[theta]^2)$$

This is $\Gamma^1{}_{11}$, a component of the affine connection.

`In[4]:= AffineG[1,-1,-1]`

$$Out[4]= \frac{G \, M}{(2 \, G \, M - r) \, r}$$

Here is a component of the Riemann tensor of the Schwarzschild metric. The quantity M is the mass of the spherical body, G is Newton's gravitational constant, and r is the radial coordinate.

```
In[5]:= RiemannR[-1,-2,-1,-2]
```

$$Out[5] = \frac{G\ M}{2\ G\ M\ -\ r}$$

The components of the Ricci tensor are zero because the Schwarzschild metric is a vacuum solution of the Einstein gravitational field equations.

```
In[6]:= RicciR[-1,-1]
```

$$Out[6] = 0$$

This is a component of the Weyl tensor.

```
In[7]:= WeylC[-1,-2,-1,-2]
```

$$Out[7] = \frac{G\ M}{2\ G\ M\ -\ r}$$

The spatially flat Robertson-Walker metric,

$$ds^2 = -dt^2 + a(t)^2(dx^2 + dy^2 + dz^2),$$

describes an isotropically expanding (or contracting), spatially flat universe. Here is an input file that will cause the function **Components** to calculate the components of the various curvature tensors for this metric (the input file contains the essential content of the file **CompInRW.m**).

```
Dimension = 4
x/:  x[1] = x
x/:  x[2] = y
x/:  x[3] = z
x/:  x[4] = t

Metricg/:  Metricg[-1, -1] = a[t]^2
Metricg/:  Metricg[-2, -1] = 0
Metricg/:  Metricg[-3, -1] = 0
Metricg/:  Metricg[-4, -1] = 0
Metricg/:  Metricg[-2, -2] = a[t]^2
Metricg/:  Metricg[-3, -2] = 0
Metricg/:  Metricg[-4, -2] = 0
Metricg/:  Metricg[-3, -3] = a[t]^2
Metricg/:  Metricg[-4, -3] = 0
Metricg/:  Metricg[-4, -4] = -1

Rmsign = 1; Rcsign = 1;
CalcEinstein = 1; CalcRiemann = 1; CalcWeyl = 1;
```

Input file for Robertson-Walker metric.

You can use this file (or **CompInRW.m**) to calculate the components of the curvature tensors in the spatially flat Robertson-Walker universe.

This calculates the various curvature tensors characterizing the spatially flat Robertson-Walker universe.

```
In[8]:= Components["CompInRW.m","CompRW.m","CompRW.out"]
```

```
The following tensors have been calculated and stored
in the file CompRW.m in InputForm and
in the file CompRW.out in OutputForm:
Metricg
MatrixMetricgLower
MatrixMetricgUpper
Detg
AffineG[ua,lb,lc]
RicciR[la,lb]
ScalarR

EinsteinG[la,lb,lc,ld]

RiemannR[la,lb,lc,ld]

WeylC[la,lb,lc,ld]
You can edit CompRW.out to print a record of the results.
```

Here is a component of the Riemann tensor of this metric. The quantity $a[t]$ describes the way in which free test particles would change their physical separation in such a universe.

```
In[9]:= RiemannR[-1,-2,-1,-2]
```

$$Out[9]= a[t]^2 \, a'[t]^2$$

The Ricci tensor components are not zero because this metric corresponds to a universe containing matter or radiation.

```
In[10]:= RicciR[-1,-1]
```

$$Out[10]= 2 \, a'[t]^2 + a[t] \, a''[t]$$

Here is the Ricci tensor with one contravariant and one covariant index.

```
In[11]:= RicciR[1,-1]
```

$$Out[11]= \frac{2 \, a'[t]^2 + a[t] \, a''[t]}{a[t]^2}$$

This is the scalar curvature.

```
In[12]:= ScalarR
```

$$Out[12]= \frac{6 \, (a'[t]^2 + a[t] \, a''[t])}{a[t]^2}$$

The Weyl tensor is zero because the Robertson-Walker spacetime is related to flat spacetime by a conformal transformation of the metric.

```
In[13]:= WeylC[-1,-2,-1,-2]
```

$$Out[13]= 0$$

You should now quit the *Mathematica* session and look at the file `CompSchw.out` that has been created. You will see that it contains components of the metric tensor, affine connection, Riemann tensor, Ricci tensor, Einstein tensor, and Weyl tensor. These components are also contained in the file `CompSchw.m` in a form suitable for input into a later *MathTensor* session. You should also look at the file `CompRW.out`, which contains the corresponding tensors calculated for the spatially flat Robertson-Walker universe. The covariant components of the various tensors are listed, along with rules that calculate the contravariant and mixed components when `CompSchw.m` or `CompRW.m` is loaded into a later *MathTensor* session. The files `CompSchw.out` and `CompRW.out` are for your information and can be edited before being printed out. The files `CompSchw.m` and `CompRW.m` should not be edited, as they will serve as input when the components are required in a *MathTensor* session.

You will see that only the independent components are listed with the indices in lexical order. The symmetries of the tensors are known to the system, so the other components do not have to be calculated or listed.

■ 4.1.5 Invariants from Curvature Components

Suppose that you want to calculate some of the invariants of the spatially flat Robertson-Walker spacetime. Start up a new *MathTensor* session. It is important that you do not continue to work in the same *Mathematica* session in which you loaded `Components.m`. After starting a new *MathTensor* session, you can work as usual with tensors having symbolic as well as integer indices. Then when you are ready to evaluate components of tensor expressions in a particular spacetime, you can `Get` the appropriate file that you created earlier. That file, which you produced using the command `Components`, contains the components of the various curvature tensors you will need.

It is advisable to make the symbolic definitions you will need before loading the file containing components of the curvature tensors. The reason is that the symbols `Detg` and `ScalarR` will have values after that file is loaded. Hence, if you want to define expressions in which the literal symbols `Detg` and `ScalarR` appear, it is simplest to use them before they have values. If you decide to make further definitions involving those symbols after you have given them values, you can always store the values of `Detg` and `ScalarR` in some temporary variables and then restore them when you are ready to evaluate the expressions that you defined (see also the *Mathematica* command `Literal`).

This defines an invariant quadratic in the curvature.

$In[1]:=$ `RicciSquared = RicciR[la,lb] RicciR[ua,ub]`

$Out[1]=$ $R_{ab} R^{ab}$

This defines a second invariant quadratic in the curvature.

$In[2]:=$ **ScalarSquared = ScalarR^2**

$Out[2]=$ R^2

Now **get** the components of the curvature tensors of the spatially flat Robertson-Walker spacetime.

$In[3]:=$ **<<CompRW.m**

MetricgFlag has been turned off.

MakeSum evaluates this invariant, and the other operations simplify the result.

$In[4]:=$ **RcSqExpr =**
        Together[Expand[MakeSum[RicciSquared]]]

$$Out[4]= \frac{12\ (a'[t]^4 + a[t]\ a'[t]^2\ a''[t] + a[t]^2\ a''[t]^2)}{a[t]^4}$$

This evaluates the second invariant in the R-W spacetime.

$In[5]:=$ **ScSqExpr = Together[Expand[ScalarSquared]]**

$$Out[5]= \frac{36\ (a'[t]^4 + 2\ a[t]\ a'[t]^2\ a''[t] + a[t]^2\ a''[t]^2)}{a[t]^4}$$

You should be aware that it takes quite a long time to evaluate certain expressions, such as the contracted square of the Riemann tensor, **RiemannSquared** = RiemannR[la,lb,lc,ld] RiemannR[ua,ub,uc,ud]. The time depends on your computer and version of *Mathematica*. If you need to perform such long sums, then you may have to be prepared to let the calculation run for several hours. To speed up the calculation in such a case, *MathTensor* includes the file **RiemannSquared.m**, which contains the full sum of terms (in a 4-dimensional spacetime) that are evaluated in RiemannSquared = RiemannR[la,lb,lc,ld] RiemannR[ua,ub,uc,ud]. By loading **RiemannSquared** from this file, the calculation is speeded up by a factor of about 15. A similar file called **RicciSquared.m** is also provided.

This loads the full sum of terms that must be evaluated.

$In[6]:=$ **<<RiemannSquared.m**

Computation of this invariant may take from a few minutes to tens of minutes, depending on your computer. If it is taking too long, you can abort the calculation and skip the next step.

$In[7]:=$ **RmSqExpr = Together[Expand[RiemannSquared]]**

$$Out[7]= \frac{12\ (a'[t]^4 + a[t]^2\ a''[t]^2)}{a[t]^4}$$

According to the Gauss-Bonnet theorem, the quantity $(-g)^{1/2}(R_{abcd}R^{abcd} + R^2 - 4R_{ab}R^{ab})$ is a perfect four-divergence. Here, we see it is equal to $8(d/dt)(a'(t)^3)$ in the spatially flat R-W universe.

```
In[8]:= GaussBonnetExpr =
  Together[Expand[(-Detg)^(1/2) (RmSqExpr + ScSqExpr - 4
  RcSqExpr)]]
```

$$Out[8] = \frac{24\ \text{Sqrt}[a[t]^6]\ a'[t]^2\ a''[t]}{a[t]^3}$$

If you wish, you can repeat this calculation for the Schwarzschild metric by getting the file `CompSchw.m`. The calculation of `RmSqExpr` will take about 30% longer and should yield the result $48G^2M^2/r^6$. Because the Ricci tensor is zero in the Schwarzschild spacetime, `GaussBonnetExpr` is obtained simply by multiplying this by `(-Detg)^(1/2)`, which gives $48G^2M^2\sin(\theta)/r^4$. This can be written as $48G^2M^2\rho/r^5$, where $\rho = \sqrt{x^2 + y^2}$ and $r = \sqrt{\rho^2 + z^2}$.

■ 4.1.6 Simplification and Series Expansion in Components

It is possible for you to specify how simplification should be performed by `Components`. To do this, you must define in your metric input file the commands `CompSimp`, `CompSimpRules`, and `CompSimpOptions`. (If you are using a version of *MathTensor* earlier than 2.0, you do not have access to this feature and can ignore these commands. If you are using *MathTensor* version 2.1 or 2.1.5, then wherever `CompSimpRules` appears below, you should replace it by `CompSimpRules[1]`.) The default values already contained in `Components` will be used for any of these that you do not define in your input file. Here are their default definitions.

```
CompSimpOptions := { SetOptions[Together, Trig->False],
                SetOptions[Expand, Trig->False] }

Evaluate[CompSimpOptions] (* required for options to take effect *)

CompSimp[a_] := Together[Expand[a/.CompSimpRules] ]

CompSimpRules = {Cos[theta]^2 -> 1 - Sin[theta]^2,
                Cos[theta]^4 -> (1 - Sin[theta]^2)^2}
```

Defaults for simplification in `Components`.

`CompSimp` is the simplification function and `CompSimpRules` is the list of transformation rules that `Components` applies to each expression it calculates. `CompSimpOptions` is a list of `SetOptions` commands determining the options used by the simplification commands in `CompSimp`. In the default case, the `SetOptions` commands in the list `CompSimpOptions` cause `Expand` and `Together` not to apply trigonometric simplification (in *Mathematica* 1.2, the `SetOptions` commands should not be included). The `CompSimpRules` listed will work with many metrics, such as Schwarzschild and Kerr, that contain trigonometric functions. If you know the trig simplification rules you should apply, it is usually faster to list them in `CompSimpRules` than to set the option `Trig->True`.

As an alternate, but potentially slow, simplification procedure, you may wish to use `Simplify` inside of `Components`. You can put the following line in the input file that you create, replacing the above `CompSimp`, containing `Together` and `Expand`, by

```
CompSimp[a_] := Simplify[a/.CompSimpRules]
```

Or, if you wish to do no simplification at all, you can set `CompSimpRules = {}` and define

```
CompSimp[a_] := a/.CompSimpRules
```

The effect of doing no simplification on the time taken by `Components` will vary greatly depending on the complexity of intermediate expressions that appear in each particular case. Sometimes the time is reduced, sometimes it is increased.

To make `Components` apply transformation rules of your choice, you can include a statement such as the following.

```
CompSimpRules = {Cos[theta]^2 -> 1 - Sin[theta]^2,
                 Cos[theta]^4->(1-Sin[theta]^2)^2,
                 r -> (x^2 + y^2 + z^2)^(1/2),
                 G -> 1}
```

Sample user-defined transformation rules.

The transformation rules you actually include in your list will of course depend on the variables appearing in the particular metric you have specified. You may need to run `Components` several times to determine the optimal simplification rule sets.

Sometimes you may wish to set `CompSimpRules = {}` and let *Mathematica* do the trig simplification by setting `Trig->True` in `CompSimpOptions`. Here is an example of how you would do that in your input file for `Components`.

```
CompSimpOptions := { SetOptions[Together, Trig->True],
                     SetOptions[Expand, Trig->True] }

Evaluate[CompSimpOptions] (*causes new options to take effect*)
```

```
CompSimp[a_] := Together[Expand[a/.CompSimpRules] ]

CompSimpRules = {} (* you can include your rules here *)
```

Using automatic trigonometric simplification.

Setting `Trig->True` will slow down most computations but may give simpler results in some cases.

If your metric has a small parameter, say q, you can use your ability to choose `CompSimp` in order to cause `Components` to expand everything in a power series in q. For example, to expand to second order in q, you would include the following line in your input file.

```
{CompSimp[a_] := Series[Expand[a/.CompSimpRules], {q,0,2}]}
```

Rule producing series expansion to second order in q.

It is important to include `Expand` in order to avoid some cases in which `Series` may otherwise have difficulty. You can check that no terms have been lost to the desired order by doing the calculation to higher order (in this case, you would replace `{q,0,2}` by `{q,0,3}`).

Similarly, you can expand to third order in powers of $1/r$ in the asymptotic region far from a mass distribution by including the following line.

```
CompSimp[a_] :=
  Together[
    Series[Expand[a/.CompSimpRules], {r,Infinity,3}]
  ]
```

Rule for third-order asymptotic expansion.

You should not convert series to `Normal` expressions inside of `CompSimp` because that can cause *Mathematica* to drop certain powers in the calculation. However, if you wish, you can use `Normal` in the usual way after you have loaded the output file created by `Components` into a fresh *Mathematica* and *MathTensor* session.

Here are a few examples that illustrate the new features of `Components`. The input file is given first, followed by an example *MathTensor* session in which the output file that was created by `Components` is loaded, and some of the components that were calculated are displayed.

■ 4.1.7 **Schwarzschild with Alternate Simplification**

If the calculation of components is taking a very long time for a particular metric, you may want to do less simplification in order to make the calculation faster (but sometimes this will have the opposite effect because internal expressions get so long). Then you can simplify individual components further after loading the output file into a later session of *MathTensor*. You would also want to calculate only the tensors of particular interest to you by choosing, for example, CalcWeyl = 0 in the input file, if the Weyl tensor is not needed. Here is an example input file in which only Together is used to do simplification and the Weyl tensor is not to be calculated. The input file is based on the usual one for the Schwarzschild metric, with the lines

    CompSimpOptions := {SetOptions[Together, Trig->False]}

    Evaluate[CompSimpOptions]

    CompSimp[a_] := Together[a/.CompSimpRules]

and with CalcWeyl set to zero. Because CompSimpRules are not defined, the default value given earlier is automatically used. Here is the complete input file, called ex1In.m.

```
Dimension = 4

x/: x[1] = r
x/: x[2] = theta
x/: x[3] = phi
x/: x[4] = t

Metricg/: Metricg[-1, -1] = (1 - (2*G*M)/r)^(-1)
Metricg/: Metricg[-2, -1] = 0
Metricg/: Metricg[-3, -1] = 0
Metricg/: Metricg[-4, -1] = 0
Metricg/: Metricg[-2, -2] = r^2
Metricg/: Metricg[-3, -2] = 0
Metricg/: Metricg[-4, -2] = 0
Metricg/: Metricg[-3, -3] = r^2*Sin[theta]^2
Metricg/: Metricg[-4, -3] = 0
Metricg/: Metricg[-4, -4] = -(1 - (2*G*M)/r)

Rmsign = 1
Rcsign = 1

CalcEinstein = 1
CalcRiemann = 1
CalcWeyl = 0
```

```
CompSimpOptions := {SetOptions[Together, Trig->False]}
Evaluate[CompSimpOptions]
CompSimp[a_] := Together[a/.CompSimpRules]
```

ex1In.m.

Now use `Components` to create an output file called `ex1Out.m` by running the following commands in a *Mathematica* session (without loading *MathTensor*).

```
Share[]
<<Components.m
Components["ex1In.m","ex1Out.m","ex1Out.out"]
Quit
```

Example Components session.

After you `Quit` the *Mathematica* session and start a new *Mathematica* and *MathTensor* session, you can load the file `ex1Out.m` and can display and manipulate the results that were calculated with your modified form of `CompSimp`. Here is such a session, beginning after you have loaded *MathTensor*.

Get the file `ex1Out.m`.

$In[1]:=$ `<<ex1Out.m`

`MetricgFlag has been turned off.`

Display the contravariant components of the metric tensor. This lists only the components with $j < i$ for this symmetric tensor (g^{11}, g^{21}, g^{22}, g^{31}, g^{32}, g^{33}, g^{41}, etc.). The result is not as compact as that obtained earlier using the default simplification rules.

$In[2]:=$ `Table[Metricg[i,j],{i,4},{j,i}]`

$$Out[2]= \{\{ \frac{\text{Csc[theta]}^2 \; (-2 \; G \; M \; \text{Sin[theta]}^2 + r \; \text{Sin[theta]}^2)}{r} \},$$

$$\{0, \; r^{-2}\}, \; \{0, \; 0, \; \frac{\text{Csc[theta]}^2}{r^2}\}, \; \{0, \; 0, \; 0, \; \frac{r}{2 \; G \; M - r}\}\}$$

This performs more simplification.

$In[3]:=$ `Simplify[%]`

$$Out[3]= \{\{1 - \frac{2 \; G \; M}{r}\}, \; \{0, \; r^{-2}\}, \; \{0, \; 0, \; \frac{\text{Csc[theta]}^2}{r^2}\},$$

$$\{0, \; 0, \; 0, \; \frac{r}{2 \; G \; M - r}\}\}$$

This shows that the Ricci tensor is already simplified to zero for this vacuum solution of Einstein's equations.

```
In[4]:= Table[RicciR[-i,-j],{i,4},{j,i}]
Out[4]= {{0}, {0, 0}, {0, 0, 0}, {0, 0, 0, 0}}
```

This displays some of the nonzero components of the Riemann tensor (in this case, the others are 0). The components listed are R_{2121}, R_{3131}, R_{3232}, R_{4141}, R_{4242}, and R_{4343}.

```
In[5]:= Table[RiemannR[-i,-j,-i,-j],{i,2,4},{j,i-1}]

Out[5]= {{    G M                  G M Sin[theta]
           {-------},     {-----------------,
            2 G M - r          2 G M - r

>         2 G M r Sin[theta] },

           -2 G M
>         {-------,   (G M Csc[theta]
             3
            r

                                          2                    2     2
>           (-2 G M Sin[theta]  + r Sin[theta] )) / r ,

                              2                    2     2
>         (G M (-2 G M Sin[theta]  + r Sin[theta] )) / r }}
```

Now **Simplify** carries out further simplification.

```
In[6]:= Simplify[%]

                                          2
Out[6]= {{    G M                  G M Sin[theta]
           {-------},     {-----------------,
            2 G M - r          2 G M - r

                            2
>         2 G M r Sin[theta] },

           -2 G M   G M (-2 G M + r)
>         {-------, ----------------,
             3              2
            r              r

          G M (-2 G M + r) Sin[theta]
>         ---------------------------}}
                    2
                   r
```

This calculates one half of the invariant squared Riemann tensor, making use of the fact that the components of R_{abcd} in this case are zero unless $a = c$ and $b = d$, or $a = d$ and $b = c$. Only the terms with $a = c$ and $b = d$ are summed, so you get only half the full value of the invariant.

```
In[7]:= Simplify[MakeSum[
          RiemannR[la,lb,lc,ld] RiemannR[ua,ub,uc,ud],
                                  {la->lc, lb->ld}] ]

              2  2
           24 G  M
Out[7]= --------
              6
             r
```

■ 4.1.8 Asymptotic Behavior in Schwarzschild

Here is an input file that will cause **Components** to series expand quantities to third order in powers of r^{-1} and to apply **Simplify** to each series. The metric is the Schwarzschild metric, as in the previous example.

```
Dimension = 4

x/: x[1] = r
x/: x[2] = theta
x/: x[3] = phi
x/: x[4] = t

Metricg/: Metricg[-1, -1] = (1 - (2*G*M)/r)^(-1)
Metricg/: Metricg[-2, -1] = 0
Metricg/: Metricg[-3, -1] = 0
Metricg/: Metricg[-4, -1] = 0
Metricg/: Metricg[-2, -2] = r^2
Metricg/: Metricg[-3, -2] = 0
Metricg/: Metricg[-4, -2] = 0
Metricg/: Metricg[-3, -3] = r^2*Sin[theta]^2
Metricg/: Metricg[-4, -3] = 0
Metricg/: Metricg[-4, -4] = -(1 - (2*G*M)/r)

Rmsign = 1
Rcsign = 1

CalcEinstein = 1
CalcRiemann = 1
CalcWeyl = 0

CompSimpOptions := {SetOptions[Expand, Trig->True]}
Evaluate[CompSimpOptions]
CompSimp[a_] :=
    Simplify[
      Series[Expand[a/.CompSimpRules],{r,Infinity,3}]
    ]
CompSimpRules = {}
```

ex2In.m.

After loading `Components.m` in a new *Mathematica* session and using the command `Components["ex2In.m","ex2Out.m","ex2Out.out"]` to produce the file `ex2Out.m` containing the calculated results, you `Quit`. Then you start a new *Mathematica* session, load *MathTensor*, and `Get` the file `ex2Out.m`. Here is an example that displays and uses the results contained in the file `ex2Out.m`.

Get the file produced by Components in an earlier *Mathematica* session.

```
In[1]:= << ex2Out.m
      MetricgFlag has been turned off.
```

Display the contravariant components of **Metricg**. Note that g^{44} is displayed as a series to order r^{-4}.

$$In[2]:= \text{Table[Metricg[i,j],\{i,4\},\{j,i\}]}$$

$$Out[2]= \{\{1 - \frac{2 \ G \ M}{r} + O[\frac{1}{r}]^4\}, \ \{0, \ r^{-2} + O[\frac{1}{r}]^4\},$$

$$> \quad \{0, \ 0, \ \frac{\text{Csc[theta]}^2}{r^2} + O[\frac{1}{r}]^4\},$$

$$> \quad \{0, \ 0, \ 0, \ -1 - \frac{2 \ G \ M}{r} - \frac{4 \ G^2 \ M^2}{r^2} - \frac{8 \ G^3 \ M^3}{r^3} + O[\frac{1}{r}]^4\}\}$$

This displays the truncated Ricci tensor components, which are all zero for this vacuum solution.

$$In[3]:= \text{Table[RicciR[-i,-j],\{i,4\},\{j,i\}]//Normal}$$

$$Out[3]= \{\{0\}, \ \{0, \ 0\}, \ \{0, \ 0, \ 0\}, \ \{0, \ 0, \ 0, \ 0\}\}$$

Here are some of the Riemann tensor components. Note that some of the terms to order r^{-3} are not calculated explicitly. You can get those terms by using **Series** to higher order than 3 in the file that you input to **Components**.

$$In[4]:= \quad \text{Table[RiemannR[-i,-j,-i,-j],}$$
$$\text{\{i,2,4\},\{j,i-1\}]}$$

$$Out[4]= \{\{-(\frac{G \ M}{r}) + O[\frac{1}{r}]^2\},$$

$$> \quad \{-(\frac{G \ M \ \text{Sin[theta]}^2}{r}) + O[\frac{1}{r}]^2,$$

$$> \quad 2 \ G \ M \ \text{Sin[theta]}^2 \ r + O[\frac{1}{r}]^0\},$$

$$> \quad \{\frac{-2 \ G \ M}{r^3} + O[\frac{1}{r}]^4, \ \frac{G \ M}{r} - \frac{2 \ G^2 \ M^2}{r^2} + O[\frac{1}{r}]^3,$$

$$> \quad \frac{G \ M \ \text{Sin[theta]}^2}{r} + O[\frac{1}{r}]^2\}\}$$

■ 4.1.9 Perturbations of Flat Spacetime

You can use the series expansion feature of **Components** to perturb about a given metric. For a perfectly general perturbation, it is probably simpler to work with symbolic indices within a *MathTensor* session. But for more special perturbations, it is convenient to use **Components**. In this example, the most general purely time-dependent perturbation about flat spacetime is considered in the linear approximation. The coordinates are called $x1$, $x2$, $x3$, and t. The 10 components of the perturbation of the symmetric covariant metric tensor are called $h11[t]$, $h21[t]$, $h31[t]$, $h41[t]$, $h22[t]$, $h32[t]$, $h42[t]$, $h33[t]$, $h43[t]$, $h44[t]$. They are taken to depend only on the time coordinate t. The definition of **CompSimp** expands to first order in a small parameter q, which is introduced as a factor in each perturbation term of the metric. Here is the input file, which is called `ex3In.m`.

```
Dimension = 4

x/: x[1] = x1
x/: x[2] = x2
x/: x[3] = x3
x/: x[4] = t

Metricg/: Metricg[-1, -1] = 1 + q h11[t]
Metricg/: Metricg[-2, -1] = q h21[t]
Metricg/: Metricg[-3, -1] = q h31[t]
Metricg/: Metricg[-4, -1] = q h41[t]
Metricg/: Metricg[-2, -2] = 1 + q h22[t]
Metricg/: Metricg[-3, -2] = q h32[t]
Metricg/: Metricg[-4, -2] = q h41[t]
Metricg/: Metricg[-3, -3] = 1 + q h33[t]
Metricg/: Metricg[-4, -3] = q h43[t]
Metricg/: Metricg[-4, -4] = -1 + q h44[t]

Rmsign = 1
Rcsign = 1

CalcEinstein = 1
CalcRiemann = 1
CalcWeyl = 0

CompSimpOptions := {SetOptions[Expand, Trig->False],
                    SetOptions[Together, Trig->False]}
Evaluate[CompSimpOptions]
CompSimp[a_] := Together[Series[Expand[a/.CompSimpRules], {q,0,1}]]
CompSimpRules = {}
```

ex3In.m.

Suppose that in a separate *Mathematica* session, you have loaded `Components.m` and issued the command `Components["ex3In.m","ex3Out.m","ex3Out.out"]` to produce the file `ex3Out.m` suitable for input to a later *MathTensor* session. Here is an example of a *MathTensor* session that displays and manipulates the calculated tensor components. It is assumed that you have `Quit` the session in which `Components` was used and have started a fresh *MathTensor* session.

Load in the results calculated earlier by `Components`.	`In[1]:= << ex3Out.m` `MetricgFlag has been turned off.`

Display the independent Ricci tensor components.

$In[2]:=$ `Simplify[Table[RicciR[-i,-j],{i,4},{j,i}] ]`

$$Out[2]= \{\{\frac{h11''[t]\ q}{2} + O[q]^2\ \},$$

$$\{\frac{h21''[t]\ q}{2} + O[q]^2\ ,\ \frac{h22''[t]\ q}{2} + O[q]^2\ \},$$

$$\{\frac{h31''[t]\ q}{2} + O[q]^2\ ,\ \frac{h32''[t]\ q}{2} + O[q]^2\ ,$$

$$\frac{h33''[t]\ q}{2} + O[q]^2\ \},$$

$$\{O[q]^2,\ O[q]^2,\ O[q]^2,$$

$$\frac{-((h11''[t] + h22''[t] + h33''[t])\ q)}{2} + O[q]^2\ \}\}$$

Here is the scalar curvature invariant.

$In[3]:=$ `ScalarR`

$$Out[3]= (h11''[t] + h22''[t] + h33''[t])\ q + O[q]^2$$

Here are three components of the Riemann tensor, namely, R_{1212}, R_{2323}, and R_{3434}.

$In[4]:=$ `Simplify[Table[RiemannR[-i,-i-1,-i,-i-1],{i,1,3}]]`

$$Out[4]= \{O[q]^2,\ O[q]^2,\ \frac{-(h33''[t]\ q)}{2} + O[q]^2\ \}$$

Here is the invariant square of the Ricci tensor.

$In[5]:=$ `MakeSum[RicciR[la,lb] RicciR[ua,ub] ]`

$$Out[5]= 6\ (O[q]^2)^2 + (\frac{h11''[t]\ q}{2} + O[q]^2)^2 +$$

$$2\ (\frac{h21''[t]\ q}{2} + O[q]^2)^2 + (\frac{h22''[t]\ q}{2} + O[q]^2)^2 +$$

$$2\ (\frac{h31''[t]\ q}{2} + O[q]^2)^2 + 2\ (\frac{h32''[t]\ q}{2} + O[q]^2)^2 +$$

$$((\frac{-h11''[t]}{2} - \frac{h22''[t]}{2} - \frac{h33''[t]}{2})\ q + O[q]^2)^2 +$$

$$(\frac{h33''[t]\ q}{2} + O[q]^2)^2$$

From the displayed components of the Ricci tensor, it is clear that in vacuum, where all the components of the Ricci tensor must vanish, there is no purely time-dependent perturbation of Minkowski space that is zero at early times and nonzero at later times. On the other hand, there are nonzero vacuum perturbations that are linear in t, but these are not physical.

The general problem of evaluating symbolic tensor expressions for particular metrics is so common that it will be taken up in more detail in the next section.

■ 4.1.10   Evaluating General Tensor Expressions for Particular Metrics

A tensor that is quadratic in the curvature and has vanishing four-divergences is (in the convention with `Rmsign=1` and `Rcsign=1`)

$$H_{ab} = 2R_{;ab} + (1/2)R^2 g_{ab} - 2R_{;p}{}^p g_{ab} - 2RR_{ab}.$$

This tensor is symmetric because $R_{;ab} = R_{;ba}$.

Suppose that you want to evaluate components of this tensor in the spatially flat Robertson-Walker universe. You have already created a file called `CompRW.m` that contains the required curvature tensors. To evaluate this tensor, do the following:

1. Use `DefineTensor` to create a tensor symbol H.

2. Input the expression for H in terms of curvature tensors.

3. Use `CDtoOD` to convert all covariant derivatives in that expression to ordinary derivatives and affine connections.

4. Define H as equal to the expression just produced. In the tensor H on the left-hand side of the definition, use pattern symbols for indices, which should have the same names as do the free indices of the expression on the right-hand side.

5. When finished with symbolic processing, get the file containing the components of the required curvature tensors and affine connections.

6. Turn on evaluation of ordinary partial derivatives by means of the command `On[EvaluateODFlag]`.

7. Evaluate particular components of the tensor that you just defined by putting appropriate integer indices in it and using `MakeSum` to sum over dummy indices.

This procedure will become clear after reading the following example.

If you are using a version of *MathTensor* earlier than March 18, 1992, then you should reverse the final two steps, making sure that `EvaluateODFlag` is off when MakeSum is applied (you should use ";" to suppress printing out the long intermediate result). Then turn on EvaluateODFlag, simplify, and print out the final result. This is really necessary only if the symbolic expression that goes into MakeSum has a different form, depending on whether EvaluateODFlag is on or off. That can occur if ordinary derivatives of symbolic expressions appear but have a negative integer index in a derivative index slot. Although that is a rare occurrence, for safety you will either want to check that the form of the symbolic expression does not depend on the setting of EvaluateODFlag or make sure that EvaluateODFlag is off before you carry out the step with MakeSum above. The same goes for the step with SetComponents in the alternative procedure given below. With the more recent versions of *MathTensor*, you do not have to worry about any of this.

An alternative method is to follow steps 1, 2, and 3, assigning to the result of step 3 a name, such as expr. Then skip step 4 and do step 5. Then, with EvaluateODFlag off, use SetComponents to evaluate all the components of expr and set them equal to a name such as H[1a,1b] that you choose (here, the free indices such as 1a and 1b must match the free indices that appear in expr, as indicated in the usage message for SetComponents). Finally, turn on EvaluateODFlag, simplify, and print the components that have been calculated.

If only a limited number of components are to be calculated, the first method using MakeSum will be faster, since only the components specifically required are calculated. The method using MakeSum is illustrated in the example below.

This defines a symmetric tensor with the name H. It is not necessary to assign any symmetries to H to carry out the following procedure.

```
In[1]:= DefineTensor[H,{{2,1},1}]
PermWeight::sym: Symmetries of H assigned
PermWeight::def: Object H defined
```

This defines the expression that will be used on the right-hand side of the rule to convert H to curvature tensors.

```
In[2]:= Hexpr1[1a,1b] = 2 CD[ScalarR, 1a,1b] +
        (1/2) ScalarR^2 Metricg[1a,1b] -
        2 CD[ScalarR,1c,uc] Metricg[1a,1b] -
        2 ScalarR RicciR[1a,1b]
```

$$Out[2]= 2\,R_{;ab} + \frac{R^2\,g_{ab}}{2} - 2\,R_{;c}{}^{c}\,g_{ab} - 2\,R\,R_{ab}$$

This converts one covariant derivative to ordinary derivatives and affine connections.

$In[3] := $ `Expand[CDtoOD[Hexpr1[la,lb] ] ]`

$$Out[3] = -2\ G^p_{\ ab}\ R_{\ ;p} + \frac{R^2\ g_{ab}}{2} + 2\ G^p_{\ qr}\ R_{\ ;p}\ g_{ab}\ g^{qr} -$$

$$> \quad 2\ g_{ab}\ g^{pq}\ R_{\ ;p,q} + 2\ R_{\ ;a,b} - 2\ R\ R_{ab}$$

This converts the second covariant derivative.

$In[4] := $ `Hexpr2[la,lb] = Expand[CDtoOD[%] ]`

$$Out[4] = \frac{R^2\ g_{ab}}{2} - 2\ G^p_{\ ab}\ R_{\ ,p} + 2\ G^p_{\ qr}\ g_{ab}\ g^{qr}\ R_{\ ,p} -$$

$$> \quad 2\ g_{ab}\ g^{pq}\ R_{\ ,pq} + 2\ R_{\ ,ab} - 2\ R\ R_{ab}$$

The indices on the left are patterns that match the free indices on the right-hand side. You will have to remember to put covariant indices (negative integers) in the index slots because **Hexpr2** is properly defined only with covariant free indices. This completes the symbolic processing.

$In[5] := $ `H[la_,lb_] = Hexpr2[la,lb];`

Get the file containing the required curvature tensors and affine connections. Now you can evaluate components of H.

$In[6] := $ `<<CompRW.m`

`MetricgFlag has been turned off.`

This causes ordinary partial derivatives to be evaluated. For example, **OD[a[t],-3]** will evaluate to zero. This step can be done after the next step in versions of *MathTensor* earlier than March 18, 1992, following the procedure explained above. In this example, it would make no difference.

$In[7] := $ `On[EvaluateODFlag]`

Here is H_{11} in the spatially flat Robertson-Walker universe. It contains up to fourth derivatives of the scale factor $a(t)$, which describes the expansion of the universe.

$In[8] := $ `H[-1,-1] =`
      `Together[Expand[MakeSum[H[-1,-1] ] ] ]`

$$Out[8] = (6\ (3\ a'[t]^4 - 12\ a[t]\ a'[t]^2\ a''[t] +$$

$$> \quad 3\ a[t]^2\ a''[t]^2 + 4\ a[t]^2\ a'[t]^2\ a^{(3)}[t] +$$

$$> \quad 2\ a[t]^3\ a^{(4)}[t])) / a[t]^2$$

Here is H_{22}. The diagonal spatial
components are equal in this universe.

```
In[9]:= H[-2,-2] =
        Together[Expand[MakeSum[H[-2,-2]] ] ]
```

$$Out[9] = (6 \ (3 \ a'[t]^4 - 12 \ a[t] \ a'[t]^2 \ a''[t] +$$

$$> \qquad 3 \ a[t]^2 \ a''[t]^2 + 4 \ a[t]^2 \ a'[t] \ a^{(3)}[t] +$$

$$> \qquad 2 \ a[t]^3 \ a^{(4)}[t])) \ / \ a[t]^2$$

The mixed components of H all vanish for
this metric.

```
In[10]:= H[-2,-1] =
         Together[Expand[MakeSum[H[-2,-1]] ] ]
Out[10]= 0
```

Here is H_{44}. It contains only up to third
derivatives of $a(t)$.

```
In[11]:= H[-4,-4] =
         Together[Expand[MakeSum[H[-4,-4]] ] ]
```

$$Out[11] = (18 \ (3 \ a'[t]^4 - 2 \ a[t] \ a'[t]^2 \ a''[t] +$$

$$> \qquad a[t]^2 \ a''[t]^2 - 2 \ a[t]^2 \ a'[t] \ a^{(3)}[t])) \ / \ a[t]^4$$

This saves the definition of H and the
components that you have evaluated. The
file can be gotten at a later session.

```
In[12]:= Definition[H]>>Hcomps.m
```

You can use the general procedure illustrated in this example to evaluate expressions you encounter that involve curvature tensors. If you create knowledge-base files containing the components of other tensors, you can use the same procedure to evaluate symbolic expressions containing those tensors. The knowledge-base files you create would be similar to the file `CompRW.m` in the sense that they would contain the values of the independent components of the tensors that appear in your expressions as well as symmetries or other relevant properties of those tensors. The tensors you deal with need not have anything to do with curvature. For example, they may describe stress, strain, light propagation, or whatever.

■ 4.2 Coordinate Transformations of Tensors

Although a tensor is independent of coordinates, its components have different values in different coordinate systems. The rules for transforming the components of tensors from one coordinate system to another were explained in the first two sections of Chapter 2. Frequently, you are given the equations of a coordinate transformation and wish to find the components of a tensor in one of the coordinate systems from its components in the other. You can use the *MathTensor* command `Ttransform` to transform the components of a tensor of any rank from one coordinate system to another in a space of any number of dimensions.

■ 4.2.1 Ttransform: Syntax and Explanation

In order to discuss the syntax of `Ttransform`, let us assume that the space is 3-dimensional and that the coordinate transformation has the form

$$x' = f(x, y, z), \quad y' = g(x, y, z), \quad z' = h(x, y, z). \tag{4.3}$$

Suppose that you know the components of a tensor $t_a{}^b{}_c$ in the (x, y, z) coordinate system and want to find its components in the (x', y', z') coordinate system. Denote the components in the primed coordinate system by $tp_a{}^b{}_c$. (The name tp is used instead of t' because a prime already denotes a derivative in *Mathematica*.) The command necessary to carry out this calculation is

`Ttransform[tp, t[la,ub,lc], {x,y,z}, {f(x,y,z),g(x,y,z),h(x,y,z)}, 1]`

The first argument of `Ttransform` is the name, in the appropriate coordinate system, of the tensor whose components are to be found (note that no indices are included). The second argument is the name and index positions of the *known* components of the tensor. In this case, the components are assumed to be known when the first and third indices are covariant and the second index is contravariant. The corresponding components of `tp` are calculated from those of `t`, so no indices are needed in the first argument of `Ttransform`. The third argument is a list of the names of the coordinates that appear on the right-hand sides of the coordinate transformation equations. The fourth argument is a list giving the full right-hand sides of the coordinate transformation equations. Finally, the fifth argument is 1 if the known components of the tensor (i.e., those indicated by the second argument) are the components in the coordinate system listed in the third argument. Put another way, the fifth argument is 1 if the coordinate and tensor transformations are in the same direction.

It may also happen that you know the components $tp_a{}^b{}_c$ and wish to find the components $t_a{}^b{}_c$. In that case, you would issue the command

`Ttransform[t, tp[la,ub,lc], {x,y,z}, {f(x,y,z),g(x,y,z),h(x,y,z)}, -1]`

You have again put the *known* components in the second argument, but now you are *seeking* the components of the tensor in the coordinates listed in the third argument of `Ttransform`. In other words, the coordinate and tensor transformations are in opposite directions. You indicate these opposite directions by putting -1 as the fifth argument of `Ttransform`.

Before you use `Ttransform`, you should set the value of `Dimension` to the number of coordinates (3 in this case) and you should use `DefineTensor` to define the tensors (t and tp in this case) with their symmetries. In addition, the name used for the tensor in the *first* argument of `Ttransform` should not have a previous assignment.

Here is a summary of the syntax:

`Ttransform[newtensor,oldtensor[la,ub], {x1,x2,x3},{rhs1,rhs2,rhs3},1or-1]`
transforms the components of `oldtensor` to a new coordinate system and names
the transformed tensor `newtensor`. The indices in `oldtensor` give positions of indices for which the components are known. The indices in `newtensor` will have
the same positions and are therefore not specified. The list `{x1,x2,x3}` gives the
names of the old coordinates if the last argument of `Ttransform` is 1 (for forward
transformation) or the names of the new coordinates if the last argument is `-1`
(for inverse transformation). The value of `Dimension` should already be set to the
number of coordinates. The list `{rhs1,rhs2,rhs3}` gives the right-hand sides of
the coordinate transformation equations and should involve the coordinates named
in the previous list. Any rank tensor and any number of coordinates are permitted. The coordinate names and the components of the `newtensor` should not have
previous assignments.

`Ttransform[`*newtensor*`,`*oldtensor*`[la,ub],{x1,x2,x3},{rhs1,rhs2,rhs3},1or-1]`
the coordinate transformation function

`Ttransform` is used for tensor coordinate transformations.

■ 4.2.2 Four Examples

Here are several examples of the transformation of tensors from one coordinate
system to another. The comments explain the syntax and use of `Ttransform`. If
you wish, you can put these commands into a file and load them all at once into
MathTensor. Although the examples involve second-rank tensors, you can also use
`Ttransform` with other rank tensors.

■ 4.2.3 Example One: Familiar Calculation

Transformation of covariant metric tensor from rectangular to spherical coordinates
in 3 dimensions.

Set the dimension of the space.	*In[1]:=* `Dimension = 3` *Out[1]=* 3
The names of the spherical coordinates are defined.	*In[2]:=* `coords = {r,theta,phi}` *Out[2]=* {r, theta, phi}

This list gives the right-hand sides of the transformation equations that give the rectangular coordinates x, y, z in terms of r, theta, phi.

```
In[3]:= trans = {r Sin[theta] Cos[phi], r Sin[theta]
        Sin[phi], r Cos[theta] }
Out[3]= {r Cos[phi] Sin[theta], r Sin[phi] Sin[theta],
>     r Cos[theta]}
```

Define a new second-rank symmetric tensor called **ga**, which will be the new or transformed metric tensor.

```
In[4]:= DefineTensor[ga,{{2,1},1}]
PermWeight::sym: Symmetries of ga assigned
PermWeight::def: Object ga defined
```

Ttransform calculates the components of the new metric tensor, **ga**, from the components of the rectangular metric tensor, which are the same as the components of the Kronecker delta, **Kdelta[la,lb]**. The indices la, lb are covariant indices and instruct **Ttransform** to calculate the covariant components of the new metric tensor **ga**. The arguments of **Ttransform** are first, the name of the new tensor; second, the name and indices of the old tensor; third, the coordinates; fourth, the right-hand sides of the transformations applied to those coordinates; and fifth, 1 if the transformation of the tensor is in the same direction as is the given coordinate transformation or -1 if in the opposite direction. In this example, the transformation of coordinates is from spherical to rectangular coordinates, while the transformation of metric is from rectangular to spherical coordinates; hence the last argument is -1.

```
In[5]:= Ttransform[ga,Kdelta[la,lb],coords,trans,-1]
Components assigned to ga
```

Display the calculated transformed metric tensor.

```
In[6]:=
Print[MatrixForm[Table[ga[-i,-j],{i,1,3},{j,1,3}]]]
```

$$\begin{pmatrix} 1 & 0 & 0 \\ 0 & r^2 & 0 \\ 0 & 0 & r^2 \, Sin[theta]^2 \end{pmatrix}$$

■ 4.2.4 Example Two: Simple Shear

Next is an example from the theory of nonlinear elasticity. (You can find much more on nonlinear elasticity in Chapter 8 on "nonlinear elasticity in engineering mechanics.") A rectangular solid is deformed by shearing it in the x-direction by an amount proportional to the height y. Relative to a given external rectangular coordinate system, the physical point originally having coordinate values x, y, z moves to the new coordinate values $x' = x + Ky, y' = y, z' = z$. Coordinate axes anchored to the physical points of the solid will be deformed from rectangular to oblique by the shear deformation of the solid. The distance between points in the deformed solid is related to the coordinate separation in the deformed oblique coordinates by a metric tensor `ga[la,lb]` related to the Euclidean metric tensor `Kdelta[la,lb]` via the above-given coordinate transformation. Note that x', y', z' are the coordinates of the physical point relative to external rectangular coordinates, while x, y, z are the (fixed) coordinates of the physical point relative to the deformed oblique axes. Thus the transformation is from oblique to rectangular coordinates, while we want to transform the metric tensor from rectangular to oblique coordinates. Hence, the last argument of `Ttransform` is `-1`. Here are the lines to be input:

Clear the values of the components of ga.   `In[7]:= Clear[ga]`

Set `Dimension`.

```
In[8]:= Dimension = 3
Out[8]= 3
```

Set the coordinates.

```
In[9]:= coords = {x,y,z}
Out[9]= {x, y, z}
```

Define the transformation.

```
In[10]:= trans = {x+K*y,y,z}
Out[10]= {x + K y, y, z}
```

Define ga.

```
In[11]:= DefineTensor[ga,{{2,1},1}]
 PermWeight::sym: Symmetries of ga assigned
 PermWeight::def: Object ga defined
```

Calculate ga.

```
In[12]:= Ttransform[ga,Kdelta[la,lb],coords,trans,-1]
 Components assigned to ga
```

Display the result.

```
In[13]:= MatrixForm[Table[ga[-i,-j],{i,1,3},{j,1,3}]]
Out[13]//MatrixForm=
```

$$\begin{pmatrix} 1 & K & 0 \\ K & 1 + K^2 & 0 \\ 0 & 0 & 1 \end{pmatrix}$$

Next find the contravariant components of the metric of the deformed body. The indices ua, ub in the original tensor tell Ttransform to calculate the contravariant components.

```
In[14]:= Ttransform[ga,Kdelta[ua,ub],coords,trans,-1]

  Components assigned to ga
```

Show the result.

```
In[15]:= Print[MatrixForm[Table[ga[i,j],{i,1,3},{j,1,3}]]]
```

$$
\begin{matrix}
1 + K^2 & -K & 0 \\
-K & 1 & 0 \\
0 & 0 & 1
\end{matrix}
$$

■ 4.2.5 Example Three: Special Relativity

This example illustrates the Lorentz transformation of the Maxwell electromagnetic field tensor between two inertial frames in standard configuration.

The transformation is to a frame moving at constant velocity v along the x-direction of the x, y, z, t reference frame. The tensor in the x, y, z, t frame is MaxwellF[ua,ub] and that in the new frame is MaxwellFb[ua,ub]. MaxwellF[ua,ub] is already defined, so DefineTensor is used only on MaxwellFb. The indices ua, ub in MaxwellF[ua,ub] tell Ttransform to calculate the contravariant components. This example gives the transformation of the electric and magnetic fields under a special Lorentz transformation (or "boost") in the x-direction.

Assign the spacetime dimension.

```
In[16]:= Dimension = 4
Out[16]= 4
```

Define a factor appearing in the Lorentz transformation.

```
In[17]:= gamma = (Sqrt[1-(v/c)^2])^(-1)
```

$$
Out[17]= \frac{1}{Sqrt[1 - \dfrac{v^2}{c^2}]}
$$

Define the coordinates.

```
In[18]:= coords = {x,y,z,t}
Out[18]= {x, y, z, t}
```

trans is a Lorentz transformation in the x-direction.

$In[19]:=$ **trans = {gamma (x - v t),y,z,gamma (t - (v/c^2) x)}**

$$Out[19]= \left\{ \frac{-(t\ v) + x}{Sqrt[1 - \dfrac{v^2}{c^2}]},\ y,\ z,\ \frac{t - \dfrac{v\ x}{c^2}}{Sqrt[1 - \dfrac{v^2}{c^2}]} \right\}$$

Transformed Maxwell tensor.

$In[20]:=$ **DefineTensor[MaxwellFb,"Fb",{{2,1},-1}]**

PermWeight::sym: Symmetries of Fb assigned

PermWeight::def: Object Fb defined

Calculate the components of the transformed Maxwell field tensor, MaxwellFb, in terms of the components MaxwellF in the original frame.

$In[21]:=$
Ttransform[MaxwellFb,MaxwellF[ua,ub],coords,trans,1]

  Components assigned to Fb

Display the result as a list, as it is too long to display in matrix form. Each sublist gives the elements of a row of the 4-by-4 matrix giving the components of the transformed Maxwell field tensor.

$In[22]:=$ **Table[MaxwellFb[i,j],{i,1,4},{j,1,4}]**

$$Out[22]= \left\{\left\{0,\ \frac{F^{12} + v\ F^{24}}{Sqrt[1 - \dfrac{v^2}{c^2}]},\ \frac{F^{13} + v\ F^{34}}{Sqrt[1 - \dfrac{v^2}{c^2}]},\ F^{14}\right\},\right.$$

$$> \quad \left\{-\left(\frac{F^{12} + v\ F^{24}}{Sqrt[1 - \dfrac{v^2}{c^2}]}\right),\ 0,\ F^{23},\ \frac{v\ F^{12} + c^2\ F^{24}}{c^2\ Sqrt[1 - \dfrac{v^2}{c^2}]}\right\},$$

$$> \quad \left\{-\left(\frac{F^{13} + v\ F^{34}}{Sqrt[1 - \dfrac{v^2}{c^2}]}\right),\ -F^{23},\ 0,\ \frac{v\ F^{13} + c^2\ F^{34}}{c^2\ Sqrt[1 - \dfrac{v^2}{c^2}]}\right\},$$

$$> \quad \left.\left\{-F^{14},\ -\left(\frac{v\ F^{12} + c^2\ F^{24}}{c^2\ Sqrt[1 - \dfrac{v^2}{c^2}]}\right),\ -\left(\frac{v\ F^{13} + c^2\ F^{34}}{c^2\ Sqrt[1 - \dfrac{v^2}{c^2}]}\right),\ 0\right\}\right\}$$

■ 4.2.6 Example Four: General Relativity—Kruskal Coordinates

Transform the Schwarzschild metric of a black hole from Schwarzschild to Kruskal coordinates. This transformation does not involve the angular coordinates, so it is sufficient to work in a 2-dimensional spacetime. In Schwarzschild coordinates r, t, the Schwarzschild line element is

$$ds^2 = (1 - (2M)/r)^{-1}dr^2 - (1 - (2M)/r))dt^2.$$

Kruskal gave the transformation

$$X = (r/(2M) - 1)^{(1/2)} \exp[r/(4M)] \cosh[t/(4M)]$$

$$T = (r/(2M) - 1)^{(1/2)} \exp[r/(4M)] \sinh[t/(4M)]$$

to Kruskal coordinates X, T. Use **Ttransform** to calculate the form of the metric tensor in Kruskal coordinates.

Clear any previous assignments.

```
In[23]:= Clear[ga,gb]
```

Define the dimension.

```
In[24]:= Dimension = 2
Out[24]= 2
```

Define the coordinates.

```
In[25]:= coords = {r,t}
Out[25]= {r, t}
```

Define the transformations giving the Kruskal coordinates X,T in terms of r,t.

```
In[26]:= trans = {(r/(2 M) - 1)^(1/2) Exp[r/(4 M)]
         Cosh[t/(4 M)],
              (r/(2 M) - 1)^(1/2) Exp[r/(4 M)] Sinh[t/(4 M)]}
             r/(4 M)              r            t
Out[26]= {E         Sqrt[-1 + ---] Cosh[---],
                              2 M          4 M

            r/(4 M)            r          t
    >      E        Sqrt[-1 + ---] Sinh[---]}
                             2 M        4 M
```

Let **ga[1a,1b]** be the Schwarzschild metric for r, t. The independent covariant components of the metric are assigned below.

```
In[27]:= DefineTensor[ga,{{2,1},1}]
PermWeight::sym: Symmetries of ga assigned
PermWeight::def: Object ga defined
```

Set the $(-2, -2)$ component.

```
In[28]:= ga[-2,-2] = -(1 - (2 M)/r)
                  2 M
Out[28]= -1 + ---
                   r
```

Set the $(-2, -1)$ component.

```
In[29]:= ga[-2,-1] = 0
Out[29]= 0
```

Set the $(-1, -1)$ component.

```
In[30]:= ga[-1,-1] = (1 - (2 M)/r)^(-1)
```

$$Out[30]= \dfrac{1}{1 - \dfrac{2\,M}{r}}$$

gb will denote the transformed metric.

```
In[31]:=
DefineTensor[gb,{{2,1},1}]

PermWeight::sym: Symmetries of gb assigned

PermWeight::def: Object gb defined
```

Calculate gb from ga. The transformation of coordinates and metric are in the same direction, from Schwarzschild to Kruskal, so the last argument of Ttransform is 1. The metric components of gb[1a,1b] refer to the Kruskal coordinates X, T, but they will appear as functions of r, t, since ga[1a,1b] and the right-hand sides of the transformation equations are given as functions of r, t. In fact, that is the usual way that the Kruskal metric is written, since r and t cannot be expressed in a simple algebraic form in terms of X, T.

```
In[32]:=
Ttransform[gb,ga[1a,1b],coords,trans,1]

Components assigned to gb
```

Display the result.

```
In[33]:= Table[gb[-i,-j],{i,2},{j,2}]
```

$$Out[33]= \left\{\left\{\frac{32\,M^3}{E^{r/(2\,M)}\,r}, 0\right\}, \left\{0, \frac{-32\,M^3}{E^{r/(2\,M)}\,r}\right\}\right\}$$

This result means that the line element in Kruskal coordinates has the well-known form

$$ds^2 = 32M^3 r^{-1} \exp[-r/(2M)](dX^2 - dT^2).$$

These examples show the power and versatility of the *MathTensor* function Ttransform.

■ 4.3 Using More Than One Type of Index

There are occasions when you will want to use more than one type of index in an application of *MathTensor*. For example, you may be dealing with a gauge field having group indices as well as spacetime indices, or a 2-dimensional surface embedded in a 3-dimensional space, or spinors in spacetime. There are four different types of indices available in *MathTensor*. You can use them as required in applications like the ones mentioned. You can define symmetries for them and set up the rules and definitions that you need with more than one type of index.

When *MathTensor* first comes up, there is only one type of index available. Those indices, which have been described in the previous sections, will be referred to as regular indices. Before you can use the additional three types of indices, you must type the command **AddIndexTypes**. If you are using *MathTensor* on a computer with no virtual memory and only a small amount of random access memory, you may find that you do not have sufficient memory for the additional indices. In that case, you should either skip this section, or if your applications require more than one type of index, install more memory. Sometimes you can use regular indices from different parts of the alphabet to act like two different types of indices, but then you will not have access to the programming constructs that are available for dealing with the various types of indices.

■ 4.3.1 Types of Indices

Before discussing the new types of indices, a brief review is in order. As you know, regular covariant indices are input as `la,lb,...,lo` and regular contravariant indices as `ua,ub,...,uo`. Here are some examples, with their output form.

This defines an antisymmetric tensor t with OutputForm "t".

$In[1]:=$ `DefineTensor[t,{{2,1},-1}]`

PermWeight::sym: Symmetries of t assigned

PermWeight::def: Object t defined

The indices appear as appropriate subscripts and superscripts.

$In[2]:=$ `t[la,lb] t[ua,ub]`

$Out[2]= t_{ab}\, t^{ab}$

The function Dum replaces paired indices by system-generated dummy indices.

$In[3]:=$ `Dum[%]`

$Out[3]= t_{pq}\, t^{pq}$

The input forms of system-generated covariant and contravariant dummy indices are 11,12,... and u1,u2,..., respectively.

```
In[4]:= InputForm[%]
Out[4]//InputForm= t[11, 12]*t[u1, u2]
```

The *MathTensor* function UpLo generates unique pairs of indices, which are used in rules and definitions created, for example, by RuleUnique and DefUnique.

```
In[5]:= UpLo[{up1,up2},{lo1,lo2}]
```

Their output form consists of a $ followed by an integer.

```
In[6]:= t[lo1,lo2] t[up1,up2]
                      $1$2
Out[6]= t        t
           $1$2
```

The function Dum replaces pairs of these unique indices by system-generated dummy indices, just as it does with the pairs that you type in.

```
In[7]:= Dum[%]
                 pq
Out[7]= t    t
           pq
```

This is actually zero because t is antisymmetric.

```
In[8]:= t[la,ua]
              a
Out[8]= t
           a
```

The function Tsimplify recognizes that this is zero.

```
In[9]:= Tsimplify[%]
Out[9]= 0
```

In addition to regular indices, there are three other types of indices available in *MathTensor*. The naming and use of the other types of indices is similar to the conventions for regular indices that were just described. To see this, you must first bring the new types of indices into memory by typing AddIndexTypes. There are three types of new indices, known as type-a, type-b, and type-c indices.

By convention, all indices must appear between the same set of brackets, even if more than one type of index is present. The symmetries of a tensor (here meaning any object with indices) are declared with DefineTensor in the usual way. If a particular tensor has more than one type of index, you should reserve particular slots for each type of index that is present. For example, you may reserve slots 1 and 2 for type-a indices and slots 3 and 4 for regular indices in a given tensor having 4 slots for indices. The user must remember which slots take which type of index when inputting an expression. The symmetries that you declare with DefineTensor will almost never mix slots having different types of indices (although it is possible to declare symmetries that permute indices of different types, such symmetries seldom appear in actual applications).

The different types of indices may be thought of as referring to different spaces, as when regular indices denote ordinary spacetime indices and type-a indices denote Lie group indices.

This causes the additional types of indices to be put into memory. In addition to regular indices, you now can use indices of types a, b, and c.	$In[10] :=$ **AddIndexTypes**

This declares an object symmetric in the first pair and in the last pair of indices. The first two slots will be used for type-a indices and the second pair for regular indices.

$In[11] :=$ **DefineTensor[t22,{{2,1,3,4},1,{1,2,4,3},1}]**

    PermWeight::sym: Symmetries of t22 assigned

    PermWeight::def: Object t22 defined

Type-a indices are input with the same names as are regular indices, except that each name is prefixed with the letter "a". On output, the indices of type-a appear with a single prime, to distinguish them from regular indices. The symmetries have been used to reorder the indices.

$In[12] :=$ **t22[alb,ala,le,lf]**

$Out[12] =$ $t22_{a'b'ef}$

Here is an expression with dummy indices.

$In[13] :=$ **t22[ala,aua,le,ue]**

$Out[13] =$ $t22_{a'\ e\ a'\ e}^{\ \ a'\ \ e}$

Dum replaces each type of dummy index by the proper type of system-generated dummy index. Again the prime identifies type-a indices.

$In[14] :=$ **Dum[%]**

$Out[14] =$ $t22_{p'\ p}^{\ \ p'\ p}$

The names of system-generated dummy indices of type-a are the same as regular system-generated dummies, except for a leading "a".

$In[15] :=$ **InputForm[%]**

$Out[15]//InputForm =$ t22[al1, au1, l1, u1]

The function UpLoa generates unique type-a dummy pairs of indices.

$In[16] :=$ **UpLoa[{aup1,aup2},{alo1,alo2}]**

After **AddIndexTypes** has been invoked, you use UpLo as before to declare new regular unique dummy indices. Normally, you will not be using UpLo explicitly. It appears in rules and definitions created with **RuleUnique** and **DefUnique**, and no problem arises.

$In[17] :=$ **UpLo[{up1,up2},{lo1,lo2}]**

The unique dummy indices created by UpLoa appear in the output with names like the unique regular indices created by UpLo, except that the "$" is replaced by "$a". You will never see these names if you use ApplyRules to apply the rules created by RuleUnique. RuleUnique uses UpLo and UpLoa internally. There are also UpLob and UpLoc for indices of types b and c.

$In[18]:=$ t22[alo1,alo2,lo1,lo2] t22[aup1,aup2,up1,up2]

$Out[18]=$ $t22_{\$a1\$a2\$3\$4}{}^{\$a1\$a2\$3\$4}\, t22$

The command Dum replaces the unique dummy indices of each type by appropriate system-generated dummy indices. When ApplyRules is used, this is done automatically. In rare cases when you create applications in which you see the unique dummy indices, you can use Dum to replace them. Usually, all this is hidden from the user.

$In[19]:=$ Dum[%]

$Out[19]=$ $t22_{p'q'pq}{}^{p'q'pq}\, t22$

Recall that t is antisymmetric. Because t22 is symmetric in the second pair of indices, this quantity is zero.

$In[20]:=$ t[la,lb] t22[ala,alb,ua,ub]

$Out[20]=$ $t_{ab}\, t22_{a'b'}{}^{ab}$

Tsimplify works on expressions with more than one type of index.

$In[21]:=$ Tsimplify[%]

$Out[21]=$ 0

Here is an example in which simplification involves both types of indices. The terms and factors have been reordered by *Mathematica* in the output line.

$In[22]:=$ t22[ala,alb,ua,ub] t22[aub,auc,la,lc] t22[aua,alc,lb,uc] +
  t22[ala,alb,ua,ub] t22[aua,auc,lb,lc] t22[aub,alc,la,uc]

$Out[22]=$ $t22_{a'b'}{}^{ab}\, t22_{c'}{}^{b'\,c}\, t22_{bc}{}^{a'c'}\, +$

$>\quad t22_{a'b'}{}^{ab}\, t22_{c'\,b}{}^{a'\,c}\, t22_{ac}{}^{b'c'}$

Simplification is again accomplished by means of Tsimplify.

$In[23]:=$ Tsimplify[%]

$Out[23]=$ $2\; t22_{a'b'}{}^{ab}\, t22_{c'\,a}{}^{b'\,c}\, t22_{bc}{}^{a'c'}$

The naming of type-b and type-c indices follows the same general rule of prepending regular index names by the appropriate letter (b or c). In the output, type-b indices have two primes and type-c indices have three primes. You can use up to four different types of indices in expressions.

$In[24]:=$ {t[bla,blb], t[cla,clb]}

$Out[24]=$ $\{t_{a''b''},\; t_{a'''b'''}\}$

`AddIndexTypes`	make indices of types a, b, and c available
`la,lb,...,lo`	regular indices
`ala,alb,...,alo`	type-a indices
`bla,blb,...,blo`	type-b indices
`cla,clb,...,clo`	type-c indices
t`[ala,alb,blf,blg,lm]`	an object with three types of indices
`UpLo,UpLoa,UpLob,UpLoc`	functions producing unique dummy indices

Four types of indices are available.

■ 4.3.2   Tests and Commands for Various Types of Indices

When you create rules involving various types of indices, you will often require tests that can be used to restrict the patterns that cause the rules to be triggered or be applied. For example, you may wish to have lower or upper indices of a particular type (regular, a, b, or c) present. The tests demonstrated here for regular and type-a indices also have their obvious counterparts for type-b and type-c indices.

Start a new session of *MathTensor* and activate all four types of indices.

```
In[1]:= AddIndexTypes
```

`LowerIndexQ` returns `True` only on regular lower indices.

```
In[2]:= {LowerIndexQ[ld], LowerIndexQ[ald],
         LowerIndexQ[ud], LowerIndexQ[aud]}
```
```
Out[2]= {True, False, False, False}
```

`LowerIndexaQ` returns `True` only on lower indices of type-a.

```
In[3]:= {LowerIndexaQ[ld], LowerIndexaQ[ald],
         LowerIndexaQ[ud], LowerIndexaQ[aud]}
```
```
Out[3]= {False, True, False, False}
```

`LowerIndexAllTypesQ` returns `True` only on lower indices of any type.

```
In[4]:= {LowerIndexAllTypesQ[ld],
         LowerIndexAllTypesQ[ald],
         LowerIndexAllTypesQ[ud], LowerIndexAllTypesQ[aud]}
```
```
Out[4]= {True, True, False, False}
```

`UpperIndexQ` returns `True` only on regular upper indices.

```
In[5]:= {UpperIndexQ[ud], UpperIndexQ[aud],
         UpperIndexQ[ld], UpperIndexQ[ald]}
```
```
Out[5]= {True, False, False, False}
```

UpperIndexaQ returns True only on upper indices of type-a. There is also **UpperIndexAllTypesQ** which returns True on any type of upper index.

```
In[6]:= {UpperIndexaQ[ud], UpperIndexaQ[aud],
    UpperIndexaQ[ld], UpperIndexaQ[ald]}

Out[6]= {False, True, False, False}
```

IndexAllTypesQ returns True on any type of index.

```
In[7]:= {IndexAllTypesQ[ud], IndexAllTypesQ[aud],
    IndexAllTypesQ[ld], IndexAllTypesQ[ald]}

Out[7]= {True, True, True, True}
```

IndexQ is an exception in that it acts like **IndexAllTypesQ**. This is necessary for internal reasons.

```
In[8]:= {IndexQ[ud], IndexQ[aud],
    IndexQ[ld], IndexQ[ald]}

Out[8]= {True, True, True, True}
```

This defines a command **IndexRegQ**, which returns True only on regular indices.

```
In[9]:= IndexRegQ[a_] := LowerIndexQ[a] || UpperIndexQ[a]
```

Now the type-a indices return False.

```
In[10]:= {IndexRegQ[ud], IndexRegQ[aud],
    IndexRegQ[ld], IndexRegQ[ald]}

Out[10]= {True, False, True, False}
```

The command **IndexaQ** returns True only on type-a indices. There are also **IndexbQ** and **IndexcQ**, which act like **IndexaQ**, but on type-b and type-c indices, respectively.

```
In[11]:= {IndexaQ[ud], IndexaQ[aud],
    IndexaQ[ld], IndexaQ[ald]}

Out[11]= {False, True, False, True}
```

Here is a list containing two types of indices and two integers.

```
In[12]:= list = {la, ala, -1, 25}

Out[12]= { , , -1, 25}
         a  a'
```

This uses **Map**, or **/@**, to apply **IndexQ** to each element of **list**. **IndexQ** returns False when acting on integers.

```
In[13]:= IndexQ /@ list

Out[13]= {True, True, False, False}
```

IndexIntQ acts like **IndexQ**, except that it returns True when acting on integers.

```
In[14]:= IndexIntQ /@ list

Out[14]= {True, True, True, True}
```

`LowerIndexQ[`*index*`]`	true only if *index* is a regular lower index
`LowerIndexaQ[`*index*`]`	true only if *index* is a type-a lower index
`LowerIndexbQ, LowerIndexcQ`	like `LowerIndexaQ`, but for indices of types b and c
`LowerIndexAllTypesQ[`*index*`]`	true if *index* is a lower index of any type
`UpperIndexQ[`*index*`]`	true only if *index* is a regular upper index
`UpperIndexaQ[`*index*`]`	true only if *index* is a type-a upper index
`UpperIndexbQ, UpperIndexcQ`	like `UpperIndexaQ`, but for indices of types b and c
`UpperIndexAllTypesQ[`*index*`]`	true if *index* is an upper index of any type
`IndexaQ[`*index*`]`	true only if *index* is a type-a index
`IndexbQ, IndexcQ`	like IndexaQ, but for indices of types b and c
`IndexQ[`*index*`]`	true if *index* is a symbolic index of any type
`IndexAllTypesQ[`*index*`]`	same as `IndexQ`
`IndexIntQ[`*index*`]`	true if *index* is a symbolic index or integer
`IndexUpLoQ[`*index*`]`	true if *index* is among `lo1,up1,...,lo10,up10`
`IndexIntUpLoQ[`*index*`]`	true if either `IndexIntQ` or `IndexUpLoQ` is True
`LowerIndexQ[`*index*`] || UpperIndexQ[`*index*`]`	
	true only if *index* is a regular index

Tests used to distinguish between types of indices.

`IndexUpLoQ` is included because the indices `lo1,up1,...,lo10,up10` it recognizes appear in the statement of the rules created by `RuleUnique` and `DefUnique`. Occasionally, you may want to distinguish those indices. `IndexIntUpLoQ` is included for the same reason, as is `ArglistIntUpLo`.

When creating sets of rules, you will also need tests that recognize pairs of summation or dummy indices of each type.

PairQ is True when the indices form a regular dummy pair. Each argument may also be given as a list of indices.

```
In[15]:= {PairQ[ld,ud], PairQ[ld,le],
    PairQ[ald,aud]}
Out[15]= {True, False, False}
```

If lists of indices are used as arguments, then the result is True only when corresponding indices form regular matching pairs in the order given.

```
In[16]:= {PairQ[{la,lb,lc},{ua,ub,uc}],
   PairQ[{la,lb,lc},{ua,uc,ub}],
    PairQ[{la,lb,lc},{ua,ld,uc}] }
Out[16]= {True, False, False}
```

There are also PairaQ, PairbQ, and PaircQ, which act like PairQ, but on indices of types a, b, and c, respectively.

```
In[17]:= {PairaQ[ld,ud], PairaQ[ald,ale],
   PairaQ[ald,aud]}
Out[17]= {False, False, True}
```

PairAllTypesQ gives True when pairs of any types of indices are formed.

```
In[18]:= PairAllTypesQ[{ald,bue,lf}, {aud,ble,uf}]
Out[18]= True
```

PairQ[*index1*,*index2*]	true only if the indices are a summed pair of regular indices, such as le,ue
PairQ[{*i1*,*i2*,..},{*j1*,*j2*,..}]	true only if *i1*, *j1* and *i2*, *j2*, etc., are summed pairs of regular indices
PairaQ, PairbQ, PaircQ	like PairQ, but for indices of types a, b, and c, respectively
PairAllTypesQ[*index1*,*index2*]	true only if the indices are a summed pair of indices of any type
PairAlltypesQ[{*i1*,*i2*,..},{*j1*,*j2*,..}]	true if *i1*, *j1* and *i2*, *j2*, etc., are summed pairs of indices of any type

Tests for pairs of indices of different types.

There are also commands for raising and lowering indices of each type as well as for replacing an index by its corresponding paired summation index (for example, replacing alc by auc or auc by alc).

Raise will raise lower regular indices and leave regular upper indices unchanged. Its action on other types of indices is undefined.

```
In[19]:= {Raise[ld], Raise[ue], Raise[ald]}
Out[19]= {  d,   e, Raise[  ]}
                            d′
```

The commands Riasea, Raiseb, and Raisec act like Raise, but on indices of types a, b, and c, respectively.

```
In[20]:= {Raisea[ald], Raisea[aue], Raisea[ld]}
Out[20]= {  d′,  e′, Raisea[ ]}
                              d
```

The corresponding operators for lowering indices also exist.

```
In[21]:= {Lower[ud],Lowera[aud],
          Lower[ld],Lowera[ald]}
```

$Out[21]= \{ \ _d, \ _{d'}, \ _d, \ _{d'} \}$

The raising and lowering commands also take lists as arguments.

```
In[22]:= Lowera[{aud,ale,auf}]
```

$Out[22]= \{ \ _{d'}, \ _{e'}, \ _{f'} \}$

LowerAllTypes lowers each type of upper index, while leaving lower indices alone.

```
In[23]:= LowerAllTypes[{ud,aud,bud,cud,le}]
```

$Out[23]= \{ \ _d, \ _{d'}, \ _{d''}, \ _{d'''}, \ _e \}$

Similarly, RaiseAllTypes raises each type of index.

```
In[24]:= RaiseAllTypes[{ld,ald,bld,cld,ue}]
```

$Out[24]= \{ \ ^d, \ ^{d'}, \ ^{d''}, \ ^{d'''}, \ ^e \}$

To lower regular upper indices and raise regular lower indices, you use the command Pair.

```
In[25]:= Pair[{la,ud,lc,uf}]
```

$Out[25]= \{ \ ^a, \ _d, \ ^c, \ _f \}$

Paira does the same thing for type-a indices. Pairb and Pairc do the same for indices of types b and c, respectively.

```
In[26]:= Paira[{ala,aud,alc,auf}]
```

$Out[26]= \{ \ ^{a'}, \ _{d'}, \ ^{c'}, \ _{f'} \}$

PairAllTypes changes upper and lower indices of all types.

```
In[27]:= PairAllTypes[{ld,ald,bue,clf}]
```

$Out[27]= \{ \ ^d, \ ^{d'}, \ _{e''}, \ ^{f'''} \}$

Pair[*index*]	gives the corresponding paired summation index only if *index* is a regular index
Paira, Pairb, Pairc	like Pair, but for indices of types a, b, and c, respectively
PairAllTypes[*index*]	gives the corresponding paired summation index if *index* is an index of any type
Lower[*index*]	lowers *index* if it is a regular index
Lowera, Lowerb, Lowerc	like Lower, but for indices of types a, b, and c, respectively
LowerAllTypes[*index*]	lowers *index* if it is an index of any type
Raise[*index*]	raises *index* if it is a regular index
Raisea, Raiseb, Raisec	like Raise, but for indices of types a, b, and c, respectively
RaiseAllTypes[*index*]	raises *index* if it is an index of any type

Commands transforming between corresponding upper and lower indices.

There are also commands you can apply to a tensor to produce a list of indices of a given type.

Define two fourth-rank tensors, s and t, having no special symmetries.

```
In[28]:= DefineTensor[{s,t},{{1,2,3,4},1}]
PermWeight::def: Object s defined
PermWeight::def: Object t defined
```

Let s and t take type-a and type-b indices, respectively, in their first two slots.

```
In[29]:= expr = s[ala,aua,lc,ld] t[bud,bld,uc,ue]
```

$$Out[29] = s_{a' \ cd}^{\ a'} \, t_{\ \ d''}^{d'' \ ce}$$

The command Arglist lists the indices of expr.

```
In[30]:= indexList = Arglist[expr]
```

$$Out[30] = \{_{a'}^{\ a'}, \ _{c'}^{\ }{}_{d'}, \ _{d''}^{\ d''}, \ ^{c}{}^{e}\}$$

Matchlista chooses the dummy indices of type-a in the list.

```
In[31]:= Matchlista[indexList]
```

$$Out[31] = \{_{a'}, \ ^{a'}\}$$

Matchlistb and Matchlistc choose the dummy indices of types b and c, respectively.

$In[32]:=$ Matchlistb[indexList]

$Out[32]= \{ _{d''}, {}^{d''} \}$

Matchlist chooses the regular dummy indices. Note that the indices 1d and ue in expr are not dummy indices.

$In[33]:=$ Matchlist[indexList]

$Out[33]= \{ _{c}, {}^{c} \}$

MatchlistAllTypes chooses dummy indices of all types.

$In[34]:=$ MatchlistAllTypes[indexList]

$Out[34]= \{ _{a'}{}^{a'}, {}_{c}{}^{c}, {}_{d''}{}^{d''} \}$

Arglist[*tensor*]	lists all the symbolic indices of *tensor*
ArglistAllTypes[*tensor*]	like *Arglist*
ArglistInt[*tensor*]	lists symbolic and integer indices of *tensor*
ArglistIntUpLo[*tensor*]	like ArglistInt, but also includes indices lo1,up1,...,lo10,up10 if present
Matchlist[*list*]	lists dummy pairs of regular indices in *list*
Matchlista, Matchlistb, Matchlistc	
	like Matchlist, but for indices of types a, b, and c, respectively
MatchlistAllTypes[*list*]	lists dummy pairs of indices of any type in *list*

Commands that filter lists of indices.

■ 4.3.3 Transformation Rules with Multiple Types of Indices

After you have loaded the multiple index module with AddIndexTypes, the commands RuleUnique and DefUnique will work as previously described, but with multiple types of indices. You can use indices of types a, b, and c as well as regular indices in your rules, and you can use conditionals that distinguish between different classes of indices.

As an example, consider a nonabelian gauge field $A^i{}_\mu$, where μ denotes a space-time coordinate index and i denotes a gauge group index. You can follow this example without knowing about nonabelian gauge fields and gauge groups. The main point of this example is to show you how to set up rules with more than one type of index. You can follow this example at the level of symbolic manipulation without knowing the deeper meaning of the groups and objects under consideration.

The gauge group is characterized by structure constants, f_{ijk}, that are totally antisymmetric. To be specific, take the gauge group to be $SU(2)$. For this group, the indices of the structure constants range over the values 1, 2, and 3, and $f_{123} = 1$. For the group $SU(2)$, the structure constants satisfy the rule,

$$f_{ijk} f^i{}_{lm} = \delta_{jl}\delta_{km} - \delta_{jm}\delta_{kl}.$$

Here, δ_{jl} denotes the usual Kronecker delta.

The Yang-Mills field strength $F^i{}_{\mu\nu}$ is defined to be

$$F^i{}_{\mu\nu} = \partial_\mu A^i{}_\nu - \partial_\nu A^i{}_\mu + g f^i{}_{jk} A^j{}_\mu A^k{}_\nu,$$

where g is the Yang-Mills coupling constant. Corresponding upper and lower gauge indices, like j and k in this equation, are dummy indices summed from 1 to 3. The gauge indices are raised and lowered with the Kronecker delta, which means that the values of the structure constants are not changed by raising and lowering gauge indices. Raised and lowered gauge indices are used here to conform to the convention that summation index pairs consist of one index in each position.

Enter the above-given equations into *MathTensor* and calculate the invariant quantity $F^i{}_{\mu\nu} F_i{}^{\mu\nu}$. Use the conventions that spacetime indices such as μ are denoted by regular indices and gauge indices such as i are denoted by type-a indices. The Kronecker delta, which has input name and print symbol `Kdelta`, is already known to *MathTensor*. Let the other quantities entering into these equations have the same input names as above but preceded by "YM" for Yang-Mills. The print symbols of those names will not be preceded by the letters "YM".

Start by defining the structure constants. Their input name is `YMf`, their print name is f, and they are antisymmetric.

```
In[1]:= DefineTensor[YMf, "f",
    {{2,1,3},-1, {1,3,2},-1, {3,2,1},-1}]
PermWeight::sym: Symmetries of f assigned
PermWeight::def: Object f defined
```

This defines the gauge field $A^i{}_\mu$. The first index will be the gauge index and the second the spacetime index.

```
In[2]:= DefineTensor[YMA, "A", {{1,2},1}]
PermWeight::def: Object A defined
```

The Yang-Mills field strength $F^i{}_{\mu\nu}$ is antisymmetric under interchange of the last two slots, which will be reserved for the spacetime indices.

```
In[3]:= DefineTensor[YMF, "F", {{1,3,2},-1}]
PermWeight::sym: Symmetries of F assigned
PermWeight::def: Object F defined
```

The input and print symbols of the coupling constant are entered through **DefineTensor** using the syntax for a scalar. If the input and print symbols were the same, this step would be unnecessary.

```
In[4]:= DefineTensor[YMg, "g"]
PermWeight::def: Object g defined
```

The multiple index module is activated, making type-a, b, and c indices available in addition to regular indices.

```
In[5]:= AddIndexTypes
```

This is the rule given above involving the structure constants. Looking at the equation above that this rule is based upon, you will see that all indices are lower indices, except for one of the summation indices. Because upper indices will be ordered after lower indices in the antisymmetric structure constants, the summation index d appears as the last index, assuming it is the upper index.

```
In[6]:= RuleUnique[ structureProductRule1,
  YMf[a_,b_,c_] YMf[e_,f_,d_],
  Kdelta[b,e] Kdelta[c,f] - Kdelta[b,f] Kdelta[c,e],
  PairaQ[a,d]
  ]
```

This gives the case in which the lower summation index is the second index in the first term of the product.

```
In[7]:= RuleUnique[ structureProductRule2,
  YMf[b_,a_,c_] YMf[e_,f_,d_],
  -Kdelta[b,e] Kdelta[c,f] + Kdelta[b,f] Kdelta[c,e],
  PairaQ[a,d]
  ]
```

This gives the case in which the lower summation index is the third index in the first term of the product. It is not necessary to add rules for the cases in which the order of terms in the product is reversed, since *Mathematica* automatically checks reordering of terms in a product.

```
In[8]:= RuleUnique[ structureProductRule3,
  YMf[b_,c_,a_] YMf[e_,f_,d_],
  Kdelta[b,e] Kdelta[c,f] - Kdelta[b,f] Kdelta[c,e],
  PairaQ[a,d]
  ]
```

Finally, the three rules are joined into a single set of rules.

```
In[9]:= structureProductRule :=
{structureProductRule1, structureProductRule2,
structureProductRule3}
```

This rule replaces the Yang-Mills field strength by the expression given above involving the gauge field and structure constants. Note that ala and aua are type-a dummy indices appearing in the rule. They are replaced by a unique pair of type-a dummy indices upon each application of the rule.

```
In[10]:= RuleUnique[ fieldStrengthRule,
  YMF[a_,b_,c_],
  OD[YMA[a,c],b] - OD[YMA[a,b],c] +
  YMg YMf[a,ala,alb] YMA[aua,b] YMA[aub,c],
  IndexaQ[a]
  ]
```

Here is a product of structure constants.

$In[11] :=$ `YMf[aua,alb,alc] YMf[ala,ald,ale]`

$$Out[11] = f_{a'd'e'} \; f_{b'c'}^{a'}$$

This is a test of the first rule.

$In[12] :=$ `ApplyRules[ %, structureProductRule]`

$$Out[12] = -(Kdelta_{b'e'} \; Kdelta_{c'd'}) + Kdelta_{b'd'} \; Kdelta_{c'e'}$$

This tests the second rule.

$In[13] :=$ `ApplyRules[ YMF[aua,la,lb], fieldStrengthRule]`

$$Out[13] = -A^{a'}_{a,b} + A^{a'}_{b,a} + g \, A^{p'}_{a} \, A^{q'}_{b} \, f_{p'q'}^{a'}$$

This is the invariant to be expanded in terms of the gauge field. Primed indices are type-a indices, which represent gauge group indices, and regular (unprimed) indices are spacetime indices.

$In[14] :=$ `expr = YMF[aua,la,lb] YMF[ala,ua,ub]`

$$Out[14] = F^{ab}_{a'} \, F^{a'}_{ab}$$

An attempt to simplify this long expression is in order.

$In[15] :=$ `Expand[ ApplyRules[expr,fieldStrengthRule] ]`

$$Out[15] = 2 \, A^{p\,q\,p'}_{p',} \, A_{p,q} - 2 \, A^{p\,q\,p'}_{p',} \, A_{q,p} +$$

$$> \quad g \, A^{p'}_{p,q} \, A^{q'q} \, A^{r'p} \, f_{p'q'r'} -$$

$$> \quad g \, A^{p'}_{p,q} \, A^{q'p} \, A^{r'q} \, f_{p'q'r'} +$$

$$> \quad g \, A^{p}_{p',q} \, A^{q'q} \, A^{r'}_{p} \, f_{q'r'}^{p'} -$$

$$> \quad g \, A^{p}_{p',q} \, A^{q'} \, A^{r'q}_{p} \, f_{q'r'}^{p'} +$$

$$> \quad g^{2} \, A^{p'p}_{p} \, A^{q'q}_{q} \, A^{r'} \, A^{s'} \, f_{p'q't'} \, f_{r's'}^{t'}$$

The seven terms have simplified to four terms.

```
In[16]:= Tsimplify[%]

              p q  p'            p q  p'
Out[16]= 2 A       A      - 2 A       A       +
             p' ,   p,q         p' ,   q,p

              p'    q'q r'p
   >   4 g A       A   A    f      +
             p,q            p'q'r'

        2  p'p q'q r'     s'              t'
   >   g  A   A   A     A     f        f
                   p     q    p'q't'  r's'
```

The expressions involving Kronecker deltas can be evaluated by means of the existing *MathTensor* set of rules called **KdeltaRule**.

```
In[17]:= Expand[ ApplyRules[%,structureProductRule] ]

              p q  p'            p q  p'
Out[17]= 2 A       A      - 2 A       A      -
             p' ,   p,q         p' ,   q,p

        2                          p'p q'   r'q s'
   >   g  Kdelta      Kdelta      A   A    A   A    +
               p'q'        r's'         q        p

        2                          p'p q'   r'q s'
   >   g  Kdelta      Kdelta      A   A    A   A    +
               p'q'        r's'        p        q

              p'    q'q r'p
   >   4 g A       A   A    f
             p,q            p'q'r'
```

This is the desired result. This is the expansion that gives rise to cubic and quartic interactions in the Yang-Mills Lagrangian, which governs the strong interactions of elementary particles.

```
In[18]:= ApplyRulesRepeated[ %, KdeltaRule]

              p q  p'            p q  p'
Out[18]= 2 A       A      - 2 A       A      -
             p' ,   p,q         p' ,   q,p

        2  p   q p'   q'     2  p   q p'   q'
   >   g  A   A   A   A    + g  A   A   A   A    +
            p'  q'  q   p          p'  q'  p   q

              p'    q'q r'p
   >   4 g A       A   A    f
             p,q            p'q'r'
```

This example shows how rules with more than one type of index can be created and used. The example is from particle physics, but there is no reason why it could not have been from any other area of mathematics, science, or engineering. Powerful knowledge-base files containing sets of rules relevant to particular applications of interest to you can be built up in the same way.

Kdelta[*index1*,*index2*]	the Kronecker delta
KdeltaRule	rule set applicable to expressions containing Kronecker deltas
AbosrbKdelta[*expr*]	applies KdeltaRule to *expr*

Commands relevant to the Kronecker delta.

■ 4.3.4 Warnings about Using Kdelta

The Kronecker delta, denoted by Kdelta, is defined in *MathTensor* to have components equal to 1 when its two indices have the same absolute numerical value and components equal to 0 otherwise, regardless of whether the indices are upper, lower, or mixed. This implies that, in general, Kdelta does not transform as a tensor. Furthermore, the command AbsorbKdelta, when applied to an expression containing products involving Kdelta with symbolic indices, causes the factors of Kdelta to be absorbed in raising or lowering indices in exactly the same way that the command Absorbg causes factors of Metricg to be absorbed when MetricgFlag is off. Obviously, when Kdelta and Metricg are different the use of AbsorbKdelta can lead to incorrect results. For example, AbsorbKdelta[Kdelta[la,lb] RicciR[ub,uc]] will give the result RicciR[la,uc], which is wrong unless the metric tensor is the same as Kdelta, as in a flat Euclidean space with Cartesian coordinates. Another possible inconsistency is that Kdelta[la,lb] Metricg[ub,uc] will give Kdelta[la,uc], which is wrong unless Metricg is equal to Kdelta (other positions of indices in this expression will also give wrong results). Thus you must be careful that you use the command AbsorbKdelta only when it is appropriate.

If you use Kdelta and Metricg with indices of the same type (i.e., in the same space), then unless Kdelta and Metricg are equal, you should avoid using AbsorbKdelta. You should also make sure that you have turned off MetricgFlag so that automatic absorption of factors of Metricg in raising or lowering indices on Kdelta will not occur. However, in such a situation you will usually find it simpler to avoid Kdelta altogether and to use Metricg instead with one covariant and one contravariant index.

Nevertheless, there are applications in which Kdelta is appropriate. For example, in calculations involving the Yang-Mills field, you can use Kdelta with group indices, while Metricg is used with regular spacetime indices. Such an example was included in the previous section. Kdelta may also be useful in other contexts, such as in a Euclidean space with Cartesian coordinates. The object Kdelta has been defined as described above because the Kronecker delta is commonly used, but in using it you should be aware of the pitfalls described above.

■ 4.3.5 Pauli Spin Matrices

As an illustration of the use of multiple index types, consider the Pauli spin matrices, s^1, s^2, and s^3. One explicit representation of these matrices is given by

$$s^1 = \begin{pmatrix} 0 & 1 \\ 1 & 0 \end{pmatrix}, \tag{4.4}$$

$$s^2 = \begin{pmatrix} 0 & -i \\ i & 0 \end{pmatrix}, \tag{4.5}$$

$$s^3 = \begin{pmatrix} 1 & 0 \\ 0 & -1 \end{pmatrix}. \tag{4.6}$$

In quantum mechanics, $(1/2)s^j$ represents the operator for the j'th component of the internal angular momentum of a spin-1/2 particle, such as an electron.

The Pauli matrices satisfy the equation

$$s^i s^j = \delta^{ij} + i\epsilon^{ij}{}_k s^k, \tag{4.7}$$

where the dummy index k is summed from 1 to 3 and the multiplication on the left-hand side is matrix multiplication. (The index i should not be confused with the imaginary number i that multiplies $\epsilon^{ij}{}_k$.) Here, $\epsilon^{ij}{}_k$ is the totally antisymmetric object with $\epsilon^{123} = 1$. The space is Euclidean with Cartesian coordinates, so that lowering an index does not change the value of ϵ. The above equation is more general than the particular matrix representation chosen for the Pauli matrices.

In the following *MathTensor* session, let us represent the index j on s^j by a regular index, such as la. Furthermore, let us show the matrix (or spinor) indices explicitly and represent them by type-a indices, such as ala. Thus s[la,aua,alb] represents $s^{aa'}{}_{b'}$, where a', b' are the matrix indices of the Pauli matrix s^a. It is instructive to construct a rule for the above-given equation and to use it to carry out a calculation.

First make all four index types available. *In[1]:=* **AddIndexTypes**

Define a three index object with no symmetries. Let the second and third slots be reserved for type-a indices and the first slot for regular indices.

In[2]:= **DefineTensor[s,{{1,2,3},1}]**

    PermWeight::def: Object s defined

You are responsible for remembering
which type of index goes in each slot.
There are functions (discussed in the next
section) for testing the index type. You
can use those tests, if you wish, to make
sure your rules trigger only with the
correct index type in each slot.

```
In[3]:= s[ua,aua,alb]

Out[3]= s  aa'
             b'
```

Suppose regular indices run from 1 to 3. It
is convenient to set `Dimension` to 3, so
that, for example, `EpsUp[1,2,3]` will be 1.

```
In[4]:= Dimension = 3

Out[4]= 3
```

This makes `Metricg` into a flat Euclidean
metric having diagonal values of 1. The
dimension of the metric is 3 because
`Dimension` is set to that value. Now the
regular type indices, as in
`EpsUp[ua,ub,lc]`, can be written as upper
or lower indices without changing the
value of `EpsUp`. This is convenient because
the summation convention requires one
upper and one lower index.

```
In[5]:= MakeMetricFlat[Euclid]

MakeMetricFlat::Ecld:
    Metricg is now Euclidean in Cartesian coordinates.
```

Use `RuleUnique` to define a rule callled
`sRule` for matrix multiplication of two of
the `s[ua,aua,alb]` objects regarded as
matrices labeled by the first index, with
the second pair of indices being the matrix
indices. The condition `PairaQ[alb,lub]`
requires patterns `alb_`, `aub_` to be a
dummy pair of type-a indices. The
patterns are given names here that make
it easier to understand the rule, but the
pattern names can actually be arbitrary.

```
In[6]:= RuleUnique[sRule, s[ua_,aua_,alb_] s[ub_,aub_,alc_],
            Kdelta[ua,ub] Kdelta[aua,alc] +
              I EpsUp[ua,ub,lc] s[uc,aua,alc],
                 PairaQ[alb,aub] ]
```

Here is something we can test our rule on.

```
In[7]:= s[1,auc,ald] s[1,aud,ale]

Out[7]= s  1c'   s  1d'
              d'      e'
```

The result is the unit matrix.

```
In[8]:= ApplyRules[%,sRule]

Out[8]= Kdelta  c'
                e'
```

Here is another matrix product.

```
In[9]:= s[1,auc,ald] s[2,aud,ale]

Out[9]= s  1c'   s  2d'
              d'      e'
```

There is a sum on the right.

```
In[10]:= ApplyRules[%,sRule]
```

$$Out[10]= I \; EpsUp_{p}^{12 \; pc'} \; s_{\;\;e'}$$

Because the sum involves regular dummy indices, you can use **MakeSum** here. Otherwise **MakeSumRange** would be used. **MakeSum** could also have been included in the definition of **sRule**.

```
In[11]:= MakeSum[%]
```

$$Out[11]= I \; s_{\;\;e'}^{3c'}$$

Here is the same product with indices 1 and 2 reversed.

```
In[12]:= s[2,auc,ald] s[1,aud,ale]
```

$$Out[12]= s_{\;\;e'}^{1d'} \; s_{\;\;d'}^{2c'}$$

This gives the previous result with opposite sign.

```
In[13]:= MakeSum[ApplyRules[%,sRule] ]
```

$$Out[13]= -I \; s_{\;\;e'}^{3c'}$$

Define two vectors c[la] and d[la], which will take regular indices.

```
In[14]:= DefineTensor[{c,d},{{1},1}]
```

PermWeight::def: Object c defined

PermWeight::def: Object d defined

Take the dot product of the vectors with a matrix product of two s matrices.

```
In[15]:= c[la] s[ua,aub,alc] s[ub,auc,ald] d[lb]
```

$$Out[15]= c_{a} \; d_{b} \; s_{\;\;c'}^{ab'} \; s_{\;\;d'}^{bc'}$$

In vector notation, you have found that $(c \cdot s)(d \cdot s) = c \cdot d \, 1 + I(c \times d) \cdot s$.

```
In[16]:= MakeSum[ApplyRules[%,sRule] ]
```

$$Out[16]= c_{3} \; d_{3} \; Kdelta_{\;\;d'}^{b'} \; + \; c_{2} \; d_{2} \; Kdelta_{\;\;d'}^{b'} \; +$$

$$> \quad c_{1} \; d_{1} \; Kdelta_{\;\;d'}^{b'} \; + \; I \; c_{2} \; d_{3} \; s_{\;\;d'}^{1b'} \; - \; I \; c_{3} \; d_{2} \; s_{\;\;d'}^{1b'} \; -$$

$$> \quad I \; c_{1} \; d_{3} \; s_{\;\;d'}^{2b'} \; + \; I \; c_{3} \; d_{1} \; s_{\;\;d'}^{2b'} \; + \; I \; c_{1} \; d_{2} \; s_{\;\;d'}^{3b'} \; -$$

$$> \quad I \; c_{2} \; d_{1} \; s_{\;\;d'}^{3b'}$$

The identity you have just proved has important applications in quantum mechanics.

■ 4.3.6 Summing Expressions with Several Types of Indices

In Section 4.1.2, the commands `MakeSum`, `SetComponents`, and `MakeSumRange` were illustrated with regular dummy indices. As discussed there, the commands `MakeSum` and `SetComponents` work only with regular dummy indices, such as `la,ua`, and require that `Dimension` be set to an integer that determines the range of summation. When more than one type of dummy index is present, the ranges of summation will often be different for each type, so more flexibility is required. In dealing with the Pauli spin matrices, for example, regular indices were summed with `MakeSum` and type-a indices were used only symbolically, with dummy index pairs denoting matrix multiplication. But you may also want to perform explicit sums over type-a indices.

The command `MakeSumRange`, which was illustrated earlier with regular indices, is perfectly general. It can be used with any of the recognized types of dummy indices, and the summation ranges can include symbolic as well as integer indices. Here are examples of some of the ways of using `MakeSumRange` with more than one type of index.

The first example involves the Pauli matrices discussed in the previous section. The example illustrates the use of `MakeSumRange` to sum dummy indices of type-a over a specified range of integers. The next example illustrates summation over a range containing both symbolic and integer indices.

Make all four types of indices available.   *In[1]:=* `AddIndexTypes`

Here are the explicit Pauli matrices given   *In[2]:=* `sMatrix[1] = {{0,1},{1,0}};sMatrix[2] =`
at the start of the previous section.   `{{0,-I},{I,0}}; sMatrix[3] =`
                                                            `{{1,0},{0,-1}};`

Define the same 3-index $s^{aa'}{}_b$ objects as in   *In[3]:=* `DefineTensor[s,{{1,2,3},1}]`
the previous section.
                                                  `PermWeight::def: Object s defined`

This assigns the components of   *In[4]:=* `s[n_?PosIntegerQ, i_?PosIntegerQ,`
`s[ua,aua,alb]`. Since the final index is a   `j_?NegIntegerQ] := sMatrix[n][[i,-j]]`
lower index, it is replaced by a *negative*
integer when dealing with a specific
component.

Here is a symbolic matrix product.   *In[5]:=* `s[2,aua,alb] s[3,aub,alc]`

                                        Out[5]= $s^{2a'}{}_{b'}\, s^{3b'}{}_{c'}$

This carries out the matrix product. You have to start the list in **MakeSumRange** with the name of the *lower* member of the dummy pair of indices that you are summing.

```
In[6]:= MakeSumRange[%,{alb,-1,-2}]
```

$$Out[6]= s_1{}^{2a'}s_{c'}{}^{31} + s_2{}^{2a'}s_{c'}{}^{32}$$

Finally, display the full matrix by assigning values to the symbolic indices using **Table**. Note that the *input* names of the indices must be used, and in {alc,-1,-2,-1} the step size of −1 must be specified explicitly. As expected, this is I **sMatrix[1]**.

```
In[7]:= Table[%,{aua,2},{alc,-1,-2,-1}]//MatrixForm
```

$$Out[7]//MatrixForm=\begin{matrix}0 & I \\ I & 0\end{matrix}$$

Of course, you could have gotten the same result by multiplying the matrices directly using the dot operator.

```
In[8]:= sMatrix[2] . sMatrix[3]
```

$$Out[8]= \{\{0, I\}, \{I, 0\}\}$$

This expression involves a sum over regular indices (which run from 1 to 3) and a sum over a pair of type-a indices (which run from 1 to 2).

```
In[9]:= expr =
    Kdelta[la,lb] s[ua,aua,alb] s[ub,aub,alc]
```

$$Out[9]= Kdelta_{ab}\ s_{b'}{}^{aa'}\ s_{c'}{}^{bb'}$$

Define a convenient function to facilitate doing the sums.

```
In[10]:= range[a_,b_Integer] :=
Flatten[{a,Table[-i,{i,b}]}]
```

This generates the summation range for a regular index **la**. The **InputForm** shows what you would have to type.

```
In[11]:= range[la,3]//InputForm
```

$$Out[11]//InputForm= \{la, -1, -2, -3\}$$

This performs the sums on the dummy indices of each type, over the correct ranges.

```
In[12]:= MakeSumRange[expr,
    range[la,3],range[lb,3],range[alb,2] ]
```

$$Out[12]= s_{c'}{}^{12}s_2{}^{1a'} + s_{c'}{}^{11}s_1{}^{1a'} + s_{c'}{}^{22}s_2{}^{2a'} +$$

$$> \quad s_{c'}{}^{21}s_1{}^{2a'} + s_{c'}{}^{32}s_2{}^{3a'} + s_{c'}{}^{31}s_1{}^{3a'}$$

Display the components of the sum in matrix form. The result is 3 times the unit matrix.

```
In[13]:= Table[%,{aua,2},{alc,-1,-2,-1}]//MatrixForm
```

$$Out[13]//MatrixForm=\begin{matrix}3 & 0 \\ 0 & 3\end{matrix}$$

In special relativity, an inertial frame is a set of standard rods and clocks that are not moving relative to one another and are not undergoing acceleration. The rods can be used to set up a Cartesian coordinate system, and clocks at different locations can be synchronized by means of light pulses. Any two different inertial frames move at constant velocity relative to one another. The transformation of the space and time coordinates (x, y, z, t) of an event from one inertial frame to another is known as a Lorentz transformation. It can be represented by a constant 4×4 transformation matrix $L^a{}_b$. Here the indices a and b take values 1 to 4. The Minkowski metric, $g_{ab} =$ {{1,0,0,0},{0,1,0,0},{0,0,1,0},{0,0,0,-1}}, is not changed by the transformation, i.e.,

$$L^a{}_c L^b{}_d g_{ab} = g_{cd}. \tag{4.8}$$

Suppose that the second inertial frame is moving at constant velocity $v^{a'}$ (a' runs from 1 to 3) relative to the first. By considering the space and time coordinates of the origin of the second frame relative to the first, you can show that

$$L^{a'}{}_4 = v^{a'} L^4{}_4. \tag{4.9}$$

Continuing the previous *MathTensor* session, show that these equations determine the value of $L^4{}_4$ (see, for example, Weinberg 1972, p. 29). Note that `MakeSumRange` in this example performs summations over a range containing symbolic and integer indices.

The dimension of spacetime is 4.

```
In[14]:= Dimension = 4;
```

This makes `Metricg` into the Minkowski metric.

```
In[15]:= MakeMetricFlat[Minkowski]

MakeMetricFlat::Mnkwski:
    Metricg is now Minkowskian with Metricg[-1,-1] = 1.
```

Since `Metricg` will appear in the transformation rule involving the metric, you do not want it to be absorbed through lowering or raising indices.

```
In[16]:= Off[MetricgFlag]
```

This defines the Lorentz tranformation matrix $L^a{}_b$.

```
In[17]:= DefineTensor[L,{{1,2},1}]

PermWeight::def: Object L defined
```

This defines the velocity vector $v^{a'}$.

```
In[18]:= DefineTensor[v,{{1},1}]

PermWeight::def: Object v defined
```

This sets up `LorentzRule`, which expresses the invariance of the metric under Lorentz transformation.

```
In[19]:= RuleUnique[LorentzRule,
  L[a_,c_] L[b_,d_] Metricg[e_,f_], Metricg[c,d],
    (PairQ[a,e]&& PairQ[b,f])||
      (PairQ[a,f]&& PairQ[b,e]) ]
```

This expression should match the left-hand side of the rule.

$In[20]:=$ `L[ua,1c] L[ub,1d] Metricg[1a,1b]`

$Out[20]=$ $L^a_{\ \ c} L^b_{\ \ d} g_{ab}$

This tests that the rule works properly.

$In[21]:=$ `ApplyRules[%,LorentzRule]`

$Out[21]=$ g_{cd}

This rule embodies the equation involving the relative velocity of two inertial frames. Notice that the condition `UpperIndexaQ[a]` in `vRule` requires `a_` to match an upper index of type-a (such as aua). The type-a indices run from 1 to 3.

$In[22]:=$ `RuleUnique[vRule, L[a_,-4],`
    `v[a] L[4,-4], UpperIndexaQ[a] ]`

You can test the rule on this expression.

$In[23]:=$ `L[aua,-4]`

$Out[23]=$ $L^{a'}_{\ \ 4}$

It works.

$In[24]:=$ `ApplyRules[%,vRule]`

$Out[24]=$ $L^4_{\ \ 4} v^{a'}$

The rule is not triggered by this expression because it involves a regular index.

$In[25]:=$ `ApplyRules[L[ua,-4],vRule]`

$Out[25]=$ $L^a_{\ \ 4}$

This rule will set, for example, `Metricg[-4,a1b]` (i.e., $g_{4b'}$) to 0. Since no dummy indices appear on the right-hand side of this rule, there is no need to use `RuleUnique` in this case.

$In[26]:=$ `g1Rule = Metricg[-4,a_?IndexaQ] :> 0;`

This tests the rule.

$In[27]:=$ `Metricg[-4,a1b]/.g1Rule`

$Out[27]=$ 0

This rule sets, for example, $g_{a'b'}$ to $Kdelta_{a'b'}$, since a' and b' are each in the range 1 through 3.

$In[28]:=$ `g2Rule =`
    `Metricg[a_?IndexaQ,b_?IndexaQ] :>`
        `Kdelta[a,b];`

Here is an example application of the rule.

```
In[29]:= Metricg[ala,alb]/.g2Rule
Out[29]= Kdelta
              a'b'
```

This combines both rules into one called gRule.

```
In[30]:= gRule := {g1Rule, g2Rule}
```

You can determine the components of $L^a{}_0$ by considering this expression.

```
In[31]:= expr = L[ua,-4] L[ub,-4] Metricg[la,lb]
           a   b
Out[31]= L   L   g
           4   4  ab
```

Thus expr is equal to -(Lightc)^2. Lightc represents the speed of light and appears as c in the output line.

```
In[32]:= ApplyRules[expr,LorentzRule]
             2
Out[32]= -c
```

In expr, this sums the index la over the symbolic value ala (which takes values 1 to 3) and the integer value -4. The paired dummy index ua is automatically summed over aua and 4. The dummy pair lb, ub is also summed. Here $L^4{}_4{}^2$ stands for $(L^4{}_4)^2$.

```
In[33]:= MakeSumRange[expr,{la,ala,-4},{lb,alb,-4}]
             2 4 2      4  a'       4  b'
Out[33]= -(c  L  )  + L   L   g    + L   L   g    +
               4        4   4  4a'     4   4  4b'

         >    a'  b'
              L   L   g
              4   4  a'b'
```

This eliminates terms involving components of the metric that are zero and replaces the purely spatial components of the metric by the Kronecker delta.

```
In[34]:= %/.gRule
             2 4 2              a'  b'
Out[34]= -(c  L  )  + Kdelta    L   L
               4           a'b'  4   4
```

This imposes the rule that $L^{a'}{}_4 \to L^4{}_4 v^{a'}$.

```
In[35]:= %/.vRule
             2 4 2             4 2  a'  b'
Out[35]= -(c  L  )  + Kdelta   L   v   v
               4          a'b'  4
```

Recall that you found earlier that expr equals -Lightc^2. Define eq to be the equation that states this.

```
In[36]:= eq = % == -Lightc^2
             2 4 2             4 2  a'  b'        2
Out[36]= -(c  L  )  + Kdelta   L   v   v    == -c
               4          a'b'  4
```

Thus the value of $L^4{}_4$ is $(1 - v^2/c^2)^{-1/2}$, where $v^2 \equiv (v^1)^2 + (v^2)^2 + (v^3)^2$. The positive solution is chosen, so that time in both inertial frames will run in the same direction. This value of $L^4{}_4$ is responsible for the time dilation, according to which a moving clock runs slow relative to a set of identical stationary clocks.

```
In[37]:= Solve[eq, L[4,-4]]

                           c
Out[37]= {{L  4  ->  -----------------------},
             4        Sqrt[c  - Kdelta     v  v  ]
                            2          a' b'
                                      a'b'

                                  c
   >     {L  4  -> -(-----------------------)}}
            4        Sqrt[c  - Kdelta     v  v  ]
                          2          a' b'
                                    a'b'
```

```
MakeSumRange[expr,{la,ala,-4},{lb,alb,-4}]
```
sum dummy index `la` over values `ala` and `-4`, and sum dummy index `lb` over `alb` and `-4`. Here `expr` can be, for example, `L[ua,-4] L[ub,-4] Metricg[la,lb]`.

Summing over a range with both symbolic and integer indices.

■ 4.4 **Manipulating Equations in *MathTensor***

In order to help you with the manipulation of equations (which contain an `==` sign), there are a number of commands available in *MathTensor* that supplement those available in *Mathematica*. Some of these commands simply apply the *Mathematica* operation indicated in the name of the command to each side of an equation. For example, `EqApart[eq]` applies `Apart` to each side of an equation, and `EqCollect[eq,{x1,x2}]` applies `Collect`, with the argument `{x1,x2}`, to each side of an equation. On the other hand, `EqReverse` interchanges the left-hand and right-hand sides of `eq`, which does not correspond to a *Mathematica* command. Commands that start with `EqTwo` manipulate a pair of equations. For example, if `eq1` and `eq2` are two equations, then `EqTwoDivide[eq1,eq2]` divides each side of `eq1` by the corresponding side of `eq2`. Note that the command `EqApply` as described below follows a different syntax than the *Mathematica* command `Apply`. These *MathTensor* commands for manipulating equations are designed to work with any kind of equations, not just those involving tensor expressions.

Finally, the command `EqSolve` differs from the *Mathematica* command `Solve` in that it is designed to solve algebraically for a specified combination of symbols, such as a product or sum of symbols. This ability is useful, for example, when one is trying to solve a tensor equation for a term that involves a product of tensors contracted over some indices, such as the combination `RiemannR[la,lb,lc,ld] RicciR[ub,ud]`. `EqSolve` will not make use of the inverse metric or other inverse tensors to solve tensor equations. Here is a list of the commands for manipulating equations.

EqApart Applies `Apart` to each side of an equation.

EqApply `EqApply[eq, op, x]` applies `op` to each side of the equation `eq`, with x as the second argument. For example, `EqApply[y==z,Plus,3]` gives `Plus[y,3]==Plus[z,3]`, or `y+3==z+3`.

EqCancel Applies `Cancel` to each side of an equation.

EqCollect `EqCollect[eq,x]` collects together terms involving the same power of x on each side of an equation. If x is a list, collects terms having the same powers of the elements of the list.

EqDivide `EqDivide[eq,x]` divides each side of `eq` by `x`.

EqExpand Applies `Expand` to each side of an equation.

EqExpandAll Applies `ExpandAll` to each side of an equation.

EqFactor Applies `Factor` to each side of an equation.

EqFactorTerms Applies `FactorTerms` to each side of an equation.

EqMinus Multiplies each side of an equation by `-1`.

EqPlus `EqPlus[eq,x]` adds x to each side of `eq`.

EqPower `EqPower[eq,x]` raises each side of `eq` to the power `x`.

EqPowerExpand `EqPowerExpand[eq]` expands all powers of products and powers on each side of `eq`. For example, `EqPowerExpand[((x + y)^3)^(1/3) == 0] -> x + y == 0`.

EqReverse Reverses the sides of an equation.

EqSimplify Applies `Simplify` to each side of an equation.

EqSolve `EqSolve[eq,expr]` solves `eq` for `expr`, where `expr` can be a product of objects such as tensors. The user should be aware that `EqSolve` does not understand tensor analysis and should only be used when purely algebraic operations that do not break the bonds of dummy indices can be used to solve for the requested object.

EqSubtract `EqSubtract[eq,x]` subtacts x from each side of `eq`.

EqTimes `EqTimes[eq,x]` multiplies each side of `eq` by `x`.

EqTogether Applies `Together` to each side of eq.

EqTwoDivide `EqTwoDivide[eq1,eq2]` divides each side of eq1 by the corresponding side of eq2, where eq1 and eq2 are equations.

EqTwoPlus `EqTwoPlus[eq1,eq2]` adds each side of eq1 to the corresponding side of eq2.

EqTwoSubtract `EqTwoSubtract[eq1,eq2]` subtracts each side of eq2 from the corresponding side of eq1.

EqTwoTimes `EqTwoTimes[eq1,eq2]` multiplies each side of eq1 by the corresponding side of eq2.

Here is a *MathTensor* session illustrating the use of several of these commands for manipulating equations.

Suppose that you want to solve this equation for **x**. You could use `Solve`, but will get back the solutions of a cubic equation.

```
In[1]:= eq1 = x^3 + y^3 + 3 x^2 y + 3 y^2 x +
          5 == y^2 + 4 z^2 + 4 y z - 3
```
$$Out[1] = 5 + x^3 + 3 x^2 y + 3 x y^2 + y^3 ==$$
$$> \quad -3 + y^2 + 4 y z + 4 z^2$$

You can get simpler results by manipulating the equation directly if you know that x and y are real. First subtract 5 from each side.

```
In[2]:= EqSubtract[eq1,5]
```
$$Out[2] = x^3 + 3 x^2 y + 3 x y^2 + y^3 ==$$
$$> \quad -8 + y^2 + 4 y z + 4 z^2$$

Factor each side.

```
In[3]:= EqFactor[%]
```
$$Out[3] = (x + y)^3 == -8 + y^2 + 4 y z + 4 z^2$$

Raise each side to the 1/3 power.

```
In[4]:= EqPower[%,1/3]
```
$$Out[4] = ((x + y)^3)^{1/3} == (-8 + y^2 + 4 y z + 4 z^2)^{1/3}$$

Expand the power of a power.

```
In[5]:= EqPowerExpand[%]
```
$$Out[5] = x + y == (-8 + y^2 + 4 y z + 4 z^2)^{1/3}$$

This gives the desired solution for **x**.

```
In[6]:= EqSubtract[%,y]
```
$$Out[6] = x == -y + (-8 + y^2 + 4 y z + 4 z^2)^{1/3}$$

Here is a second equation. Manipulate eq1 and eq2 to find x in terms of y.

$In[7]:= \texttt{eq2 = y^2 + 4 y z == 8 - 4 z^2}$

$Out[7]= y^2 + 4\ y\ z == 8 - 4\ z^2$

Add the 4 z^2 to both sides of eq2.

$In[8]:= \texttt{EqPlus[eq2, 4 z^2]}$

$Out[8]= y^2 + 4\ y\ z + 4\ z^2 == 8$

Reverse the sides of the equation.

$In[9]:= \texttt{EqReverse[\%]}$

$Out[9]= 8 == y^2 + 4\ y\ z + 4\ z^2$

Now subtract each side from eq1.

$In[10]:= \texttt{EqTwoSubtract[eq1,\%]}$

$Out[10]= -3 + x^3 + 3\ x^2\ y + 3\ x\ y^2 + y^3 == -3$

Add 3 to each side.

$In[11]:= \texttt{EqPlus[\%,3]}$

$Out[11]= x^3 + 3\ x^2\ y + 3\ x\ y^2 + y^3 == 0$

This equation is easily solved for x by inspection, but let us proceed to the finish.

$In[12]:= \texttt{EqFactor[\%]}$

$Out[12]= (x + y)^3 == 0$

Now the equation is linear.

$In[13]:= \texttt{EqPowerExpand[EqPower[\%,1/3]]}$

$Out[13]= x + y == 0$

Here is the solution for x of eq1 and eq2. If you had used Solve[{eq1,eq2},x], the solution would have appeared more complicated.

$In[14]:= \texttt{EqSubtract[\%,y]}$

$Out[14]= x == -y$

The terms in this equation can be grouped in different ways.

$In[15]:= \texttt{eq3 = EqPlus[eq2,a y^2 + b z^2 + c y z]}$

$Out[15]= y^2 + a\ y^2 + 4\ y\ z + c\ y\ z + b\ z^2 ==$
$> \qquad 8 + a\ y^2 + c\ y\ z - 4\ z^2 + b\ z^2$

This groups terms by powers of z.

$In[16]:= \texttt{EqCollect[eq3,z]}$

$Out[16]= y^2 + a\ y^2 + (4\ y + c\ y)\ z + b\ z^2 ==$
$> \qquad 8 + a\ y^2 + c\ y\ z + (-4 + b)\ z^2$

This groups terms by powers of y and z.

$In[17] := $ `EqCollect[eq3,{y,z}]`

$Out[17] = (1 + a)\ y^2 + (4 + c)\ y\ z + b\ z^2 == $

$> \quad 8 + a\ y^2 + c\ y\ z + (-4 + b)\ z^2$

Here is another equation.

$In[18] := $ `eq4 = x^4 - 2 x^2 + 1 == 0`

$Out[18] = 1 - 2\ x^2 + x^4 == 0$

Applying `EqFactor` shows that there are two double roots, 1 and −1.

$In[19] := $ `EqFactor[eq4]`

$Out[19] = (-1 + x)^2\ (1 + x)^2 == 0$

`EqFactor` is not equipped to handle a second argument in the manner of `Factor`.

$In[20] := $ `EqFactor[eq4, Modulus->3]`

$Out[20] = $ `EqFactor[`$1 - 2\ x^2 + x^4 == 0$`, Modulus -> 3]`

In such a situation, you can use `EqApply`, which in this case applies `Factor`, with the second argument `Modulus->3`, to each side of `eq4`. The double roots found are −1 and −2, which is equal to 1 modulo 3, that is, `Mod[-2,3]->1`.

$In[21] := $ `EqApply[eq4, Factor, Modulus->3]`

$Out[21] = (1 + x)^2\ (2 + x)^2 == 0$

Suppose that you want to solve this equation for `MaxwellF[la,lb]*MaxwellF[ua,ub]`.

$In[22] := $ `3 MaxwellF[la,lb] MaxwellF[ua,ub] +`
`ScalarR == 2 RicciR[la,lb] RicciR[ua,ub]`

$Out[22] = R + 3\ F_{ab}\ F^{ab} == 2\ R_{ab}\ R^{ab}$

`EqSolve` gives the solution.

$In[23] := $ `EqSolve[%, MaxwellF[la,lb] MaxwellF[ua,ub] ]`

$$Out[23] = \{\{F_{ab}\ F^{ab} \to \frac{-(R - 2\ R_{ab}\ R^{ab})}{3}\}\}$$

These examples should be sufficient to illustrate how the listed commands for manipulating equations work.

■ 4.5 Unit Systems, Constants, Sign Conventions

You have a choice of unit systems in which certain equations and rules known to *MathTensor* will be expressed. For example, by giving the command `RationalizedMKS`, you can tell *MathTensor* to express Maxwell's equations, and other rules that it knows that are relevant to electromagnetism, in rationalized MKS or SI units. Here are the unit systems for expressing Maxwell's equations that you can choose in *MathTensor*. The command that chooses the system of units is usually put into a file called `Conventions.m`, together with values that determine sign conventions. No units are chosen by default. You may either set them temporarily in a *MathTensor* session, or you may set them permanently by editing the last few lines of the `Conventions.m` file.

emuUnits Electromagnetic units

esuUnits Electrostatic units

GaussianUnits Gaussian units

HeavisideLorentzUnits Heaviside-Lorentz units

RationalizedMKSUnits Rationalized MKS or SI units

SIUnits Rationalized MKS or SI units

Units Command that tells which unit system is chosen

In addition to an electromagnetic system of units, you have the option of choosing to use natural or gravitational units. But note that if you choose `RationalizedMKSUnits` or `SIUnits` for doing electromagnetism, you should not also choose natural units because that would make the speed of light in vacuum equal to 1, which would be inconsistent with the electromagnetic units chosen.

GravitationalUnits Units in which `NewtonG` and `Lightc` are both equal to 1

NaturalUnits Units in which `hbar`, Planck's constant divided by 2π, and `Lightc` are both equal to 1

Here are some constants that appear in equations and rules pertaining to electromagnetism in *MathTensor*. The constants `hbar` and `NewtonG` do not appear in classical electromagnetism but do appear in other contexts. The values of the constants `Maxwellk1` and `Maxwellk3` are assigned when a unit system is chosen by means of one of the commands described above. More information on their values can be found in the `Conventions.m` file and in the textbook, J. D. Jackson, *Classical Electrodynamics* (John Wiley and Sons, New York, 1962), pp. 611–616.

Eps0 The permittivity constant, ϵ_0, of the vacuum in rationalized MKS or SI units

Lightc The speed of light in vacuum

Maxwellk1 A constant in Maxwell's equations that is set by *MathTensor* in accordance with the unit system chosen by the user. When no system of units is chosen, this constant appears explicitly in Maxwell's equations.

Maxwellk3 A constant in Maxwell's equations that is set by *MathTensor* in accordance with the unit system chosen by the user. When no system of units is chosen, this constant appears explicitly in Maxwell's equations.

Mu0 The permeability constant, μ_0, of the vacuum in rationalized MKS or SI units

hbar Planck's constant h divided by 2π

NewtonG The Newtonian gravitational constant

There are also several variables that determine the sign conventions. Their values are usually assigned in the `Conventions.m` file. You can change their values temporarily in a *MathTensor* session or permanently by editing the `Conventions.m` file. The default values of the sign conventions agree with those in the textbook, C. W. Misner, K. S. Thorne, J. A. Wheeler, *Gravitation* (W. H. Freeman and Company, San Francisco, 1973).

AskSignsFlag If set to `True` in `Conventions.m`, then *MathTensor* will ask you to choose sign conventions. Its default value is `False`.

DetgSign The sign of the determinant of the metric tensor, `Metricg`. Its default value is -1.

EpsilonSign Sign of the Levi-Civita antisymmetric tensor density with covariant indices in ascending order. Its default value is 1.

MetricgSign Sign of the diagonal spatial components of the metric tensor in a locally inertial or normal coordinate system or in flat spacetime. Its default value is 1.

Rcsign When `Rcsign` is 1, the Ricci tensor, `RicciR`, is obtained from the Riemann tensor `RiemannR` by contracting the first and third indices. When `Rcsign` is -1, it is obtained by contracting the first and fourth indices. The default value of `Rcsign` is 1.

Rmsign When `Rmsign` is 1, then $R^a{}_{bcd} = -\Gamma^a{}_{bc,d} + \cdots$. When `Rmsign` is -1, the opposite convention is used. The default value of `Rmsign` is 1.

■ 4.6 Electromagnetism: Objects and Rules

The following objects and rules relevant to electromagnetism are known to *MathTensor* in a form suitable for curved spacetime. A few of them appeared in examples given in previous sections of this chapter. In Part 3 of this book, many of them will be illustrated, particularly in the chapter on special relativity and electromagnetism. The present section is a brief summary of these objects and rules.

LorentzGaugeRule Transformation rule for the generally covariant Lorentz gauge condition: $A^a{}_{;a} \rightarrow 0$

MaxwellA The Maxwell vector potential A_a

MaxwellCyclicEquation The input line, `MaxwellCyclicEquation[a,b,c]` gives the Maxwell equation, $F_{ab;c} + F_{bc;a} + F_{ca;b} == 0$.

MaxwellCyclicRule `MaxwellCyclicRule[a,b,c]` produces the transformation rule, $F_{ab;c} \rightarrow -F_{bc;a} - F_{ca;b}$.

MaxwellDivergenceEquation `MaxwellDivergenceEquation[ua,ub,lb]` gives the Maxwell equation, $F^{ab}{}_{;b} == \text{constant} J^a$, where the constant depends on the unit system that you have chosen.

MaxwellDivergenceRule Transformation rule used without indices that replaces any expression of the form $F^{ab}{}_{;b}$ by the quantity $\text{constant} J^a$, where the constant depends on the unit system

MaxwellF The Maxwell electromagnetic field tensor

MaxwellJ The electromagnetic current density 4-vector

MaxwellT The electromagnetic stress-energy tensor

MaxwellVectorPotentialRule Transformation rule used without indices that replaces any expression of the form F_{ab} by the quantity $A_{b;a} - A_{a;b}$

There is also a file called `SpecialRelativityEM.m`, which the user has the option of loading into a *MathTensor* session and which redefines the above quantities for special relativity. It also introduces values for the components of `Metricg` and `MaxwellF` that are suitable for special relativity in the unit system and sign conventions specified in `Conventions.m` or chosen during the *MathTensor* session (see the earlier subsection on units). Additional quantities that are defined in the file `SpecialRelativityEM.m` are the following:

MaxwellB The magnetic induction 3-vector

MaxwellE The electric field 3-vector

Maxwellj The current density 3-vector

Maxwellrho The charge density

■ 4.7 Flags and Miscellaneous Commands or Objects

Flags are variables that take the values `True` or `False` and determine whether a particular rule or set of rules is applied. The command `On[flag]` will set a *MathTensor* flag called *flag* to `True` and will update rules and expressions. The command `Off[flag]` will set *flag* to `False` and will update rules and expressions. By convention, the names of *MathTensor* flags end with the word "Flag." Here are the flags used in *MathTensor*.

AskSignsFlag If set to `True` in `Conventions.m`, then *MathTensor* will ask you to choose sign conventions. Its default value is `False`.

EvaluateODFlag If `True`, the ordinary partial derivative `OD[{expr}, {negint}]`, where *negint* is a negative integer, will be turned into the *Mathematica* derivative `D[{expr}, {coord}]`, where *coord* is the coordinate $x[int]$, with *int* being the absolute value of *negint*. It has the default value `False`.

MetricgFlag If `True`, the metric tensor `Metricg` will be used to raise or lower indices on tensors wherever possible. It has the default value `True`.

XDtoCDFlag If `True`, exterior derivatives are converted to covariant derivatives when the command `FtoC` (form to components) is issued. If `False`, ordinary partial derivatives are used when `FtoC` converts an exterior derivative to components form. The default value is `True`.

XDtoCDflag Same as `XDtoCDFlag` (both spellings for this flag are retained for compatibility with earlier versions of *MathTensor*).

VectorAFlag When `True`, the first covariant derivative, `CD[Varg[la,lb],ub]`, of the variation, `Varg[la,lb]`, of the metric is abbreviated by `VectorA[la]` as a shorthand notation.

Finally, here is a list of miscellaneous commands and objects that have not been discussed previously.

Downlist The list of all lower indices, including the ones the user types and the ones generated as dummy indices by *MathTensor*.

DumAllTypes The same as `Dum`, but undefined before the multiple index module has been loaded. Use `Dum` instead.

Evenlist Produces the sublist consisting of the even-numbered elements of a list.

FreeList When applied to a list of indices, gives the sublist of "free" indices, which are not paired with corresponding upper or lower indices.

FtoCrule Rule that converts differential form expressions to their components. Use the command `FtoC` instead.

InListQ Returns `True` if a specified element is a member of a list. Unlike `MemberQ`, if the element is a pattern, it will not match members of the list that fit the pattern.

IntInArgQ Returns `True` when acting on an expr (which can be a sum of products of tensors) containing at least one integer index and `False` otherwise.

Invert Interchanges upper and lower dummy indices.

LieDtoCDrule Rule to replace an expression containing Lie Derivatives by an equivalent expression containing covariant derivatives. Use the command `LieDtoCD` instead.

LowerAllPairs Lowers the upper index of every paired set of indices in a tensor expression.

MakeAllSymmetries Forms a group of all symmetries and weights of a tensor.

MakePermWeightGroup Generates a group of symmetries and weights from a smaller set of symmetries and weights.

MatchlistOrd Like `Matchlist`, but does not put each lower index before the corresponding upper index unless it appears first in the tensor expression.

MetricgFlagOff Same as `Off[MetricgFlag]`

MetricgFlagOn Same as `On[MetricgFlag]`

NegIntegerQ Returns `True` on a negative integer (not 0).

NoIntInArgQ Returns `False` when acting on an expr (which can be a sum of products of tensors) containing at least one integer index and `True` otherwise.

NonTensorPart Returns the nontensorial factors (having no indices) in a product.

Oddlist Produces the sublist consisting of the odd-numbered elements of a list.

OrderedArgsQ Compares the lists of indices of two tensor expressions and returns `True` if the index list of the first expression is lexically earlier than that of the second expression. The expressions should not be (or expand to) sums.

PIntegrate Used to do integrations by parts in variational derivative calculations.

Pairdum When applied to a system-generated regular dummy index, gives the corresponding upper or lower dummy index.

PermWeight Assigns a list of symmetries and weights to a tensor. Use `DefineTensor` instead.

PosIntegerQ Returns `True` on a positive integer (not 0).

PrettyOff Same as `Off[TensorForm]`

PrettyOn Same as `On[TensorForm]`

RicciToAffineRule Rule used by `RicciToAffine` to replace the Ricci tensor by the corresponding expression in terms of affine connections

Rulelists Given two lists of equal lengths, produces a list of transformation rules to replace the corresponding elements of the first list by those of the second list.

ScalarRtoAffineRule Rule used by `ScalarRtoAffine` to replace the scalar curvature by the corresponding expression in terms of affine connections.

ShowNumbers Splits an expression into separate numbered terms.

ShowTime Function produced by Roman Maeder that shows the time of operations when the command `On[ShowTime]` is issued. This is normally not on and can be turned off by `Off[ShowTime]`.

SwapDum Interchange upper and lower dummy indices on a specified sublist of dummy indices in an expression.

SymmetriesOfSymbol Returns the list of symmetries of a specified tensor.

SyntaxCheckOff Same as `Off[SyntaxCheck]`

SyntaxCheckOn Same as `On[SyntaxCheck]`

TensorPart Returns the tensorial factors in a product.

TensorPartSameQ Returns `True` if the tensor parts of two specified products are the same.

TraceFreeRicciR The trace-free part of the Ricci tensor

Unlist Removes the outermost curly brackets from a list.

Uplist The list of all upper indices, including the ones the user types and the ones generated as dummy indices by *MathTensor*

Part B
Differential Forms in *MathTensor*

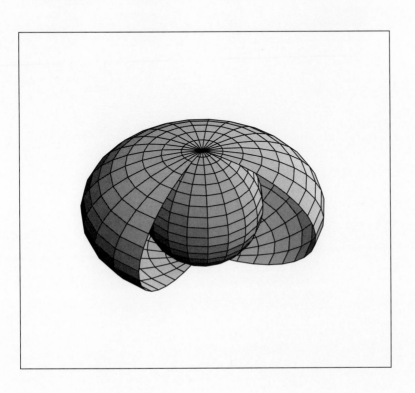

Chapter 5
Differential Form Operations

■ Introduction

Differential forms are objects corresponding to covariant antisymmetric tensors. The degree of the form corresponds to the rank of the corresponding tensor. Because of the total antisymmetry of the corresponding tensors, differential forms may be conveniently manipulated without reference to indices using a set of operations that preserve the antisymmetry, thus taking one differential form into another. Furthermore, many of these operations, such as exterior product and exterior derivative, are independent of the metric structure of the manifold.

In this chapter, you will find the mathematical definition of each differential form operation, as well as an illustration of its implementation in *MathTensor*. Additional applications of differential forms using *MathTensor* are given in the next chapter. If you are not familiar with differential forms, you may wish to look back at the brief introductory material on differential forms in Chapter 2, Section 3. In addition, examples of many of the *MathTensor* commands relevant to differential forms are given in Chapter 3, Section 4.

A good way to learn about differential forms is to supplement the examples in this chapter and the next by one or more of the following references, which discuss differential forms: T. Eguchi, P. B. Gilkey, and A. J. Hanson, Physics Reports **66**, 213–393 (1980); H. Flanders, *Differential Forms* (Academic Press, New York, 1963); M. Crampin and F. A. E. Pirani, *Applicable Differential Geometry* (Cambridge University Press, Cambridge, 1986); C. W. Misner, K. S. Thorne, and J. A. Wheeler, *Gravitation* (Freeman, San Francisco, 1973); S. Chandrasekhar, *The Mathematical Theory of Black Holes* (Oxford University Press, Oxford, 1983); and R. M. Wald, *General Relativity* (University of Chicago Press, Chicago, 1984).

If $x^1, x^2, \ldots, x^n$ denote a set of coordinate functions in an n-dimensional space, then the differentials, or exterior derivatives of the coordinate functions, are denoted by $dx^1, dx^2, \ldots, dx^n$. These differentials can be multiplied by means of the Cartan exterior, or wedge, product, denoted by $\wedge$. The differentials anticommute in the exterior product. Thus

$$dx^1 \wedge dx^2 = -dx^2 \wedge dx^1.$$

The exterior derivatives $dx^1, dx^2, \ldots, dx^n$ form a coordinate basis of 1-forms, in the sense that any 1-form ω can be expanded as a linear combination

$$\omega = v_1 dx^1 + v_2 dx^2 + \cdots + v_n dx^n.$$

Any set of n linearly independent 1-forms, e^a, constructed as linear combinations of the dx^j, form a basis. In general, the basis 1-forms e^a need not be exterior derivatives of coordinate functions.

Exterior products of more than n basis 1-forms vanish by antisymmetry because at least one pair of 1-forms in the product must be the same. The independent exterior products, $dx^1 \wedge dx^2 \ldots \wedge dx^p$, for any given integer p such that $p \leq n$, form a basis for writing any p-form. Thus a general p-form can be written as

$$\omega = (1/p!)\, \omega_{i_1,i_2,\ldots,i_p}\, dx^{i_1} \wedge dx^{i_2} \wedge \ldots \wedge dx^{i_p}.$$

The components of ω form the totally antisymmetric covariant tensor, $\omega_{i_1,i_2,\ldots,i_p}$. The factor of $(1/p!)$ is present in ω because the summations run over *all* values of the indices, so that each independent exterior product of p basis forms appears in the sum $p!$ times. For example, in 3 dimensions the above expressions for $p = 2$ can be written in terms of independent exterior products of basis 1-forms as

$$\omega = \omega_{12} dx^1 \wedge dx^2 + \omega_{13} dx^1 \wedge dx^3 + \omega_{23} dx^2 \wedge dx^3.$$

In terms of n independent linear combinations, e^a, of the coordinate differentials, the p-form ω is reexpressed as,

$$\omega = (1/p!)\omega_{a_1,a_2,\ldots,a_p} e^{a_1} \wedge e^{a_2} \wedge \ldots \wedge e^{a_p},$$

where the $\omega_{a_1,a_2,\ldots,a_p}$ are linear combinations of the $\omega_{i_1,i_2,\ldots,i_p}$. Note that the index names are used here to distinguish between components in the two different bases. For an arbitrary set of basis vectors e^a, related to the coordinate differentials by

$$dx^i = b^i{}_a e^a,$$

with constant coefficients $b^i{}_a$, you find that the components in the two basis are related by

$$\omega_{a_1,a_2,\ldots,a_p} = \omega_{i_1,i_2,\ldots,i_p} b^{i_1}{}_{a_1} b^{i_2}{}_{a_2} \ldots b^{i_p}{}_{a_p}.$$

In *MathTensor*, you can work at the level of differential forms without indices. At any point you can give a command, called FtoC for "form to components," that will give the components of a differential form expression. Since the differential form carries no indices, as one of the arguments of FtoC, you must specify an ordered list of indices that you want to appear as the indices of the antisymmetric tensor represented by the components. The components can then be treated in *MathTensor* like any other indexed tensors. You can think of the indices as those of basis vectors that need *not* necessarily be a coordinate basis (i.e., a basis formed from differentials of coordinate functions).

The exterior derivative of a p-form ω is a $(p+1)$-form, denoted by $d\omega$. By definition, if ω has the expansion given above in terms of the coordinate differentials, then

$$d\omega = (1/p!)(\partial_j \omega_{i_1,i_2,\ldots,i_p})dx^j \wedge dx^{i_1} \wedge dx^{i_2} \wedge \ldots \wedge dx^{i_p},$$

where $\partial_j \equiv \frac{\partial}{\partial x^j}$. This $(p+1)$-form can be rewritten as

$$d\omega = (1/(p+1)!) \left(\sum_{\mathcal{P}} \text{sign}(\mathcal{P})(\partial_{i_1} \omega_{i_2,i_3,\ldots,i_{p+1}}) \right) dx^{i_1} \wedge dx^{i_2} \wedge dx^{i_3} \wedge \ldots \wedge dx^{i_{p+1}},$$

where the explicit sum is over all permutations $\mathcal{P}$ of the $(p+1)$ indices and $\text{sign}(\mathcal{P})$ is the sign of the indicated permutation. Thus, in a coordinate representation, the $i_1, i_2, \ldots, i_{p+1}$ component of $d\omega$ is

$$(d\omega)_{i_1,i_2,\ldots i_{p+1}} \equiv \sum_{\mathcal{P}} \text{sign}(\mathcal{P})(\partial_{i_1} \omega_{i_2,i_3,\ldots,i_{p+1}}),$$

which is a totally antisymmetric tensor of rank $(p+1)$. In the arbitrary basis e^a considered above, the components of $d\omega$ are

$$(d\omega)_{a_1,a_2,\ldots a_{p+1}} \equiv \sum_{\mathcal{P}} \text{sign}(\mathcal{P})(\partial_{a_1} \omega_{a_2,a_3,\ldots,a_{p+1}}),$$

where $\omega_{a_2,a_3,\ldots,a_{p+1}}$ was defined above, and $\partial_a \equiv b^i{}_a \partial_i$.

In addition to the exterior product and exterior derivative defined above, there are many more operators that take differential forms to other differential forms. These operators are defined in the later sections of this chapter together with examples illustrating their implementation in *MathTensor*.

The command **DefineForm** is used to define differential forms having the names and degrees that you specify. You can then operate on these forms to obtain new differential form expressions. If you want the components of such an expression, you apply the command **FtoC**, which takes a form to its components. These components carry the set of indices that you specify as an argument of **FtoC**. You may also want to expand a differential form expression as an explicit linear combination of coordinate basis forms, $dx^1 \wedge dx^2 \ldots \wedge dx^p$. You can produce such an expansion by issuing the command **CoordRep**. These commands are illustrated in the next section.

But first, the following table gives a summary of the differential form commands and operations that are available in *MathTensor*. For each operation, the input form that you type is given first, followed by the name and then the print form that shows in the ouput line. The exterior product XP[w1,w2] of two forms is normally written in mathematical notation with an infix operator, as $w1 \wedge w2$, which is the way it appears in the output line. If you wish to use the standard infix symbol for inputting the exterior product, you can issue the *Mathematica* command

$$\texttt{\$PreRead = StringReplace[\#, \{" $\wedge$ " -> "\textasciitilde XP\textasciitilde"\}]\&}$$

Then you can type, for example, w1 ^ w2 ^ w3 instead of XP[w1,w2,w3]. Notice that spaces have been included on each side of ^. That is done so that you can still access the infix operator for Power. Thus you can type x^2 with no spaces for the second power of x, but w1 ^ w2 for the exterior product of two forms, w1 and w2. You are free to employ this form of input if you wish, although in this book the functional form using XP will be shown in the input line. If you prefer the infix form of input, then you can put the above assignment for \$PreRead in your init.m file. You can also change other input names by including the replacements you wish inside the list appearing as the second argument of StringReplace in the above assignment of \$PreRead.

`DefineForm[w, p]`	define p-form w, where p is an integer
`DefineForm[{w1,w2,..}, {p1,p2,..}]`	
	define forms of the specified names and degrees
`FtoC[{expr},{list}]`	take the form expression *expr* to components, using the indices in *list*
`CoordRep[expr]`	represent a differential form expression in a coordinate basis
`CollectForm[expr]`	group *expr* in terms of the coordinate basis forms
`DegreeForm[form]`	gives the degree of *form*
`ZeroDegreeQ[form]`	returns `True` if *form* is a 0-form
`RankForm[form]`	name of DegreeForm in version 2.1.5 and earlier
`ZeroFormQ[form]`	name of ZeroDegreeQ in version 2.1.5 and earlier
`FormComponentQ[h[ua,lb,lc]]`	test if $h^a{}_{bc}$ is a *component* of a form or tensor-valued form
`XP[s,w]`	exterior product of forms s and w, $s \wedge w$
`XD[w]`	exterior derivative, dw
`HodgeStar[w]`	Hodge star operator, $*(w)$
`CoXD[w]`	codifferential, $delta(w)$
`GenLap[w]`	generalized or Hodge Laplacian, $GenLap(w)$
`Lap[w]`	standard or Bochner Laplacian, $Lap(w)$
`IntP[w1, wp]`	interior product of a 1-form with a p-form
`LD[wp, w1]`	Lie derivative of a p-form with respect to a 1-form, $LD(wp, w1)$
`LDtoXDrule`	rule replacing LD by XD and IntP
`LDtoXD[expr]`	replaces LD by XD and IntP in *expr*
`MatrixXP[m1,m2]`	matrix exterior product of matrices **m1** and **m2** of forms
`MatrixMap[op,m]`	maps the operator *op* to each element of the matrix **m**
`XDtoCDflag`	`Off[XDtoCDflag]` causes exterior derivative components to be expressed in terms of ordinary rather than covariant derivatives

Differential form commands, operators, and flags in *MathTensor*.

■ 5.1 Basic Differential Form Operations

■ 5.1.1 Defining Forms and Taking Their Components

You define a form by means of the command `DefineForm`. You take the components of a form, or any expressions involving differential forms, by means of the command `FtoC`. You should *not* use the same name for two different forms. Also be careful not to use upper or lower index names, such as `ua`, `u1`, `l2`, as the names of forms and avoid names to which you have assigned values.

The command `FtoC` gives the components of the form with respect to an arbitrary basis. The indices of the components refer to the basis vectors. As explained in the first section of this chapter, those basis vectors may or may not be a coordinate basis.

You can also expand a form explicitly in terms of a coordinate basis by first setting the value of `Dimension` and then using the command `CoordRep`. The command `CollectForm` factors out the basis forms so that you can clearly see the components of the form in the coordinate representation. The command `CoordRep` assumes that the coordinates are `x[1]`, `x[2]`, ..., `x[n]`, where n is an integer equal to the value of `Dimension`. You can give these coordinates specific names appropriate to your application, if you wish.

This defines a 2-form called `w2`. The message that is printed can be turned off in the usual way, if desired.	`In[1]:= DefineForm[w2,2]`
	`PermWeight::sym: Symmetries of w2 assigned`
	`PermWeight::def: Object w2 defined`

You can also use lists in `DefineForm` to define several forms. In this case `f`, `w1`, and `w3` are a 0-form, 1-form, and 3-form, respectively.	`In[2]:= DefineForm[{f,w1,w3},{0,1,3}]`
	`DefineForm::frmdef: defined 0-form`
	`PermWeight::def: Object w1 defined`
	`PermWeight::sym: Symmetries of w3 assigned`
	`PermWeight::def: Object w3 defined`

You type the forms with no indices.	`In[3]:= {f,w1,w2,w3}` `Out[3]= {f, w1, w2, w3}`
The predicate `ZeroDegreeQ` returns `True` only on 0-forms. In versions 2.1.5 and earlier of *MathTensor* this predicate was called `ZeroFormQ`.	`In[4]:= ZeroDegreeQ /@ %` `Out[4]= {True, False, False, False}`

The command `DegreeForm` gives the degree or rank of a form. In versions 2.1.5 and earlier, this was called `RankForm`.

```
In[5]:= DegreeForm /@ %%
Out[5]= {0, 1, 2, 3}
```

These are the components of `w3` in an arbitrary basis (not necessarily a coordinate basis). You must specify the indices you want as a list.

```
In[6]:= FtoC[w3,{1a,1b,1c}]
Out[6]= w3
          abc
```

If you give the wrong number of indices, you are warned.

```
In[7]:= FtoC[w3,{1a,1b}]

  all::wrongnumber: The number of indices should be 3
```

The components are antisymmetric tensors and are given the same name as the form by `DefineForm`.

```
In[8]:= {w3[1b,1a,1c], w2[1b,1a]}
Out[8]= {-w3   , -w2  }
           abc     ab
```

A component of a form is a 0-form. The older predicate `ZeroFormQ` gives `False` here, which is not very useful.

```
In[9]:= ZeroDegreeQ[w3[1a,1b,1c] ]
Out[9]= True
```

This correctly gives 0 for the degree of the component of a form, recognizing that it is a 0-form. The older function `RankForm` returns 3 here, which is the number of indices of the tensor. This can be useful at times. `DegreeForm` and `RankForm` behave the same when acting on the form itself, such as `w3`, with no indices.

```
In[10]:= DegreeForm[w3[1a,1b,1c] ]
Out[10]= 0
```

The predicate `FormComponentQ` distinguishes between the component of a form and the form itself.

```
In[11]:= FormComponentQ /@ {w3[1a,1b,1c], w3 }
Out[11]= {True, False}
```

To expand a form in terms of coordinate differentials, you should first assign the dimension of the space.

```
In[12]:= Dimension = 3;
```

Here is the expansion of the 2-form `w2` in terms of exterior products of coordinate differentials. By convention, the coordinate names are $x[1]$, $x[2]$, ...

```
In[13]:= CoordRep[w2]
Out[13]= -(w2   dx[1] ^ dx[2]) - w2   dx[1] ^ dx[3] -
            21                    31

>      w2   dx[2] ^ dx[3]
         32
```

You can give the coordinates names. For example, you might choose these names for cylindrical coordinates.

```
In[14]:= x[1] = r; x[2] = theta; x[3] = z;
```

The coordinate names are used in the expansion of the 3-form w3. The minus sign occurs because the indices of the component w3[-1,-2,-3] are put in ascending order, with −3 first.

```
In[15]:= CoordRep[w3]
Out[15]= -(w3     dr ^ dtheta ^ dz)
             321
```

■ 5.1.2 The Exterior Product

The exterior product in *MathTensor* is denoted by XP.

This unsets the value of Dimension.

```
In[16]:= Dimension=.
```

The exterior product of a 0-form or scalar function with a *p*-form is the same as the ordinary product.

```
In[17]:= XP[f,w1]
Out[17]= f w1
```

Here is the exterior product of w1 and w3. This object is a 4-form.

```
In[18]:= XP[w1,w3]
Out[18]= w1 ^ w3
```

It is antisymmetric because both forms are of odd degree or rank. Automatic reordering occurs to facilitate simplification.

```
In[19]:= XP[w3,w1]
Out[19]= -w1 ^ w3
```

An even form commutes with other forms. The exterior product of an odd form with itself is zero by antisymmetry.

```
In[20]:= {XP[w2,w1], XP[w2,w2], XP[w3,w3], XP[w1,w1]}
Out[20]= {w1 ^ w2, w2 ^ w2, 0, 0}
```

You can have more than two arguments in the exterior product. Currently, *MathTensor* will only reorder and simplify exterior products of up to four arguments, since more than four are seldom required.

```
In[21]:= XP[w3, w2, w1]
Out[21]= -w1 ^ w2 ^ w3
```

Here are the components of this 3-form. You can, if you wish, take the components of the 6-form, XP[w1,w2,w3], but it will take a while to compute and print them.

```
In[22]:= FtoC[XP[w1,w2],{1a,1b,1c}]
Out[22]= w1  w2   - w1  w2   + w1  w2
           c   ab      b   ac     a   bc
```

This sets the dimension to 3 again.

```
In[23]:= Dimension = 3;
```

Now these quantities are zero because they are 4-forms, which have higher degree than the dimension of the manifold or space.

```
In[24]:= {XP[w2,w2], XP[w1,w3]}
Out[24]= {0, 0}
```

This 3-form is not zero.

```
In[25]:= XP[w1,w2]
Out[25]= w1 ^ w2
```

Here is its expansion in terms of coordinate basis 3-forms. There is only one such basis form in 3 dimensions. The command `CollectForm` regroups terms by factoring out basis forms so that components can be clearly seen.

```
In[26]:= CollectForm[CoordRep[%] ]
Out[26]= (-(w1  w2   ) + w1  w2   - w1  w2   )
              1   32       2   31      3   21

>      dr ^ dtheta ^ dz
```

Finally, this demonstrates how you can alter the form of your input for the exterior product. Now you can type `^` , with a space on each side, as an infix form of XP so that the input and output look the same.

```
In[27]:= $PreRead = StringReplace[#, {" ^ " -> "~XP~"}]&
Out[27]= StringReplace[#1, { ^  -> ~XP~}] &
```

Define two more 1-forms.

```
In[28]:= DefineForm[{h1,g1},{1,1}]
 PermWeight::def: Object h1 defined
 PermWeight::def: Object g1 defined
```

Now you can input this 3-form by typing the exterior product as an infix operator. The spaces around the `^` permit you to continue using `^` without spaces when raising to powers. The output will show the difference in spacing, so that you can distinguish the two.

```
In[29]:= w1 ^ h1 ^ g1
Out[29]= -g1 ^ h1 ^ w1
```

`InputForm` still shows the functional form of the input. You can still type the functional form rather than the infix form for your input, and that is what will be done here. However, you are free to use the infix form if you like and to put the above assignment of `$PreRead` into your `init.m` file.

```
In[30]:= InputForm[%]
Out[30]//InputForm= -XP[g1, h1, w1]
```

■ 5.1.3 The Exterior Derivative

The exterior derivative is denoted by XD. When FtoC is applied to an exterior derivative, it takes the components in an arbitrary coordinate basis. Because the exterior derivative is independent of the metric structure, the derivatives appearing in its components can be either covariant or ordinary derivatives (the affine connections always drop out). There is a flag called XDtoCDFlag that controls whether covariant or ordinary derivatives are used in components (the same flag is also denoted by XDtoCDflag for compatibility with older versions). The default is to use covariant derivatives because the result is often simpler. For example, the covariant derivatives, but not the ordinary derivatives, of the Levi-Civita tensor Epsilon are zero. You can use ordinary derivatives by turning off XDtoCDflag.

Here is the exterior derivative of a scalar function or 0-form.	`In[31]:= XD[f]`
	
	`Out[31]= df`

Its components by default are written with covariant derivatives.	`In[32]:= FtoC[%,{la}]` $Out[32]= f_{;a}$
Because f is a scalar, the covariant and ordinary derivative are the same in this case.	`In[33]:= CDtoOD[%]` $Out[33]= f_{,a}$

Here is the exterior derivative of the 1-form w1, which was defined in the previous section.	`In[34]:= expr = XD[w1]`
	
	`Out[34]= dw1`

Here are the components of this 2-form.	`In[35]:= FtoC[%,{la,lb}]` $Out[35]= -w1_{a;b} + w1_{b;a}$
You can check explicitly that the affine connections in the covariant derivative drop out.	`In[36]:= CDtoOD[%]` $Out[36]= -w1_{a,b} + w1_{b,a}$
This turns off XDtoCDflag.	`In[37]:= Off[XDtoCDflag]`
Now the components are written directly with ordinary derivatives. You will recognize the components of the curl of a vector.	`In[38]:= FtoC[expr,{la,lb}]` $Out[38]= -w1_{a,b} + w1_{b,a}$

This is the exterior derivative of a 2-form.	`In[39]:= XD[w2]`
	
	`Out[39]= dw2`

Here are its components. In 3 dimensions, there is only one independent component, which is the divergence of the pseudo-vector having components w_{23}, w_{31}, and w_{12}.	`In[40]:= FtoC[%,{la,lb,lc}]` $Out[40]= w2_{ab,c} - w2_{ac,b} + w2_{bc,a}$

Now let us work in 2 dimensions. First, a brute force method of expressing forms in terms of coordinate differentials will be used. Then the quicker and more elegant method of using **CoordRep** will be demonstrated.

```
In[41]:= Dimension = 2;
```

This expresses this 1-form in terms of the exterior derivatives of a set of coordinate functions, x and y. Note that in contrast to forms of higher degree, it is not strictly necessary to use **DefineForm** to define 0-forms (i.e., u and v here).

```
In[42]:= oneform = u XD[x] + v XD[y]
Out[42]= u dx + v dy
```

In taking the exterior derivative, the fact that $ddf = 0$ has been used for each coordinate function. A form that can be expressed globally as the exterior derivative of another form is said to be exact.

```
In[43]:= XDoneform = XD[oneform]
Out[43]= du ^ dx + dv ^ dy
```

This defines the expansion of du in terms of the basis dx and dy. The variables uPx and uPy represent $\partial u/\partial x$ and $\partial u/\partial y$, respectively.

```
In[44]:= XD[u] ^= uPx XD[x] + uPy XD[y]
Out[44]= uPx dx + uPy dy
```

This is the corresponding expansion of dv. The operator **UpSet**, or ^=, assigns this rule involving XD[v] to the symbol v rather than to the **Protected** symbol XD.

```
In[45]:= XD[v] ^= vPx XD[x] + vPy XD[y]
Out[45]= vPx dx + vPy dy
```

This 2-form expressed in the dx, dy basis has one component, which you recognize as the curl in 2 dimensions.

```
In[46]:= Factor[XDoneform]
Out[46]= (-uPy + vPx) dx ^ dy
```

Here is a general 2-form in 2 dimensions. The exterior derivative of u has already been defined in terms of dx and dy.

```
In[47]:= twoform = u XP[XD[x],XD[y] ]
Out[47]= u dx ^ dy
```

This vanishes in 2 dimensions.

```
In[48]:= XD[twoform]
Out[48]= 0
```

This is $du \wedge dv$.

```
In[49]:= XP[XD[u], XD[v] ]
Out[49]= -(uPy vPx dx ^ dy) + uPx vPy dx ^ dy
```

If you imagine u and v to be new coordinates obtained from x and y, then you will see that the area element $du \wedge dv$ is related to the original area element $dx \wedge dy$ by a factor given by the Jacobian determinant of the transformation.

```
In[50]:= Factor[%]
Out[50]= (-(uPy vPx) + uPx vPy) dx ^ dy
```

You can do the same calculation more quickly and elegantly by using `CoordRep`.

This assigns the coordinates the names x and y.

```
In[51]:= x[1] = x; x[2] = y;
```

Here is the exterior product of exterior derivatives of two 0-forms, s and t. As noted before, it is not strictly necessary to use `DefineForm` to define a 0-form, so that the symbols s and t are automatically regarded as 0-forms. They are analogous to the symbols u and v in the previous calculation.

```
In[52]:= XP[XD[s],XD[t] ]
Out[52]= ds ^ dt
```

By turning off `XDtoCDFlag`, you cause functions like `CoordRep` and `FtoC` to express exterior derivatives in terms of ordinary, rather than covariant, derivatives.

```
In[53]:= Off[XDtoCDFlag]
```

Here is the previous result. The derivatives are not evaluated because `EvaluateODFlag` is off by default. This is important because if it were on, you would incorrectly get 0, since s and t show no explicit functional dependence on the coordinates x and y.

```
In[54]:= CollectForm[CoordRep[%%] ]
Out[54]= (s    t   - s    t  ) dx ^ dy
           ,1  ,2    ,2  ,1
```

You can also work with explicit functions of the coordinates when using `CoordRep`. Let us demonstrate this by finding "area" element $dr \wedge d\theta$ in terms of $dx \wedge dy$, where r, θ are cylindrical coordinates and x, y are rectangular coordinates, as defined by the above transformation equations. The function `ArcTan[x,y]` is the angle whose tangent is y/x.

```
In[55]:= r = Sqrt[x^2 + y^2]; theta = ArcTan[x, y];
```

You want to evaluate ordinary derivatives, since the functional dependence is given.

```
In[56]:= On[EvaluateODFlag]
```

This calculates $dr \wedge d\theta$ in terms of the coordinate differentials dx and dy. You may be more familiar with the inverse relation, that $dx \wedge dy = r dr \wedge d\theta$.

```
In[57]:= Simplify[CoordRep[XP[XD[r], XD[theta] ] ] ]

               dx ^ dy
Out[57]= ---------------
                  2    2
            Sqrt[x  + y ]
```

Unset the values of r and theta.

```
In[58]:= r =. ; theta=. ;
```

To get the inverse relation directly, change the name of the coordinates to r and theta, which now have no values.

```
In[59]:= x[1] = r; x[2] = theta;
```

Define the xx and y in terms of r and theta. It is important to note that because x is the name of the list of coordinates, you should not assign a value to the symbol x (you can let x[1] = x as was done before, but you cannot give x a value). Therefore xx is assigned a value here instead of x.

```
In[60]:= xx = r Cos[theta]; y = r Sin[theta];
```

This gives the familiar result for the area element $dxx \wedge dy$ in terms of $dr \wedge d\theta$ in cylindrical coordinates.

```
In[61]:= Simplify[CoordRep[XP[XD[xx], XD[y] ] ] ]
Out[61]= r dr ^ dtheta
```

You can work directly with a *p*-form such as w1 and if necessary use FtoC to take components in a general basis, or you can use CoordRep to explicitly expand forms in terms of a particular coordinate basis like dx, dy. Both techniques were illustrated in the examples above.

Here is a final example to illustrate an important property of the exterior derivative.

Let the dimension be arbitrary.

```
In[62]:= Dimension=. ; Update[]
```

Here is the exterior product of a 1-form, 2-form, and 3-form.

```
In[63]:= XP[w1,w2,w3]
Out[63]= w1 ^ w2 ^ w3
```

Its exterior derivative yields a sum of three triple exterior products.

```
In[64]:= XD[%]
Out[64]= -w1 ^ w2 ^ dw3 + w1 ^ w3 ^ dw2 + w2 ^ w3 ^ dw1
```

The exterior derivatives of the terms of this sum add to zero. This is an example of the Poincaré lemma, which states that $ddw = 0$, where w is any differential form.

```
In[65]:= XD[%]
Out[65]= 0
```

■ 5.2 Advanced Differential Form Operations

None of the operations on differential forms discussed so far in this Chapter require the space to have a metric for raising and lowering indices. Now let us assume that there is a metric tensor. Then a 1-form field `w1` having components `w1[la]` corresponds to a contravariant vector field `w1[ua]`. The Lie derivative `LD` and interior product `IntP`, as defined below, each involve a 1-form. Actually, it is only the corresponding contravariant vector field that enters into their definitions. Since it is possible to have a vector field defined *ab initio*, without a metric, the definitions of the Lie derivative and interior product do not strictly require there to be a metric. However, in the subsequent discussions it is assumed that there is a correspondence between 1-forms and contravariant vectors set up by a metric.

■ 5.2.1 The Lie Derivative

The Lie derivative of a tensor field with respect to a vector (or 1-form) was defined in Chapter 2 as the rate of change of the tensor at a given coordinate point under an infinitesimal coordinate transformation generated by the vector. In Chapter 2 and in Chapter 3, Section 3.4, the *MathTensor* operator `LieD` was demonstrated. It takes the Lie derivative of a tensor having symbolic indices and yields a new tensor of the same rank. Thus, if `t[la,lb,lc]` is a tensor field, the `{la,lb,lc}` component of its Lie derivative with respect to `v` is `LieD[t[la,lb,lc], v]`.

The Lie derivative of a form `w` with respect to a 1-form `v` is a form of the same degree as `w`. Since it carries no indices, the operator for taking the Lie derivative of a form is denoted by `LD` to distinguish it from `LieD`. For example, the Lie derivative of `w` with respect to `v` is input as `LD[w, v]`. Because the components of `w` are those of an antisymmetric tensor, the form `LD[w, v]` can be defined as having components that are given by the Lie derivative, `LieD`, of the components of `w`.

To summarize, the Lie derivative of a *p*-form `wp` with respect to a 1-form `w1` is input as `LD[wp, w1]`. It is a *p*-form. Let `{la,lb,...}` be a list of *p* symbolic lower indices. Then the `{la,lb,...}` component of `LD[wp, w1]` is `LieD[wp[la,lb,...], w1]`.

Define a 1-form `v` and a 2-form `w`.

```
In[1]:= DefineForm[{v,w}, {1,2}]

PermWeight::def: Object v defined

PermWeight::sym: Symmetries of w assigned

PermWeight::def: Object w defined
```

Here is the Lie derivative of `w` with respect to `v`. This Lie derivative is a 2-form.

```
In[2]:= lie = LD[w,v]

Out[2]= LD (w)
          v
```

Its components are given by LieD.	$In[3]:=$ `FtoC[lie,{la,lb}]`
	$Out[3]=$ $\text{LieD}_v (w_{ab})$

The command `LieDtoOD` expresses these components in terms of ordinary derivatives.

$In[4]:=$ `LieDtoOD[%]`

$$Out[4]= w_{ab,p}\, v^p - v^p{}_{,b}\, w_{pa} + v^p{}_{,a}\, w_{pb}$$

You can also express the components in terms of covariant derivatives.

$In[5]:=$ `LieDtoCD[%%]`

$$Out[5]= w_{ab;p}\, v^p - v^p{}_{;b}\, w_{pa} + v^p{}_{;a}\, w_{pb}$$

This converts the covariant derivatives to ordinary derivatives and affine connections. The latter drop out, giving the result obtained by `LieDtoOD`. The Lie derivative is independent of the metric (as long as the index on the vector remains raised).

$In[6]:=$ `CDtoOD[%]`

$$Out[6]= w_{ab,p}\, v^p - v^p{}_{,b}\, w_{pa} + v^p{}_{,a}\, w_{pb}$$

This uses an identity (see Crampin and Pirani, p.132) to express LD[w,v] in terms of the interior product and exterior derivative. (The interior product is defined in the next section.)

$In[7]:=$ `LDtoXD[lie]`

$Out[7]=$ `IntP(v, dw) + dIntP(v, w)`

This shows that the components agree with those found before. If you had turned off `XDtoCDFlag`, the result would involve ordinary rather than covariant derivatives.

$In[8]:=$ `FtoC[%,{la,lb}]`

$$Out[8]= w_{ab;p}\, v^p - v^p{}_{;b}\, w_{pa} + v^p{}_{;a}\, w_{pb}$$

Make the space 3-dimensional.

$In[9]:=$ `Dimension = 3;`

Here is LD[w,v] expanded in a coordinate basis.

$In[10]:=$ `CoordRep[lie]`

$Out[10]=$ $-(\text{LieD}_v (w_{21})\ dx[1] \wedge dx[2])\ -$

$\quad >\quad \text{LieD}_v (w_{31})\ dx[1] \wedge dx[3] - \text{LieD}_v (w_{32})\ dx[2] \wedge dx[3]$

This unsets the dimension.

$In[11]:=$ `Dimension=.`

This exterior product is a 4-form. It would be zero if the dimension were still 3.

$In[12]:=$ `XP[w,w]`

$Out[12]=$ `w ^ w`

The Lie derivative acts on exterior products like the ordinary derivative acts on ordinary products.

```
In[13]:= LD[%,v]

Out[13]= 2 w ^ LD (w)
                 v
```

■ 5.2.2 The Interior Product

The interior product of a 1-form **w1** with a p-form **wp** is input in *MathTensor* as IntP[w1, wp]. It is the $(p-1)$-form having {lb,lc,...} component given by w1[ua] wp[la,lb,lc,...], that is, by contracting the index of the contravariant vector corresponding to **w1** with the first index of the component of **wp**. The value of p must be at least 1. Common mathematical notations for the interior product IntP[v, w] are $v \lfloor w$ and $i_v w$. The output form used in *MathTensor* is IntP(v, w), which is similar to the input form. (Crampin and Pirani, pp. 108, 109, discuss the properties of the interior product.)

Recall that **v** was defined as a 1-form and **w** as a 2-form. Hence, this interior product is a 1-form.

```
In[14]:= IntP[v,w]

Out[14]= IntP(v, w)
```

Here are its components.

```
In[15]:= FtoC[%, {la}]

          p
Out[15]= v  w
            pa
```

This uses the identity,
IntP[w1,XP[wp,wq]] =
XP[IntP[w1,wp], wq] +
(-1)^p XP[wp, IntP[w1,wq]].

```
In[16]:= IntP[v, XP[w,w] ]

Out[16]= 2 w ^ IntP(v, w)
```

This uses the same identity. The first term reduces to an ordinary product because IntP[v,v] is a 0-form.

```
In[17]:= IntP[v, XP[v,w] ]

Out[17]= w IntP(v, v) - v ^ IntP(v, w)
```

Set the dimension to 3 and let the coordinates be {x, y, z}.

```
In[18]:= Dimension=3;x[1]=x;x[2]=y;x[3]=z;
```

Here is the expansion of this interior product in terms of coordinate basis forms. The minus signs come from interchanging indices.

```
In[19]:= CollectForm[CoordRep[IntP[v,w] ] ]

          3        2              3        1
Out[19]= (v  w   + v  w   ) dx + (v  w   - v  w   ) dy +
            31       21             32       21

              2          1
     >    (-(v  w   ) - v  w   ) dz
               32         31
```

This is just the directional derivative of the function **f**, which is a 0-form, along the **v** direction. It is expressed here using the interior product.

```
In[20]:= LD[f, v]
Out[20]= IntP(v, df)
```

Here it is in terms of components.

```
In[21]:= FtoC[%,{}]
                  p
Out[21]= f     v
          ;p
```

The covariant derivative of a scalar is the same as the ordinary derivative.

```
In[22]:= CDtoOD[%]
                  p
Out[22]= f     v
          ,p
```

■ 5.2.3 The Hodge Star Operator

The number of basis p-forms is the same as the number of basis $(n - p)$-forms in a space of n dimensions. The Hodge star operator sets up a duality relationship between the space of p-forms and the space of $(n - p)$-forms. The Hodge star operator, which is denoted by the symbol $*$, takes a p-form ω into an $(n - p)$-form, $*\omega$. The components of $*\omega$ are

$$(p!)^{-1} \omega_{j_1 j_2 \cdots j_p} \, \epsilon^{j_1 j_2 \cdots j_p}{}_{i_1 i_2 \cdots i_{n-p}} \, (g/\,|g|).$$

In a general curved space, unlike the exterior product and exterior derivative, the result of the Hodge star operation depends on the metric structure and dimension of the space. Here, g is the metric determinant and ϵ is the Levi-Civita antisymmetric *tensor*. In *MathTensor*, you will recall that $g/\,|g|$ is called **DetgSign** and is set in the file **Conventions.m**. Its default value is -1. If you wish to work with differential forms in a Euclidean space, you will want to set **DetgSign** to 1 either directly or in your **init.m** or **Conventions.m** file. In addition, if you are working in a flat space in rectangular coordinates, you will want to set **Detg** to 1.

You can automatically set up a flat metric in rectangular coordinates with Euclidean signature by first setting the value of **Dimension** and then entering the command **MakeMetricFlat[Euclid]**. (Similarly, you can set up a flat metric in rectangular coordinates with a Minkowskian (or Lorentzian) signature by entering the command **MakeMetricFlat[Minkowski]**.) The appropriate values of **DetgSign**, **Detg**, and **AffineG** will automatically be set by this command and covariant derivatives will be changed to ordinary derivatives.

Let us work in a 4-dimensional space of Euclidean signature. The `HodgeStar` operator requires that `Dimension` has been set to an integer.

```
In[1]:= Dimension = 4; DetgSign = 1;
```

Define 1- and 2-forms called `w1` and `w2`.

```
In[2]:= DefineForm[{w1,w2},{1,2}]
PermWeight::def: Object w1 defined
PermWeight::sym: Symmetries of w2 assigned
PermWeight::def: Object w2 defined
```

Also define 3- and 4-forms called `w3` and `w4`.

```
In[3]:= DefineForm[{w3,w4},{3,4}]
PermWeight::sym: Symmetries of w3 assigned
PermWeight::def: Object w3 defined
PermWeight::sym: Symmetries of w4 assigned
PermWeight::def: Object w4 defined
```

This takes the `HodgeStar` of each of the forms.

```
In[4]:= HodgeStar /@ {w1, w2, w3, w4}
Out[4]= {*(w1), *(w2), *(w3), *(w4)}
```

This confirms that `HodgeStar` takes p-forms to $(n-p)$-forms.

```
In[5]:= DegreeForm /@ %
Out[5]= {3, 2, 1, 0}
```

Here are the components of $*(w1)$. The $-$ sign comes from reordering of indices in `Epsilon`.

```
In[6]:= w1Star[la_,lb_,lc_] =
FtoC[HodgeStar[w1],{la,lb,lc}]
```
$$Out[6]= -(\text{Epsilon}\,{}^{\ \ \ \ p}_{abc}\ w1\,{}_{p}\,)$$

Here is the result of applying the `HodgeStar` operation twice. In a space of Euclidean signature, double application of $*$ to a p-form yields the original form multiplied by $(-1)^{p(n-p)}$.

```
In[7]:= HodgeStar[HodgeStar[w1] ]
Out[7]= -w1
```

There is an operator called `DualStar` that corresponds to `HodgeStar` but works at the level of components. It is not obvious that this result gives the components of the form $-w1$.

```
In[8]:= DualStar[w1Star[la,lb,lc],{ua,ub,uc,ud}]
```
$$Out[8]= \frac{-(\text{Epsilon}\,{}^{\ \ \ \ p}_{abc}\ \text{Epsilon}\,{}^{abcd}\ w1\,{}_{p}\,)}{6}$$

`EpsilonProductTensorRule` converts the product of ϵ-tensors to terms involving Kronecker deltas, giving the contravariant components of $-w1$.

```
In[9]:= ApplyRules[%,EpsilonProductTensorRule]
```
$$Out[9]= -w1^{d}$$

Here are the components of $*w2$.

$In[10]:=$ `FtoC[HodgeStar[w2],{la,lb}]`

$$Out[10]= \frac{Epsilon^{pq}_{ab} \, w2_{pq}}{2}$$

This is the component of the 0-form $*w4$.

$In[11]:=$ `FtoC[HodgeStar[w4],{}]`

$$Out[11]= \frac{Epsilon^{pqrs} \, w4_{pqrs}}{24}$$

Operations can be nested. Here is the exterior derivative of $*(w3)$. The result is a 2-form.

$In[12]:=$ `XD[HodgeStar[w3] ]`

$Out[12]=$ `d*(w3)`

These are its components. `FtoC` works on nested differential form operations. The flag `XDtoCDflag` is on by default, so that covariant derivatives appear. This is important here because the ordinary derivative of the tensor `Epsilon` is not zero in curved space or in curvilinear coordinates. Additional terms would appear if `XDtoCDflag` were off.

$In[13]:=$ `FtoC[%,{la,lb}]`

$$Out[13]= \frac{w3_{pqr;b} \, Epsilon^{pqr}_{a}}{6} - \frac{w3_{pqr;a} \, Epsilon^{pqr}_{b}}{6}$$

Change the dimension to 3.

$In[14]:=$ `Dimension = 3;`

This sets up a 3-dimensional Euclidean metric in rectangular coordinates.

$In[15]:=$ `MakeMetricFlat[Euclid]`

`MakeMetricFlat::Ecld:`
`    Metricg is now Euclidean in Cartesian coordinates.`

Let the coordinates be called {x,y,z}.

$In[16]:=$ `x[1]=x; x[2]=y; x[3]=z;`

Here is a list of `HodgeStar` acting on the coordinate differentials. Each term is a 2-form.

$In[17]:=$ `HodgeStar /@ {XD[x], XD[y], XD[z]}`

$Out[17]=$ `{*(dx), *(dy), *(dz)}`

This expands each of these 2-forms in terms of coordinate basis vectors.

$In[18]:=$ `CoordRep /@ %`

$Out[18]=$ `{dy ^ dz, -dx ^ dz, dx ^ dy}`

This is a 3-form.

$In[19]:=$ `HodgeStar[1]`

$Out[19]=$ `*(1)`

Here is its expansion in a coordinate basis. Applying **HodgeStar** and **CoordRep** once more would yield the original 0-form, namely, 1.

```
In[20]:= CoordRep[%]
Out[20]= dx ^ dy ^ dz
```

■ 5.2.4 The Codifferential Operator

The codifferential is an operator that takes a p-form, w, to a $(p-1)$-form, δw. In an n-dimensional space, the codifferential of w is defined as

$$\delta w = (g/\left|g\right|)(-1)^{(np+n+1)} * d * w.$$

Here, $*$ is the Hodge star, d is the exterior derivative, and g is the determinant of the metric tensor, the sign of which in *MathTensor* is denoted by **DetgSign**. With this definition, the components of the codifferential of a form are the negative of the covariant divergence acting on the first index of the components of the form. Thus an equivalent way of defining the codifferential of a p-form w is as the $(p-1)$-form δw having components $-w^b{}_{a_1,a_2,\ldots,a_{p-1};b}$. In *MathTensor*, the codifferential operator is denoted by **CoXD** and appears in **OutputForm** as **delta**.

Let us set the dimension of the space to 3.

```
In[1]:= Dimension = 3;
```

Define a 0-form, 2-form, and 3-form.

```
In[2]:= DefineForm[{w0,w2,w3},{0,2,3}]
DefineForm::frmdef: defined 0-form
PermWeight::sym: Symmetries of w2 assigned
PermWeight::def: Object w2 defined
PermWeight::sym: Symmetries of w3 assigned
PermWeight::def: Object w3 defined
```

The codifferential of a 0-form vanishes.

```
In[3]:= CoXD[w0]
Out[3]= 0
```

Here is the codifferential of **w3**. **delta(w3)** is a 2-form.

```
In[4]:= CoXD[w3]
Out[4]= delta(w3)
```

Here are its components. The definition of **CoXD** is arranged so that you will get the negative of the covariant divergence with respect to the first index in any dimension and for any form.

```
In[5]:= FtoC[%,{1a,1b}]
                   p
Out[5]= -w3
                pab;
```

The codifferential of a codifferential is zero because $\delta^2\omega$ involves $d^2\omega$, which is zero. (To prove this directly in terms of components, it is simplest to show that $w3^{abc}{}_{;ab} = 0$, with indices in the positions shown.) A form that can be expressed globally as the codifferential of another form is said to be co-exact.

```
In[6]:= CoXD[%%]

Out[6]= 0
```

Here is the coordinate basis expansion of `CoXD[w3]`. Terms with two equal indices in w3 do not appear because of the antisymmetry of form components.

```
In[7]:= CoordRep[%%]
                   3                          2
Out[7]= w3       dx[1] ^ dx[2] - w3       dx[1] ^ dx[3] +
          321;                      321;

             1
>     w3       dx[2] ^ dx[3]
        321;
```

Here is $\delta dw2$, which is a 2-form.

```
In[8]:= CoXD[XD[w2] ]
Out[8]= delta(dw2)
```

These are its components.

```
In[9]:= expr1 = FtoC[%,{1a,1b}]
               p          p          p
Out[9]= -w2       + w2       - w2
           pa;b       pb;a       ab;p
```

Here is $d\delta w2$.

```
In[10]:= XD[CoXD[w2] ]
Out[10]= ddelta(w2)
```

You will see that its components are similar to those of $\delta dw2$, except for sign and the presence of a covariant Laplacian term (with negative sign).

```
In[11]:= expr2 = FtoC[%,{1a,1b}]
              p           p
Out[11]= w2       - w2
            pa; b       pb; a
```

In flat space, this sum of components will reduce to the negative of the ordinary Laplacian. Because the other terms involve commutators of covariant derivatives, they vanish when the curvature vanishes.

```
In[12]:= expr1 + expr2
               p          p           p          p          p
Out[12]= -w2       + w2       + w2       - w2       - w2
            pa;b       pa; b       pb;a       pb; a       ab;p
```

■ 5.2.5 The Hodge and Bochner Laplacian Operators

From the result of the last section, it is natural to define the operator

$$d\delta + \delta d$$

as a generalized Laplacian operator. It is known as the Hodge Laplacian and is denoted by `GenLap` in *MathTensor*. The ordinary Laplacian or Bochner Laplacian is denoted in *MathTensor* by Lap. For example, if w is a 2-form with components w_{ab}, then Lap(w) has components $w_{ab;p}{}^p$. GenLap(w) has components that differ from those of Lap(w) in sign and by terms involving the curvature tensor. Both Laplacian operators take p-forms to p-forms.

Adding Lap to GenLap will leave only terms proportional to the curvature.	`In[13]:= GenLap[w2] + Lap[w2]`
	
	`Out[13]= GenLap(w2) + Lap(w2)`

Take the components of this expression. The next step is to commute covariant derivatives to display the curvature explicitly.

`In[14]:= lapsum = FtoC[%, {la,lb}]`

$$Out[14] = -w2_{pa;b}{}^{p} + w2_{pa;\ b}{}^{p} + w2_{pb;a}{}^{p} - w2_{pb;\ a}{}^{p}$$

To apply CommuteCD, you must recall, or use InputForm to see, the input names of the indices.

`In[15]:= InputForm[%]`

`Out[15]//InputForm=`
`  -CD[w2[l1, la], lb, u1] + CD[w2[l1, la], u1, lb] +`
`   CD[w2[l1, lb], la, u1] - CD[w2[l1, lb], u1, la]`

This commutes the derivative indices in the second term of lapsum.

`In[16]:= lapsum[[2]] = CommuteCD[lapsum[[2]],u1,lb]`

$$Out[16] = w2_{pa;b}{}^{p} + R_{pb}{}^{p}{}_{a}\,w2 - R_{paqb}\,w2^{pq}$$

This shows that the second term of lapsum has been replaced by the result of the commutation. It also changes the name of lapsum to lapsum2 (this renaming avoids a bug in some versions of *Mathematica*).

`In[17]:= lapsum2 = Expand[lapsum]`

$$Out[17] = w2_{pb;a}{}^{p} - w2_{pb;\ a}{}^{p} + R_{pb}{}^{p}{}_{a}\,w2 - R_{paqb}\,w2^{pq}$$

This commutes the covariant derivatives in the second term of lapsum2.

`In[18]:= lapsum2[[2]] = CommuteCD[lapsum2[[2]],u1,la]`

$$Out[18] = -w2_{pb;a}{}^{p} - R_{pa}{}^{p}{}_{b}\,w2 - R_{paqb}\,w2^{pq}$$

This gives the components of GenLap(w2) + Lap(w2) in terms of the components of the Riemann tensor and of w2. Thus GenLap(w2) equals -Lap(w2) plus these curvature terms.

`In[19]:= result = Expand[lapsum2]`

$$Out[19] = R_{pb}{}^{p}{}_{a}\,w2 - R_{pa}{}^{p}{}_{b}\,w2 - 2\,R_{paqb}\,w2^{pq}$$

In this chapter, the differential form commands that are available in *MathTensor* were defined and illustrated through brief examples. The next chapter deals with several longer applications of these differential form commands.

Chapter 6
Differential Form Applications

The operations defined in the previous chapter permit you to apply differential forms to a wide range of problems. A number of interesting examples are illustrated there. Introductory material on differential forms (with references) can be found in the introductory section of the previous chapter, as well as in Chapter 2, Section 3. In addition, examples of many of the *MathTensor* commands relevant to differential forms are given in Chapter 3, Section 4.

The present chapter deals with several longer applications drawn from calculus, physics, and differential geometry. The first application is to the statement of Stokes' theorem in terms of differential forms. You will use *MathTensor* to express, in various dimensions, the integrands that appear in Stokes' theorem in terms of components and coordinate differentials. In the next application, you will express Maxwell's equations of electromagnetism in terms of differential forms and will find the wave equation obeyed by the electromagnetic vector potential in curved space-time. Then you will turn to the Cartan structure equations in curved space with torsion. You will use tensor-valued differential forms to obtain a condition for consistency of the structure equations and to derive the Bianchi identities. Finally, you will consider the matrix expression of the structure equations in 3-dimensional flat Euclidean space. You will set up orthonormal basis forms directed along spherical coordinates and will use them to show that the curvature 2-form is zero.

■ 6.1 The Theorem of Stokes

Consider an n-dimensional space containing a bounded p-dimensional manifold M, with $p \leq n$. Stokes' theorem states that if ω is a $(p-1)$-form, then

$$\int_M d\omega = \int_{\partial M} \omega.$$

The integral on the left-hand side is over the p-dimensional manifold M, and the integral on the right-hand side is an oriented integral over the $(p-1)$-dimensional boundary ∂M of M. You can use the *MathTensor* command `CoordRep` to expand in a coordinate basis the quantities appearing in the integrands of Stokes' theorem.

For example, consider these cases, which will be illustrated in the following *MathTensor* session.

1. A space of $n = 2$ dimensions, containing an area M having dimension $p = 2$, bounded by a closed curve ∂M. In this case, ω is a 1-form w1.

2. A space of $n = 3$ dimensions, containing a surface M having dimension $p = 2$, bounded by a closed curve ∂M. As in the previous case, ω is a 1-form w1.

3. A space of $n = 3$ dimensions, containing a volume M of dimension $p = 3$, bounded by a closed surface ∂M. In this case, ω is a 2-form w2.

This insures that ordinary (rather than covariant) derivatives appear when you expand exterior derivatives.

```
In[1]:= Off[XDtoCDFlag]
```

In the first case, $n = 2$. Let the coordinates be x and y.

```
In[2]:= Dimension=2; x[1]=x; x[2]=y;
```

The bounded manifold M is an area with $p = 2$, so the form involved is a 1-form, w1.

```
In[3]:= DefineForm[w1,1]
  PermWeight::def: Object w1 defined
```

Here is the integrand on the left-hand side of Stokes' theorem.

```
In[4]:= XD[w1]
Out[4]= dw1
```

This expands the integrand in terms of the coordinate basis. You recognize the curl here.

```
In[5]:= CollectForm[CoordRep[%] ]
Out[5]= (w1    - w1   ) dx ^ dy
          2,1     1,2
```

This is the integrand on the right-hand side of the theorem, which says that the surface integral of the curl of a vector is equal to the oriented line integral of the vector around the curve bounding the surface.

```
In[6]:= CoordRep[w1]
Out[6]= w1   dx + w1   dy
         1          2
```

For the second case, the space is 3-dimensional. Let the third coordinate be z.

```
In[7]:= Dimension = 3; x[3]=z;
```

The integrand of the left-hand side of Stokes' theorem, with M a 2-dimensional surface and ω a 1-form w1, is the same exterior derivative as before.

```
In[8]:= XD[w1]
Out[8]= dw1
```

This is the dot product of the surface element with the 3-dimensional curl of w1.

```
In[9]:= CollectForm[CoordRep[%] ]
Out[9]= (w1    - w1   ) dx ^ dy +
          2,1     1,2

>    (w1    - w1   ) dx ^ dz + (w1    - w1   ) dy ^ dz
       3,1     1,3               3,2     2,3
```

Again the right-hand side of Stokes' theorem involves a line integral around the bounding curve.

```
In[10]:= CoordRep[w1]

Out[10]= w1  dx + w1  dy + w1  dz
          1         2        3
```

The final case is a volume bounded by a closed surface. The form ω is now a 2-form w2.

```
In[11]:= DefineForm[w2,2]

  PermWeight::sym: Symmetries of w2 assigned

  PermWeight::def: Object w2 defined
```

Here is the integrand on the left-hand side of the theorem.

```
In[12]:= XD[w2]

Out[12]= dw2
```

The expansion involves only one term, since there is only one independent basis 3-form in 3 dimensions.

```
In[13]:= CollectForm[CoordRep[%] ]

Out[13]= (-w2     + w2     - w2    ) dx ^ dy ^ dz
            32,1     31,2     21,3
```

Here is the integrand on the right-hand side of the theorem.

```
In[14]:= CoordRep[w2]

Out[14]= -(w2    dx ^ dy) - w2    dx ^ dz - w2    dy ^ dz
           21                31              32
```

If you let $w2_{12} = V^1$, $w2_{13} = -V^2$, and $w2_{23} = -V^1$, then you will see that the left-hand side of Stokes' theorem is the volume integral of the divergence of $\vec{V}$, and the right-hand side is the dot product of $\vec{V}$ with the (outward) surface element, integrated over the bounding surface. One can show that V^a transforms under rotations as a vector. Thus, for $n = 3$ and $p = 3$, Stokes' theorem is equivalent to Gauss's divergence theorem,

$$\int_{\text{vol}} \vec{\nabla} \cdot \vec{V} \, d^3x = \int_{\text{surf}} \vec{V} \cdot d\vec{S}.$$

■ 6.2 Differential Forms and Maxwell's Equations

The electromagnetic field equations of Maxwell are very naturally expressed in terms of differential forms. The electromagnetic field tensor F_{ab} is an antisymmetric tensor in spacetime and thus corresponds to the components of a differential form. Covariant derivatives appear below because you are working in a curved spacetime. Although they could replaced by ordinary derivatives in expressions that result from taking exterior derivatives of the 2-form f and the 1-form a, they cannot be so replaced in expressions involving the codifferential, δ or CoXD, or in the Lorentz gauge condition. Thus it is simplest to retain covariant derivatives in all equations.

Let us choose Heaviside-Lorentz or rationalized Gaussian units. You can use any of the other available systems of electromagnetic units but will then have to adjust some constants later.

```
In[1]:= HeavisideLorentzUnits
Out[1]= {Heaviside-Lorentz}
```

Here are the components of Maxwell's divergence equation. J_a is the current density 4-vector, and c is the speed of light in vacuum, `Lightc`.

```
In[2]:= MaxwellDivergenceEquation[la,lb,ub]
```

$$Out[2]= F_{ab;}{}^{b} == \frac{J_a}{c^2}$$

Let us define an electromagnetic field 2-form called f. The components f_{ab} correspond to F_{ab} in the above Maxwell equation.

```
In[3]:= DefineForm[f,2]
 PermWeight::sym: Symmetries of f assigned
 PermWeight::def: Object f defined
```

This is the codifferential of f. It is a 1-form.

```
In[4]:= CoXD[f]
Out[4]= delta(f)
```

Its components agree with the left-hand side of Maxwell's divergence equation.

```
In[5]:= FtoC[%,{la}]
```

$$Out[5]= -f_{pa;}{}^{p}$$

Define a 1-form j corresponding to the current density.

```
In[6]:= DefineForm[j,1]
 PermWeight::def: Object j defined
```

Then Maxwell's divergence equation can be written in terms of forms in this way.

```
In[7]:= eqdiv = CoXD[f] == j/Lightc^2
```

$$Out[7]= delta(f) == \frac{j}{c^2}$$

This checks that the components agree with those obtained above from `MaxwellDivergenceEquation` when the antisymmetry of f_{ab} is taken into account.

```
In[8]:= FtoC[%,{la}]
```

$$Out[8]= -f_{pa;}{}^{p} == \frac{j_a}{c^2}$$

Here are the components of the homogeneous Maxwell equation.

```
In[9]:= MaxwellCyclicEquation[la,lb,lc]
```

$$Out[9]= F_{ab;c} - F_{ac;b} + F_{bc;a} == 0$$

The exterior derivative of **f** is a 3-form.

```
In[10]:= XD[f]
Out[10]= df
```

These are the components of df.

```
In[11]:= FtoC[%,{1a,1b,1c}]
Out[11]= f     - f     + f
          ab;c    ac;b    bc;a
```

Hence this is the homogeneous Maxwell equation in differential form notation.

```
In[12]:= XD[f] == 0
Out[12]= df == 0
```

Thus the Maxwell equations are simply $\delta f = j/c^2$ and $df = 0$ in terms of differential forms.

```
In[13]:= FtoC[%,{1a,1b,1c}]
Out[13]= f     - f     + f     == 0
          ab;c    ac;b    bc;a
```

Define a 1-form, a. In a region of trivial topology, $df = 0$ implies that the electromagnetic field 2-form f is *exact*, meaning that $f = da$, where a is the vector potential 1-form.

```
In[14]:= DefineForm[a,1]
 PermWeight::def: Object a defined
```

This is the equation relating the electromagnetic field to the 4-vector potential a.

```
In[15]:= eqvecpot = f == XD[a]
Out[15]= f == da
```

Here it is in component form.

```
In[16]:= FtoC[%,{1b,1c}]
Out[16]= f    == -a     + a
          bc        b;c    c;b
```

This Maxwell equation now follows from the Poincaré lemma.

```
In[17]:= XD[eqvecpot]
Out[17]= df == 0
```

What about the other Maxwell equation? Here it is in terms of the vector potential. This takes a more familiar form in the Lorentz gauge.

```
In[18]:= eqdiv2 = eqdiv /. f->XD[a]
                         j
Out[18]= delta(da) == --
                         2
                        c
```

This is the Lorentz gauge condition.

```
In[19]:= CoXD[a] == 0
Out[19]= delta(a) == 0
```

Here is its familiar coordinate expression.

```
In[20]:= FtoC[%,{}]
            p
Out[20]= -a   == 0
           p;
```

This is obviously 0 if the Lorentz gauge is imposed. Hence, the Hodge Laplacian, $(\delta d + d\delta)a$, equals δda in the Lorentz gauge.

```
In[21]:= XD[CoXD[a] ]
Out[21]= ddelta(a)
```

Then the inhomogeneous Maxwell equation, $\delta f = \delta da = j/c^2$, takes this form, which in flat spacetime reduces to the familiar Laplace equation for the vector potential.

```
In[22]:= GenLap[a] == j/Lightc^2

                        j
Out[22]= GenLap(a) == ---
                        2
                       c
```

These are the components.

```
In[23]:= eqMaxdiv = FtoC[%,{lb}]

                                      j
               p       p       p      b
Out[23]= a        - a      - a     == ---
            p;b       p; b      b;p    2
                                      c
```

The `eqMaxdiv[[1]]` refers to the entire lhs of the equation. Only the covariant derivatives in the first term on the lhs are commuted because the order of derivative indices in CommuteCD matches the derivative indices in that particular term.

```
In[24]:= eqMaxdiv[[1]] = CommuteCD[eqMaxdiv[[1]],lb,u1]

                 p         p
Out[24]= -a        + a   R
             b;p        p   b
```

Here is this Maxwell equation in the Lorentz gauge. In addition to a simple Laplacian term, there is a term involving the Ricci tensor, as was already found in Chapter 3, Section 3.4.4.

```
In[25]:= eqMaxdiv

                                   j
                 p         p       b
Out[25]= -a        + a   R     == ---
             b;p        p   b      2
                                  c
```

■ 6.3 Tensor-valued Forms: Cartan Structure Equations

It is sometimes helpful to define differential forms that take values in the space of tensors. For example, given the fact that the Riemann tensor is antisymmetric in its second pair of indices, you can define the second-rank tensor-valued differential form

$$r^a{}_b = (1/2)R^a{}_{bcd}\, e^c \wedge e^d,$$

where e^a is a set of basis 1-forms. You can view $r^a{}_b$ as a differential form that carries tensor indices a and b. (It can also be viewed as a tensor that has components that are differential forms.) Using this tensor-valued form $r^a{}_b$, you can deal with the second pair of indices carried by $R^a{}_{bcd}$ at the level of differential forms, thus reducing index shuffling and simplifying calculations. The tensor-valued form $r^a{}_b$ is known as the curvature 2-form. (It is often written as $R^a{}_b$.)

You can take advantage of the possibility of using basis vectors e^a that are not exact coordinate differentials. This is done by choosing the e^a at a point x^μ so that the line element

$$g_{\mu\nu}\, dx^\mu \otimes dx^\nu = \eta_{ab}\, e^a \otimes e^b.$$

Here, $\otimes$ is the ordinary tensor product and η_{ab} is the diagonal Minkowski metric in a spacetime of Lorentzian signature or the diagonal Euclidean metric in a Riemannian space. Then these e^a form an orthonormal basis at the point. A linear combination of coordinate differentials that form an orthonormal basis is given by

$$e^a = e^a{}_\mu\, dx^\mu,$$

where the $e^a{}_\mu$ are the components at the point of a coordinate transformation or diffeomorphism from the original coordinates to a coordinate system that is normal or locally inertial at the point. That is,

$$\eta^{ab} = g^{\mu\nu} e^a{}_\mu e^b{}_\nu$$

and

$$g_{\mu\nu} = \eta_{ab} e^a{}_\mu e^b{}_\nu.$$

The vectors $e^a{}_\mu$ for $a = 1, 2, \ldots$, form an orthonormal set at the point and are known in 4 dimensions as an orthonormal vierbein or tetrad. Vierbein indices, $a, b, \ldots$, are raised and lowered by η_{ab}, while coordinate indices, $\mu, \nu, \ldots$, are raised and lowered by $g_{\mu\nu}$. The vectors $e_a{}^\mu$ satisfy $e_a{}^\mu e^b{}_\mu = \delta^a{}_b$ and $e_a{}^\mu e^a{}_\nu = \delta^\mu{}_\nu$.

The e^a at a given point are simply the coordinate differentials of normal coordinates at that point. In general, there is no set of coordinates that is normal at every point of a region. Nevertheless, one can choose a set of orthonormal vectors e^a at each point, forming a locally continuous vierbein field. Note that the orthonormal basis e^a is a tensor-valued (or vector-valued) 1-form. The field of basis 1-forms e^a is not exact in general.

The components of the tensor-valued 2-form $r^a{}_b$, defined above, are the components $R^a{}_{bcd}$ of the Riemann tensor at the origin of a normal coordinate system. What if you are interested in the components in the original coordinate system x^μ? The components of the basis forms e^a at each point are just the transformation matrices needed to take components of tensors in the normal coordinates at that point to the corresponding components in the coordinate system x^μ. Thus, given a vierbein field (or n-bein field in n dimensions), you obtain the ordinary tensor components $R^\mu{}_{\nu\lambda\sigma}$ at each point by the transformation

$$R^\mu{}_{\nu\lambda\sigma} = R^a{}_{bcd}\, e_a{}^\mu e^b{}_\nu e^c{}_\lambda e^d{}_\sigma.$$

It also follows that the tensor-valued 2-form $r^\mu{}_\nu$, defined as $r^a{}_b e_a{}^\mu e^b{}_\nu$, is

$$r^\mu{}_\nu = R^\mu{}_{\nu\lambda\sigma}\, dx^\lambda \wedge dx^\sigma.$$

The way the basis 1-forms e^a change from point to point determines a set of 1-forms called the affine spin connections, or Ricci rotation coefficients, $\omega^a{}_b$. This tensor-valued 1-form is defined as

$$\omega^a{}_b = \omega^a{}_{b\mu}\, dx^\mu,$$

with components

$$\omega^a{}_{b\mu} = e^a{}_\nu\, e_b{}^\nu{}_{;\mu}.$$

Here the covariant derivative is defined by

$$e_b{}^\nu{}_{;\mu} = e_b{}^\nu{}_{,\mu} + \Gamma^\nu{}_{\sigma\mu}\, e_b{}^\sigma.$$

The covariant derivative is also assumed to obey the Leibnitz rule for derivatives and to be the same as the ordinary derivative when acting on a scalar. We have not assumed that $\Gamma^\nu{}_{\sigma\mu}$ is symmetric or that covariant derivatives of the metric tensor are zero. It is only when those assumptions are made that the Cartan formalism is a representation of standard Riemannian geometry.

For more complete discussions of these matters, we refer the reader to T. Eguchi, P. B. Gilkey, and A. J. Hanson, Physics Reports **66**, 213–393 (1980); C. W. Misner, K. S. Thorne, and J. A. Wheeler, *Gravitation* (Freeman, San Francisco, 1973); S. Chandrasekhar, *The Mathematical Theory of Black Holes* (Oxford University Press, Oxford, 1983); and R. M. Wald, *General Relativity* (University of Chicago Press, Chicago, 1984). Here, we discuss the Cartan equations of structure, which define the curvature and torsion. We then use *MathTensor* to verify the Cartan consistency condition. If you want to write rules involving both vierbein and coordinate indices, you can make use of the additional index types provided by *MathTensor* or you can simply use a convention, such as the one that `la,lb,lc` denote vierbein indices and `lm,ln,lo` denote coordinate indices.

In fact, none of the equations that you type below will depend on the fact that the basis e^a is orthonormal. Thus you can regard the basis as arbitrary in these equations. In particular, this will permit you to consider the special case in which the e^a are a coordinate basis dx^a, thus gaining a quick insight into the relation between the Cartan formalism and the standard tensor formalism.

You define a tensor-valued 1-form, in this case the basis vector 1-form, by including the tensor index in the name of the form.

```
In[1]:= DefineForm[e[ua], 1]
  PermWeight::def: Object e defined
```

Here is the exterior product of two basis vectors. The system understands that these are tensor-valued forms.

```
In[2]:= XP[e[ua],e[ub]]
```

$$Out[2] = e^a \wedge e^b$$

Here are the components of this exterior product. You can regard the indices (1m,1n) as referring to coordinate indices like (μ, ν) in the discussion above. Alternatively you can issue the command **AddIndexTypes** and then use (alm,aln) as coordinate indices.

```
In[3]:= FtoC[%,{1m,1n}]
```

$$Out[3] = -(e^a{}_n \, e^b{}_m) + e^a{}_m \, e^b{}_n$$

This defines the curvature 2-form, which carries two tensor indices. Again, the tensor indices are included in the name of the form.

```
In[4]:= DefineForm[r[ua,lb], 2]

  PermWeight::sym: Symmetries of r assigned

  PermWeight::def: Object r defined
```

It prints with its tensor indices showing, but you have to remember that it is also a 2-form.

```
In[5]:= r[uc,ld]
```

$$Out[5] = r^c{}_d$$

These are its components. (An upper-case R was used in the introductory discussion.)

```
In[6]:= FtoC[r[ua,lb],{1m,1n}]
```

$$Out[6] = r^a{}_{bmn}$$

This defines the affine spin connection 1-form, $\omega^a{}_b$.

```
In[7]:= DefineForm[w[ua,lb], 1]

  PermWeight::def: Object w defined
```

It is possible to generalize standard Riemannian geometry by introducing the vector-valued torsion 2-form T^a. If one is given the affine spin connection field, then the torsion is defined by

$$T^a = de^a + \omega^a{}_b \wedge e^b.$$

This is the first structure equation of Cartan. In terms of the basis e^a, the torsion has the form

$$T^a = (1/2) \, T^a{}_{bc} \, e^b \wedge e^c.$$

The second structure equation of Cartan defines the curvature 2-form in terms of the affine spin connection by

$$r^a{}_b = d\omega^a{}_b + \omega^a{}_c \wedge \omega^c{}_b.$$

The two structure equations require for consistency that the torsion and curvature 2-forms are related by

$$dT^a + \omega^a{}_b \wedge T^b = r^a{}_b \wedge e^b.$$

As an exercise, let us use *MathTensor* to derive this consistency condition as well as a second consistency condition.

The torsion 2-form, T^a, will appear as t^a.

```
In[8]:= DefineForm[t[ua], 2]
 PermWeight::sym: Symmetries of t assigned
 PermWeight::def: Object t defined
```

This defines `Cartan1` as the first structure equation.

```
In[9]:= Cartan1 = XD[e[ua]] + XP[w[ua,lb],e[ub] ] == t[ua]
```
$$Out[9] = de^a - e^b \wedge w^a{}_b == t^a$$

It is convenient to define a rule called `Cartan1Rule`, which is based on the equation `Cartan1`. This rule can be used to replace the exterior derivative of basis vectors by torsion and affine spin connection.

```
In[10]:= RuleUnique[Cartan1Rule, XD[e[ua_] ],
          t[ua] - XP[w[ua,lb], e[ub] ] ]
```

This defines `Cartan2` as the second structure equation.

```
In[11]:= Cartan2 = XD[w[ua,lb] ] + XP[w[ua,lc],w[uc,lb] ]
== r[ua,lb]
```
$$Out[11] = dw^a{}_b + w^a{}_c \wedge w^c{}_b == r^a{}_b$$

This defines `Cartan2Rule`, which replaces the exterior derivative of the affine spin connection by curvature and the spin connection.

```
In[12]:= RuleUnique[Cartan2Rule, XD[w[ua_,lb_] ],
          r[ua,lb] - XP[w[ua,lc], w[uc,lb] ] ]
```

This combines the two rules into one rule called `CartanRule`. (You may receive a warning about spelling, which can be ignored.)

```
In[13]:= CartanRule := {Cartan1Rule, Cartan2Rule}
```

The consistency equation involves the exterior derivative of the torsion, so this is the first step in the derivation.

```
In[14]:= XD[Cartan1]
```
$$Out[14] = e^b \wedge dw^a{}_b - w^a{}_b \wedge de^b == dt^a$$

`CartanRule` eliminates the exterior derivatives of the basis and affine spin connections, resulting in the Cartan consistency equation. If you want to go back and see more of the calculations involved, you can apply `Cartan1Rule` and `Cartan2Rule` one at a time.

```
In[15]:= ApplyRules[%, CartanRule]
```
$$Out[15] = e^p \wedge r^a{}_p - t^p \wedge w^a{}_p == dt^a$$

You can derive a second consequence of the two structure equations of Cartan. This time take the exterior derivative of the second structure equation.

$In[16] := $ **XD[Cartan2]**

$$Out[16] = -w^a{}_c \wedge dw^c{}_b + w^c{}_b \wedge dw^a{}_c == dr^a{}_b$$

Again use **CartanRule** to eliminate exterior derivatives of the affine spin connection. The result is the generalized Bianchi identity.

$In[17] := $ **ApplyRules[%, CartanRule]**

$$Out[17] = -r^p{}_b \wedge w^a{}_p + r^a{}_p \wedge w^p{}_b == dr^a{}_b$$

Give this equation a name for use below.

$In[18] := $ **Bianchi = %;**

None of the equations that you have entered into *MathTensor* require that the basis e^a is an orthonormal basis. All of them hold also when e^a is an arbitrary set of basis-vector 1-forms. In order to see the relation to Riemannian geometry in a simple way, let the e^a be a coordinate basis dx^a. Then the indices $(a, b, \ldots)$ are ordinary coordinate indices, and the components of e^a in this coordinate basis are $e^a{}_b = \delta^a{}_b$. It now follows immediately from the definition of the affine spin connection, namely,

$$\omega^a{}_{b\mu} = e^a{}_\nu \, e_b{}^\nu{}_{;\mu},$$

that

$$\omega^a{}_{bc} = \Gamma^a{}_{bc}.$$

Here, we used the definition of the covariant derivative given above and have replaced index μ by c, since the e^a have been taken as a coordinate basis. We also assume that

$$g_{ab;c} = 0,$$

so that $\Gamma^a{}_{bc}$ is the standard Levi-Civita connection, which is symmetric in indices (b, c). Then, if you replace e^a by dx^a and use the symmetry of the connection in the first structure equation of Cartan, you find that the torsion vanishes:

$$\begin{aligned} T^a &= de^a + \omega^a{}_b \wedge e^b \\ &= \omega^a{}_{bc} \, dx^c \wedge dx^b = 0 \end{aligned}$$

As a final example, let us use this coordinate basis to show that the components of the curvature 2-form $r^a{}_b$ are related to the affine connections in the standard way. The starting point is the second Cartan structure equation.

Here is the second structure equation.

$In[19] := $ **Cartan2**

$$Out[19] = dw^a{}_b + w^a{}_c \wedge w^c{}_b == r^a{}_b$$

Turning off `XDtoCDflag` will cause ordinary derivatives to appear when going from differential forms to their components.

$In[20] := $ `Off[XDtoCDflag]`

Because $w^a{}_{bc}$ is the Levi-Civita connection in this basis, this expression is the standard one for the Riemann tensor components.

$In[21] := $ `FtoC[%%,{1d,1e}]`

$$Out[21] = -w^a{}_{bd,e} + w^a{}_{be,d} + w^a{}_{be}w^p{}_{pd} - w^p{}_{bd}w^a{}_{pe} == r^a{}_{bde}$$

This can be compared term by term with the previous expression.

$In[22] := $ `RiemannToAffine[RiemannR[ua,lb,ld,le] ]`

`MetricgFlag::off:`
   `MetricgFlag is turned off by this operation`

$$Out[22] = G^p{}_{be}G^a{}_{pd} - G^p{}_{bd}G^a{}_{pe} - G^a{}_{bd,e} + G^a{}_{be,d}$$

This recalls the Bianchi identity that you derived above.

$In[23] := $ `Bianchi`

$$Out[23] = -r^p{}_b \wedge w^a{}_p + r^a{}_p \wedge w^p{}_b == dr^a{}_b$$

You can check that the terms involving the connections are just those necessary to turn the ordinary derivatives of $r^a{}_{bcd}$ into covariant derivatives. Hence, this is equivalent to the well-known tensor form of the Bianchi identity.

$In[24] := $ `FtoC[%,{1c,1d,1e}]`

$$Out[24] = r^a{}_{pde}w^p{}_{bc} - r^a{}_{pce}w^p{}_{bd} + r^a{}_{pcd}w^p{}_{be} -$$
$$> \quad r^p{}_{bde}w^a{}_{pc} + r^p{}_{bce}w^a{}_{pd} - r^p{}_{bcd}w^a{}_{pe} ==$$
$$> \quad r^a{}_{bcd,e} - r^a{}_{bce,d} + r^a{}_{bde,c}$$

Before we close this section, it is appropriate to remark briefly on the contrasting properties of the $\omega^a{}_{b\mu}$ in an orthonormal basis and in a coordinate basis. When the basis 1-forms e^a are orthonormal (as defined at the beginning of this section), you can show that the previous definition of the $\omega^a{}_{b\mu}$ in terms of covariant derivatives of the $e^a{}_\mu$ implies that

$$\omega_{ab\mu} + \omega_{ba\mu} = \eta_{ab,\mu} = 0.$$

This is 0 because the η_{ab} are constants. Hence, $\omega_{ab\mu}$ is antisymmetric in its first two indices.

On the other hand, when the basis 1-forms are taken as the original coordinate basis, $e^a = dx^a$, then both metrics are the same, and $\eta_{ab,\mu}$ in the previous derivation is replaced by $g_{ab,\mu}$. Because the g_{ab} are not constants, you are left with the result,

$$\omega_{abc} + \omega_{bac} = g_{ab,c},$$

where μ has now been replaced by c, since only one coordinate system is involved. Also with this coordinate basis, as shown above, $\omega^a{}_{bc} = \Gamma^a{}_{bc}$, and vanishing torsion is equivalent to *symmetry* of $\omega^a{}_{bc}$ on the *last* two indices. Then this equation involving $g_{ab,c}$ (which states that $g_{ab;c} = 0$) can be solved to show that $\omega^a{}_{bc}$ is the standard metric affine connection, $(1/2)g^{ae}(g_{be,c} + g_{ce,b} - g_{bc,e})$.

■ 6.4 Structure Equations in Euclidean Space

Consider Euclidean 3-dimensional space. Let x^1, x^2, x^3 be rectangular Cartesian coordinates. The invariant line element is

$$ds^2 = \delta_{\mu\nu}\,dx^\mu \otimes dx^\nu,$$

where $\otimes$ is the ordinary tensor product and $\delta_{\mu\nu}$ is the Kronecker delta, which is the metric tensor in this flat space with rectangular coordinates.

Define a basis of 1-forms, e^a, as at the beginning of the previous section, such that at each point,

$$\begin{aligned} ds^2 &= \delta_{\mu\nu}\,dx^\mu \otimes dx^\nu \\ &= \delta_{ab}\,e^a \otimes e^b, \end{aligned}$$

where all sums run from 1 to 3. Each basis 1-form can be expanded in terms of the rectangular coordinate basis, as

$$e^a = e^a{}_\mu\,dx^\mu,$$

where the components $e^a{}_\mu$ are 0-forms and are continuous functions of position. Then the previous relation is equivalent to

$$\delta_{\mu\nu} = \delta_{ab}e^a{}_\mu e^b{}_\nu.$$

Orthonormality of the $e^a{}_\mu$ is expressed by the relation

$$\delta^{ab} = \delta^{\mu\nu}e^a{}_\mu e^b{}_\nu.$$

This states that $e^1{}_\mu$, $e^2{}_\mu$, $e^3{}_\mu$ at any given point form an orthonormal triad of vectors. The orientation of these vectors will in general vary from point to point.

You can see how the Cartan structure equations arise in the present context by starting with the equation $e^a = e^a{}_\mu\,dx^\mu$. It is convenient to write it as a matrix equation,

$$\mathbf{e} = \mathbf{B}^{-1}\mathbf{dx}.$$

Here, $\mathbf{e}$ is the column matrix of 1-forms e^a, $\mathbf{dx}$ is the column matrix of 1-forms dx^μ, and $\mathbf{B}^{-1}$ is the 2×2 matrix of 0-forms $e^a{}_\mu$, and matrix multiplication is implied. Then

$$\mathbf{dx} = \mathbf{Be}.$$

These matrix-valued forms (which are simply matrix representations of tensor-valued forms) can be manipulated almost like they were ordinary forms with the following definitions [see, for example, H. Flanders, *Differential Forms* (Academic Press, New York, 1963)]. The exterior product of two matrix-valued forms is defined to be their matrix product, with multiplication of matrix elements replaced by exterior multiplication. (In *MathTensor*, the operator `MatrixXP` performs this operation.) The exterior derivative of a matrix-valued form is taken by applying the exterior derivative to each matrix element. (In *MathTensor*, the operator `MatrixMap` will do this.) Unlike the exterior product of a 1-form with itself, the exterior product of a matrix-valued 1-form with itself is not necessarily 0. This is because its matrix elements involve exterior products of different 1-forms. For the same reason, you cannot simply anticommute the exterior product of two matrix 1-forms. Thus you must be careful about the order of matrix-valued forms in exterior products. The order cannot be changed using the same rules as for ordinary differential forms.

Taking the exterior derivative of the previous equation, you find

$$\mathbf{d}(\mathbf{dx}) = 0 = \mathbf{Bde} + \mathbf{dB} \wedge \mathbf{e},$$

or

$$\mathbf{de} = -\omega \wedge \mathbf{e},$$

where

$$\omega \equiv (\mathbf{B}^{-1}\mathbf{dB}).$$

Because $\mathbf{B}$ is a matrix-valued 0-form, ω is a matrix-valued 1-form. If you compare the equation for $\mathbf{de}$ with the definition of torsion in the previous section, you see that the torsion is 0 in the present space and that the matrix elements, $\omega^a{}_b$, of ω are just the components of the affine spin connection 1-form. Next take the exterior derivative of $\mathbf{de}$, obtaining

$$\begin{aligned} 0 &= -\mathbf{d}\omega \wedge \mathbf{e} + \omega \wedge \mathbf{de} \\ &= -\mathbf{d}\omega \wedge \mathbf{e} - \omega \wedge \omega \wedge \mathbf{e}. \end{aligned}$$

It follows that

$$\mathbf{d}\omega + \omega \wedge \omega = \mathbf{r},$$

where $\mathbf{r}$ is a matrix-valued 2-form satisfying $\mathbf{r} \wedge \mathbf{e} = 0$. Comparing this equation for $\mathbf{d}\omega$ with the definition of curvature in the previous section, you see that the components $r^a{}_b$ of **r** are the tensor components of the tensor-valued curvature 2-form. The expansion of the curvature 2-form in the basis e^a was earlier written as $r^a{}_b = (1/2)R^a{}_{bcd}e^c \wedge e^d$, where $R^a{}_{bcd}$ is antisymmetric under exchange of c and d. The condition that $\mathbf{r} \wedge \mathbf{e} = 0$ then implies that $R^a{}_{bcd} + R^a{}_{dbc} + R^a{}_{cdb} = 0$, the familiar cyclic identity satisfied by the Riemann tensor (when the torsion is 0).

In the present flat space, the dx^μ of rectangular coordinates themselves form an orthonormal triad of 1-forms. If the matrix **e** is taken to be the same as the matrix **dx**, then $d\mathbf{e}$ is 0 by the Poincaré lemma and the affine spin connection matrix ω is 0. It follows that in the present space, the curvature matrix **r** is 0. Because the components of **r** are tensors, the curvature 2-form is 0 in any coordinate system. However, the affine spin connection components $\omega^a{}_b$ do not transform as tensors and are therefore not 0 in other systems of coordinates. Therefore it is nontrivial to confirm that the curvature 2-form is 0 directly in spherical coordinates. Let us carry out that calculation in *MathTensor*.

If t^1, t^2, t^3 denotes an orthogonal curvilinear coordinate system, such as spherical coordinates, the orthonormal triad at each point can be chosen such that e^a points in the direction of increasing t^a, for $a = 1, 2, 3$. Then, e^a is proportional to dt^a but is not equal to it because of the normalization condition. Suppose that the line element in these orthogonal curvilinear coordinates is

$$ds^2 = g_{ab}\, dt^a \otimes dt^b,$$

with g_{ab} a *diagonal* metric. Then it is not difficult to show that the triad

$$e^1 = \sqrt{g_{11}}\, dt^1, \;\; e^2 = \sqrt{g_{22}}\, dt^2, \;\; e^3 = \sqrt{g_{33}}\, dt^3,$$

satisfies the required relation, $ds^2 = \delta_{ab}\, e^a \otimes e^b$. The components $e^a{}_\mu$ refer to the dx^μ basis and are thus given by

$$
\begin{aligned}
e^1{}_\mu &= \sqrt{g_{11}}\, \frac{\partial t^1}{\partial x^\mu}, \\[2mm]
e^2{}_\mu &= \sqrt{g_{22}}\, \frac{\partial t^2}{\partial x^\mu}, \\[2mm]
e^3{}_\mu &= \sqrt{g_{33}}\, \frac{\partial t^3}{\partial x^\mu}.
\end{aligned}
$$

Then you can show that the first relation these components must satisfy, namely $\delta_{\mu\nu} = \delta_{ab}e^a{}_\mu e^b{}_\nu$, follows from the equation for transformation of the covariant components of the metric tensor from g_{ab} in t^a coordinates to $\delta_{\mu\nu}$ in x^μ coordinates. Similarly, the second relation, $\delta^{ab} = \delta^{\mu\nu}e^a{}_\mu e^b{}_\nu$, follows from the transformation of the contravariant components of the metric tensor from $\delta^{\mu\nu}$ in x^μ coordinates to g^{ab} in t^a coordinates. Thus the matrix $\mathbf{B}^{-1} \equiv (e^a{}_\mu)$ is

$$\mathbf{B}^{-1} = (\sqrt{g_{ab}}) \left(\frac{\partial t^a}{\partial x^\mu} \right),$$

where the parentheses denote matrices having the indicated matrix elements and the product is a matrix product. Because (g_{ab}) is diagonal, the inverse matrix, $\mathbf{B}$, is

$$\mathbf{B} = \left(\frac{\partial x^\mu}{\partial t^a} \right) \left(\sqrt{g^{ab}} \right),$$

as is easily checked, using $g^{ab} = 1/g_{ab}$ for this diagonal metric, and $\left(\frac{\partial x^\mu}{\partial t^a} \right) \left(\frac{\partial t^a}{\partial x^\nu} \right) = \delta^\mu{}_\nu$.

Specifically, in spherical coordinates r, θ, ϕ, with

$$ds^2 = dr^2 + r^2 d\theta^2 + r^2 \sin^2(\theta) d\phi^2,$$

the appropriate triad of 1-forms are

$$e^1 = dr, \ e^2 = rd\theta, \ e^3 = r\sin(\theta)d\phi.$$

Rectangular coordinates x, y, z are given by

$$x = r\sin(\theta)\cos(\phi), \ y = r\sin(\theta)\sin(\phi), \ z = r\cos(\theta).$$

The above matrix for $\mathbf{B}$, with x^μ being x, y, z and t^a being r, θ, ϕ, is readily found.

This gives rectangular in terms of spherical coordinates.	`In[1]:= x = r Sin[theta] Cos[phi]; y = r Sin[theta] Sin[phi]; z = r Cos[theta];`
This calculates $\mathbf{B}$ as the matrix product given previously.	`In[2]:= B = { {D[x,r],D[x,theta],D[x,phi]}, {D[y,r],D[y,theta],D[y,phi]}, {D[z,r],D[z,theta],D[z,phi]} }. { {1,0,0}, {0,r^(-1),0}, {0,0,(r Sin[theta])^(-1)} }`

```
Out[2]= {{Cos[phi] Sin[theta], Cos[phi] Cos[theta],
>        -Sin[phi]}, {Sin[phi] Sin[theta],
>        Cos[theta] Sin[phi], Cos[phi]},
>        {Cos[theta], -Sin[theta], 0}}
```

Here is $\mathbf{B}^{-1}$. It is the same as the transpose of $\mathbf{B}$, which means that $\mathbf{B}$ is a rotation (or orthogonal) matrix.

```
In[3]:= Binv = Simplify[Inverse[B] ]
Out[3]= {{Cos[phi] Sin[theta], Sin[phi] Sin[theta],
>       Cos[theta]}, {Cos[phi] Cos[theta],
>       Cos[theta] Sin[phi], -Sin[theta]},
>     {-Sin[phi], Cos[phi], 0}}
```

You must set the dimension of the space before using `CoordRep` below.

```
In[4]:= Dimension = 3;
```

This assigns the coordinates that are used by `CoordRep` in expanding a form in terms of a coordinate basis. It is important to first `Clear` the symbol x, since it was assigned a value above.

```
In[5]:= Clear[x]; x[1] = r; x[2]=
  theta; x[3] = phi;
```

Turn off `XDtoCDFlag` so that the exterior derivatives you will be taking are evaluated using ordinary rather than covariant derivatives when you give the command `CoordRep` below.

```
In[6]:= Off[XDtoCDFlag]
```

Turn on `EvaluateODFlag` so that the ordinary derivatives are explicitly computed.

```
In[7]:= On[EvaluateODFlag]
```

Here is the exterior derivative of $\mathbf{B}$. The *MathTensor* function `MatrixMap` maps or applies the operator in its first argument to the elements of the matrix in its second argument. `CoordRep` expands the exterior derivatives in terms of the dr, $d\theta$, $d\phi$ coordinate basis (because you have set $x[1]=r$, $x[2]=theta$, and $x[3]=phi$). The operator `CoordRep[XD[#]]&` applies `XD` followed by `CoordRep`.

```
In[8]:= dB = MatrixMap[CoordRep[XD[#]]&, B] //
    Simplify
Out[8]= {{-(Sin[phi] Sin[theta] dphi) +
>       Cos[phi] Cos[theta] dtheta,
>     -(Cos[theta] Sin[phi] dphi) -
>       Cos[phi] Sin[theta] dtheta, -(Cos[phi] dphi)},
>     {Cos[phi] Sin[theta] dphi +
>       Cos[theta] Sin[phi] dtheta,
>     Cos[phi] Cos[theta] dphi -
>       Sin[phi] Sin[theta] dtheta, -(Sin[phi] dphi)},
>     {-(Sin[theta] dtheta), -(Cos[theta] dtheta), 0}}
```

This calculates the matrix-valued 1-form $\omega = \mathbf{B}^{-1}d\mathbf{B}$. Its components are those of the affine spin connection, $\omega^a{}_b$. It is an antisymmetric matrix, as it must be when $\mathbf{B}$ is a rotation. This agrees with the property, proved earlier, that $\omega_{ab} = -\omega_{ba}$.

```
In[9]:= omega = Simplify[Binv.dB]
Out[9]= {{0, -dtheta, -(Sin[theta] dphi)},
>     {dtheta, 0, -(Cos[theta] dphi)},
>     {Sin[theta] dphi, Cos[theta] dphi, 0}}
```

This takes the exterior derivative of `omega` and expands it in the coordinate basis.

```
In[10]:= domega = MatrixMap[CoordRep[XD[#]]&, omega] //
           Simplify
Out[10]= {{0, 0, Cos[theta] dphi ^ dtheta},
>         {0, 0, -(Sin[theta] dphi ^ dtheta)},
>         {-(Cos[theta] dphi ^ dtheta),
>           Sin[theta] dphi ^ dtheta, 0}}
```

Here is $\omega \wedge \omega$. The operator `MatrixXP` takes the exterior, or wedge, product of the two matrices, in the manner defined earlier.

```
In[11]:= omegaomega = MatrixXP[omega,omega]
Out[11]= {{0, 0, -(Cos[theta] dphi ^ dtheta)},
>         {0, 0, Sin[theta] dphi ^ dtheta},
>         {Cos[theta] dphi ^ dtheta,
>           -(Sin[theta] dphi ^ dtheta), 0}}
```

This shows that the curvature 2-form $r^a{}_b$ and Riemann tensor $R^a{}_{bcd}$ are 0 in this space. This completes the calculation in spherical coordinates that you set out to do.

```
In[12]:= curvature = domega + omegaomega
Out[12]= {{0, 0, 0}, {0, 0, 0}, {0, 0, 0}}
```

The examples in this chapter should help you to apply *MathTensor* in learning about and doing your own calculations with differential forms.

Part C
Applications of *MathTensor*

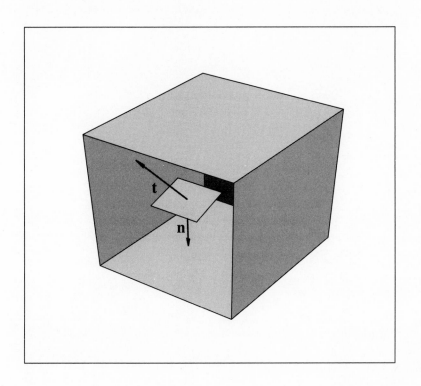

Chapter 7
Electromagnetism and Special Relativity

With your present understanding of the basic operations of *MathTensor*, you are prepared to follow the example applications of *MathTensor* that you will find in this part of the book. You already have a working knowledge of *MathTensor*. The particular chapters that you choose to look at will depend on your background and interests. Although a chapter or example may not be in your field of expertise, you may still gain valuable pointers to guide you in developing your own applications.

The example applications in the present chapter include a discussion of Maxwell's field equations in special and general relativity and derivations of the electromagnetic wave equation and the Lorentz force density in curved spacetime. There is also a discussion of the collision of particles in special relativity, followed by a detailed solution for the relativistic scattering of two particles of equal mass. The problem is first solved in the frame of reference in which the total momentum is zero (the center-of-momentum or barycentric frame). The solution in the laboratory frame (the rest frame of the target particle before collision) is then found by means of Lorentz transformations.

Chapter 8 is on nonlinear elasticity in engineering mechanics. It starts with an introduction and review of the theory of nonlinear elasticity and then turns to the detailed solution of several examples using *MathTensor*.

Chapter 9 deals with calculating invariants in curved spacetime and with obtaining field equations by variation of actions with respect to field variables. This includes obtaining the Einstein gravitational field equations, as well as a proof of the invariance under metric variations of a famous combination of products of the Riemann tensor and its contractions.

■ 7.1 Maxwell's Electromagnetic Field Equations

■ 7.1.1 Units and Maxwell's Equations in *MathTensor*

In dealing with electromagnetism in *MathTensor* you can choose to use any of the common systems of units. Although you will be able to set up your favorite unit

system by issuing a single command during a session or by editing a line in the file
`Conventions.m`, you will probably find it helpful to understand how *MathTensor*
deals with units in Maxwell's equations.

In curved spacetime, Maxwell's equations (in the absence of dielectric or magnetic media and of magnetic monopoles) can be written in any of the common systems of units in the form

$$F^{ab}{}_{;b} = 4\pi c^{-2} k_1 J^a$$

and

$$F_{ab;c} + F_{ca;b} + F_{bc;a} = 0.$$

The semicolon denotes covariant differentiation and may be replaced by ordinary differentiation in the last equation. Here, F_{ab} is the electromagnetic field tensor, `MaxwellF[la,lb]`, J^a is the current density 4-vector, and the value of the constant k_1 depends on the system of units. In SI or rationalized MKS units, $k_1 = (4\pi\epsilon_0)^{-1}$; in esu units and Gaussian units, $k_1 = 1$; in emu units, $k_1 = c^{-2}$; and in Heaviside-Lorentz or rationalized Gaussian units, $k_1 = (4\pi)^{-1}$. (SI and rationalized MKS are different names for the same system of units, as are Heaviside-Lorentz and rationalized Gaussian.) There is also a second constant, k_3, relevant to units, which enters into the relation between the components of F_{ab} and those of the electric and magnetic field 3-vectors, $\vec{E}$ and $\vec{B}$.

It is simplest to introduce k_3 by considering the fields at the origin of a locally inertial, or freely falling, frame of reference. The metric there can be taken to be that of special relativity. In special relativity,

$$ds^2 = (\text{MetricgSign})\left(-c^2 dt^2 + dx^2 + dy^2 + dz^2\right),$$

where `MetricgSign` depends on your choice of conventions and is set to 1 or -1 in the file `Conventions.m`. With either convention for `MetricgSign`, the independent values of F_{ab} and the 3-vectors $\vec{E}$ and $\vec{B}$ are related as follows. (The indices of 3-vectors can be written in the raised position, since the spatial metric is Euclidean here.)

$$F_{12} = k_3 B^3, \quad F_{31} = k_3 B^2, \quad F_{23} = k_3 B^1$$

and

$$F_{14} = E^1, \quad F_{24} = E^2, \quad F_{34} = E^3.$$

In SI or rationalized MKS units and in esu and emu units, $k_3 = 1$; while in Gaussian units, as well as in Heaviside-Lorentz or rationalized Gaussian units, $k_3 = c^{-1}$. There is a file called `SpecialRelativityEM.m`, which you can `Get` during a *MathTensor* session, that sets up the metric of special relativity and the relation between the fields given here.

The values of k_1 and k_3 agree with the constants of the same name in J. D. Jackson, *Classical Electrodynamics* (John Wiley and Sons, New York, 1962) pp. 611-616, in which further discussion of units can be found.

In *MathTensor*, you can choose any of these electromagnetic unit systems by typing an appropriate command. If you type ?Units, you will see the appropriate commands, which are esuUnits, emuUnits, GaussianUnits, HeavisideLorentzUnits, RationalizedGaussianUnits, RationalizedMKSUnits, and SIUnits. You will also see listed the commands NaturalUnits and GravitationalUnits, which may be chosen in addition to any of the previous electromagnetic system of units, except for SI or rationalized MKS units. In natural units, the speed of light, c, and Planck's constant divided by 2π, $\hbar$, are set equal to 1, and the only unit is the centimeter. In gravitational units, the Newtonian gravitational constant, G, and the speed of light are set equal to 1. Natural and gravitational units are each incompatible with SI or rationalized MKS units because the speed of light is not 1 in SI units.

The command Units will list the unit system or systems that have been chosen. You can clear the unit systems that are in effect by issuing the command ClearUnits.

The electromagnetic stress tensor or energy-momentum tensor, T^{ab}, in curved spacetime is known to *MathTensor* and is given in arbitrary units and sign conventions by

$$T^{ab} = (\text{MetricgSign})\, c^4 (4\pi k_1)(F^a{}_p F^{bp} - (1/4)g^{ab} F_{pq} F^{pq}).$$

The input form of the symmetric tensor T^{ab} is MaxwellT[ua,ub]. You can use ApplyRules, with the rule MaxwellTtoFrule, to replace the stress tensor by the equivalent expression in terms of the field tensor MaxwellF. In addition, the right-hand side of the above equation for T^{ab} is represented by MaxwellTexpression[ua,ub].

Finally, the electromagnetic field F_{ab} is expressed in terms of the vector potential A_a by

$$F_{ab} = A_{b;a} - A_{a;b}.$$

Covariant derivatives can be replaced by ordinary partial derivatives in this expression. The rule that replaces F_{ab} by the equivalent expression involving A_a, or MaxwellA[la], is called MaxwellVectorPotentialRule.

esuUnits	choose esu units
emuUnits	choose emu units
GaussianUnits	choose Gaussian units
HeavisideLorentzUnits	choose Heaviside-Lorentz units
RationalizedGaussianUnits	same as Heaviside-Lorentz units
SIUnits	choose SI units
RationalizedMKSUnits	same as SI units
Maxwellk1	a constant, k_1, relevant to electromagnetic unit systems
Maxwellk3	a constant, k_3, relevant to electromagnetic unit systems

Electromagnetic unit systems in *MathTensor*.

In addition to any one of the electromagnetic unit systems above, with the exception of SI or rationalized MKS units, you may also choose either natural or gravitational units.

Lightc	the speed of light in vacuum, c
hbar	Planck's constant divided by 2π, $\hbar$
NewtonG	the Newtonian gravitational constant, G
NaturalUnits	choose natural units ($c = 1$, $\hbar = 1$)
GravitationalUnits	choose gravitational units ($c = 1$, $G = 1$)

Universal constants and related unit systems in *MathTensor*.

The input forms of objects relevant to electromagnetism in *MathTensor* are summarized in the next two tables.

MaxwellF[la,lb]	electromagnetic field tensor F_{ab}
MaxwellA[la]	the vector potential A_a
MaxwellJ[ua]	the current density 4-vector J^a
MaxwellT[la,lb]	electromagnetic stress tensor T_{ab}
MaxwellTexpression	the expression for T_{ab} in terms of F_{ab}

4-vectors and tensors relevant to electromagnetism.

MaxwellTtoFrule	replace T_{ab} by expression with F_{ab}
MaxwellVectorPotentialRule	replace F_{ab} by expression with A_a
LorentzGaugeRule	replace $A^a{}_{;a}$ by 0
MaxwellDivergenceRule	replace $F^{ab}{}_{;b}$ by expression with J^a
MaxwellCyclicRule[la,lb,lc]	replace $F_{ab;c}$ by $-F_{bc;a} - F_{ca;b}$

Rules relevant to electromagnetism.

MaxwellDivergenceEquation[ua,ub,lb]	
	Maxwell's equation involving $F^{ab}{}_{;b}$ and J^a
MaxwellCyclicEquation[la,lb,lc]	
	Maxwell's equation, $F_{ab;c} + F_{bc;a} + F_{ca;b} = 0$

Maxwell's electromagnetic field equations in free space.

In special relativity, or at the origin of a locally inertial coordinate system, one also deals with the electric and magnetic 3-vectors $\vec{E}$ and $\vec{B}$. The Minkowski metric of special relativity in Cartesian coordinates, together with the appropriate special relativistic relations between F_{ab} and $\vec{E}$ and $\vec{B}$, are contained in the file **SpecialRelativityEM.m**, which you can **Get** from within a *MathTensor* session (the name of this file may be somewhat different on your computer). The components, $\vec{j}$ and ρ, of the current-density 4-vector, J^a are also defined in this file.

MetricgSign	the sign of g_{11} in locally inertial coordinates
x,y,z,t	the Cartesian coordinate names in special relativity
MaxwellE[i]	electric field $\vec{E}$, with $i = 1, 2$, or 3
MaxwellB[i]	magnetic field $\vec{B}$, with $i = 1, 2$, or 3
Maxwellj[i]	current density 3-vector $\vec{j}$, with $i = 1, 2$, or 3
Maxwellrho	charge density ρ, with $i = 1, 2$, or 3

Electric and magnetic fields, three-current density, and charge density.

Next, let us turn to some applications of *MathTensor* in electromagnetism.

■ 7.1.2 Electromagnetic Wave Equation in Curved Spacetime

To obtain the electromagnetic wave equation in curved spacetime in the Lorentz gauge, consider the lhs of one of Maxwell's eqs.

In vacuum, this is zero by one of Maxwell's equations.

```
In[1]:= expr = CD[ MaxwellF[la,ub], lb]
```
$$Out[1]= F^{\;\;\;b}_{a\;;b}$$

Use of the vector potential enforces the other Maxwell equation. The first term is the Laplacian of the vector potential. To simplify the second term by imposing the Lorentz gauge condition, you must first commute the covariant derivatives.

```
In[2]:= expr = ApplyRules[expr, MaxwellVectorPotentialRule
]
```
$$Out[2]= -A^{\;\;\;p}_{a;\;p} + A^{\;\;p}_{\;\;;ap}$$

This gives the input form of the second term so that you can recall the input forms of the indices that have output form p.

```
In[3]:= InputForm[expr[[2]] ]
Out[3]//InputForm= CD[MaxwellA[u1], la, l1]
```

This commutes the covariant derivative indices in the second term of expr. A term with the Ricci tensor is generated.

```
In[4]:= expr[[2]] = CommuteCD[expr[[2]], la,l1]
```
$$Out[4]= A^{\;\;\;\;p}_{\;\;p;\;a} + A^{\;\;p}R^{\;\;\;p}_{\;\;a}$$

Here is the expression that we have arrived at.

```
In[5]:= expr
```
$$Out[5]= A^{\;\;\;\;p}_{\;\;p;\;a} - A^{\;\;\;p}_{a;\;p} + A^{\;\;p}R^{\;\;\;p}_{\;\;a}$$

Finally, imposing the Lorentz gauge condition causes simplification.

```
In[6]:= ApplyRules[%, LorentzGaugeRule]
```

$$Out[6] = -A^p{}_{a;p} + A^p{}_p R_a$$

Setting the above expression to zero gives the electromagnetic wave equation in curved spacetime. The operator acting on the vector potential is the de Rham wave operator.

■ 7.1.3   Lorentz Force Density from the Maxwell Stress Tensor

An electromagnetic field exerts a force on a system of charged particles described by the current density 4-vector J^a. The density of force exerted by the field on the particles is proportional to the expression,

$$F^a{}_b J^b,$$

which, when integrated over volume, is equivalent to the Lorentz force acting on each charge [for example, see S. Weinberg, *Gravitation and Cosmology* (John Wiley & Sons, Inc., New York, 1972), pp. 43–45]. The local conservation law of the total stress energy-momentum tensor of the particles and electromagnetic field implies that the four-divergence of the Maxwell stress tensor, $T^{ab}{}_{;b}$, must be equal to this force density acting on the system of charges. Here is how to derive this equality using *MathTensor*.

This clears whatever unit system that was set in **Conventions.m**.

```
In[7]:= ClearUnits
Out[7]= {}
```

This sets up rationalized Gaussian or Heaviside-Lorentz units. If you prefer to use another system of units, you may. However, your output lines will then be somewhat different.

```
In[8]:= HeavisideLorentzUnits
Out[8]= {Heaviside-Lorentz}
```

Here is the covariant four-divergence of the electromagnetic stress tensor.

```
In[9]:= CD[MaxwellT[ua,ub],lb]
```

$$Out[9] = T^{ab}{}_{;b}$$

This replaces `MaxwellT` by the corresponding expression involving `MaxwellF` and also takes covariant derivatives.

```
In[10]:= ApplyRules[%, MaxwellTtoFrule]
                4  pq  a                            4      a  pq
            -(c  F    F  )                      c  F      F
                    ;   pq        4  pq      a           pq;
  Out[10]= ———————————————————  - c  F      F      - —————————————— +
                    4                      ;p  q               4

            4  a   pq
        >  c  F   F
               p ;q
```

This places dummy indices in a standard order, finding a simplification. The input form of $F_{pq;}{}^a$ is `CD[MaxwellF[l1,l2],ua]`. Because it has a factor of 1/2, applying `MaxwellCyclicRule[l1,l2,ua]` to generate two terms may cause further simplification.

```
In[11]:= CanDum[%]
                4   a  pq
            -(c  F   F  )
                pq;                 4  a   pq      4   p  qa
  Out[11]= ———————————————  + c  F   F     - c  F    F
                  2                  p ;q           pq;
```

Only one term remains. Now use Maxwell's equation to produce J^a.

```
In[12]:= ApplyRules[%, MaxwellCyclicRule[l1,l2,ua] ]
                4   p  qa
  Out[12]= -(c  F    F  )
                 pq;
```

This is the Lorentz force density.

```
In[13]:= ApplyRules[%, MaxwellDivergenceRule]
            2  pa
  Out[13]= c  F   J
                  p
```

The factor of c^2 appears here because with $x^4 = t$, one has $g_{44} = c^2$, $F_{14} = E^1$, and $J^4 = \rho$. Thus, for example, $c^2 F^{41} J_4 = E^1 \rho$, which is the correct contribution to the part of the Lorentz force law involving E^1. You may want to try the above example again with your favorite system of units.

■ 7.2 Special Relativistic Collisions

Experiments involving fast-moving particles undergoing collisions have confirmed that Einstein's special theory of relativity correctly predicts the outcome. In special relativity, as in Newtonian mechanics, an *inertial* frame is one relative to which a free particle moves in a straight line at constant speed. If S is an inertial frame, then any other frame S' moving at constant velocity relative to S is also an inertial frame. The fundamental laws governing particles and fields have the same form when expressed in any inertial frame.

Unlike Newtonian mechanics, in special relativity there is a limiting speed. Particles or quanta of electromagnetic radiation, i.e., photons, move in empty space at this limiting speed c, which is approximately 3×10^8 meter/sec. This speed c is the same measured relative to any inertial frame. No particle can move faster than this invariant speed c.

Associated with any particle is another invariant called its rest mass, m. A photon has $m = 0$ and cannot be brought to rest (it always moves at speed c). Any particle that moves at speeds less than c can be brought to rest. It has a positive value of m, which is the value of the particle's mass measured when it is at rest.

An *event E* is something that occurs at a specific time and position. For example, think of two billiard balls making contact for an instant when they collide. The position and time of contact is an event. It may be specified by giving its Cartesian coordinates, x, y, z, and its time of occurrence t, relative to a given inertial frame S. The time of occurence t is ideally to be measured using a clock at rest in the given inertial frame at the position of the event. (Assume that all clocks are identically constructed standard clocks that run at the same rate when not moving relative to each other. In addition, assume that clocks at different positions of the inertial frame have had their settings synchronized by using the fact that light signals in empty space travel at the constant speed c.)

The position x', y', z', and time t' of the same event E can also be determined using measuring rods and clocks at rest and synchronized relative to a second inertial frame S'. The relation between the space and time coordinates of event E in two different inertial frames is known as a Lorentz transformation. It is always possible to set up coordinate systems in two inertial frames S and S' in such a way that the origins and coordinate axes of the two frames coincide at the instant when the clocks at the origins read $t = 0$ and $t' = 0$ (recall that t is measured by a clock at rest in frame S, and t' is measured by a clock at rest in frame S'). Furthermore, the orientation of the axes can be chosen such that the origin of S' is moving in the positive x-direction relative to S. Let v be the speed of this motion of S' as measured relative to S. The frames S and S' are then said to be in standard configuration. The Lorentz transformation relating the coordinates of the same event E relative to the two frames is given by

$$
\begin{aligned}
x' &= \gamma(v)\,(x - vt) \\
y' &= y \\
z' &= z \\
t' &= \gamma(v)\,\left(t - (v/c^2)x\right).
\end{aligned}
$$

Here,

$$
\gamma(v) = \left(1 - \frac{v^2}{c^2}\right)^{-1/2}.
$$

The consequences of the Lorentz transformation are discussed in numerous text-books, including the ones already listed on general relativity.

Because the relative velocity of the two inertial frames is constant, the Lorentz transformation is linear. Therefore, if we define $x^1 = x$, $x^2 = y$, $x^3 = z$, and $x^4 = t$, then x^a transforms as a first-rank tensor, or 4-vector, under Lorentz transformations. Another 4-vector associated with the motion of a particle is its four-momentum p^a, which has components relative to inertial frame S given by

$$
\begin{aligned}
p^1 &= \gamma(u) m u_x, \\
p^2 &= \gamma(u) m u_y, \\
p^3 &= \gamma(u) m u_z, \\
p^4 &= \gamma(u) m.
\end{aligned}
$$

Here, (u_x, u_y, u_z) is the velocity 3-vector of the particle, m is its rest mass, and $\gamma(u) = \left(1 - (u^2/c^2)\right)^{-1/2}$, where u is the magnitude of the three-velocity. The first three components are the relativistic three-momentum of the particle, and the last component is interpreted to be E/c^2, where E is the total energy of the particle (including its kinetic energy and any other forms of energy it may contain). (Notice that p^4 has been defined to have the same dimensions as p^1/c, just as t has the same dimensions as x/c.) The components p'^a of the four-momentum relative to frame S' are related to the components p^a relative to S by the same linear Lorentz transformation that relates x'^a to x^a:

$$
\begin{aligned}
p'^1 &= \gamma(v)\left(p^1 - v p^4\right), \\
p'^2 &= p^2, \\
p'^3 &= p^3, \\
p'^4 &= \gamma(v)\left(p^4 - (v/c^2) p^1\right).
\end{aligned}
$$

The total energy and three-momentum of a particle do not transform independently of one another.

Recall that in Newtonian mechanics, the vector sum of the three-momenta associated with each of the colliding particles before any collision is equal to the vector sum of the three-momenta of the particles after collision. This *conservation* of total three-momentum is true for elastic collisions (in which the total kinetic energy is also conserved) and for inelastic collisions (in which some of the kinetic energy is converted to other forms of energy, such as heat, during the collision). In special relativity, the mixing of three-momentum with energy by Lorentz transformation to another inertial frame implies that if the total three-momentum is conserved in any inertial frame, then the sum of the fourth components of the relativistic momenta of the colliding particles must also be conserved. This conservation law holds even if the collision is inelastic. Therefore the fourth component of relativistic momentum of a particle must be interpreted as the total energy of the particle, including, in addition to kinetic energy, all other forms of energy the particle may be carrying.

The conservation of relativistic four-momentum in a collision may be summarized as

$$\sum p^a{}_{\text{before}} = \sum p^a{}_{\text{after}},$$

where the a-component of the total momentum of the particles present before collision appears on the left-hand side and the analogous sum after collision appears on the right-hand side (here, a is 1, 2, 3, or 4). Because the Lorentz transformation is linear, the form of this conservation law does not change when expressed in any other inertial frame.

The following example uses *MathTensor* to predict the outcome of the elastic collision of two particles of equal mass, such as two electrons.

■ 7.2.1 Elastic Collision of Two Particles of Equal Mass

A target particle of mass m is initially at rest at the origin of an inertial frame S (the laboratory frame of reference). A second particle of mass m starts from a large negative value of x and moves in the positive x-direction at an initial constant speed, u_i, until it approaches sufficiently near to the origin to interact with the target particle. After the two particles are far enough apart to cease interacting, the target particle is moving away from the origin with constant speed w_f making an angle ϕ with the x-axis (see Fig. 7–1), and the other particle is moving away from the origin with constant speed u_f making an angle θ with the x-axis. The y-axis is chosen so that the plane containing the particles is the xy plane. It is assumed that the collision is elastic, so that the rest masses of the particles do not change and no additional particles are created in the process of collision.

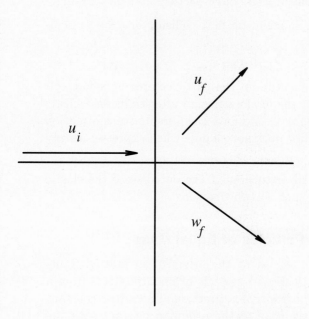

Fig. 7–1 Laboratory frame S: Target particle initially at rest at origin.

Given the initial speed u_i and the angle θ at which the incoming particle is scattered, find the prediction of special relativity for the final speeds u_f, w_f, and the angle ϕ at which the target particle is scattered.

To solve this problem, make use of conservation of relativistic four-momentum, which in this example takes the form

$$p_i{}^a + q_i{}^a = p_f{}^a + q_f{}^a,$$

where q^a refers to relativistic four-momentum of the target particle and p^a to relativistic four-momentum of the particle that is originally incoming. Subscripts i refer to initial values before collision and subscripts f to final values after collision. One way to solve this problem would be to substitute expressions for the momenta into these conservation equations and to solve for the desired speeds and angles. A somewhat simpler way is to transform to the inertial frame S' in which the total initial relativistic *three*-momentum $p_i'^n + q_i'^n$ (with $n = 1, 2, 3$) is zero. The frame S' is called the center-of-momentum frame (or the barycentric frame). In Newtonian mechanics, it coincides with the frame in which the center of mass is at rest. It is clear that S' must be moving in the positive x-direction relative to S at the speed v necessary to give the two particles equal and opposite three-momenta. Thus the lab frame S and the center-of-momentum frame S' are in standard configuration.

■ 7.2.2 Solution in Center-of-Momentum Frame

In the center-of-momentum frame, the solution of the conservation equations $p_i'^a + q_i'^a = p_f'^a + q_f'^a$ is immediate. Before collision, you have

$$p_i'^n = -q_i'^n.$$

It follows that after collision,

$$p_f'^n = -q_f'^n.$$

Thus the relativistic three-momenta have equal magnitudes and are directed away from each other after collision. Let the constant angle that the final three-momentum $p_f'^n$ makes with the x'-axis be θ'. Then $q_f'^n$ makes an angle $\theta' + \pi$ with the x'-axis.

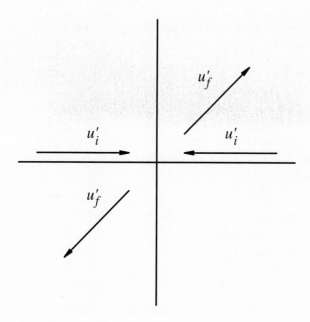

Fig. 7–2 C-of-m frame S': Particles approach symmetrically before collision.

The Lorentz transformations of the y- and z-components of momenta are trivial, so you find $p_i'^2 = 0$, $p_i'^3 = 0$, $q_i'^2 = 0$, and $q_i'^3 = 0$. That is, the three-momentum before collision of the incoming particle makes angle 0 with the x'-axis, and that of the target particle before collision makes angle π with the x'-axis.

Let u_i' denote the speed of each particle before collision and u_f' the speed of each particle after collision relative to the center-of-momentum frame. The fourth component of the conservation law gives

$$2\gamma(u_i')m = 2\gamma(u_f')m,$$

which implies that

$$u_i' = u_f' \equiv u'.$$

The problem now reduces to making Lorentz transformations in order to relate the quantities u_i, u_f, w_f, θ, and ϕ in the lab frame S to the quantities u' and θ' in the center-of-momentum frame S'. You can then use those relations to express the unknowns u_f, w_f, and ϕ in terms of the given quantities u_i and θ.

■ 7.2.3 Transformation to Laboratory Frame

The speed v of frame S' relative to frame S can be found by considering the target particle before collision. It is at rest at the origin of the lab frame S and is moving in the negative x'-direction at speed u' in the center-of-momentum frame S'. But the origin of S is moving at speed v in the negative x'-direction relative to S'. Hence,

$$v = u'.$$

The Lorentz transformations of each of the momenta from frame S' to frame S give a set of equations relating the speeds and angles in the lab frame to the speed u' and angle θ' in the center-of-momentum frame. Then you can solve for u' and θ' in terms of the given quantities u_i and θ. Finally, you can solve for the unknowns u_f, w_f, and ϕ in terms of u' and θ', which are now known.

It is convenient to use *MathTensor* and *Mathematica* to perform the Lorentz transformations and solve the resulting equations. Because there are three Lorentz transformations involved, you will construct a function in *MathTensor* to calculate the components of the Lorentz transformed momenta. The *MathTensor* function **Ttransform** may be used as the basic building block for this construction. But first list the components of the momenta of the particles in each frame of reference.

The momentum components of the incoming particle *before* collision in frame S' are

$$p_i'^1 = \gamma(u')mu',$$

$$p_i'^2 \;=\; 0, \quad p_i'^3 = 0,$$
$$p_i'^4 \;=\; \gamma(u')m.$$

In S, the corresponding components of momentum are

$$p_i{}^1 \;=\; \gamma(u_i)mu_i,$$
$$p_i{}^2 \;=\; 0, \quad p_i{}^3 = 0,$$
$$p_i{}^4 \;=\; \gamma(u_i)m.$$

The momentum components of the same particle *after* collision in frame S' are

$$p_f'^{\,1} \;=\; \gamma(u')mu' \cos(\theta'),$$
$$p_f'^{\,2} \;=\; \gamma(u')mu' \sin(\theta'),$$
$$p_i'^{3} \;=\; 0,$$
$$p_f'^{\,4} \;=\; \gamma(u')m.$$

In S, the corresponding components of momentum are

$$p_f{}^1 \;=\; \gamma(u_f)mu_f \cos(\theta),$$
$$p_f{}^2 \;=\; \gamma(u_f)mu_f \sin(\theta),$$
$$p_f{}^3 \;=\; 0,$$
$$p_f{}^4 \;=\; \gamma(u_f)m.$$

The momentum components of the target particle *after* collision in S' are

$$q_f'^{\,1} \;=\; -\gamma(u')mu' \cos(\theta'),$$
$$q_f'^{\,2} \;=\; -\gamma(u')mu' \sin(\theta'),$$
$$q_f'^{3} \;=\; 0,$$
$$q_f'^{\,4} \;=\; \gamma(u')m.$$

In S, the corresponding components of momentum are

$$q_f{}^1 \;=\; \gamma(w_f)mw_f \cos(\phi'),$$
$$q_f{}^2 \;=\; -\gamma(w_f)mw_f \sin(\phi'),$$
$$q_f{}^3 \;=\; 0,$$
$$q_f{}^4 \;=\; \gamma(w_f)m.$$

You will not require the momentum components of the target particle before collision, since their Lorentz transformation would only confirm the equation $u' = v$, which you have already obtained.

The Lorentz transformation of space and time coordinates from S' to S is

$$x = \gamma(v)(x' + vt'), \tag{7.1}$$
$$t = \gamma(v)(t' + vx'/c^2), \tag{7.2}$$
$$y = y', \quad z = z'. \tag{7.3}$$

First construct a function to carry out this transformation on 4-vectors. Make use of the fact that in the present problem, the relative velocity v is equal to u', as was derived above.

The spacetime is 4-dimensional.

```
In[1]:= Dimension = 4;
```

These are the space and time coordinates. They will be needed in a list appearing in Ttransform.

```
In[2]:= coords = {x,y,z,t}

Out[2]= {x, y, z, t}
```

Also required is a list of the right-hand sides of the transformation equations involving the previously listed coordinates. The information that $v = u'$ has been used to replace v by uSp, which represents u', the speed of the particles in frame S'. The specific function gamma will be specified later. You can think of the Sp appended to the u in uSp as representing the frame of reference S' in which the speed u' is measured.

```
In[3]:= trans = {gamma[uSp] (x + uSp t), y, z,
            gamma[uSp] (t + uSp x/Lightc^2)}

Out[3]= {(t uSp + x) gamma[uSp], y, z,

              uSp x
    >    (t + —————) gamma[uSp]}
                2
               c
```

This defines the function lorentz, which will Lorentz transform from S' to S the tensor (or vector) specified in its second argument, giving the transformed tensor the name in the first argument of lorentz. Symbolic indices are included in the second argument to indicate which components are to be transformed.

```
In[4]:= lorentz[a_,b_] :=
         Ttransform[a,b,coords,trans,1]
```

The tensor ppi[ua] represents $p_i'^{\,a}$, the initial momentum 4-vector of the incoming particle in the center-of-momentum frame S'.

```
In[5]:= DefineTensor[ppi,{{1},1}]

  PermWeight::def: Object ppi defined
```

This defines the same 4-vector in the lab frame S.

```
In[6]:= DefineTensor[pi,{{1},1}]

  PermWeight::def: Object pi defined
```

Now the contravariant components of the initial four-momentum in the lab frame have been calculated.

```
In[7]:= lorentz[pi, ppi[ua] ]
 Components assigned to pi
```

Here is the first component.

```
In[8]:= pi[1]
                          1          4
Out[8]= gamma[uSp] (ppi  + uSp ppi )
```

Here is the fourth component. They are the Lorentz transform of the corresponding components in the center-of-momentum frame.

```
In[9]:= pi[4]
              1     2    4
        gamma[uSp] (uSp ppi  + c  ppi )
Out[9]= ───────────────────────────────
                        2
                       c
```

Now set the values of the initial components in the center-of-momentum frame, as given above. As noted before, uSp represents u', the speed of the incoming particle in the center-of-momentum frame S'.

```
In[10]:= ppi[1] = gamma[uSp] m uSp
Out[10]= m uSp gamma[uSp]
```

These are the second and third components.

```
In[11]:= ppi[2] = 0; ppi[3] = 0;
```

This is the fourth component.

```
In[12]:= ppi[4] = gamma[uSp] m
Out[12]= m gamma[uSp]
```

Now pi[1], for example, is expressed in terms of the incoming particle's speed in frame S', its mass, and the speed v of frame S relative to frame S'.

```
In[13]:= pi[1]
                            2
Out[13]= 2 m uSp gamma[uSp]
```

This sets up an equation (note the ==), setting the value of pi[1], as expressed in terms of the initial speed uiS of the incoming particle in frame S, equal to the Lorentz transform of the corresponding momentum in frame S'. The equation is assigned the name eqpi1.

```
In[14]:= eqpi1 = gamma[uiS] m uiS == pi[1]
                                              2
Out[14]= m uiS gamma[uiS] == 2 m uSp gamma[uSp]
```

Here is the analogous equation for the fourth component of the initial momentum of the incoming particle in the lab frame.

```
In[15]:= eqpi4 = Simplify[gamma[uiS] m == pi[4] ]
                             2     2          2
                         m (c  + uSp ) gamma[uSp]
Out[15]= m gamma[uiS] == ─────────────────────────
                                    2
                                   c
```

This divides eqpi1 by eqpi4. The result gives u_i in terms of u'.

```
In[16]:= Simplify[EqTwoDivide[eqpi1,eqpi4] ]
```

$$Out[16]= \text{uiS} == \frac{2\ c^2\ \text{uSp}}{c^2 + \text{uSp}^2}$$

This solves for u' in terms of the given quantity u_i. The second solution is the physical one, in which uSp goes to zero as uiS goes to zero.

```
In[17]:= Solve[%,uSp]
```

$$Out[17]= \{\{\text{uSp} \to$$

$$> \frac{\dfrac{2\ c^2}{\text{uiS}} + \dfrac{2\ c\ \text{Sqrt}[c - \text{uiS}]\ \text{Sqrt}[c + \text{uiS}]}{\text{uiS}}}{2}\},$$

$$> \{\text{uSp} \to \frac{\dfrac{2\ c^2}{\text{uiS}} - \dfrac{2\ c\ \text{Sqrt}[c - \text{uiS}]\ \text{Sqrt}[c + \text{uiS}]}{\text{uiS}}}{2}\}\}$$

This defines a rule called uSpRule involving the solution of interest. It replaces uSp in terms of uiS, or u' in terms of u_i.

```
In[18]:= uSpRule = Simplify[%[[2,1]] ]
```

$$Out[18]= \text{uSp} \to \frac{c\ (c - \text{Sqrt}[c - \text{uiS}]\ \text{Sqrt}[c + \text{uiS}])}{\text{uiS}}$$

This defines the final momentum $p'_f[ua]$ of the originally incoming particle after collision, as measured in frame S'.

```
In[19]:= DefineTensor[ppf,{{1},1}]
PermWeight::def: Object ppf defined
```

This defines the corresponding final momentum in frame S.

```
In[20]:= DefineTensor[pf,{{1},1}]
PermWeight::def: Object pf defined
```

Before Lorentz transforming, you can set the values of the components of p'_f to those listed earlier. Here thetaSp is the angle θ' in frame S'.

```
In[21]:= ppf[1] = gamma[uSp] m uSp Cos[thetaSp]
Out[21]= m uSp Cos[thetaSp] gamma[uSp]
```

This is p'^2_f.

```
In[22]:= ppf[2] = gamma[uSp] m uSp Sin[thetaSp]
Out[22]= m uSp gamma[uSp] Sin[thetaSp]
```

Here are the third and fourth components.

```
In[23]:= ppf[3] = 0; ppf[4] = gamma[uSp] m
Out[23]= m gamma[uSp]
```

This expresses the components of pf by means of Lorentz transformation in terms of those of ppf.

```
In[24]:= lorentz[pf,ppf[ua] ]
Components assigned to pf
```

For example, here is pf[1] or $p_f{}^1$. The assigned values of the ppf[ua] components have been used.

```
In[25]:= pf[1]
                              thetaSp  2           2
Out[25]= 2 m uSp Cos[-------]  gamma[uSp]
                                 2
```

This uses the expression for pf[1] or $p_f{}^1$ in frame S to set up an equation (called eqpf1) in terms of the quantities in frame S'. You can ignore messages warning about possible spelling errors (or turn off the message General::spell1 if you wish).

```
In[26]:= eqpf1 =
  gamma[ufS] m ufS Cos[thetaS] == pf[1]
Out[26]= m ufS Cos[thetaS] gamma[ufS] ==

                       thetaSp  2           2
>     2 m uSp Cos[-------]  gamma[uSp]
                          2
```

Here is the corresponding equation for the second component.

```
In[27]:= eqpf2 =
  gamma[ufS] m ufS Sin[thetaS] == pf[2]
Out[27]= m ufS gamma[ufS] Sin[thetaS] ==

>     m uSp gamma[uSp] Sin[thetaSp]
```

Here is the equation for the fourth component.

```
In[28]:= eqpf4 =
  gamma[ufS] m == pf[4]
Out[28]= m gamma[ufS] ==

              2        2                          2
        m (c  + uSp  Cos[thetaSp]) gamma[uSp]
>     ---------------------------------------------
                           2
                          c
```

This divides eqpf2 by eqpf1, calling the result eqthetaS. Since uSp is known in terms of the given speed ui, this equation effectively gives thetaSp in terms of thetaS, or θ' in terms of the given angle θ.

```
In[29]:= eqthetaS = Simplify[ EqTwoDivide[eqpf2, eqpf1] ]
                              thetaSp
                         Tan[-------]
                                 2
Out[29]= Tan[thetaS] == ---------------
                          gamma[uSp]
```

Here it is explicitly.

```
In[30]:= Solve[eqthetaS,thetaSp]
Out[30]= {{thetaSp -> 2 ArcTan[gamma[uSp] Tan[thetaS]]}}
```

This rule can be used to replace θ' in terms of u' and θ. Now you can solve for the unknowns u_f, w_f, and ϕ in terms of u' (uSp) and θ' (thetaSp), both of which are known in terms of the given quantities u_i and θ.

```
In[31]:= thetaSpRule = %[[1,1]]
Out[31]= thetaSp -> 2 ArcTan[gamma[uSp] Tan[thetaS]]
```

This divides each side of eqpf4 by m. The resulting equation gives gamma[ufS], and hence ufS or u_f, in terms of u' and θ'. It is not particularly illuminating to use thetaSpRule followed by uSpRule to express the result explicitly in terms of the given u_i and θ.

```
In[32]:= EqDivide[eqpf4, m]
Out[32]= gamma[ufS] ==
```

$$> \qquad \frac{(c^2 + uSp^2\ Cos[thetaSp])\ gamma[uSp]^2}{c^2}$$

This defines qf[ua], which represents the final four-momentum $q_f{}^a$ of the target particle in the lab frame S.

```
In[33]:= DefineTensor[qf,{{1},1}]
PermWeight::def: Object qf defined
```

The 4-vector qpf[ua] represents the corresponding four-momentum $q'_f{}^a$ in the center-of-momentum frame S'.

```
In[34]:= DefineTensor[qpf,{{1},1}]
PermWeight::def: Object qpf defined
```

This assigns the value of $q'_f{}^1$, the first component of the four-momentum of the target particle after collision in the center-of-momentum frame S'.

```
In[35]:= qpf[1] = - gamma[uSp] m uSp Cos[thetaSp]
Out[35]= -(m uSp Cos[thetaSp] gamma[uSp])
```

This is the second component.

```
In[36]:= qpf[2] = - gamma[uSp] m uSp Sin[thetaSp]
Out[36]= -(m uSp gamma[uSp] Sin[thetaSp])
```

Here are the last two components.

```
In[37]:= qpf[3] = 0; qpf[4] = gamma[uSp] m
Out[37]= m gamma[uSp]
```

Do a Lorentz transformation to assign the components of qf[ua] or $q_f a$ in the lab frame.

```
In[38]:= lorentz[qf, qpf[ua] ]
Components assigned to qf
```

On the left-hand side of this equation is the expression for qf[1] in terms of the speed wf (or w_f) and angle phi (or ϕ) measured in the lab frame S. The right-hand side is the result of the Lorentz transformation from S' to S.

```
In[39]:= eqqf1 =
gamma[wf] m wf Cos[phi] == qf[1]
Out[39]= m wf Cos[phi] gamma[wf] ==
```

$$> \qquad 2\ m\ uSp\ gamma[uSp]\ Sin\left[\frac{thetaSp}{2}\right]^2$$

This is the analogous equation for qf[2] or $q_f{}^2$.

```
In[40]:= eqqf2 =
 -gamma[wf] m wf Sin[phi] == qf[2]
Out[40]= -(m wf gamma[wf] Sin[phi]) ==
>     -(m uSp gamma[uSp] Sin[thetaSp])
```

This is the equation for the fourth component of the final momentum of the target particle in the lab frame.

```
In[41]:= eqqf4 =
  gamma[wf] m == qf[4]
```

$$Out[41]= \text{m gamma[wf] } ==$$

$$> \quad \frac{\text{m (c}^2 - \text{uSp}^2 \text{ Cos[thetaSp]) gamma[uSp]}^2}{\text{c}^2}$$

Notice the similarity of `eqqf4` to this equation for `pf[4]` or $p_f{}^4$. You can solve for `gamma[wf]` in the same way that you solved earlier for `gamma[ufS]`. Only `phi` or ϕ remains to be found.

```
In[42]:= eqpf4
```

$$Out[42]= \text{m gamma[ufS] } ==$$

$$> \quad \frac{\text{m (c}^2 + \text{uSp}^2 \text{ Cos[thetaSp]) gamma[uSp]}^2}{\text{c}^2}$$

This gives `phi` in terms of `thetaSp` and `uSp`.

```
In[43]:= eqphi = Simplify[ EqTwoDivide[eqqf2, eqqf1] ]
```

$$Out[43]= -\text{Tan[phi]} == -\left(\frac{\text{Cot}[\frac{\text{thetaSp}}{2}]}{\text{gamma[uSp]}}\right)$$

This multiplies each side by -1 to get rid of the minus signs.

```
In[44]:= eqphi = EqTimes[%,-1]
```

$$Out[44]= \text{Tan[phi]} == \frac{\text{Cot}[\frac{\text{thetaSp}}{2}]}{\text{gamma[uSp]}}$$

You can use `thetaSpRule` and `uSpRule` to express `Tan[phi]` in terms of the quantities given in the lab frame. The result is surprisingly simple.

```
In[45]:= Simplify[eqphi//.{thetaSpRule, uSpRule}]
```

$$Out[45]= \text{Tan[phi]} ==$$

$$> \quad \frac{\text{Cot[thetaS]}}{\text{gamma}[\frac{\text{c (c - Sqrt[c - uiS] Sqrt[c + uiS]) 2}}{\text{uiS}}]}$$

This substitution expresses the function `gamma` in terms of its argument.

```
In[46]:= Simplify[%/. gamma[a_] ->
  (1-a^2/Lightc^2)^(-1/2)]
```

$$Out[46]= \text{Tan[phi]} == (1 -$$

$$> \quad \frac{(\text{c - Sqrt[c - uiS] Sqrt[c + uiS]})^2}{\text{uiS}^2}) \text{ Cot[thetaS]}$$

A second way to get at this result is to multiply each side of `eqphi` by each side of `eqthetaS`.

```
In[47]:= EqTwoTimes[eqphi,eqthetaS]

Out[47]= Tan[phi] Tan[thetaS] == gamma[uSp]
                                            -2
```

Then apply `uSpRule`.

```
In[48]:= Simplify[%/.uSpRule]

Out[48]= Tan[phi] Tan[thetaS] ==

             c (c - Sqrt[c - uiS] Sqrt[c + uiS]) -2
 >     gamma[------------------------------------]
                            uiS
```

Finally put in the explicit function for **gamma**. This is equivalent to the previous result for `Tan[phi]`. When $(u_i)^2$ is small with respect to c^2, the right-hand side approaches 1, which implies that in the nonrelativistic limit, $\theta + \phi \rightarrow \pi/2$, a well-known result.

```
In[49]:= Simplify[%/. gamma[a_] ->
(1-a^2/Lightc^2)^(-1/2)]

Out[49]= Tan[phi] Tan[thetaS] ==

                                               2
             (c - Sqrt[c - uiS] Sqrt[c + uiS])
 >     1 - -----------------------------------
                          2
                       uiS
```

This completes the solution for the relativistic scattering of two particles of equal rest mass m, given the initial speed u_i and the final scattering angle θ in the lab frame.

Chapter 8

Nonlinear Elasticity in Engineering Mechanics

Nonlinear elasticity is an active field of mechanics with many important applications in civil and mechanical engineering. In this chapter, you will see how *MathTensor* can be used to solve complicated problems in nonlinear elasticity. The outline of the theory and notation given here follows the classic text, A. E. Green and W. Zerna, *Theoretical Elasticity* (Oxford University Press, London, 1968), which has appeared in a 1993 Dover edition. You can find more detailed explanations there.

The first part of this chapter is a brief introduction to the theory of nonlinear elasticity, including curvilinear coordinate systems and metrics associated with a body in its unstrained and strained states, basis vectors, and the stress tensor and its expression in terms of invariants for an elastically isotropic body.

Following the summary of the basic theory, the examples of simple shear of a rectangular solid and torsional deformation of a cylinder from the text of Green and Zerna will be illustrated, emphasizing the use of *MathTensor*. This chapter is designed to help you apply *MathTensor* to your own engineering problems or research in elasticity. We thank Prof. Gautam Dasgupta (Columbia University) for helpful suggestions.

■ 8.1 Finite Deformation of a Body

■ 8.1.1 Deformation Metrics and Strain

Let B_0 represent the undeformed state of a 3-dimensional body. Let B represent the deformed state of the same body after it has undergone a deformation resulting from the action of external forces (see Fig. 8–1). The basic problem is to deduce a set of forces that produce a specified deformation.

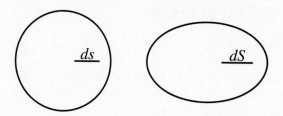

Fig. 8–1 Distances ds and dS between the same two molecules in B_0 and B.

Rigid translations or rotations of a body do not change the relative positions of molecules or the relative configuration of forces causing a deformation. Therefore to get at the relation between the deformation and forces, it is sufficient and most convenient to work with quantities that depend on changes in the relative positions of the molecules, not on their absolute positions. A convenient measure of the relative position of two molecules is the distance between the molecules.

Let θ^a be a 3-dimensional system of coordinates, which in general may be curvilinear. (Here, we depart somewhat from the notation of Green and Zerna. They use lower indices on the coordinates themselves and upper indices on the differentials of the same coordinates. We use upper indices on both the coordinates and their differentials.) Suppose that the coordinate system is deformed with the body so that a given molecule has the *same* values of the coordinates θ^a when the body is in its undeformed or deformed states. Thus the θ^a are a body-fixed coordinate system undergoing deformation as the body is deformed. The square of the physical distance between two given *nearby* molecules of the body is quadratic in the coordinate separations, $d\theta^a$, and has the general form

$$ds^2 = g_{ab}d\theta^a d\theta^b \qquad (8.1)$$

in the undeformed state B_0 and

$$dS^2 = G_{ab}d\theta^a d\theta^b \qquad (8.2)$$

in the deformed state B. In general, the physical distance between two molecules changes as the body is deformed, even though the coordinate separation $d\theta^a$ does not change (see Fig. 8–1).

You will recognize the quantities g_{ab} and G_{ab} as metric tensors (see Chapter 1). The first is associated with the body in its undeformed state B_0 and the second with the body in its deformed state B. The metrics vary from point to point in the body. [1]

   The values of ds and dS are physically measurable quantities and do not change if θ^a undergoes a coordinate transformation to new body-fixed coordinates θ'^a. Hence, the two metrics g_{ab} and G_{ab} each transform as covariant tensors. Therefore half their difference is a tensor, which characterizes the change in the relative positions of molecules:

$$\gamma_{ab} \equiv (1/2)(G_{ab} - g_{ab}). \tag{8.3}$$

The tensor γ_{ab} is called the *strain* tensor. It is the most basic quantity upon which the forces required to produce a deformation depend. The strain tensor has been defined here prior to basis vectors in order to bring out its fundamental nature.

■ 8.1.2 Basis Vectors

Choose an origin fixed in space and let $\mathbf{r}$ denote the position vector of a molecule of the body in its undeformed state B_0. Let $\mathbf{R}$ be the position vector of the same molecule of the body in its deformed state B. Now consider a different nearby molecule at position $\mathbf{r} + \mathbf{dr}$ in B_0 and $\mathbf{R} + \mathbf{dR}$ in B (see Fig. 8–2).

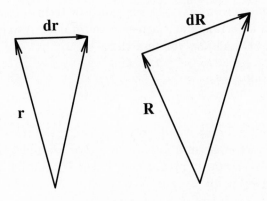

Fig. 8–2 Position vectors $\mathbf{r}$, $\mathbf{dr}$ in B_0, and $\mathbf{R}$, $\mathbf{dR}$ in B.

---

[1]The quantity G_{ab} is closely related to the right Cauchy-Green deformation tensor — see, for example, A. J. M. Spencer, *Continuum Mechanics* (Longman Group Ltd., London, 1980), pp. 70–75, and compare values for simple shear, as calculated later in this chapter. See also Section 8.1.3.

Suppose that θ^a are the coordinates of the first molecule and $\theta^a + d\theta^a$ of the second molecule. You can define basis vectors $\mathbf{g}_a$ at the position of the first molecule in the undeformed body by writing

$$\mathbf{dr} = d\theta^a \mathbf{g}_a. \tag{8.4}$$

The three vectors $\mathbf{g}_a$ constitute basis vectors for the θ^a coordinate system in B_0. It is clear, for example, that $\mathbf{g}_1$ points in the direction of increasing θ^1 in the undeformed body. Similarly, you can define basis vectors $\mathbf{G}_a$ by writing

$$\mathbf{dR} = d\theta^a \mathbf{G}_a. \tag{8.5}$$

The $\mathbf{G}_a$ are basis vectors for the θ^a coordinate system in B. They point in the direction of increasing θ^a in the deformed configuration.

The square of the physical distance between the two molecules in the undeformed state B_0 is

$$ds^2 = \mathbf{dr} \cdot \mathbf{dr} = \mathbf{g}_a \cdot \mathbf{g}_b d\theta^a d\theta^b \tag{8.6}$$

and in the deformed state is

$$dS^2 = \mathbf{dR} \cdot \mathbf{dR} = \mathbf{G}_a \cdot \mathbf{G}_b d\theta^a d\theta^b. \tag{8.7}$$

Here, the scalar or dot product of two vectors has the usual form in terms of the components of the vectors relative to a rectangular Cartesian coordinate system. Comparing these equations with Eqs. (1) and (2), you find that

$$\mathbf{g}_a \cdot \mathbf{g}_b = g_{ab} \tag{8.8}$$

and

$$\mathbf{G}_a \cdot \mathbf{G}_b = G_{ab}. \tag{8.9}$$

It follows that, in general, these basis vectors are not unit vectors. For example, G_1 has length $(G_{11})^{1/2}$. They are also not necessarily orthogonal, so the θ^a coordinate axes form an oblique system at any given point.

Define the vector

$$\mathbf{G}^a \equiv G^{ab} \mathbf{G}_b, \tag{8.10}$$

where G^{ab} is the matrix inverse of G_{ab}. Then by taking the dot product of this equation with $\mathbf{G}_c$, you obtain

$$\mathbf{G}_c \cdot \mathbf{G}^a = \delta_c{}^a. \tag{8.11}$$

This means, for example, that at any given point of the body, the vector $\mathbf{G}^1$ points in the direction orthogonal to both $\mathbf{G}_2$ and $\mathbf{G}_3$. From Eq. (10), it follows that the length of $\mathbf{G}^1$ is $(G^{11})^{1/2}$. Similar statements can be made about the other raised basis vectors $\mathbf{G}^2$ and $\mathbf{G}^3$. You can also define similar raised basis vectors $\mathbf{g}^a$ using the metric and basis vectors corresponding to the undeformed body.

If possible, the θ^a coordinate system is chosen so that the surfaces of the body are surfaces in which one of the coordinates is held constant. For example, for an undeformed cylinder you would very naturally choose cylindrical coordinates. Because the θ^a coordinates are body-fixed, the surfaces of the deformed body will also be surfaces in which one of the coordinates is fixed.

If θ^1 is constant on a surface of the body, then in the deformed state B the vectors $\mathbf{G}_2$ and $\mathbf{G}_3$ at any point on the surface will be tangent to the surface, while the vector $\mathbf{G}^1$ (*not* $\mathbf{G}_1$) will be normal to the surface. These vectors are useful in finding the tangential and normal components of surface forces.

In practice, a Cartesian rectangular coordinate system is often introduced with the coordinates of a molecule expressed relative to an orthogonal set of axes fixed in space. Let $\mathcal{C}$ be this space-fixed Cartesian system of coordinates. A molecule having given body-fixed coordinates $(\theta^1, \theta^2, \theta^3)$ will have different coordinates before and after deformation of the body relative to the space-fixed Cartesian system $\mathcal{C}$. Let the molecule in the undeformed state B_0 of the body have coordinates in $\mathcal{C}$ given by $(x^1(\theta^1, \theta^2, \theta^3), x^2(\theta^1, \theta^2, \theta^3), x^3(\theta^1, \theta^2, \theta^3))$. In the deformed state B of the body, let the same molecule have coordinates relative to $\mathcal{C}$ given by $(y^1(\theta^1, \theta^2, \theta^3), y^2(\theta^1, \theta^2, \theta^3), y^3(\theta^1, \theta^2, \theta^3))$. In general, the θ^a coordinate system may be curvilinear. The metric in Cartesian coordinates $\mathcal{C}$ is δ_{ab}. If the above functions for the x^a and y^a are known, then the undeformed and deformed metrics g_{ab} and G_{ab} relative to the body-fixed θ^a coordinates can be found by making the appropriate coordinate transformation of these covariant metric tensors (as given in Chapter 1). In the undeformed state of the body, the result is

$$g_{ab} = (\partial x^c / \partial \theta^a)(\partial x^d / \partial \theta^b)\,\delta_{cd}. \tag{8.12}$$

In the deformed state of the body, you obtain the same form, but with the functions y^a replacing x^a.

$$G_{ab} = (\partial y^c / \partial \theta^a)(\partial y^d / \partial \theta^b)\,\delta_{cd}. \tag{8.13}$$

When the functions x^a and y^a are known, these equations may be used to calculate the metrics g_{ab} and G_{ab}. This calculation is easily done using the *MathTensor* function `Ttransform`, as is illustrated in the examples.

■ 8.1.3   Relation to Cauchy-Green Strain Tensors

It is illuminating to relate the metric tensor to other tensors commonly used in the theory of elasticity. Suppose you were to choose the body-fixed coordinates θ^a to coincide with an orthogonal Cartesian coordinate system in the undeformed state of the body (as in our first example of simple shear). In the notation of the previous section, this means that $\theta^a = x^a$. Because the body-fixed coordinates of a molecule do not change upon deformation, it follows from Eq. (12) and Eq. (13) that

$$g_{ab} = \delta_{ab} \tag{8.14}$$

and

$$G_{ab} = (\partial y^c/\partial x^a)(\partial y^d/\partial x^b)\,\delta_{cd}. \tag{8.15}$$

Referred to the original orthogonal Cartesian coordinate system (i.e., the space-fixed Cartesian system), the coordinates y^a give the position of a molecule in the deformed state, which was at position x^a in the undeformed state. The 3×3 matrix **F**, with elements

$$(\partial y^a/\partial x^b), \tag{8.16}$$

is known as the deformation gradient (index a gives the row and index b the column). (In some literature, the deformation gradient is defined as the gradient of the displacement, $(y^a - x^a)$, rather than of y^a.)

The *right Cauchy-Green strain tensor* is defined as

$$F^T F, \tag{8.17}$$

where the superscript T denotes the transposed matrix. Comparing this definition with Eq. (15), you see that the elements of the right Cauchy-Green strain tensor are the covariant components G_{ab} of the metric of the deformed body.

The contravariant components of the metric tensor of the deformed body are obtained from the contravariant metric tensor, δ^{ab}, of the undeformed body by the transformation

$$G^{ab} = (\partial y^a/\partial x^c)(\partial y^b/\partial x^d)\,\delta^{cd}. \tag{8.18}$$

These are the components of the *left Cauchy-Green strain tensor*, which is defined as the matrix

$$FF^T. \tag{8.19}$$

Thus if you were to work in an orthogonal Cartesian coordinate system, then the covariant and contravariant metric tensors of the deformed body would be the same as the right and left Cauchy-Green strain tensors, respectively. Our use of general curvilinear body-fixed coordinates θ^a generalizes the theory based on Cartesian tensors in a natural and effective way.

■ 8.1.4 The Stress Tensor

Consider a small surface element dA at a point inside the body in its deformed state B. Let

$$\mathbf{n} = n_a \mathbf{G}^a \qquad (8.20)$$

be a unit vector normal to the surface element. Thus $\mathbf{n} \cdot \mathbf{n} = 1 = n_a n_b G^{ab}$.

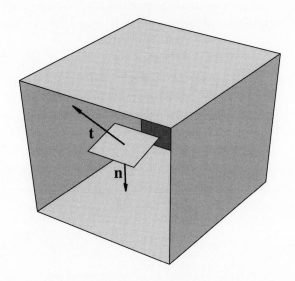

Fig. 8–3 Surface element, normal $\mathbf{n}$, and traction $\mathbf{t}$.

Let the positive side of the surface be the side toward which $\mathbf{n}$ points. The material of the body on the positive side of the surface exerts a force per unit area $\mathbf{t}$ on the material on the negative side of the surface (see Fig. 8–3). The vector $\mathbf{t}$ is called the traction vector. It is not necessarily perpendicular to the surface element. The stress tensor τ^{ab} is defined by

$$\mathbf{t} \equiv \tau^{ab} n_a \mathbf{G}_b. \qquad (8.21)$$

It can be shown, as a consequence of the equation of motion involving the balance of torques and angular momenta, that the stress tensor is symmetric, $\tau^{ab} = \tau^{ba}$.

If the surface element lies, for example, in the surface $\theta^1 = $ constant, then $\mathbf{n}$ can be chosen to point in the direction of $\mathbf{G}^1$, with $n_2 = 0$, $n_3 = 0$, and $n_1 = (G^{11})^{-1/2}$. Then the force per unit area acting on the surface element would be

$$\mathbf{t} = (G^{11})^{-1/2} \tau^{1b} \mathbf{G}_b. \qquad (8.22)$$

In order to guarantee equilibrium, the traction vector **t** near the surface bounding the body must approach the externally applied surface force per unit area **P**.

If there are no external body forces, such as would be produced by a gravitational field acting on each mass element of the body, and if the mass elements of the body are not undergoing acceleration, then Newton's laws of motion require that the traction forces must integrate to zero over the surface of any internal volume element of the body. It can be shown that as a consequence of the Gauss divergence theorem, this balance of traction forces in the deformed state is equivalent to the equation

$$\tau^{ab}{}_{;b} = 0, \tag{8.23}$$

where the semicolon denotes the covariant derivative with respect to the metric G_{ab} of the deformed body. When an external body force **F** per unit mass is acting on the mass element at the point under consideration and the mass element has acceleration **f**, then Eq. (23) will contain additional terms to take into account the body forces and accelerations:

$$\tau^{ab}{}_{;b} + \rho \mathbf{F}^a = \rho \mathbf{f}^a. \tag{8.24}$$

Here, ρ is the mass per unit volume of the body at the point under consideration.

■ 8.1.5 Displacement and Strain

The displacement vector **v** is the vector from the position of a molecule in the undeformed state B_0 to its position in the deformed state B:

$$\mathbf{v} = \mathbf{R} - \mathbf{r}. \tag{8.25}$$

The strain tensor γ_{ab} can be expressed in terms of the components of the displacement vector. This is proved in Green and Zerna as follows.

From Eqs. (4) and (5), you see that

$$\partial \mathbf{r}/\partial \theta^a = \mathbf{g}_a, \quad \partial \mathbf{R}/\partial \theta^a = \mathbf{G}_a. \tag{8.26}$$

Therefore

$$\partial \mathbf{v}/\partial \theta^a = \mathbf{G}_a - \mathbf{g}_a. \tag{8.27}$$

Then from Eqs. (3), (8), and (9), you find

$$\gamma_{ab} = (1/2)(\mathbf{G}_a \cdot \mathbf{G}_b - \mathbf{g}_a \cdot \mathbf{g}_b). \tag{8.28}$$

Using Eq. (27) to eliminate $\mathbf{g}_a$, you obtain

$$\gamma_{ab} = (1/2)(\mathbf{G}_a \cdot \mathbf{v}_{,b} + \mathbf{G}_b \cdot \mathbf{v}_{,a} - \mathbf{v}_{,a} \cdot \mathbf{v}_{,b}), \tag{8.29}$$

where $\partial \mathbf{v}/\partial \theta^a$ has been abbreviated as $v_{,a}$. This can be expressed in terms of components of the displacement vector.

With the basis vectors $\mathbf{G}^a$ of the deformed state B, the displacement vector can be written as

$$\mathbf{v} = V_a \mathbf{G}^a. \tag{8.30}$$

It can be shown that in general

$$\mathbf{v}_{,b} = V_{a;b} \mathbf{G}^a, \tag{8.31}$$

where $V_{a;b}$ is the covariant derivative of V_a with respect to θ^b, calculated using the affine connections formed from the metric G_{ab} of the deformed state B. Using Eq. (11), you then obtain from Eq. (29) the result,

$$\gamma_{ab} = (1/2)(V_{a;b} + V_{b;a} - G^{cd} V_{c;a} V_{d;b}). \tag{8.32}$$

The strain tensor γ_{ab} can also be expressed in terms of the components v_a of the displacement vector $\mathbf{v}$ with respect to the basis vectors $\mathbf{g}^a$ of the undeformed state B_0. The result has the same form as Eq. (32), but with the components V_a replaced by v_a, G^{cd} replaced by g^{cd}, and covariant derivatives calculated using the metric g^{cd}.

These equations offer an alternate way to calculate the strain tensor. If the coordinate system is Cartesian, then the covariant derivatives reduce to ordinary partial derivatives, and the equations are simplified. However, in the examples considered here, it will be convenient to calculate the strain tensor directly by means of Eq. (3).

■ 8.1.6 Stress and Strain in an Elastic Body

The total energy of the body can be expressed as the sum of its kinetic energy and internal energy U. Here, U refers to the energy associated with the internal degrees of freedom of the body. For example, U includes the potential energy associated with the forces acting between the molecules of the body. This potential energy depends on the configuration of the molecules and will change as the body is deformed. In addition, U includes the energy of the random thermal motions of the molecules. The latter changes as the temperature of the body changes or as heat energy flows internally or across the surface of the body. It can be shown (see Green and Zerna) that the rate of change of the internal energy is given by

$$\dot{U} = \int \tau^{ab} \dot{\gamma}_{ab} dv. \tag{8.33}$$

Here, the dot denotes differentiation with respect to time, holding the coordinates θ^a constant, and the integration is over the volume of the body. Thus the rate of change of the internal energy is the volume integral of the product of the stress tensor with the rate of change of the strain tensor.

Suppose that the deformation is reversible, in the sense that it takes place through a sequence of near equilibrium states, and that it occurs at constant temperature, or at constant entropy. Then the internal energy will often depend only on the initial and final configurations of the molecules and can be expressed as a volume integral over a potential function E. That is, $U = \int \rho E dv$, where ρ is the instantaneous value of the mass density. Because the mass of a given volume of molecules does not change, the quantity ρdv is independent of time, so that

$$\dot{U} = \int \rho \dot{E} dv. \tag{8.34}$$

It follows that

$$\tau^{ab} \dot{\gamma}_{ab} = \rho \dot{E}. \tag{8.35}$$

In an elastic body, the stress tensor τ^{ab} and the potential E depend only on the instantaneous value of the strain tensor γ_{ab} (apart from the given initial configuration of the body). Expressing $\dot{E}$ in terms of partial derivatives with respect to γ_{ab} and cancelling factors of $\dot{\gamma}_{ab}$, you finally obtain

$$\tau^{ab} = \frac{1}{2}\rho \left(\frac{\partial E}{\partial \gamma^{ab}} + \frac{\partial E}{\partial \gamma^{ba}} \right). \tag{8.36}$$

In this expression, when indices a and b are not equal, the variables γ^{ab} and γ^{ba} are regarded as independent when taking partial derivatives.

■ 8.1.7 Elastically Isotropic Body

Suppose that density of the body is constant in its undeformed state B_0. In addition, suppose that the body is elastically isotropic, which means that its elastic potential E at any given point can be expressed as a function of invariants (which do not change when the body or coordinate system is rotated about the given point).

There are three independent invariants, I_1, I_2, and I_3, that can be formed from the metrics g_{ab} and G_{ab} of the body in its undeformed and deformed states, respectively. The three invariants can be defined as

$$I_1 = g^{ab} G_{ab} = (2g)^{-1} e^{acd} e^{bef} G_{ab} g_{ce} g_{df}, \tag{8.37}$$

$$I_2 = G^{ab} g_{ab} (G/g) = (2g)^{-1} e^{acd} e^{bef} g_{ab} G_{ce} G_{df}, \tag{8.38}$$

and

$$I_3 = G/g = g^{-1} e^{acd} e^{bef} G_{ab} G_{ce} G_{df}. \tag{8.39}$$

Here, G and g are the determinants of G_{ab} and g_{ab}, respectively, and e^{abc} is the totally antisymmetric three-index object (permutation symbol) normalized so that $e^{123} = 1$. Notice that in I_1, I_2, and I_3, the tensor G_{ab} appears once, twice, and three times, respectively. These invariants are not necessarily constant. They may depend on scalar functions of the coordinates (as in the example of torsional deformation of a cylinder given later).

For a body consisting of an elastically isotropic material, the elastic potential E may depend on I_1, I_2, and I_3, as well as on possible further scalar functions of the coordinates. When E is a function only of the three invariants I_1, I_2, and I_3, the body is said to be elastically homogeneous as well as isotropic. Only such bodies will be considered further.

From the last expression for each invariant, it is a relatively simple matter to evaluate the partial derivatives with respect to $\gamma_{ab} = (1/2)(G_{ab} - g_{ab})$ in Eq. (36), with E regarded as a function of the three invariants I_a. The final result (see Green and Zerna, Chapter 2) can be written in the form

$$\tau^{ab} = \Phi g^{ab} + \Psi B^{ab} + p G^{ab}, \tag{8.40}$$

where Φ, Ψ, and p are functions formed from partial derivatives of the elastic potential with respect to the invariants I_1, I_2, and I_3, respectively. Φ, Ψ, and p are invariant functions of the coordinates, since they depend only on the I_j. The tensor B^{ab} is defined as

$$B^{ab} = g^{-1} e^{acd} e^{bef} g_{ce} G_{df} = I_1 g^{ab} - g^{ac} g^{bd} G_{cd} \tag{8.41}$$

and is obtained from partial derivatives of I_2 with respect to the strain tensor.

With the form of the stress tensor in Eq. (40), you can find the forces acting on an elastically homogeneous and isotropic body of constant undeformed density when the body undergoes a given deformation. The results will be expressed in terms of the functions Φ, Ψ, and p. If the elastic potential is known, p can be calculated (in the case of an incompressible body, the function p must be obtained from equilibrium and boundary conditions). The procedure for finding the components of stress and the surface forces in terms of Φ, Ψ, and p will be illustrated in several examples using *MathTensor*.

■ 8.2 Simple Shear Deformation of a Solid

■ 8.2.1 Finding the Metric Tensors

Consider a rectangular solid block of uniform density in 3 dimensions. Let (x, y, z) denote the coordinates of a point in the solid relative to a fixed rectangular coordinate system. Suppose that you next deform the solid so that each point is deformed in the x-direction by a distance proportional to the y-coordinate of the point (see Fig. 8–4). Such a deformation is called simple shear.

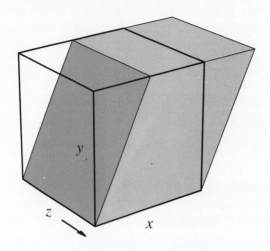

Fig. 8–4 Simple Shear. The body-fixed θ^i axes initially coincide with the
space-fixed x-, y-, and z-axes, but after deformation, the θ^2 axis
coincides with the oblique edge of the sheared body.
The direction of the z-axis is shown.

Relative to the fixed rectangular coordinate system, a point that had coordinates (x, y, z) in the undeformed body, has coordinates (x', y', z') after the shear deformation, where

$$x' = x + Ky, \quad y' = y, \quad z' = z. \tag{8.42}$$

Here, K is a constant, giving the tangent of the angle through which edges of the solid that were originally parallel to the y-axis are turned by the shear deformation.

Consider now a set of axes formed by the edges of the solid that intersect at a corner of the solid (which we assume to be at the origin). The appropriate body-fixed coordinates θ^a, defined in the previous sections, are the coordinates based on these body-fixed axes. Before deformation, the coordinates of a molecule are $\theta^1 = x$, $\theta^2 = y$, and $\theta^3 = z$, and these coordinate values do not change in the θ^a coordinate system as the solid is deformed.

Originally, these edges of the body coincide with the rectangular axes fixed in space. But after deformation, the edges form an oblique coordinate system. As noted, the coordinates of each physical point (i.e., molecule) of the solid do not change relative to these oblique body-fixed axes. Each point of the solid initially has the same coordinates (x, y, z) relative to the space-fixed and body-fixed axes. However, after the shear deformation a given molecule of the body has the same coordinates (x, y, z) relative to the body-fixed oblique axes but has coordinates (x', y', z') relative to the space-fixed rectangular axes. The relation between the two sets of coordinates is given by the above transformation equations.

In the undeformed state, B_0, the body-fixed θ^a coordinate system coincides with the rectangular space-fixed coordinate system. The distance between two nearby molecules in the undeformed state has the usual form in rectangular coordinates. This form corresponds to Eq. (1), with the metric of the undeformed state of the body given by

$$g_{ab} = \delta_{ab}. \tag{8.43}$$

Here, δ_{ab} is the Kronecker delta, which is 1 if $a = b$ and 0 otherwise. It is the metric tensor of a rectangular orthogonal coordinate system. (In *MathTensor*, the Kronecker delta δ_{ab} is typed in as `Kdelta[1a,1b]` and appears in the output line as Kdelta$_{ab}$.)

Next consider the deformed state, B, of the body. Two nearby molecules of the deformed solid have coordinate separations (dx', dy', dz') relative to the space-fixed rectangular axes and (dx, dy, dz) relative to the body-fixed oblique axes. The square of the distance between the two molecules relative to the space-fixed orthogonal axes is then

$$dS^2 = (dx')^2 + (dy')^2 + (dz')^2 = \delta_{ab}dx'^a dx'^b, \tag{8.44}$$

where (a, b) are summed from 1 to 3 and $x'^1 = x'$, $x'^2 = y'$, and $x'^3 = z'$. This same squared distance, expressed in terms of the coordinate separation of the molecules relative to the oblique body-fixed axes, has the form

$$dS^2 = \text{ga}_{ab}dx^a dx^b, \tag{8.45}$$

where ga$_{ab}$ is the metric tensor in the oblique coordinate system (i.e., the θ^a coordinate system). Comparison of Eq. (45) with Eq. (2) shows that $G_{ab} = \text{ga}_{ab}$. (Here, ga is regarded as a single symbol representing the name of the metric.) The first thing you have to find is this metric ga$_{ab}$ of the body in its deformed state B.

The *MathTensor* function `Ttransform` can do this calculation. In this case, it is performing the coordinate transformation of Eq. (13). The *MathTensor* session is already given as one of the brief examples in Chapter 1. Here are the steps of the calculation.

Let `coords` be a list of the body-fixed coordinates of a point.

```
In[1]:= coords = {x,y,z}
Out[1]= {x, y, z}
```

The space is 3-dimensional.

```
In[2]:= Dimension = Length[coords]
Out[2]= 3
```

Next list the right-hand sides of the transformation equations giving the space-fixed coordinates x', y', z' of the point in the deformed body.

```
In[3]:= trans = {x + K y, y, z}
Out[3]= {x + K y, y, z}
```

Define the metric tensor `ga[la,lb]` of the body-fixed oblique coordinates, x, y, z.

```
In[4]:= DefineTensor[ga,{{2,1},1}]
  PermWeight::sym: Symmetries of ga assigned
  PermWeight::def: Object ga defined
```

Use `Ttransform` to calculate the components of metric `ga`. The last argument is −1 because the given transformation equations are *from* oblique coordinates having metric `ga` *to* rectangular coordinates having metric `Kdelta`, while `ga` is to be found in terms of `Kdelta`. That is, the coordinate and tensor transformations are in opposite directions.

```
In[5]:= Ttransform[ga,Kdelta[la,lb],coords,trans,-1]
  Components assigned to ga
```

These are the calculated components of `ga`.

```
In[6]:= MatrixForm[Table[ga[-i,-j],{i,3},{j,3}] ]
Out[6]//MatrixForm=
```

$$\begin{pmatrix} 1 & K & 0 \\ K & 1 + K^2 & 0 \\ 0 & 0 & 1 \end{pmatrix}$$

■ 8.2.2 Finding the Invariants I_1, I_2, and I_3

Now that you have the metrics $g_{ab} = \delta_{ab}$ and $G_{ab} = ga_{ab}$, you can calculate the invariants given in Eqs. (37), (38), and (39). The inverse undeformed metric is obviously $g^{ab} = \delta^{ab}$, but calculation is necessary to find the inverse deformed metric ga^{ab}. (The term "undeformed metric" refers to the metric of the undeformed state

B_0, and "deformed metric" refers to that of the deformed state B.)

This builds a matrix from the components of ga_{ab}.

```
In[7]:= gaLowerMatrix = Table[ga[-i,-j],{i,3},{j,3}]

Out[7]= {{1, K, 0}, {K, 1 + K , 0}, {0, 0, 1}}
                               2
```

This is the matrix inverse, the components of which are those of ga^{ab}.

```
In[8]:= gaUpperMatrix = Inverse[gaLowerMatrix]

Out[8]= {{1 + K , -K, 0}, {-K, 1, 0}, {0, 0, 1}}
               2
```

The components of ga^{ab} are now assigned.

```
In[9]:= ga[a_,b_]/;PosIntegerQ[a]&&PosIntegerQ[b] :=
        gaUpperMatrix[[a,b]]
```

The determinant of ga_{ab} is unity, as is that of δ_{ab}, so that the shear deformation does not change volume.

```
In[10]:= detga = Det[gaLowerMatrix]
Out[10]= 1
```

From Eq. (39), we immediately see that $I_3 = 1$.

```
In[11]:= I3 = 1
Out[11]= 1
```

Here is the invariant I_1 of Eq. (37).

```
In[12]:= I1 = Simplify[ MakeSum[Kdelta[ua,ub] ga[la,lb] ]
         ]

Out[12]= 3 + K
               2
```

Here is I_2 of Eq. (38). In this example, I_1 and I_2 are equal.

```
In[13]:= I2 = Simplify[ MakeSum[ga[ua,ub] Kdelta[la,lb]
         I3] ]

Out[13]= 3 + K
               2
```

These results show that for simple shear, the three invariants are constants. It follows that Φ, Ψ, and p are constant as well, depending only on the angle of shear through K, but independent of position in the body.

■ 8.2.3 Finding the Stress Tensor

The stress tensor is calculated from Eq. (40), with B^{ab} given by Eq. (41).

Define a symmetric tensor B^{ab}.

```
In[14]:= DefineTensor[B,{{2,1},1}]
         PermWeight::sym: Symmetries of B assigned
         PermWeight::def: Object B defined
```

This defines a rule based on Eq. (41) for obtaining the components of B^{ab}. **MakeSum** will sum over the paired dummy indices.

```
In[15]:= B[a_,b_]/;PosIntegerQ[a]&&PosIntegerQ[b] :=
   I1 Kdelta[a,b] - MakeSum[Kdelta[a,ua] Kdelta[b,ub]
ga[1a,1b] ]
```

Here are the components of B^{ab}.

```
In[16]:= MatrixForm[Table[B[i,j],{i,3},{j,3}] ]
Out[16]//MatrixForm=
```

$$\begin{pmatrix} 2 + K^2 & -K & 0 \\ -K & 2 & 0 \\ 0 & 0 & 2 + K^2 \end{pmatrix}$$

Define the symmetric tensor t^{ab} to represent the stress tensor τ^{ab}.

```
In[17]:= DefineTensor[t,{{2,1},1}]
PermWeight::sym: Symmetries of t assigned
PermWeight::def: Object t defined
```

This defines a rule based on Eq. (40) to calculate the stress tensor.

```
In[18]:= t[a_,b_]/;PosIntegerQ[a]&&PosIntegerQ[b] :=
   Phi Kdelta[a,b] + Psi B[a,b] + p ga[a,b]
```

Here is one component of the stress tensor.

```
In[19]:= t[1,1]
```
$$Out[19]= (1 + K^2) p + Phi + (2 + K^2) Psi$$

This lists the values of all the components of t^{ab}.

```
In[20]:= Table[t[i,j],{i,3},{j,3}]
```
$$Out[20]= \{\{(1 + K^2) p + Phi + (2 + K^2) Psi,$$
$$>   -(K p) - K Psi, 0\},$$
$$>   \{-(K p) - K Psi, p + Phi + 2 Psi, 0\},$$
$$>   \{0, 0, p + Phi + (2 + K^2) Psi\}\}$$

■ 8.2.4 Finding the Surface Forces

The forces acting on the external surfaces of the body may be found from the traction vector **t**. Recall that as one approaches the boundary of the body, **t** must approach the force per unit area **P** acting on the body. The traction is given by Eq. (21).

Consider the right-hand surface of the *deformed* body. It is a surface of constant θ^1 (this is obvious in the undeformed state and must be true in the deformed state because the θ^a coordinates of the molecules at the surface do not change as the body is deformed). The outer normal **n** to this surface points in the $\mathbf{G}^1$-direction, so that the traction is given by Eq. (22). Hence, the externally applied surface force is

$$\mathbf{P} = (G^{11})^{-1/2}\tau^{1b}\mathbf{G}_b. \tag{8.46}$$

This can be resolved into components normal and tangential to the right-hand surface of the deformed body. The *unit* normal to the surface is the vector $\mathbf{n} = (G^{11})^{-1/2}\,\mathbf{G}^1$. Then the normal component (referred to *unit* basis vectors) of the applied surface force is

$$\mathbf{P} \cdot \mathbf{n} = (G^{11})^{-1}\tau^{11}, \tag{8.47}$$

where Eq. (11) has been used. There is no tangential component of $\mathbf{P}$ along the $\mathbf{G}^3$ direction, since earlier you found that $t^{13} \equiv \tau^{13}$ is zero. The tangential component of the surface force along the θ^2 direction is found by projecting onto the unit vector, $\mathbf{s} = (G_{22})^{-1/2}\,\mathbf{G}_2$, which is tangent to the surface. With the help of Eq. (9), the result is

$$\mathbf{P} \cdot \mathbf{s} = (G^{11})^{-1/2}\,\tau^{1b}G_{b2}(G_{22})^{-1/2}. \tag{8.48}$$

You may find the normal and tangential components of the surface force on the upper surface of the deformed body in a similar manner, noting that the unit normal to the upper surface of the body is $\mathbf{n} = (G^{22})^{-1/2}\,\mathbf{G}^2$, and the unit tangent along the θ^1 direction is $\mathbf{s} = (G_{11})^{-1/2}\,\mathbf{G}_1$.

For the surface of the deformed body at $\theta^3 = 0$, the normal vector is $\mathbf{n} = (G^{33})^{-1/2}\,\mathbf{G}^3$. (In Fig. 8–4, the body extends from $z = -1$ to $z = 0$.) The traction vector of Eq. (21) is then

$$\mathbf{t} = (G^{33})^{-1/2}\tau^{3b}\mathbf{G}_b. \tag{8.49}$$

You found earlier that $\tau^{31} = 0$, $\tau^{32} = 0$, and

$$\tau^{33} = p + \Phi + (2 + K^2)\Psi. \tag{8.50}$$

Because the volume of the body is unchanged under simple shear deformation, the body can be assumed to be incompressible. Then constant p is determined by imposing the reasonable condition that the traction on this $\theta^3 = 0$ surface (or any surface parallel to it) is zero. This implies that $\tau^{33} = 0$, or

$$p = -\Phi - (2 + K^2)\Psi. \tag{8.51}$$

Let us use *MathTensor* to evaluate the normal and tangential components of the surface force $\mathbf{P}$ acting on the right-hand surface of the deformed body.

Make a rule to impose the relation given in Eq. (51).

```
In[21]:= pRule := p -> -Phi - (1+K^2) Psi
```

The normal component of **P** is given by Eq. (47). The components of the tensors involved were calculated earlier in this *MathTensor* session.

`In[22]:= Pnorm = (ga[1,1])^(-1) t[1,1]`

$$Out[22]= \frac{(1 + K^2)\ p + Phi + (2 + K^2)\ Psi}{1 + K^2}$$

Substitute the value of p and simplify.

`In[23]:= Simplify[% /. pRule]`

$$Out[23]= \frac{-(K^2\ Phi) + Psi - K^2\ Psi - K^4\ Psi}{1 + K^2}$$

The tangential component of **P** is found from Eq. (48). `MakeSum` carries out the sum over the dummy index pair ub, lb.

`In[24]:= Ptan = MakeSum[(ga[1,1])^(-1/2) t[1,ub]* ga[lb,-2] (ga[-2,-2])^(-1/2) ]`

$$Out[24]= -(K\ p) - K\ Psi +$$

$$> \qquad \frac{K\ ((1 + K^2)\ p + Phi + (2 + K^2)\ Psi)}{1 + K^2}$$

Notice that p drops out of this result without the need to substitute its value.

`In[25]:= Simplify[%]`

$$Out[25]= \frac{K\ (Phi + Psi)}{1 + K^2}$$

These results make definite predictions relating the components of the surface forces, which can be confirmed through experiment.

The theory of linear elasticity is obtained from the nonlinear theory in the limit of small deformation, which in this problem is found by working to first order in K (corresponding to a small angle of shear). In that limit, the normal component of the applied surface force **P** acting on the right-hand surface of the body vanishes, so that **P** is tangent to the surface. You can similarly show that in the linear limit, the normal component of the surface force acting on the upper surface of the body also vanishes. Thus, in the linear theory of elasticity, the shear is produced by purely tangential forces, in contrast to the nonlinear theory.

■ 8.3 Cylinder Twisted about Its Axis

Suppose an incompressible right circular cylinder in the undeformed state has radius a and length l. Let the axis of the cylinder extend from $z = 0$ to $z = l$ along the z-axis of a space-fixed Cartesian coordinate system. A pure torsional deformation of the cylinder is carried out by turning each cross-sectional plane of the cylinder rigidly through an angle kz proportional to its height z. The radius and length of the cylinder do not change in this torsional deformation.

The body-fixed coordinates of a molecule are most conveniently taken to be its cylindrical polar coordinates (r, θ, z) in the *deformed* state B. Thus we are taking as the body-fixed coordinates of the molecule, $\theta^1 \equiv r$, $\theta^2 \equiv \theta$, and $\theta^3 \equiv z$. The corresponding coordinates of the molecule in the deformed cylinder relative to the space-fixed Cartesian axes are

$$y^1 = r\cos(\theta),\ y^2 = r\sin(\theta),\ y^3 = z. \tag{8.52}$$

This gives the y^a as functions of the θ^a. The reason for adopting the simplest form of this transformation for the cylinder in its *deformed* state is that Eq. (23) involves covariant derivatives with respect to the deformed metric, G_{ab}, so that it is desirable to make that metric as simple as possible. Although the metric G_{ab} could be calculated from Eq. (52) by means of Eq. (13), it is well known that in cylindrical polar coordinates the square of the distance between two nearby points is $dS^2 = dr^2 + r^2 d\theta^2 + dz^2$. Therefore, from Eq. (2), the only nonzero components of G_{ab} are

$$G_{11} = 1,\ G_{22} = r^2,\ G_{33} = 1. \tag{8.53}$$

In Fig. 8–5, the curved line running diagonally from the bottom to the top of the cylinder shows the position of molecules on the surface having body-fixed coordinate $\theta = 0$ in the *undeformed* state. In the torsionally deformed state of the cylinder, the molecules on this curve have moved to positions in which they form a straight vertical line (shown joining with the curved line at the bottom of the cylinder). This straight vertical line has body-fixed coordinate $\theta = 0$ in the *deformed* state. The angle of displacement of a molecule at height z as a result of the torsional deformation is proportional to z, as can be seen in Fig. 8–5.

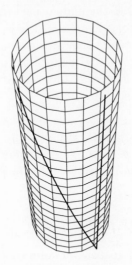

Fig. 8–5 Torsional deformation of a cylinder. Curves $\theta = 0$ are shown.

Relative to the *space-fixed* Cartesian x-axis, a molecule at height z that makes an angle θ after deformation, makes an angle $(\theta - kz)$ before deformation, where k is a constant. Hence, the Cartesian coordinates of the molecule in the undeformed state B_0 are

$$x^1 = r\cos(\theta - kz),\ \ x^2 = r\sin(\theta - kz),\ \ x^3 = z. \tag{8.54}$$

The undeformed metric g_{ab} may be calculated from Eq. (12), recalling that the coordinates θ^a are denoted here by r, θ, and z. Let us use **Ttransform** to carry out this calculation.

■ 8.3.1 Metrics

The undeformed metric g_{ab} is denoted in the following *MathTensor* session by gb[1a,1b] and is found by transforming the Cartesian metric δ_{ab} to the metric g_{ab} employing the coordinate transformation given in Eq. (54). (In the example of simple shear, the *deformed* metric was denoted by ga$_{ab}$. To avoid confusion, the notation gb$_{ab}$ is used here for the *undeformed* metric of the cylinder.)

This is a list of the body-fixed coordinates of a molecule of the cylinder.

```
In[1]:= coords = {r, theta, z}

Out[1]= {r, theta, z}
```

The dimension equals the number of coordinates.

```
In[2]:= Dimension = Length[coords]
Out[2]= 3
```

This lists the right-hand side of the transformation of Eq. (54) from r, θ, z to Cartesian coordinates x^1, x^2, x^3 when the body is in its undeformed state.

```
In[3]:= trans = {r Cos[theta - k z],
        r Sin[theta - k z], z}
Out[3]= {r Cos[theta - k z], r Sin[theta - k z], z}
```

The symmetric tensor gb[1a,1b] represents the metric g_{ab} of the undeformed state in body-fixed coordinates r, θ, z.

```
In[4]:= DefineTensor[gb,{{2,1},1}]
  PermWeight::sym: Symmetries of gb assigned
  PermWeight::def: Object gb defined
```

The metric gb[1a,1b] is obtained from the Cartesian metric Kdelta[1a,1b] using Ttransform. The last argument is -1 because gb[1a,1b] is obtained by transformation from the Cartesian metric Kdelta[1a,1b] by using the coordinate transformation that goes in the opposite direction, i.e., from r, θ, z to Cartesian coordinates x^1, x^2, x^3.

```
In[5]:= Ttransform[gb, Kdelta[1a,1b],coords,trans,-1]
  Components assigned to gb
```

This gives the calculated components of gb[1a,1b] in the form of a matrix.

```
In[6]:= MatrixForm[Table[gb[-i,-j],{i,3},{j,3}] ]
Out[6]//MatrixForm=
        1          0            0

                    2            2
        0          r          -(k r )

                     2          2 2
        0        -(k r )     1 + k  r
```

To find the inverse metric gb[ua,ub], it is straightforward to use matrix inversion.

```
In[7]:= gbLowerMatrix = Table[gb[-i,-j],{i,3},{j,3}]
                         2       2
Out[7]= {{1, 0, 0}, {0, r , -(k r )},

               2        2  2
   >    {0, -(k r ), 1 + k  r }}
```

Here is the inverse matrix.

```
In[8]:= gbUpperMatrix = Inverse[gbLowerMatrix]

                          2  2
                     1 + k  r
Out[8]= {{1, 0, 0}, {0, --------, k}, {0, k, 1}}
                          2
                         r
```

This assigns values just found to the components of gb[ua,ub]. You will recall that contravariant components have positive integers as indices.

```
In[9]:= gb[a_,b_]/;PosIntegerQ[a]&&PosIntegerQ[b] :=
        gbUpperMatrix[[a,b]]
```

The components of G_{ab}, the metric of the deformed state B in body-fixed coordinates r, θ, z, were given in Eq. (53). It is convenient to denote G_{ab} in this *MathTensor* session by `Metricg[la,lb]`. By using the built-in `Metricg[la,lb]`, you will be able to easily take covariant derivatives with respect to the metric of the deformed state, which are required later. (Alternatively, you could use the notation `ga[la,lb]` for the metric of the deformed state, as was done in the case of simple shear. Then, when covariant derivatives with respect to `ga[la,lb]` were required, you could set the components of `Metricg[la,lb]` to those of `ga[la,lb]` so that the method illustrated below could be used to find the affine connections and covariant derivatives. The *MathTensor* commands `Components` and `AffineToMetric`, which are used in that method, assume that the metric is called `Metricg[la,lb]`.)

This is the matrix of values that you want to assign to `Metricg[la,lb]`.

```
In[10]:= gLowerMatrix = {{1,0,0},{0,r^2,0},{0,0,1}}

Out[10]= {{1, 0, 0}, {0, r , 0}, {0, 0, 1}}
                          2
```

This assigns values to `Metricg[la,lb]`, the metric of the undeformed state B_0 of the cylinder. Covariant indices have negative integers as values.

```
In[11]:= Metricg[a_,b_]/;NegIntegerQ[a]&&NegIntegerQ[b] :=
           gLowerMatrix[[a,b]]
```

Here is the inverse matrix.

```
In[12]:= gUpperMatrix = Inverse[gLowerMatrix]

Out[12]= {{1, 0, 0}, {0, r , 0}, {0, 0, 1}}
                          -2
```

This assigns the computed values to the covariant components, `Metricg[ua,ub]`.

```
In[13]:= Metricg[a_,b_]/;PosIntegerQ[a]&&PosIntegerQ[b] :=
           gUpperMatrix[[a,b]]
```

■ 8.3.2 Invariants I_1, I_2, and I_3

The metric in the undeformed state is `gb[la,lb]` and that in the deformed state is `Metricg[la,lb]`. From the covariant and contravariant components of these metrics, you can calculate the invariants.

The normal behavior of `Metricg` in *MathTensor* is to automatically lower or raise indices whenever possible. Because there are two metrics involved here, we do not want `Metricg` to lower or raise indices. This can be prevented by turning the flag called `MetricgFlag` off. It is important to turn this flag off for the following calculation.

This turns off the flag, thus preventing `Metricg` from lowering or raising indices.

```
In[14]:= Off[MetricgFlag]
```

This is the metric determinant of the undeformed cylinder. For I_3 of Eq. (39), the determinants of both metrics are required.

```
In[15]:= detgb = Det[gbLowerMatrix]

Out[15]= r
         2
```

The metric determinant of the deformed cylinder has the same value, so that the deformation is volume-preserving.

```
In[16]:= detMetricg = Det[gLowerMatrix]

Out[16]= r
         2
```

The invariant I_3 is 1.

```
In[17]:= I3 = detMetricg/detgb

Out[17]= 1
```

I_1 is calculated from Eq. (37).

```
In[18]:= I1 =
  Simplify[MakeSum[gb[ua,ub] Metricg[la,lb] ] ]

Out[18]= 3 + k  r
              2  2
```

Here is I_2 of Eq. (38). It has the same value as I_1. Notice that these invariants depend on r^2.

```
In[19]:= I2 = I3*
  Simplify[MakeSum[Metricg[ua,ub] gb[la,lb] ] ]

Out[19]= 3 + k  r
              2  2
```

■ 8.3.3 Stress Tensor

The cylinder will be assumed to be incompressible (the torsion deformation is volume preserving). It will also be assumed that no body forces act and that there is no acceleration. The stress tensor is calculated from Eq. (40). Because the Φ and Ψ are functions of the invariants I_1 and I_2, they depend only on r. The function p for an incompressible body is found from the equation of equilibrium Eq. (23), and suitable boundary conditions.

The symmetric tensor B^{ab} of Eq. (41) appears in the expression for the stress tensor τ^{ab}.

```
In[20]:= DefineTensor[B,{{2,1},1}]

PermWeight::sym: Symmetries of B assigned

PermWeight::def: Object B defined
```

The components of B^{ab} are calculated by means of the present rule, which comes from Eq. (41).

```
In[21]:= B[a_,b_]/;PosIntegerQ[a]&&PosIntegerQ[b] :=
  Simplify[ I1 gb[a,b] -
    MakeSum[gb[a,ua] gb[b,ub] Metricg[la,lb] ] ]
```

This displays the components of B^{ab}.

```
In[22]:= MatrixForm[Table[B[i,j],{i,3},{j,3}] ]
Out[22]//MatrixForm=
```

$$
\begin{pmatrix}
2 + k^2 r^2 & 0 & 0 \\
0 & k^2 + \dfrac{2}{r^2} & k \\
0 & k & 2
\end{pmatrix}
$$

The stress tensor τ^{ab} will be denoted in *MathTensor* by the symmetric tensor t^{ab}.

```
In[23]:= DefineTensor[t,{{2,1},1}]
PermWeight::sym: Symmetries of t assigned
PermWeight::def: Object t defined
```

This rule for the stress tensor embodies Eq. (40).

```
In[24]:= t[a_,b_]/;PosIntegerQ[a]&&PosIntegerQ[b] :=
    Simplify[Phi gb[a,b] + Psi B[a,b] + p Metricg[a,b] ]
```

Here is the calculated value of the (2,2) component of the stress tensor.

```
In[25]:= t[2,2]
```

$$
Out[25]= \frac{p + Phi + 2\ Psi + k^2\ Phi\ r^2 + k^2\ Psi\ r^2}{r^2}
$$

This produces the list, $\{\{t^{11}\},\{t^{12},t^{22}\},\{t^{13},t^{23},t^{33}\}\}$, of the independent values of the symmetric matrix t^{ab}. This is the stress tensor of the cylinder under torsional deformation.

```
In[26]:= Table[t[i,j],{i,3},{j,i}]
Out[26]= {{p + Phi + 2 Psi + k^2 Psi r^2},
```

$$
> \quad \{0, \frac{p + Phi + 2\ Psi + k^2\ Phi\ r^2 + k^2\ Psi\ r^2}{r^2}\},
$$

```
>    {0, k (Phi + Psi), p + Phi + 2 Psi}}
```

Before proceeding further, save to the file **Cyl.m** the stress tensor and the lists of components of the metric of the deformed body.

```
In[27]:= Save["Cyl.m", t, gLowerMatrix, gUpperMatrix]
```

Then **Quit** the current *Mathematica* session.

■ 8.3.4 Equilibrium Equations

The function *p*, which appears in the expression for the stress tensor, does not follow from the elastic potential for an incompressible body. Rather, in the absence of body forces and accelerations, it is determined through the mechanical equilibrium equation Eq. (23), with suitably chosen boundary conditions.

The covariant derivatives in Eq. (23) involve the affine connections (defined in Chapter 1) of the deformed metric. To evaluate those covariant derivatives, you may use the *MathTensor* function `Components` contained in the file `Components.m`. To use `Components`, you must first `Quit` your current *Mathematica* session after saving the definitions and values that you will require later. The `Save` and `Quit` were done in the final steps above.

With your editor, prepare a file called `CylIn.m` containing the components of the metric of the deformed body. These components were listed in `gLowerMatrix` (you saved this list in the file `Cyl.m`). The file will contain the data required by the function `Components`. Here is the file `CylIn.m`.

```
Dimension = 3 (* dimension of the space *)

x/: x[1] = r        (* name the coordinates *)
x/: x[2] = theta
x/: x[3] = z

Metricg/: Metricg[-1, -1] = 1    (* Give the independent covariant *)
Metricg/: Metricg[-2, -1] = 0    (* components of the metric, with *)
Metricg/: Metricg[-3, -1] = 0    (* indices ordered.  For example, *)
Metricg/: Metricg[-2, -2] = r^2  (* -2 is less than -1.    *)
Metricg/: Metricg[-3, -2] = 0    (* The AffineG[ua,lb,lc] *)
Metricg/: Metricg[-3, -3] = 1    (* will be calculated.    *)

Rmsign = 1 (* sign conventions - irrelevant here *)
Rcsign = 1

CalcEinstein = 0  (* Do not calculate the Einstein, *)
CalcRiemann = 0   (* Riemann or Weyl tensors. *)
CalcWeyl = 0
```

The file `CylIn.m` for use with `Components`.

After preparing the file `CylIn.m`, start a new *Mathematica* session but do *not* load *MathTensor*. Instead `Get` the file `Components.m`. Below, it is assumed that you have started the new *Mathematica* session without loading *MathTensor*.

Get the file `Components.m`, which contains the `Components` command.

```
In[1]:= << Components.m

=========================================================
MathTensor (TM) 2.2 (UNIX (R)) (January 6, 1994)
               Components Package
by Leonard Parker and Steven M. Christensen
Copyright (c) 1991-1994 MathSolutions, Inc.
Runs with Mathematica (R) Versions 1.2 and 2.X.
Licensed to machine gravity.
=========================================================
```

This executes the `Components` command. The first argument is the file containing the data about the dimension, coordinates, and metric. The second and third arguments are the names of files created by `Components`. The file `CylOut.m` will contain the desired affine connections in a form suitable for input to a future *MathTensor* session. The file `CylOut.out` will contain the same information but in the form it would appear in output lines (i.e., OutputForm).

```
In[2]:= Components["CylIn.m", "CylOut.m", "CylOut.out"]


The following tensors have been calculated and stored

in the file CylOut.m in InputForm and

in the file CylOut.out in OutputForm:

Metricg
MatrixMetricgLower
MatrixMetricgUpper
Detg
AffineG[ua,lb,lc]
RicciR[la,lb]
ScalarR

You can edit CylOut.out to print a record of the results.
```

This completes the session in which the components of the affine connection (`AffineG`) are calculated by `Components`. Now `Quit` this *Mathematica* session. Always use the command `Components` in an independent *Mathematica* session.

You should now start a new *Mathematica* session and load *MathTensor*. Earlier, you saved the components t^{ab} of the stress tensor in the file `Cyl.m`. The file `CompOut.m`, which was created by `Components`, contains the components of the affine connection that you will need when you calculate the covariant derivatives of the stress tensor. Therefore you `Get` both files, `Cyl.m` and `CylOut.m`, and then proceed with the calculation of the equilibrium equation Eq. (23). In the following, it is assumed that you have already loaded *MathTensor* into your new *Mathematica* session.

This loads the contravariant components, `t[ua,ub]`.

```
In[1]:= << Cyl.m
                            -2
Out[1]= {{1, 0, 0}, {0, r  , 0}, {0, 0, 1}}
```

This loads the components of `AffineG[ua,lb,lc]`. It also turns off `MetricgFlag`. `AffineG[ua,lb,lc]` appears in output lines as $G^a{}_{bc}$.

```
In[2]:= << CylOut.m
 MetricgFlag has been turned off.
```

This checks that the components of this symmetric tensor are now present. You may have noticed some delay because the components are calculated from a formula. You can avoid this overhead of time by assigning values directly to the components as follows.

```
In[3]:= Table[t[i,j],{i,3},{j,i}]
```

$$Out[3]= \{\{p + Phi + 2\ Psi + k^2\ Psi\ r^2\},$$

$$\{0,\ \frac{p + Phi + 2\ Psi + k^2\ Phi\ r^2 + k^2\ Psi\ r^2}{r^2}\},$$

$$\{0,\ k\ (Phi + Psi),\ p + Phi + 2\ Psi\}\}$$

The values on the right-hand side of the assignment are evaluated using the formula. The independent components `t[i,j]`, such as `t[1,3]`, are then assigned those values so that the computation need not be repeated again. In the present case, this speed-up is not needed, but it is worth knowing about.

```
In[4]:= Do[t[i,j] = t[i,j], {j,3},{i,j}]
```

Here is the covariant divergence of the stress tensor. The equilibrium condition, Eq. (23), says that this quantity is zero.

```
In[5]:= CD[t[ua,ub],lb]
```

$$Out[5]= t^{ab}{}_{;b}$$

This converts the covariant derivatives to ordinary partial derivatives, OD, and affine connection terms involving `AffineG`, which appears as G.

```
In[6]:= CDtoOD[%]
```

$$Out[6]= t^{pa}{}_{,p} + G^{a}{}_{pq}\ t^{pq} + G^{p}{}_{pq}\ t^{qa}$$

Notice that the free index ua matches the input form of the free index in the line above, which appears as the second argument of `SetComponents`. This calculates all the indicated components and assigns them to `divStress[ua]`, with the appropriate integer indices and with sums carried out over dummy indices.

```
In[7]:= SetComponents[divStress[ua], %]
  Components assigned to divStress
```

Here is $t^{1b}{}_{;b}$. The ordinary partial derivatives are denoted by commas followed by a coordinate index. The derivative will be evaluated after the dependence of various quantities on the coordinates is specified.

```
In[8]:= divStress[1] = Simplify[divStress[1] ]
```

$$Out[8]= -(k^2\ Phi\ r) + 2\ k\ Psi\ r^2\ k_{,1} + p_{,1} + Phi_{,1} +$$

$$2\ Psi_{,1} + k^2\ r^2\ Psi_{,1} + 2\ k^2\ Psi\ r\ r_{,1}$$

This is $t^{2b}{}_{;b}$.

`In[9]:= divStress[2] = Simplify[divStress[2] ]`

$Out[9]= \text{Phi k}_{,3} + \text{Psi k}_{,3} + 2\text{ k Phi k}_{,2} + 2\text{ k Psi k}_{,2} +$

$> \quad \dfrac{p_{,2}}{r^2} + \text{k Phi}_{,3} + k^2\,\text{Phi}_{,2} + \dfrac{\text{Phi}_{,2}}{r^2} + \text{k Psi}_{,3} +$

$> \quad k^2\,\text{Psi}_{,2} + \dfrac{2\,\text{Psi}_{,2}}{r^2} - \dfrac{2\,p\,r_{,2}}{r^3} - \dfrac{2\,\text{Phi}\,r_{,2}}{r^3} - \dfrac{4\,\text{Psi}\,r_{,2}}{r^3}$

Finally, here is $t^{3b}{}_{;b}$.

`In[10]:= divStress[3] = Simplify[divStress[3] ]`

$Out[10]= \text{Phi k}_{,2} + \text{Psi k}_{,2} + p_{,3} + \text{Phi}_{,3} + \text{k Phi}_{,2} +$

$> \quad 2\,\text{Psi}_{,3} + \text{k Psi}_{,2}$

This rule will be used to put in the coordinate dependencies. We do not yet know p, so we allow for general coordinate dependence in it.

`In[11]:= dependRule =`
`{Phi->Phi[r],Psi->Psi[r],p->p[r,theta z]}`

$Out[11]= \{\text{Phi} \to \text{Phi[r]}, \text{Psi} \to \text{Psi[r]},$

$> \quad p \to p[r, theta, z]\}$

This puts in the coordinate arguments.

`In[12]:= rDiv = divStress[1] /. dependRule`

$Out[12]= p[r, theta, z]_{,1} + \text{Phi[r]}_{,1} + 2\,\text{Psi[r]}_{,1} +$

$> \quad k^2\,r^2\,\text{Psi[r]}_{,1} - k^2\,r\,\text{Phi[r]} + 2\,k\,r^2\,k\,\text{Psi[r]}_{,1} +$

$> \quad 2\,k^2\,r\,r_{,1}\,\text{Psi[r]}$

The same is done for the θ-component.

$In[13]:=$ **thetaDiv = divStress[2] /. dependRule**

$$Out[13]= \frac{p[r, theta, z]_{,2}}{r^2} + k\,Phi[r]_{,3} + k^2\,Phi[r]_{,2} +$$

$$> \quad \frac{Phi[r]_{,2}}{r^2} + k\,Psi[r]_{,3} + k^2\,Psi[r]_{,2} + \frac{2\,Psi[r]_{,2}}{r^2} -$$

$$> \quad \frac{2\,r\,p[r, theta, z]_{,2}}{r^3} + k_{,3}\,Phi[r] + 2\,k\,k_{,2}\,Phi[r] -$$

$$> \quad \frac{2\,r\,Phi[r]_{,2}}{r^3} + k_{,3}\,Psi[r] + 2\,k\,k_{,2}\,Psi[r] -$$

$$> \quad \frac{4\,r\,Psi[r]_{,2}}{r^3}$$

Now the z-component is also prepared.

$In[14]:=$ **zDiv = divStress[3] /. dependRule**

$$Out[14]= p[r, theta, z]_{,3} + Phi[r]_{,3} + k\,Phi[r]_{,2} +$$

$$> \quad 2\,Psi[r]_{,3} + k\,Psi[r]_{,2} + k_{,2}\,Phi[r] + k_{,2}\,Psi[r]$$

The derivatives are now carried out by turning on a flag called **EvaluateODFlag**. If this flag had been turned on before the coordinate arguments were put into the various functions, the derivatives would have evaluated to zero, as if those functions were constants.

$In[15]:=$ **On[EvaluateODFlag]**

Here is $t^{1b}{}_{;b}$. The symbol $p^{(0,1,0)}[r, theta, z]$ stands for the derivative of p with respect to the first argument.

$In[16]:=$ **rDiv**

$$Out[16]= -(k^2\,r\,Phi[r]) + 2\,k^2\,r\,Psi[r] + Phi'[r] +$$

$$> \quad 2\,Psi'[r] + k^2\,r^2\,Psi'[r] + p^{(1,0,0)}[r, theta, z]$$

The expression for $t^{2b}{}_{;b}$ is much simpler. The derivative is with respect to the second argument, **theta**.

$In[17]:=$ **thetaDiv**

$$Out[17]= \frac{p^{(0,1,0)}[r, theta, z]}{r^2}$$

Similarly, $t^{3b}{}_{;b}$ has only one term. Equilibrium demands that `thetaDiv` and `zDiv` are each zero. These two equilibrium equations clearly require that `p[r, theta, z] = p[r]`.

```
In[18]:= zDiv
             (0,0,1)
Out[18]= p        [r, theta, z]
```

This is the `FullForm` of the term `p^(1,0,0)[r,theta,z]` that appears in `rDiv`. You want to know this form in order to see how to set up a rule to replace that term by `p'[r]`.

```
In[19]:= FullForm[rDiv[[6]] ]
Out[19]//FullForm= Derivative[1, 0, 0][p][r, theta, z]
```

Here is the appropriate rule.

```
In[20]:=
pDependRule={Derivative[1,0,0][p][r,theta,z]->p'[r]}
            (1,0,0)
Out[20]= {p        [r, theta, z] -> p'[r]}
```

Now p appears as a function of r alone. Equilibrium requires that the expression is zero. You can use `DSolve` to find the solution of this differential equation for `p[r]`.

```
In[21]:= rDiv /. pDependRule
             2               2
Out[21]= -(k  r Phi[r]) + 2 k  r Psi[r] + p'[r] +
                                      2  2
>    Phi'[r] + 2 Psi'[r] + k  r  Psi'[r]
```

This solves the equation for `p[r]`, with independent variable `r`. `C[1]` is a constant of integration.

```
In[22]:= DSolve[% == 0, p[r], r]
Out[22]= {{p[r] ->
                  2
>        C[1] + k  Integrate[r Phi[r], r] - Phi[r] +
                   2  2
>        (-2 - k  r ) Psi[r]}}
```

Create a rule to replace `p[r]` by its solution.

```
In[23]:= pSolRule = %[[1]]
Out[23]= {p[r] ->
                  2
>        C[1] + k  Integrate[r Phi[r], r] - Phi[r] +
                   2  2
>        (-2 - k  r ) Psi[r]}
```

By integrating the equation of equilibrium (Eq. 23), you have found, for the incompressible cylinder undergoing torsional deformation, that

$$p(r) = k^2 \int^r r' \, \Phi(r')dr' - \Phi(r) - (2 + k^2 r^2)\Psi(r), \qquad (8.55)$$

where the constant of integration, `C[1]`, has been absorbed into the undetermined lower limit on the integral. The lower limit must be determined by choosing a suitable boundary condition. This is done by considering the external force per unit area exerted on the outer curved surface of the deformed cylinder.

■ 8.3.5 Surface Forces on the Deformed Cylinder

Recall that the external force $\mathbf{P}$ exerted per unit area must equal the traction force per unit area, $\mathbf{t}$, which is given by Eq. (21). Because the cylinder is incompressible, you have some choice in the amount of force per unit area to exert on the curved surface of the cylinder at $r = a$. The simplest choice consistent with equilibrium is to take that surface force to be zero.

The unit normal to the surface at $r = a$, which appears in the expression for $\mathbf{t}$ is $\mathbf{G}^1/(G^{11})^{1/2} = \mathbf{G}^1$, since the contravariant (1,1) component of the deformed body metric tensor in this case is 1. Then from Eq. (21) or Eq. (22),

$$\mathbf{t} = \tau^{1b}\mathbf{G_b}. \tag{8.56}$$

Looking back at the components of $\mathbf{t[ua,ub]}$, which you calculated above using *MathTensor*, you see that $\tau^{1b} \equiv t^{1b}$ is zero for $b = 2, 3$. Hence, $\mathbf{t} = \tau^{11}\mathbf{G}_1$. Therefore the boundary condition that the traction vector is zero on the surface at $r = a$ requires that $\tau^{11} \equiv \mathbf{t}^{11} = 0$. From the calculated value of $\mathbf{t}^{11}$, you then find

$$p(a) = -\Phi(a) - (2 + k^2r^2)\Psi(a). \tag{8.57}$$

Comparing this with Eq. (55), you find that the integral term must vanish at $r = a$, so

$$p(r) = k^2 \int_a^r r'\, \Phi(r')dr' - \Phi(r) - (2 + k^2r^2)\Psi(r). \tag{8.58}$$

The applied surface forces on the flat upper and lower surfaces of the deformed cylinder produce the torsional deformation. The unit normal to the upper flat surface at $z = l$ is $\mathbf{G}^3/(G^{33})^{1/2} = \mathbf{G}^3$. Substituting this for the normal vector in Eq. (21) and using the condition that the applied surface force per unit area equals the traction at the surface, you find that the applied surface force is

$$\mathbf{P} = \tau^{3b}\mathbf{G}_b = \tau^{32}\mathbf{G}_2 + \tau^{33}\mathbf{G}_3, \tag{8.59}$$

where the vanishing of $t^{31} \equiv \tau^{31}$ has been used. The normal component is then

$$\mathbf{P} \cdot \mathbf{G}^3 = \tau^{33}. \tag{8.60}$$

The tangential force per unit area is in the direction of increasing θ (if τ^{32} is positive) and is found by projecting $\mathbf{t}$ onto the unit vector $\mathbf{s} = \mathbf{G}_2/(G_{22})^{1/2}$ tangent to the surface. The result is (using Eq. (9) and the fact that $G_{23} = 0$)

$$\mathbf{P} \cdot \mathbf{s} = \tau^{32}(G_{22})^{1/2}. \tag{8.61}$$

For the lower surface at $z = 0$, the only difference in the calculation is that the outward normal, and hence the traction **t**, has the opposite sign. Thus the tangential component has the opposite sign, as you would expect for a torsional deformation.

Let us evaluate these expressions for the normal and tangential components of the applied surface force on the upper surface of the cylinder. First, define

$$\text{IntPhi}(r) \equiv \int_a^r r' \, \Phi(r') dr' . \tag{8.62}$$

This rule will replace p[r] by the solution with the boundary condition that we imposed. IntPhi[r] is define by Eq. (62).

```
In[24]:= pSolRule2 = pSolRule /.
  {C[1]->0,
   Integrate[r Phi[r], r] -> IntPhi[r]}
Out[24]= {p[r] ->

>      k  IntPhi[r] - Phi[r] + (-2 - k  r ) Psi[r]}
```

This rule is needed because when the components of t[ua,ub] were calculated, the coordinate dependencies were not included. Therefore it is Phi, Psi, and p that must be acted upon.

```
In[25]:= pSolRule3 = {Phi -> Phi[r], Psi -> Psi[r], p ->
pSolRule2[[1,2]]}
Out[25]= {Phi -> Phi[r], Psi -> Psi[r],

>      p -> k  IntPhi[r] - Phi[r] + (-2 - k  r ) Psi[r]}
```

This is the normal component found in Eq. (60).

```
In[26]:= pNorm = Simplify[t[3,3]/.pSolRule3]

Out[26]= k  (IntPhi[r] - r  Psi[r])
```

The tangential component follows from Eq. (61). *Mathematica* does not evaluate Sqrt[r^2] = r because it does not know which sign to use.

```
In[27]:= pTan = t[3,2] (Metricg[-2,-2])^(1/2)/.pSolRule3

Out[27]= k Sqrt[r ] (Phi[r] + Psi[r])
```

Notice that in the limit of small deformation (i.e., linear elasticity), the constant **k** is small, and the normal component of force acting on the cylinder vanishes. A similar vanishing of normal components was observed earlier in the limit of small shear deformation of a rectangular solid.

Chapter 9
General Relativity Examples

Tensor analysis lies at the heart of Einstein's theory of gravitation. The properties of spacetime are characterized in a coordinate-independent way by means of invariants. You can use *MathTensor* to calculate these invariants for particular spacetimes. This is done in Section 9.1. The gravitational field equations of Einstein are most directly obtained by taking the simplest invariant formed from the Riemann tensor (i.e., the scalar curvature) as the integrand of an integral over spacetime known as the action. Requiring that the variation of this action vanish with respect to small changes in the metric gives rise to the Einstein equations in vacuum. You can use *MathTensor* to carry out this variational calculation as illustrated in Section 9.2.1. By integrating an invariant that is quadratic in the Riemann tensor over spacetime, you can form a most interesting quantity known as the Gauss-Bonnet invariant. In Section 9.2.1, *MathTensor* is used to prove that this quantity is a topological invariant, meaning that its variation vanishes under changes of the metric.

■ 9.1 Reissner-Nordström Invariants

One of the more difficult calculations that is often done in gravitational theory is to compute invariants constructed from the Riemann tensor and its covariant derivatives. This type of computation is common in quantum field theory in curved spacetimes in applications like point-splitting regularization. In this section, we will look at a few sample invariants

$$R^2, R_{ab}R^{ab}, R_{abcd}R^{abcd}, R_{;a}{}^{a}, R_{ab;c}R^{ab\,;c}$$

for the Reissner-Nordström spacetime. This spacetime represents the curvature around a charged black hole. The mass of the black hole is m and its charge is q. We also set the gravitational constant G equal to one and select the coordinates (r, θ, ϕ, t), that are written as (r, th, ph, t).

■ 9.1.1 Computing the Riemann Tensor and Related Objects

The first step in computing the invariants uses the Components function. In the standard way discussed earlier, a file called Reissner_NordstromIn.m is created and the Components function is used to create Reissner_NordstromOut.m and Reissner_NordstromOut.out files.

```
CompSimpOptions := {SetOptions[Expand,Trig->False],
SetOptions[Together,Trig->False]}
Evaluate[CompSimpOptions]
CompSimpRules = {Cos[theta]^2 -> 1 - Sin[theta]^2,
Cos[theta]^4 -> (1- Sin[theta]^2)^2}
CompSimp[a_] := Together[Expand[a /. CompSimpRules]]

Dimension = 4
x[1] = r; x[2] = th ; x[3] = ph; x[4] = t

Metricg[-1,-1] = 1/(1-2 m/r+q^2/r^2)
Metricg[-2,-1] = 0; Metricg[-3,-1] = 0
Metricg[-4,-1] = 0
Metricg[-2,-2] = r^2
Metricg[-3,-2] = 0; Metricg[-4,-2] = 0
Metricg[-3,-3] = r^2 Sin[th]^2
Metricg[-4,-3] = 0
Metricg[-4,-4] = -(1-2 m/r+q^2/r^2)

Rmsign = 1 ; Rcsign = 1; CalcEinstein = 1; CalcRiemann = 1; CalcWeyl = 1
```

Reissner_NordstromIn.m .

■ 9.1.2 Invariant Definitions

We begin the computation of the invariants by giving the basic definition of each one and performing the summation on the indices.

We will be working in 4 dimensions.

$In[1]:=$ **Dimension = 4**

$Out[1]=$ 4

Define the first invariant, which is the square of the Riemann scalar.

$In[2]:=$ **InvariantOne = ScalarR^2**

$Out[2]=$ R^2

Define the second invariant, the "square" of the Ricci tensor, and then write out the object as a sum of its components.

$In[3]:=$ **InvariantTwo = MakeSum[RicciR[la,lb] RicciR[ua,ub]]**

$Out[3]=$ $R_{11}R^{11} + 2 R_{21}R^{12} + 2 R_{31}R^{13} + 2 R_{41}R^{14} +$

$>$ $\quad R_{22}R^{22} + 2 R_{32}R^{23} + 2 R_{42}R^{24} + R_{33}R^{33} +$

$>$ $\quad 2 R_{43}R^{34} + R_{44}R^{44}$

The third invariant is the "square of the Riemann tensor." We suppress the output of a long expression.

```
In[4]:= InvariantThree = MakeSum[RiemannR[la,lb,lc,ld]
RiemannR[ua,ub,uc,ud]];
```

To find the fourth invariant, we must convert the covariant derivatives to ordinary derivatives before we do the index summations.

```
In[5]:= InvariantFour =
MakeSum[CDtoOD[CDtoOD[CD[ScalarR,la,ua]]]];
```

The fifth invariant is defined similarly.

```
In[6]:= InvariantFive =
MakeSum[CDtoOD[CD[RicciR[la,lb],lc]
CD[RicciR[ua,ub],uc]]];
```

■ 9.1.3 Evaluation of the Invariants

We now combine the results of the two previous sections to get the values of the invariants for the Reissner-Nordström spacetime. After the values of the tensors are substituted into the various invariants, we take the derivatives by setting `EvaluateODFlag` to `True`. *The calculations in this section can take a very long time, often many hours, on some computers with slower CPUs or low memory.*

EvaluateODFlag is set to True.

```
In[7]:= On[EvaluateODFlag]
```

The file containing the previously computed Riemann tensor and related components can now be loaded.

The previous output file that contains the Reissner-Nordström results is read into *MathTensor*.

```
In[8]:= <<Reissner_NordstromOut.m
MetricgFlag has been turned off.
```

The computation of each invariant is carried out by simplification.

Because `ScalarR` is zero for this metric, its square is zero.

```
In[9]:= Simplify[InvariantOne]
Out[9]= 0
```

Now, consider `InvariantFour`. Simplification gives the obvious result. In this case, more simplification could have been done in the `Reissner_NordstromOut.m` file and the vanishing of this invariant would have been automatic, since `ScalarR` is zero.

```
In[10]:= Simplify[InvariantFour]
Out[10]= 0
```

Work on `InvariantTwo` gives a simple result.

```
In[11]:= Simplify[InvariantTwo]
```

$$Out[11]= \frac{4\,q^4}{r^8}$$

If we take the charge to zero, we get the standard Schwarzschild black hole result.

$In[12]:= \% \; /. \; q\text{->}0$

$Out[12]= 0$

There is an alternate way to compute this invariant. *MathTensor* has a file called `RicciSquared.m`, that has precomputed the explicit sum of terms appearing in the 4-dimensional, contracted square of the Ricci tensor.

Load in the file that contains $R_{ab}R^{ab}$ written explicitly as a sum with integer indices.

$In[13]:= \text{<<RicciSquared.m}$

Ask for the invariant and then simplify the object. We obtain the same results as previously.

$In[14]:= \text{Simplify[RicciSquared]}$

$$Out[14]= \frac{4 \; q^4}{r^8}$$

The next two invariants are much more complicated. `InvariantThree` is more efficiently computed by loading in another file `RiemannSquared.m`.

Load in the file that contains the precomputed 4-dimensional object, $R_{abcd}R^{abcd}$.

$In[15]:= \text{<<RiemannSquared.m}$

We ask for the simplifed `RiemannSquared`

$In[16]:= \text{Simplify[RiemannSquared]}$

$$Out[16]= \frac{8 \; (7 \; q^4 - 12 \; m \; q^2 \; r + 6 \; m^2 \; r^2)}{r^8}$$

Again, the limit of the charge going to zero gives the standard Schwarzschild result.

$In[17]:= \% \; /. \; q\text{->} \; 0$

$$Out[17]= \frac{48 \; m^2}{r^6}$$

Finally, we look at `InvariantFive`.

Simplifying gives us another simple result that has a zero charge-free limit.

$In[18]:= \text{Simplify[InvariantFive]}$

$$Out[18]= \frac{80 \; q^4 \; (q^2 - 2 \; m \; r + r^2)}{r^{12}}$$

In computing invariants or other objects with many summations, the more summations there are, the longer the computation will take. It is a good idea to save `MakeSum` calculations to a file for future use.

■ 9.2   Variations and Field Equations

One very common computation done in physics and engineering is functional variation. For example, we might want to derive field equations using the so-called Variational Principle. To do this, it is necessary to compute how an object like the action functional $S[\phi]$ changes under infinitesimal variations of the dynamical variable ϕ. $\phi[x]$ can itself be a function of position and time, x. This section will show how such variations are done in *MathTensor*.

■ 9.2.1   Metric Variations and the Einstein Action

The gravitational field equations for Einstein's General Theory of Relativity can be derived from a very simple action. In standard notation (ignoring coupling constants), the Einstein action is

$$S[g_{\mu\nu}] = \int g^{1/2} R d^4 x,$$

where the square brackets indicate functional dependence on the metric. The dependence on the metric comes in the Riemann scalar and the determinant of the metric, which defines the volume integral over spacetime. In the computations that follow, the integral is not given explicitly, but its existence is assumed at each stage.

The functional variation is performed by computing the first-order changes in objects depending on the metric, when

$$g_{\mu\nu} + \delta g_{\mu\nu}$$

replaces each metric. In practice, we compute the basic variations like

$$\delta g^{\mu\nu}, \delta g, \delta\Gamma^{\alpha}{}_{\beta\gamma}$$

and from those compute variations of objects like

$$R, R_{\mu\nu}, R^{\alpha}{}_{\beta\gamma\delta}$$

and so forth.

It is important to create a knowledge base of basic variations and add the more complex variations as they are computed. If this is not done, *MathTensor* will need to compute them, wasting time. The metric variations built into *MathTensor* are limited to a few of the basic ones.

In most cases, it is best to set `MetricgFlag` equal to `False` before doing a variation with respect to the metric. The `Variation` function does this automatically.

Enter the Einstein action. We assume that this object is inside an integral over spacetime.

$$In[1] := \text{Sqrt[Detg] ScalarR}$$
$$Out[1] = \text{Sqrt[g] R}$$

Vary with respect to the metric. The `Variation` function is designed to handle the case of variations with respect to the metric tensor. It is straightforward to define the `Variation` function so that it can work for other kinds of variations also. The pretty print form for the variation of the metric `Varg` is `h`.

$$In[2] := \text{Variation[\%,Metricg]}$$
MetricgFlag::off:
    MetricgFlag is turned off by this operation
$$Out[2] = \text{Sqrt[g] h}^{pq}{}_{pq;} - \text{Sqrt[g] h}^{p}{}_{p}{}^{q}{}_{;q} +$$
$$> \quad \frac{\text{Sqrt[g] R g}^{pq}\, h_{pq}}{2} - \text{Sqrt[g] R}^{pq}\, h_{pq}$$

We use the `PIntegrate` function, which can also be generalized to other field types, to partially integrate the covariant derivatives off of the `Varg` factors in the first two terms. This can generate so-called boundary terms, which are ignored in this elementary calculation. We use the fact that `CD[Detg,a]` vanishes. If we remove the `Detg` term and the `Varg` terms and set the first variation equal to zero, we get Einstein's vacuum field equations.

$$In[3] := \text{PIntegrate[\%,Metricg]}$$
$$Out[3] = \frac{\text{Sqrt[g] R g}^{pq}\, h_{pq}}{2} - \text{Sqrt[g] R}^{pq}\, h_{pq}$$

Divide out the `Sqrt[Detg]` factor.

$$In[4] := \text{Expand[- \%/Sqrt[Detg]]}$$
$$Out[4] = \frac{-(\text{R g}^{pq}\, h_{pq})}{2} + \text{R}^{pq}\, h_{pq}$$

The `VariationalDerivative` function is designed to remove, in this case, `Varg[ua,ub]` and any integration, giving the variational derivative with free indices `1a` and `1b`. Setting this to zero gives the Einstein vacuum equations.

$$In[5] := \text{VariationalDerivative[\%,Metricg,ua,ub]} == 0$$
$$Out[5] = \frac{-(\text{R g}_{ab})}{2} + \text{R}_{ab} == 0$$

`Varg[la,lb]`	the variation of the metric tensor
`Variation[{`*expr*`},Metricg]`	vary *expr* with respect to the metric tensor
`VariationalDerivative[{`*expr*`},Metricg,ua,ub]`	pull off the `Varg[ua,ub]` terms
`PIntegrate[{`*expr*`},Metricg]`	partially integrate a covariant derivative off of a `Varg` term

Metric variation functions included in *MathTensor*.

■ 9.2.2 The Gauss-Bonnet Invariant

There is a particular combination of geometrical objects with very interesting properties that can be built from the Riemann tensor. The so-called Gauss-Bonnet Invariant can be shown to be invariant under changes of the metric. It is called a topological invariant. It has the form

$$\int g^{\frac{1}{2}}(R_{abcd}R^{abcd} - 4R_{ab}R^{ab} + R^2)d^4x,$$

and when its variation is taken with respect to the metric, the result vanishes identically.

In the next *MathTensor* session, we show what is required to prove this and why it is a difficult hand calculation. Here is a part of the *MathTensor* file that contains the various definitions needed of a proof in either 2 or 4 dimensions:

```
GaussBonnetMetricProductFourDimensions[a_,b_,c_,d_,e_,f_,g_,h_,i_,j_] :=
 Block[{terms,list,siglist},
       terms = 0;
       list = Permutations[{f,g,h,i,j}];
       siglist = Map[Signature,list];
       Do[terms = terms + siglist[[ii]] *
               Metricg[a,list[[ii,1]]] * Metricg[b,list[[ii,2]]] *
               Metricg[c,list[[ii,3]]] * Metricg[d,list[[ii,4]]] *
               Metricg[e,list[[ii,5]]], {ii,1,Length[list]}];
       terms]
GaussBonnetInvariantFourDimensionsX := Sqrt[Detg] *
(RiemannR[ua,ub,uc,ud] RiemannR[la,lb,lc,ld] - 4 RicciR[ua,ub] RicciR[la,lb] +
ScalarR^2)
```

Part of the GaussBonnetInvariant.m file.

Feed in the above file.

$In[6]:=$ **<<GaussBonnetInvariant.m**

Ask for the form of the 4-dimensional invariant we will be considering as a possible invariant. This object is normally written in an integral over a 4-dimensional spacetime.

$In[7]:=$ **GaussBonnetInvariantFourDimensionsX**

$Out[7]=$ $\text{Sqrt}[g] \ (R^2 - 4 \ R_{ab} \ R^{ab} + R_{abcd} \ R^{abcd})$

Take the first variation of the object with respect to the metric. It is clear why a computer program is helpful in deriving such large expressions. We note that there are several terms with covariant derivatives on **Varg**, which we remember is represented by **h**. To eventually be able to factor out these terms, we will have to use the **PIntegrate** function to take off the covariant derivatives.

$In[8]:=$ **Variation[%,Metricg]**

$Out[8]=$ $2 \ \text{Sqrt}[g] \ R \ h^{pq}{}_{pq;} - 2 \ \text{Sqrt}[g] \ R \ h^{p}{}_{p}{}^{q}{}_{;q} +$

$>$ $2 \ \text{Sqrt}[g] \ h^{pq}{}_{;r}{}^{r} \ R_{pq} - 4 \ \text{Sqrt}[g] \ h^{p}{}_{q;}{}^{rq} \ R_{pr} +$

$>$ $2 \ \text{Sqrt}[g] \ h^{p}{}_{p}{}^{qr}{}_{;} \ R_{qr} + 2 \ \text{Sqrt}[g] \ h^{r}{}_{pq;r}{}^{pq} \ R -$

$>$ $4 \ \text{Sqrt}[g] \ h^{q}{}_{pq;r} \ R^{pr} + 2 \ \text{Sqrt}[g] \ h^{p}{}_{p}{}^{}{}_{;qr} \ R^{qr} -$

$>$ $2 \ \text{Sqrt}[g] \ h^{pq}{}_{;} \ R^{rs}{}_{prqs} - 2 \ \text{Sqrt}[g] \ h^{prqs} \ R_{pq;rs} +$

$>$ $\dfrac{\text{Sqrt}[g] \ R^2 \ g^{pq} \ h_{pq}}{2} - 2 \ \text{Sqrt}[g] \ g^{pq} \ R_{rs} \ R^{rs} \ h_{pq} +$

$>$ $\dfrac{\text{Sqrt}[g] \ g^{pq} \ R_{rstu} \ R^{rstu} \ h_{pq}}{2} +$

$>$ $4 \ \text{Sqrt}[g] \ R^{qr} \ R_{r}{}^{p} \ h_{pq} - 2 \ \text{Sqrt}[g] \ R \ R^{pq} \ h_{pq} -$

$>$ $\dfrac{\text{Sqrt}[g] \ R^{qrs} \ R_{pqrs} \ R^{pt} \ h_{t}}{2} + 4 \ \text{Sqrt}[g] \ R^{pr} \ R_{r}{}^{q} \ h_{pq} +$

$>$ $\text{Sqrt}[g] \ R_{pqrs}{}^{ptrs} \ R_{}{}^{q} \ h_{t} + \dfrac{\text{Sqrt}[g] \ R^{prs} \ R_{pqrs}{}^{qt} \ h_{t}}{2} -$

$>$ $\text{Sqrt}[g] \ R_{pqrs}{}^{spq} \ R^{rt} \ h_{t} + \text{Sqrt}[g] \ R_{pqrs}{}^{rpq} \ R^{st} \ h_{t}$

Use PIntegrate twice to move some covariant derivatives around. Suppress the long output.

In[9]:= PIntegrate[PIntegrate[%,Metricg],Metricg]

Repeatedly apply the RiemannRules and Canonicalize to simplify the expression. Again, we suppress the output.

In[10]:= ApplyRulesRepeated[%,RiemannRules];

RiemannRule18::Applied: RiemannRule18 has been used.

RiemannRule23::Applied: RiemannRule23 has been used.

RiemannRule16::Applied: RiemannRule16 has been used.

RiemannRule16::Applied: RiemannRule16 has been used.

RiemannRule18::Applied: RiemannRule18 has been used.

RiemannRule23::Applied: RiemannRule23 has been used.

RiemannRule18::Applied: RiemannRule18 has been used.

RiemannRule18::Applied: RiemannRule18 has been used.

Get rid of the extraneous overall factors. Eliminate the Varg factors, and then simplify the results with Tsimplify.

In[11]:= Tsimplify[VariationalDerivative[Expand[%/Sqrt[Detg]],Metricg,ua,ub]]

$$Out[11]= \frac{R^2 g_{ab}}{2} - 2 R R_{ab} + 4 R_{qb}{}^q R_a - 2 g_{ab} R_{rs} R^{rs} +$$

$$> \quad 4 R_{pq} R^{p}{}_{a}{}^{q}{}_{b} + 2 R_{pars} R^{prs}{}_b + \frac{g_{ab} R_{rstu} R^{rstu}}{2}$$

We now want to prove that this object is identically equal to zero. An interesting way to do this is to convert the Riemann tensors in this result into Weyl tensors.

Set the dimension of spacetime to 4.

In[12]:= Dimension = 4

Out[12]= 4

Using `RiemannToWeylRule`, the Riemann tensors are converted to Weyl tensors plus Ricci tensor and Riemann scalar terms with metric tensor factors. The metric tensors are absorbed by using the `Absorbg` function and then the whole expression is simplified with `Tsimplify`.

```
In[13]:=
Tsimplify[Absorbg[ApplyRules[%%,RiemannToWeylRule]]]
```

$$
Out[13]= -2\ g^{rs}_{\ \ ab}\ R\ C^{p}_{\ prs} - \frac{R\ g_{ab}\ C^{pr}_{\ \ pr}}{3} + 2\ R^{r}_{\ b}\ C^{p}_{\ par} -
$$

$$
> \frac{4\ R\ C^{p}_{\ pab}}{3} + 2\ R^{r}_{\ ra}\ C^{p}_{\ p\ b} + 2\ C^{pqr}_{\ paqr}\ C^{pqr}_{\ \ \ b} +
$$

$$
> \frac{g_{ab}\ C^{pqrs}\ C_{pqrs}}{2}
$$

We define a new rule that expresses the fact that the Weyl tensor is trace-free on all of its index pairs.

```
In[14]:= RuleUnique[WeylTraceRule,Weyl[la_,lb_,lc_,ld_],0,
  PairQ[la,lb] || PairQ[la,lc] || PairQ[la,ld] ||
  PairQ[lb,lc] || PairQ[lb,ld] || PairQ[lc,ld]]
```

We now want to prove that this object is identically zero in 4 dimensions.

```
In[15]:= Canonicalize[ApplyRules[%%,WeylTraceRule]]
```

$$
Out[15]= 2\ C^{rpq}_{\ pqra}\ C_{\ b} + \frac{g_{ab}\ C^{pqrs}\ C_{pqrs}}{2}
$$

We do this by first generating a product of five metric tensors with indices ordered in a certain way (this takes a while even on a fast RISC workstation). This is done using the `GaussBonnetMetricProductFourDimensions` object defined in `GaussBonnetInvariant.m`. In this file, we have the object

$$
\sum (\pm) g^{af} g^{bg} g^{ch} g^{di} g^{ej},
$$

where the summation is over all 120 possible permutations of the f, g, h, i, and j indices and where the sign is chosen to be + if the permutation is even and − if the permutation is odd.

A very long expression is generated, so we have told *Mathematica* not to print out the result. This is the hardest part of the calculation to do by brute force.

```
In[16]:= MetricProduct = GaussBonnetMetricProductFourDi-
mensions[ua,ub,uc,ud,ue,uf,ug,uh,ui,uj];
```

The figure below shows a few of the many terms in `MetricProduct`:

```
GaussBonnetMetricProdctFourDimensions[a_,b_,c_,d_,e_,f_,g_,h_,i_,j_] :=
   Metricg[a, j]*Metricg[b, i]*Metricg[c, h]*Metricg[d, g]*
   Metricg[e, f] - Metricg[a, i]*Metricg[b, j]*Metricg[c, h]*
   Metricg[d, g]*Metricg[e, f] -
   Metricg[a, j]*Metricg[b, h]*Metricg[c, i]*Metricg[d, g]*
   Metricg[e, f] + Metricg[a, h]*Metricg[b, j]*Metricg[c, i]*
   Metricg[d, g]*Metricg[e, f] + 118 more terms ...
```

`GaussBonnetMetricProductFourDimensions`: A few terms.

We now multiply our long expression by two Weyl tensors with indices in a particular order. Again, we do not print out the long result.

```
In[17]:= Invariant = Expand[MetricProduct *
WeylC[1b,1c,1i,1j] WeylC[1d,1e,1g,1h]];
```

We absorb the metrics by raising and lowering indices on the Riemann tensor terms in **Invariant** and then canonicalize to reduce the number of terms. We also divide by eight and then lower the free indices.

```
In[18]:= Canonicalize[Expand[Absorbg[Invariant]/8]] /.
{ua->1a,uf->1b}
```

$$Out[18]= \frac{g_{ab} C^{pq}_{pq} C^{rs}_{rs}}{2} + 2 C^{pq}_{pq} C^{r}_{rab} +$$

$$> \quad 2 C^{p}_{pqb} C^{qr}_{ra} + 2 C^{p}_{pqa} C^{qr}_{rb} - 2 g_{ab} C^{p}_{pqr} C^{rqs}_{s} -$$

$$> \quad 2 C^{p}_{pqr} C^{q\ r}_{a\ b} - 2 C^{p}_{pqr} C^{r\ q}_{a\ b} + 2 C^{rpq}_{pqra} {}_{b} +$$

$$> \quad \frac{g_{ab} C^{pqrs}_{pqrs} C}{2}$$

Finally, we use the trace-free property of the Weyl tensor and canonicalize to obtain the same structure we generated by the variation calculation.

```
In[19]:= Canonicalize[ApplyRules[%,WeylTraceRule]]
```

$$Out[19]= 2 C^{rpq}_{pqra} C_{b} + \frac{g_{ab} C^{pqrs}_{pqrs} C}{2}$$

To prove that the object we have just generated is zero identically, we look at the generating function `GaussBonnetMetricProductFourDimensions`. This function takes the product

$$g^{af} g^{bg} g^{ch} g^{di} g^{ej}$$

and antisymmetrizes completely on the f, g, h, i, j indices. This generates $5! = 120$

terms. We are in 4 dimensions, so the values of each index can take on only four values, say 1, 2, 3, or 4. Because antisymmetric objects with duplicated indices are identically zero, the antisymmetric object above must be zero. If we take this zero object and multiply it by $C_{bcij}C_{ghde}$, we will still get zero. *MathTensor* carries out this arduous calculation in several steps, gives us our Weyl tensor result, and completes the proof of the topological invariance of GaussBonnetInvariantFourDimensionsX. Anyone who has tried this sort of computation by hand knows the difficulty in keeping the indices on 120 terms straight. This calculation also produces a proof of an identity in a form that is apparently not well known.

Appendix
Listing of *MathTensor* Objects

This *Appendix* contains an alphabetical listing and explanation of built-in commands and objects for *MathTensor* version 2.2 of February 1994. You can access the corresponding up-to-date usage messages on-screen for your version of *MathTensor* by doing `?<command>` in a *MathTensor* session.

Objects marked with a (*) are those that appear after the command `AddIndexTypes` has been issued in a *MathTensor* session. Loading additional sets of indices with `AddIndexTypes` will modify the behavior of some objects. Such objects have two entries in this list, one of which is marked with a (*). The latter entry describes the object after it has been modified by the command `AddIndexTypes`.

- ## Absorb

  Absorb[expr,metricName] will raise or lower indices using the tensor metricName appearing as the second argument. For example, if type-a indices refer to a subspace with metric called metrica and
  expr = RicciR[ala,alb] metrica[aua,aub], then Absorb[expr,metrica] gives RicciR[ala,aua]. (This is not automatically converted to ScalarR because the indices would not be present and the subspace referred to would be unclear.) Absorb[sum,metricName,n] acts on the nth term of the expression sum. See also AddIndexTypes.

- ## Absorbg

  Absorbg[expr] causes Metricg's with indices summed on some other tensor to be absorbed by raising or lowering the summed indices. Absorbg[expr,n] absorbs Metricg on the nth term of expr.

- ## AbsorbKdelta

  AbsorbKdelta[expr] will cause Kronecker deltas, Kdelta, in expr to act on indices in tensors that are paired with indices in Kdelta.
  AbsorbKdelta[expr,n], where expr is a sum of terms, will cause any Kdelta appearing in term n of the sum to be absorbed by changing index names and raising and lowering indices if possible. For space or spacetime indices, this is not what you want because the results will generally be different from those using the metric tensor Metricg to raise or lower indices. You should use Metricg with one covariant and one contravariant index instead of Kdelta, unless you are dealing with particular spaces, such as a Euclidean space in Cartesian coordinates, or a group space in Yang-Mills gauge theory. See also Kdelta, KdeltaRule.

- ## AddIndexTypes

  The command AddIndexTypes causes the multiple index module to be loaded into memory. In addition to regular indices, this makes available to the user three new types of indices called type-a, type-b, and type-c indices. The input form of a type-a index is the same as that of a regular index, except that the index name is prefixed by the letter a. For example, you would type alc instead of lc. Similarly, the names of type-b indices start with the letter b and type-c with the letter c. The output forms of these indices are like those of regular indices, but have one, two, or three primes for types a, b, and c, respectively.

- ## AffineDrule

  AffineDrule is a transformation rule that orders indices in expressions such as OD[AffineG[ua,la,lc],lb] and OD[AffineG[ud,lb,ld],la].

- ## AffineG

  AffineG[ua,lb,lc] is the affine connection associated with the covariant derivative CD. The function CDtoOD reduces CD to ordinary derivatives OD and affine connections AffineG.

- ## AffineToMetric

  AffineToMetric[expr] converts all AffineG's in an expression to ordinary derivatives of the metric.

- ## AffineToMetricRule

  AffineToMetricRule converts all AffineG's in an expression to ordinary derivatives of the metric.

- ## aIndices

  aIndices are made available by the command AddIndexTypes and are input by typing ala, alb,..., alo for lower indices, and aua, aub,..., auo for the corresponding upper indices. In output lines, ale, for example, appears as a subscripted e' index and aue as a superscripted e' index. See also AddIndexTypes, RegularIndices, bIndices, cIndices.

- ## AllSymmetries

  AllSymmetries[tensor[la,lb,...]] returns a complete list of the permutations and weights of tensor[la,lb,...] under permutations of the indices. This list forms a group. It is created automatically when DefineTensor is used to enter a short list of symmetries. AllSymmetries will also return the complete list of symmetries of *MathTensor* system-defined tensors. For example, AllSymmetries[RicciR[la,lb]] gives {{1,2},1,{2,1},1}. See also Symmetries, MakePermWeightGroup, MakeAllSymmetries.

■ **Antisymmetrize**

Antisymmetrize[expr,{la,lb,...}], where expr contains sums and products of tensors and la,lb,... are among the indices, will yield the tensor formed from expr and antisymmetrized with respect to indices la,lb,.... Thus Antisymmetrize[f[la,lb,lc],{la,lb}] gives (1/2)(f[la,lb,lc]-f[lb,la,lc]). Factor and function names should not be the same as index names when applying Antisymmetrize.

■ **ApplyRules**

ApplyRules[expr,Rules] will apply the rules, Rules, once to the expression, expr, and replace newly generated dummy index names by standard dummy index names. An example set of rules included in *MathTensor* is RiemannRules. To apply to the nth term in an expression, use ApplyRules[expr,Rules,n]. See also ApplyRulesRepeated, SuperApplyRules, CanApplyRules.

■ **ApplyRulesRepeated**

ApplyRulesRepeated[expr,Rules] will canonicalize an expression expr, apply the rules Rules repeatedly, and finally canonicalize again. One example set of Rules is RiemannRules. This function differs from ApplyRules in that Rules are applied repeatedly. To apply to the nth term in an expression, use ApplyRulesRepeated[expr,Rules,n]. See ApplyRules, SuperApplyRules, CanApplyRulesRepeated.

■ **Arglist**

Arglist[expr] returns a list (like {lc,la,ua,lb}) consisting of the arguments of the tensors in a product of tensors. Thus Arglist[f[lc,ld]*g[la,ub]] returns {lc,ld,la,ub}. The ordering of the indices is retained. Integers and symbols other than recognized symbolic indices are not included in the returned list. See also ArglistInt.

■ **ArglistAllTypes**

ArglistAllTypes works just like Arglist, except that the list it returns includes all indices of the types listed by IndexTypes. The indices listed in IndexTypes are the ones that have been loaded into memory using AddIndexTypes and also SpaceTimeIndices.

■ ArglistInt

`ArglistInt[expr]` acts like `Arglist[expr]`, except that integers as well as recognized symbolic indices are included in the returned list. See also `Arglist`, `ArglistIntUpLo`.

■ ArglistIntUpLo

`ArglistIntUpLo[expr]` acts like `ArglistInt[expr]`, except that members of the list {lo1,up1,..., lo10, up10} as well as integers and recognized symbolic indices are included in the returned list. The lo1,...,up10 symbols can appear in rules created by `RuleUnique` and `DefUnique`. Sometimes you may want to define functions that recognize these special symbols as possible indices. See also `Arglist`, `ArglistInt`.

■ AskSignsFlag

`AskSignsFlag` is set to `True` or `False` in the file `Conventions.m`. If `False`, then the sign conventions are taken from `Conventions.m`. If `True`, then the sign conventions are set by a dialogue each time that *MathTensor* is loaded into a *Mathematica* session.

■ BianchiFirstPairRule

`BianchiFirstPairRule[la,lb,lc,ld,le]` performs the Bianchi identity on a Riemann tensor covariant derivative of the form `CD[RiemannR[la,lb,lc,ld],le]` using the `la,lb,` and `le` indices.

■ BianchiSecondPairRule

`BianchiSecondPairRule[la,lb,lc,ld,le]` performs the Bianchi identity on a Riemann tensor covariant derivative of the form `CD[RiemannR[la,lb,lc,ld],le]` using the `lc,ld,` and `le` indices.

■ bIndices

`bIndices` are made available by the command `AddIndexTypes` and are input by typing `bla, blb,...,` `blo` for lower indices and `bua, bub,...,` `buo` for the corresponding upper indices. In output lines, `ble`, for example, appears as a subscripted e′′ index and `bue` as a superscripted e′′ index. See also `AddIndexTypes`, `RegularIndices`, `aIndices`, `cIndices`.

■ CanAll

CanAll[expr] applies various internal canonicalizer functions to an expression to produce a unique canonical form. CanAll or Canonicalize automatically make use of the most efficient of the group of canonicalization functions available so that those other functions, with the possible exception of CanFree, need never be used directly.

■ CanApplyRules

CanApplyRules[expr,Rules] combines the functions CanAll and ApplyRules. First, expr is Canonicalized, then ApplyRules is used, and finally CanAll is run again. CanApplyRules can be slower than ApplyRules, but more Rules are likely to be found and provide a simpler expression. CanApplyRules[expr,Rules,n] applies CanApplyRules to the nth term in expr. See ApplyRules and CanAll.

■ CanApplyRulesFast

CanApplyRulesFast[expr,Rules] combines the functions CanAll and ApplyRules. CanApplyRulesFast is just like CanApplyRules except that no initial canonicalization is performed. It is assumed that expr is already canonical. Because CanAll is not performed first, this function is faster than CanApplyRules. CanApplyRulesFast[expr,Rules,n] applies CanApplyRulesFast to the nth term in expr. See CanApplyRules.

■ CanApplyRulesRepeated

CanApplyRulesRepeated[expr,Rules], applies CanAll and ApplyRulesRepeated, then Canonicalize again. CanApplyRulesRepeated[expr,Rules,n] applies CanApplyRulesRepeated to the nth term in expr. See ApplyRulesRepeated, Canonicalize.

■ CanDum

CanDum[expr,n] will replace all paired indices by pairs li, ui from Downdummylist and Updummylist in such a way that the li are in ascending order and each ui comes after the corresponding li. Furthermore, the lowest i in li will start at n, and the numbering will run consecutively. In contrast, Dum replaces lower indices by lower indices and upper by upper but does not put the lower index first in each pair. CanDum[expr] takes n as 1.

- ## CanFree

  `CanFree[expr]` will canonicalize tensor expressions that have, in addition to dummy indices, free indices. In almost all cases with free indices, it is sufficient to use `CanAll` or `Canonicalize` directly.

- ## CanInvert

  `CanInvert[expr]` runs `Dum` and then `Invert` on `expr`.

- ## Cannn

  `Cannn` is used internally by the canonicalizers. Its algorithm is quadratic in the number of dummy indices.

- ## CannnDum

  `CannnDum[expr]` is similar to but more powerful than `CanDum`. However, its algorithm takes a time that increases quadratically with the number of paired indices. `CannnDum` can be used directly by the user, but the use of `CanAll` or `Canonicalize` is recommended.

- ## CanNonInvert

  `CanNonInvert[expr]` is equivalent to `Dum[expr]`. When an expression is not manifestly covariant or contains `OD`'s, so that indices should not be raised or lowered, `CanNonInvert`, `Dum`, or `Tsimplify` can be used to perform simplification.

- ## Canonicalize

  `Canonicalize[expr]` applies various internal canonicalizer functions to an expression to produce a unique canonical form. `Canonicalize` or `CanAll` automatically make use of the most efficient of the group of canonicalization functions available so that those other functions, with the possible exception of `CanFree`, need never be used directly.

■ **CanSame**

CanSame[expr] will replace all paired indices by pairs li, ui from Downdummylist and Updummylist in such a way that the li are in ascending order and each ui comes after the corresponding li. In contrast to CanDum, the li and ui that appear in the final expression will be the same ones that appeared in the original expression, except for the improved ordering. CanSame is used to help treat sets of repeating tensors appearing as subsets of larger products. Changing the names of the indices could cause conflict with names already used in other terms of the larger product. The user would normally not directly use CanSame.

■ **CanSuperApplyRules**

CanSuperApplyRules[expr,Rules] is the most powerful function for applying Rules but is also the slowest. It applies CanApplyRules over and over until no changes occur. CanSuperApplyRules[expr,Rules,n] applies CanSuperApplyRules to the nth term in expr.

■ **CD**

CD[tensor expression,index1,index2,...]. For example, CD[f[la]*h[ua,lb]+j[lb],lc,ld] is the second covariant derivative, first with respect to lc and then to ld.

■ **CDtoOD**

CDtoOD[expr] replaces covariant derivatives of the form CD by the corresponding expression in terms of ordinary partial derivatives OD and affine connections, AffineG. CDtoOD will not work on expressions with concrete indices and may need to be applied repeatedly to an expr. CDtoOD[expr,n] applies CDtoOD to the nth term of expr.

■ **cIndices**

cIndices are made available by the command AddIndexTypes and are input by typing cla, clb,..., clo for lower indices and cua, cub,..., cuo for the corresponding upper indices. In output lines, cle, for example, appears as a subscripted e′′′ index and cue as a superscripted e′′′ index. See also AddIndexTypes, RegularIndices, aIndices, bIndices.

■ ClearComponents

`ClearComponents[tensor[la,lb]]` will clear any values assigned to components of tensor having integer indices in the range `-Dimension` to `Dimension`, where `Dimension` must be a positive integer. The rank of the tensor to be cleared is indicated by the number of indices specified (2 in the above example). `ClearComponents` does not work fully in *Mathematica* 1.2 due to a bug in the `UnSet` function. This bug is fixed in versions 2.X.

■ ClearUnits

`ClearUnits` will clear the values of various constants that are set when a system of units is chosen. See also `Maxwellk1`, `Maxwellk3`, `Lightc`, `hbar`, `NewtonG`, `emuUnits`, `esuUnits`, `GaussianUnits`, `HeavisideLorentzUnits`, `RationalizedGaussianUnits`, `RationalizedMKSUnits`, `SIUnits`, `NaturalUnits`, `GravitationalUnits`.

■ CollectForm

`CollectForm[form]` groups a *p*-form that is expressed as a linear combination of coordinate basis *p*-forms (as produced by application of the command `CoordRep`), according to the independent coordinate basis exterior products of the same degree as the form. `Dimension` must already be set to an integer, and the names of the coordinates should have already been assigned, as in `x[1] = r; x[2] = theta; x[3] = phi,...` See also `CoordRep`.

■ CommuteCD

`CommuteCD[CD[tensor,i1,...,i2,i3,...,i4],i2,i3]` commutes the `i2` and `i3` covariant derivatives generating the appropriate Riemann tensor terms. To apply `CommuteCD` to the nth term in an expression, use `CommuteCD[tensor,i1,...,i2,i3,...,i4],i2,i3,n]`. `CommuteCD` works only with abstract indices, not numerical ones.

■ **Components**

Components[inputfile,outputfile1,outputfile2] reads the value of
Dimension, the coordinate names, the covariant metric components, and other
options from inputfile. It then calculates, in accordance with the options
specified in inputfile, the contravariant metric components, the metric determinant, the affine connections, and the covariant components of the Ricci,
Einstein, Riemann, and Weyl tensors, and the scalar curvature. These results are put into outputfile1 in a form that can be read in at later sessions
by Get and into outputfile2 in user editable form. As a guide in creating
inputfile, the file CompInSchw may be copied, edited, and renamed to be
used as inputfile. The arguments of Components must be quoted. Use the
saved components in a new session. See also SaveDef, MakeSum, Components,
Perturb.

■ **CompSimp**

CompSimp is used by Components to do simplification. CompSimp can be defined
by the user in the input file for Components. It is possible to define a set
of simplification rules, called CompSimpRules, used by CompSimp inside
Components. See a sample input file, such as CompInSchw.m, for examples of
how to define CompSimp and CompSimpRules. The default value of CompSimp
first applies Expand and then applies Together. The default CompSimpRules
list is the empty set.

■ **CompSimpOptions**

CompSimpOptions is a list of SetOptions statements associated with the simplification commands used by CompSimp.

■ **CompSimpRules**

CompSimpRules is a list of rules used by Components to do simplification.
CompSimpRules can be defined by the user in the input file for Components.
See a sample input file, such as CompInSchw.m, for examples of how to define
CompSimpRules and CompSimp. The default CompSimpRules list is the empty
list. If you have the old form, CompSimpRules[1], in your metric input files,
it must be changed to CompSimpRules for the files to work.

■ CoordRep

CoordRep[form] expresses a differential form expression in terms of a linear combination of basis exterior products of coordinates. Dimension must already be set to an integer, and the names of the coordinates should have already been assigned, as in x[1] = r; x[2] = theta; x[3] = phi,.... See also CollectForm.

■ CoXD

CoXD[w] is the codifferential, delta, of a p-form w. CoXD[w] is a $(p-1)$-form. The codifferential of a scalar function or 0-form is zero. In standard differential form notation, if w is a p-form in an n-dimensional space, then our definition of CoXD[w] or delta w is delta w = DetgSign (-1)^(np+n+1) * d * w, where DetgSign is the sign of the determinant of the metric tensor. See also FtoC, HodgeStar, XD, GenLap, Lap, DetgSign.

■ DefineForm

DefineForm[name,p], where p is an integer, defines a differential form called name of degree or rank p. For example, the components of the 2-form w defined by DefineForm[w,2] would be the antisymmetric object w[1a,1b]. Only the name w of the form , not its indices, should be typed when using it as a form. DefineForm[name[index1,index2],p], where p is an integer, defines a tensor-valued p-form called name[index1,index2]. For example, the components of the tensor-valued 2-form r[ua,1b] defined by DefineForm[r[ua,1b],2] would be r[ua,1b,1c,1d], with antisymmetry under interchange of 1c,1d. Only r[ua,1b] would be typed when using it as a form. DefineForm[{w,x,...},{2,1,...}] defines a 2-form w, a 1-form x,.... The names of forms or tensor-valued forms should all be different. See also RankForm, FtoC, XP, XD, CoXD, HodgeStar, GenLap, Lap.

■ DefineTensor

DefineTensor[name,printString,permWeightList] defines the tensor called name that prints as printString and has symmetries specified by permWeightList. For example,
DefineTensor[anti,"a",{{2,1},-1}]. Note that name is not quoted and printString is a quoted symbol or string. The length of each permutation in permWeightList must equal the number of indices of the tensor. If a tensor has no symmetries, permWeightList is {{1,2,...,rank},1}, where rank is the number of indices. In general, the smallest set of permutations and weights that give the desired symmetry should be entered as a list in DefineTensor. For a scalar, the form is DefineTensor[scalar,printString].
DefineTensor[name,permWeightList] gives the same print string as name.
DefineTensor[name1,name2,...,permWeightList] defines tensors name1, name2,... having the same print strings as their names and each having the same symmetry specified by permWeightList. See also PermWeight, Symmetries, AllSymmetries.

■ DefUnique

DefUnique[lhs,rhs], where lhs is the left-hand side of a rule and rhs is a tensor expression with dummy indices, uses SetDelayed (:=) to define lhs in terms of rhs in such a way that unique dummy indices are generated each time the definition is called. For example,
DefUnique[f[la_,lc_], t[la,lb] t[ub,lc]] produces a definition such that typing f[le,lf] will produce t[le,ll1] t[uu1,lf], where ll1,uu1 are a unique pair of dummy indices, that change each time that f is typed with two indices as arguments. The print forms of ll1, uu1 are as a subscript $1 and a superscript $1, respectively. DefUnique[lhs,rhs,cond] defines lhs to be rhs with unique dummy indices only if the conditional cond holds. A possible cond in the above example would be PairQ[la,lc].

■ DefUnique(*)

DefUnique[lhs,rhs], where lhs is the left-hand side of a rule and rhs is a tensor expression with dummy indices, uses SetDelayed (:=) to define lhs in terms of rhs in such a way that unique dummy indices are generated each time the definition is called. For example, DefUnique[f[la_,lc _],t[la,lb] t[ub,lc]] produces a definition such that typing f[le,lf] will produce t[le,ll1] t[uu1,lf], where ll1,uu1 are a unique pair of dummy indices, that change each time that f is typed with two indices as arguments. Dummy indices of each available type can be used. The print forms of the dummy indices are $1, $a1, $b1, and $c1 for regular and types a, b, and c indices. DefUnique[lhs,rhs,cond] defines lhs to be rhs with unique dummy indices only if the conditional cond holds. A possible cond in the above example would be PairQ[la,lc]. There are also PairaQ, PairbQ, and PaircQ.

■ DefUniqueAllTypes(*)

DefUniqueAllTypes is an alternate name for DefUnique when multiple index types are present. See the usage message for DefUnique. See also AddIndexTypes.

■ DegreeForm

DegreeForm[expr] gives the degree of a differential form expression. Unlike RankForm, DegreeForm recognizes that the components of a form are scalars of degree zero. DegreeForm also gives the correct degree when acting on a tensor-valued form and zero when acting on its components. RankForm will give the correct degree of a tensor-valued form but will not give zero for its components. Thus DegreeForm gives the correct degree of any form, while RankForm gives the correct degree only for forms not involving components of forms as factors (such forms may arise when using CoordRep). See also CoordRep, RankForm, TensorRankOfForm.

■ Detg

Detg is the determinant of the metric tensor.

■ DetgSign

DetgSign equals Abs[Detg]/Detg, giving the sign of the determinant of the metric tensor.

■ **DiffFormOpQ**

DiffFormOpQ[op] is True if op is a differential forms operator, such as XD, XP, HodgeStar, CoXD, GenLap, or Lap.

■ **Dimension**

Dimension is the dimension of spacetime.

■ **Downdummylist**

Downdummylist is the list of covariant dummy indices.

■ **Downlist**

Downlist is the union of Downdummylist and Downuserlist.

■ **Downuserlist**

Downuserlist is the list of tensor indices that may be used for covariant indices.

■ **DualStar**

DualStar[F[la,lb],{ua,ub,uc,ud}] gives the antisymmetric tensor produced by the action of Epsilon on the tensor F. In this example, the dimension of the space is 4 and F is of rank 2. The result is an antisymmetric second-rank tensor equal to (1/2!)F[la,lb] Epsilon[ua,ub,uc,ud]. If F were of rank p, then the factor of (1/2!) would be replaced by (1/p!) and the sum would be over the p indices of the tensor. Generally, F would be an antisymmetric tensor. See also HodgeStar, Epsilon, DefineTensor, DefineForm.

■ Dum

Dum[expr,n] will replace all paired indices by pairs li,ui from Downdummylist and Updummylist in such a way that the li are in ascending order, replacing lower indices with lower indices and upper with upper. The numbering of the dummy indices will start with the second argument, n. Dum[expr] takes n as 1. If you want to multiply together two tensor expressions, then Dum or CanDum can be used with argument n to make sure that the expressions to be multiplied have no common sets of dummy indices. After you load the multiple index module using the command AddIndexTypes, the usage message for Dum will explain how to start dummy indices of each type at a number other than 1.

■ Dum(*)

Dum[expr,{n,na,nb,nc}] will replace paired indices of all four types (regular, type-a, type-b, and type-c) by system-generated dummy indices. The numbering of regular dummy indices will start with integer n, that of type-a with na, type-b with nb, and type-c with nc. If fewer than four integers are entered in the second argument, the remaining integers will be assumed to be ones. Dum[expr] will start the numbering with 1 for each index-type.

■ DumAllTypes(*)

DumAllTypes is another name for Dum when multiple index types are present. See the usage message for Dum. See also AddIndexTypes.

■ EinsteinG

EinsteinG[la,lb] is the Einstein tensor.

■ EinsteinToRicciRule

EinsteinToRicciRule is used to replace any EinsteinG in an expression by its definition in terms of the Ricci tensor and the Riemann scalar. This is used only in 4 dimensions.

■ emuUnits

Entering the input line emuUnits will set up the emu system of units in electromagnetism by assigning the constants Maxwellk1 and Maxwellk3 values, Maxwellk1 = Lightc^2 ; Maxwellk3 = 1. See also Maxwellk1, Maxwellk3, emuUnits, esuUnits, GaussianUnits, HeavisideLorentzUnits, RationalizedGaussianUnits, RationalizedMKSUnits, SIUnits.

■ **Eps0**

Eps0 is the permittivity constant in MKS or SI units.

■ **EpsDown**

EpsDown[a,b,c,...] is antisymmetric under interchange of any two indices.
All traces vanish, as do any cases with equal indices. At the same time,
if Dimension is an integer and all the indices are negative integers in the
range -1 to -Dimension, then
EpsDown[-1,-2,...,-Dimension] = EpsilonSign, where negative integers
represent concrete covariant indices. EpsilonSign is 1 or -1 and is set in
the file Conventions.m. EpsilonSign can also be altered interactively. After Dimension is set to an integer, the user should type Update[ ] in order
to activate the rules that depend on the dimension. See EpsUp, Epsilon,
EpsilonProductTensor.

■ **EpsDownToEpsilonRule**

EpsDownToEpsilonRule takes expressions with EpsDown into ones with Epsilon.

■ **EpsDownToEpsUpRule**

EpsDownToEpsUpRule takes expressions with EpsDown into ones with EpsUp.

■ **Epsilon**

Epsilon[a,b,c,...] is a tensor that is antisymmetric under interchange of
any two indices. All traces vanish, as do any cases with equal indices. At
the same time, if Dimension is an integer, then
Epsilon[-1,-2,...,-Dimension] = EpsilonSign*(Abs[Detg])^(1/2), where
EpsilonSign is 1 or -1 and is set in the file Conventions.m. EpsilonSign
can be altered interactively. With all indices contravariant, one has
Epsilon[1,2,...,Dimension] = EpsilonSign*Detg^(-1)*(Abs[Detg])^(1/2).
Also, Epsilon[...] = (Abs[Detg])^(1/2)*EpsDown[...]. After setting
Dimension to an integer, the user should type Update[ ] in order to ac-
tivate the rules that depend on the dimension. See also EpsDown, EpsUp,
EpsilonProductTensor, EpsilonProductTensorRule.

- ## EpsilonProductTensor

  EpsilonProductTensor is the product of two Epsilon tensors. It is expanded in terms of Kronecker deltas and metric tensors when Dimension is set to an integer. In 4, 3, and 2 dimensions, respectively, it is
  EpsilonProductTensor[a,b,c,d,e,f,g,h] = Epsilon[a,b,c,d]*Epsilon[e,f,g,h] when Dimension = 4;
  EpsilonProductTensor[a,b,c,d,e,f] = Epsilon[a,b,c]*Epsilon[e,f,g] when Dimension = 3; and
  EpsilonProductTensor[a,b,c,d] = Epsilon[a,b]*Epsilon[e,f] when Dimension = 2. Here Epsilon is the antisymmetric tensor. The sign of the result depends on DetgSign = Abs[Detg]/Detg, that is assigned a value in Conventions.m. The value can be changed interactively by typing DetgSign = 1 or -1 and then Update[ ]. See EpsilonProductTensorRule.

- ## EpsilonProductTensorRule

  expr/.EpsilonProductTensorRule replaces the product of two Epsilons (or two EpsDowns or two EpsUps) in a tensor expression, expr, by the appropriate expression involving products of metric tensors or Kronecker deltas. Dimension must be an integer for this replacement to occur. See also EpsilonProductTensor, Epsilon.

- ## EpsilonSign

  EpsilonSign determines the sign of the Levi-Civita antisymmetric tensor density.

- ## EpsilonToEpsDownRule

  EpsilonToEpsDownRule takes expressions with Epsilon into ones with EpsDown.

- ## EpsilonToEpsUpRule

  EpsilonToEpsUpRule takes expressions with Epsilon into ones with EpsUp.

- ## EpsUp

  EpsUp[a,b,c,...] is antisymmetric under interchange of any two indices. All traces vanish, as do any cases with equal indices. At the same time, if Dimension is an integer and all the indices are integers in the range 1 to Dimension, then EpsUp[1,2,...,Dimension] = EpsilonSign, where EpsilonSign is 1 or -1 and is set in the file Conventions.m. EpsilonSign can be altered interactively. The user should type Update[ ] after Dimension is set to an integer in order to activate the rules that depend on the dimension. See also EpsDown, Epsilon, EpsilonProductTensor.

■ **EpsUpToEpsDownRule**

EpsUpToEpsDownRule takes expressions with EpsUp into ones with EpsDown.

■ **EpsUpToEpsilonRule**

EpsUpToEpsilonRule takes expressions with EpsUp into ones with Epsilon.

■ **EqApart**

EqApart[lhs_ == rhs_] applies Apart to each side of the equation. See Apart in the *Mathematica* book.

■ **EqApply**

EqApply[lhs_ == rhs_, operator_, a___] applies operator to each side of the equation, with a as the second argument, unless the argument a is omitted. (This syntax differs from Apply.)

■ **EqCancel**

EqCancel[lhs_ == rhs_] applies Cancel to each side of the equation. See Cancel in the *Mathematica* book.

■ **EqCollect**

EqCollect[lhs_ == rhs_,x_] collects together terms involving the same power of x on each side of the equation. If x is a list, collects terms having the same powers of the elements of the list. See Collect in the *Mathematica* book.

■ **EqDivide**

EqDivide[lhs_ == rhs_, a_] divides each side of the equation by the argument a. See Divide in the *Mathematica* book.

■ **EqExpand**

EqExpand[lhs_ == rhs_] applies Expand to each side of the equation. See Expand in the *Mathematica* book.

■ **EqExpandAll**

EqExpandAll[lhs_ == rhs_] applies ExpandAll to each side of the equation. See ExpandAll in the *Mathematica* book.

■ EqFactor

EqFactor[lhs_ == rhs_] applies Factor to each side of the equation. See Factor in the *Mathematica* book.

■ EqFactorTerms

EqFactorTerms[lhs_ == rhs_] applies FactorTerms to each side of the equation. See FactorTerms in the *Mathematica* book.

■ EqMinus

EqMinus[lhs_ == rhs_] multiplies each side of the equation by -1. See Minus in the *Mathematica* book.

■ EqPlus

EqPlus[lhs_ == rhs_, a__] adds the arguments a to each side of the equation. See Plus in the *Mathematica* book.

■ EqPower

EqPower[lhs_ == rhs_, a_] raises each side of the equation to the power a. See Power in the *Mathematica* book.

■ EqPowerExpand

EqPowerExpand[lhs_ == rhs_] expands all powers of products and powers on each side of the equation. For example, ((x + y)^3)^(1/3) -> x + y. See PowerExpand in the *Mathematica* book.

■ EqReverse

EqReverse[lhs_ == rhs_] reverses the sides of the equation.

■ EqSimplify

EqSimplify[lhs_ == rhs_] applies Simplify to each side of the equation. See Simplify in the *Mathematica* book.

- **EqSolve**

  `EqSolve[lhs == rhs, expr]` solves the equation `lhs == rhs` for the expression `expr`. This function is needed because the regular *Mathematica* `Solve` will not solve for complicated products of objects.

- **EqSubtract**

  `EqSubtract[lhs_ == rhs_, a_]` subtracts the arguments `a` from each side of the equation. See `Subtract` in the *Mathematica* book.

- **EqTimes**

  `EqTimes[lhs_ == rhs_, a_]` multiplies each side of the equation by the arguments `a`. See `Times` in the *Mathematica* book.

- **EqTogether**

  `EqTogether[lhs_ == rhs_]` applies `Together` to each side of the equation. See `Together` in the *Mathematica* book.

- **EqTwoDivide**

  `EqTwoDivide[lhs1_ == rhs1_, lhs1_ == rhs2_]` divides the first equation by the second.

- **EqTwoPlus**

  `EqTwoPlus[lhs1_ == rhs1_, lhs2_ == rhs2_]` adds two equations.

- **EqTwoSubtract**

  `EqTwoSubtract[lhs1_ == rhs1_, lhs1_ == rhs2_]` subtracts the second equation from the first.

- **EqTwoTimes**

  `EqTwoTimes[lhs1_ == rhs1_, lhs2_ == rhs2_]` multiplies two equations.

■ **esuUnits**

Entering the input line `esuUnits` will set up the esu system of units in electromagnetism by assigning the constants `Maxwellk1` and `Maxwellk3` values, `Maxwellk1 = 1`; `Maxwellk3 = 1`. See also `Maxwellk1`, `Maxwellk3`, `emuUnits`, `GaussianUnits`, `HeavisideLorentzUnits`.

■ **Euclid**

`Euclid` is a possible argument of `MakeMetricFlat`.

■ **EvaluateODFlag**

When `EvaluateODFlag = True`, `OD` is evaluated explicitly.

■ **Evenlist**

`Evenlist[expr]` gives the even-numbered elements of a list.

■ **Explode**

`Explode[expr]` turns an expression into a list of characters that make up `expr`.

■ **FirstCubicRiemannRule**

`FirstCubicRiemannRule` relates the product of three Riemann tensors with summed indices mixed to the product of three Riemann tensors with summed indices in lexical order.

■ **FirstQuadraticRiemannRule**

`FirstQuadraticRiemannRule` relates the product of two Riemann tensors with crossed summed indices to the product of two Riemann tensors with summed indices in lexical order, i.e., the Riemann tensor squared.

■ **FormComponentQ**

`FormComponentQ[expr]`, where `expr` has the same `Head` as a single differential form or tensor-valued differential form, returns `True` if `expr` is a component of the form or tensor-valued form and `False` if it is the form itself. For other types of expressions, `FormComponentQ` will return `True` or `False`, but with no particular significance. On a scalar, it returns `True`.

■ **FreeList**

`FreeList[list_of_indices]` gives the list of free indices, that is, of indices in list_of_indices that are not paired with corresponding up or down indices.

■ **FtoC**

FtoC[expr, {la,lb,...}], where expr is a differential form expression that may involve exterior products, exterior derivatives, and other differential form operators, returns the components of expr with indices la,lb,.... There must be p indices specified if expr is a *p*-form. The components are the coefficients of the independent basis *p*-forms in the expansion of expr. For example, if w is a *p*-form with components w[la,lb,...], then
w = (1/p!) w[la,lb,...] e[ua]^e[ub]^..., where the e[ua] are the basis 1-forms and the sum is over all values of the indices. See also XDtoCDflag, XP, XD, CoXD, HodgeStar, GenLap, Lap.

■ **GaussianUnits**

Entering the input line GaussianUnits will set up the Gaussian system of units in electromagnetism by assigning the constants Maxwellk1 and Maxwellk3 values, Maxwellk1 = 1 ; Maxwellk3 = Lightc^(-1). See also Maxwellk1, Maxwellk3, emuUnits, esuUnits, GaussianUnits, HeavisideLorentzUnits, RationalizedGaussianUnits, RationalizedMKSUnits, SIUnits.

■ **GenLap**

GenLap stands for the generalized Laplacian, delta d + d delta, where delta is the codifferential, CoXD, and d is the exterior derivative, XD. GenLap[w] is a *p*-form if w is a *p*-form. Among the components of GenLap[w] are the components of -Lap[w], where Lap[w] is the standard or raw Laplacian having components CD[w[la,lb,...],le,ue]. The other terms in the components of the generalized Laplacian involve the curvature and vanish in flat spaces. See also FtoC, Lap, CoXD, XD.

■ **GravitationalUnits**

Entering the input line GravitationalUnits will set up the system of units with the speed of light, Lightc, and the Newtonian gravitational constant, NewtonG, having the values: Lightc = 1 ; NewtonG = 1. See also NaturalUnits.

■ **hbar**

hbar is Planck's constant divided by 2 Pi.

- ## HeavisideLorentzUnits

  Entering the input line `HeavisideLorentzUnits` will set up the Heaviside-Lorentz or rationalized Gaussian system of units in electromagnetism by assigning the constants `Maxwellk1` and `Maxwellk3` values, `Maxwellk1 = (4*Pi)^(-1)` ; `Maxwellk3 = Lightc^(-1)`. See also `Maxwellk1, Maxwellk3, emuUnits, esuUnits, GaussianUnits, HeavisideLorentzUnits, RationalizedGaussianUnits, RationalizedMKSUnits, SIUnits`.

- ## HodgeStar

  `HodgeStar[w]` in n dimensions is the $(n-p)$-form representing the action of the Hodge star operation on the p-form `w`. For example, if the dimension of space is 4 and `w` is a 3-form, then `HodgeStar[w]` is a 1-form having components `(1/3!)w[la,lb,lc] Epsilon[ua,ub,uc,ld]`. To obtain these components, you must set `Dimension` to an integer value (4 in this example) and then apply the command `FtoC`. A double application of `HodgeStar` gives in general, `HodgeStar[HodgeStar[w] ] -> DetgSign (-1)^(p(n-p)) w`, where `DetgSign` is the sign of the determinant of the metric tensor. See also `FtoC, Epsilon, XD, CoXD, GenLap, Lap, DualStar, DetgSign`.

- ## Implode

  `Implode[charlist]` turns a list of characters into an expression.

- ## IndexAllTypesQ

  `IndexAllTypesQ` works like `IndexQ`, except on all index types that are present in memory.

- ## IndexAllTypesQ(*)

  `IndexAllTypesQ[index]` gives `True` if `index` is a regular index or an index of types a, b, or c. See also `IndexQ, IndexaQ, IndexbQ, IndexcQ`.

- ## IndexaQ

  `IndexaQ[x]` returns `True` if `x` is a tensor index of type-a and `False` otherwise. If `x` is an integer or a pattern such as `a_`, then `False` is returned. See also `IndexbQ, IndexcQ`.

■ **IndexaQ(*)**

IndexaQ[index] gives True if index is a type-a index and False otherwise. See also IndexQ, IndexbQ, IndexcQ, IndexAllTypesQ.

■ **IndexbQ**

IndexbQ[x] returns True if x is a tensor index of type-b and False otherwise. If x is an integer or a pattern such as a_, then False is returned. See also IndexaQ, IndexcQ.

■ **IndexbQ(*)**

IndexbQ[index] gives True if index is a type-b index and False otherwise. See also IndexQ, IndexaQ, IndexcQ, IndexAllTypesQ.

■ **IndexcQ**

IndexcQ[x] returns True if x is a tensor index of type-c and False otherwise. If x is an integer or a pattern such as a_, then False is returned. See also IndexaQ, IndexbQ.

■ **IndexcQ(*)**

IndexcQ[index] gives True if index is a type-c index and False otherwise. See also IndexQ, IndexaQ, IndexcQ, IndexAllTypesQ.

■ **IndexIntQ**

IndexIntQ[x] returns True if x is a possible tensor index or an integer and False otherwise. If x is a pattern such as a_, then False is returned. See also IndexQ, LowerIndexQ, UpperIndexQ, IndicesAndNotOrderedQ.

■ **IndexIntUpLoQ**

IndexIntUpLoQ[x] acts like IndexIntQ, except that in addition IndexIntUpLoQ returns True if x is in the list {lo1, up1, lo2, up2,..., lo10, up10}. Members of that list can appear in rules created by RuleUnique and DefineUnique and sometimes must be recognized by functions that appear in the rules created.

- ## IndexQ

  IndexQ[x] returns True if x is a possible tensor index and False otherwise. If x is an integer or a pattern such as a_, then False is returned. See also IndexIntQ, LowerIndexQ, UpperIndexQ, IndicesAndNotOrderedQ.

- ## IndexQ(*)

  IndexQ[index] gives True if index is a regular index or an index of types a, b, or c. It gives False otherwise. See also IndexaQ, IndexbQ, IndexcQ, IndexAllTypesQ.

- ## IndexRegQ

  IndexRegQ[index] gives True if index is a regular index and False otherwise. See also IndexQ, IndexAllTypesQ, IndexaQ, IndexbQ, IndexcQ.

- ## IndexTypes

  IndexTypes is a list of types of indices that Tsimplify will act upon. New index types are added to the list by the function AddIndexTypes. The possible index types are RegularIndices (always present), aIndices, bIndices, and cIndices (loaded by AddIndexTypes). See also AddIndexTypes, RegularIndices, aIndices, bIndices, cIndices.

- ## IndexUpLoQ

  IndexUpLoQ[x] returns True if and only if x is in the list {lo1, up1, lo2, up2,..., lo10, up10}. Members of that list can appear in rules created by RuleUnique and DefineUnique and sometimes must be recognized by functions that appear in the rules created.

- ## IndicesAndNotOrderedQ

  IndicesAndNotOrderedQ[el1,el2,...] returns True if every element is a tensor index or an integer and the elements of the list are not in lexical order. This function is useful when defining rules to automatically reorder indices in a tensor. See also IndexQ.

- ## InListQ

  InListQ[x,y] returns True if x is a list and y is a symbol that is an element of the list. Otherwise, False is returned. It differs from MemberQ in that the latter matches patterns also.

- ## IntInArgQ

  IntInArgQ[expr] is True if expr (that can be a sum of products of tensors)
  contains any integer indices and is False otherwise.

- ## IntP

  IntP[w1,wp], where w1 is a 1-form and wp is a p-form, is the interior product, that is defined to be a $(p-1)$-form with components
  w1[ua] wp[la,12,...,lp] formed by contracting the index of the components of w1 with the first index of the components of wp.

- ## Invert

  Invert[expr] interchanges lower and upper dummy tensor indices in expr. It
  first applies Dum to put them in program-generated form. InvertFast assumes
  that the dummy indices are already in that form. To use Invert on the nth
  term of expr, use Invert[expr,n].

- ## InvertFast

  See Invert.

- ## Kdelta

  Kdelta[index1,index2] is the symmetric Kronecker delta symbol. It is 1 if
  index1 = index2 and 0 otherwise. The indices can be in upper, lower, or
  mixed positions. It is evaluated if the indices are integers and is manipulated
  with KdeltaRule or AborbKdelta if the indices are symbols. Conventions
  on upper and lower indices are recognized. For example, Kdelta[-2,2] and
  Kdelta[2,2] are both equal to 1. Kdelta should not be used to raise or
  lower indices in a space in that the metric is not equal to Kdelta. Kdelta is
  useful when dealing with group indices on Yang-Mills fields, for example. In
  general spaces or spacetimes, Kdelta does not transform as a tensor. With
  indices referring to such spaces, you should use Metricg with one covariant
  and one contravariant index, rather than Kdelta, in order to avoid potential
  inconsistencies. For example, Kdelta[la,lb] Metricg[ub,uc] gives
  Kdelta[la,uc], that is false unless Metricg equals Kdelta. Thus Kdelta
  should be reserved for particular applications in which its use is consistent.
  For more, see AbsorbKdelta. See also KdeltaRule, AbsorbKdelta.

- ## KdeltaRule

  KdeltaRule is the set of rules used by AbsorbKdelta. KdeltaRule can be applied directly if desired using Replace or ReplaceRepeated. For important warnings about absorbing Kdelta, see AbsorbKdelta and Kdelta.

- ## Lap

  Lap[w], where w is a p-form, is the standard or raw Laplacian having components CD[w[la,lb,...],le,ue]. Lap[w] is a p-form if w is a p-form. The generalized Laplacian, GenLap, has -Lap as one term. See also GenLap, FtoC, CoXD, XD.

- ## LD

  LD[wp,w1] is the Lie derivative of the p-form wp with respect to the 1-form w1. LD[wp, w1] is a p-form with its la,lb,... component given by LieD[wp[la,lb,...], w1]. (Here, la,lb,... represent p symbolic indices.) See LieD for the explicit expression for the component. Note that LieD is defined for tensors of arbitrary symmetry, while LD is defined only for forms (that correspond to antisymmetric tensors). FtoC gives the components of LD in terms of LieD. You can then use LieDtoCD or LieDtoOD if you want them expressed in terms of covariant or ordinary derivatives.

- ## LDtoXD

  LDtoXD[expr] uses the identity LD[wp,w1] = XD[IntP[w1,wp]]+IntP[w1,XD[wp]] to replace, in expr, the Lie derivative, LD, of a p-form, wp, with respect to a 1-form, w1, by exterior derivatives, XD, and interior products, IntP. See also LDtoXDrule.

- ## LDtoXDrule

  LDtoXDrule is a rule that uses the identity LD[wp,w1] = XD[IntP[w1,wp]]+IntP[w1,XD[wp]] to replace the Lie derivative, LD, of a p-form, wp, with respect to a 1-form, w1, by exterior derivatives, XD, and interior products, IntP. See also LDtoXD.

- ## LieD

  LieD[expr,vector] is the Lie Derivative of expr with respect to vector. The index of the vector should not be typed. For example, LieD[MaxwellF[la,lb],V] takes the Lie derivative of MaxwellF[la,lb] with respect to the vector V[uc]. The expression may be a sum of products of tensors. See also LieDtoCD, LD.

■ **LieDtoCD**

LieDtoCD[expr] replaces any Lie derivatives, LieD, in expr by the equivalent expressions involving covariant derivatives, CD. See also LieDtoCDrule, LieDtoOD.

■ **LieDtoCDrule**

expr/.LieDtoCDrule replaces any Lie derivatives, LieD, in expr by the equivalent expressions involving covariant derivatives, CD. LieDtoCD[expr] is preferred to LieDtoCDrule, since it also introduces standard dummy indices in the resulting expression, as opposed to totally new ones. See also LieDtoCD, LieDtoOD.

■ **LieDtoOD**

LieDtoOD[expr] replaces any Lie derivatives, LieD, in expr by the equivalent expressions involving ordinary derivatives, OD. See also LieDtoODrule, LieDtoCD.

■ **LieDtoODrule**

expr/.LieDtoODrule replaces any Lie derivatives, LieD, in expr by the equivalent expressions involving ordinary derivatives, OD. LieDtoOD[expr] is preferred to LieDtoODrule, since it also introduces standard dummy indices in the resulting expression, as opposed to totally new ones. See also LieDtoOD, LieDtoCD.

■ **Lightc**

Lightc is the speed of light.

■ **LorentzGaugeRule**

LorentzGaugeRule is the Lorentz gauge condition on the vector potential.

■ **Lower**

Lower[index] gives the lowered index if acting on an upper index. The action of Lower on other than regular indices is undefined.

- **Lowera(*)**

  `Lowera[index]` gives the corresponding lowered index if acting on an upper index of type-a and returns `index` otherwise. The action of `Lowera` on other than type-a indices is undefined. See also `LowerAllTypes`, `Lowerb`, `Lowerc`.

- **LowerAllPairs**

  `LowerAllPairs[expr]` lowers the upper member of every paired set of indices (i.e., dummy pairs) appearing in `expr`. Here, `expr` is a product of tensors multiplied by numerical or symbolic factors, but `expr` may not be a sum of seperate terms.

- **LowerAllTypes**

  `LowerAllTypes` works like `Lower`, except on all index types that are present in memory.

- **LowerAllTypes(*)**

  `LowerAllTypes[index]` gives the corresponding lowered index if acting on an upper index of any type and returns `index` otherwise. See also `Lower`, `Lowera`, `Lowerb`, `Lowerc`.

- **Lowerb(*)**

  `Lowerb[index]` gives the corresponding lowered index if acting on an upper index of type-b and returns `index` otherwise. The action of `Lowerb` on other than type-b indices is undefined. See also `LowerAllTypes`, `Lowera`, `Lowerc`.

- **Lowerc(*)**

  `Lowerc[index]` gives the corresponding lowered index if acting on an upper index of type-c and returns `index` otherwise. The action of `Lowerc` on other than type-c indices is undefined. See also `LowerAllTypes`, `Lowera`, `Lowerb`.

- **LowerIndexAllTypesQ**

  `LowerIndexAllTypesQ[x]` returns `True` if `x` is a possible lower tensor index of any type and `False` otherwise. If `x` is an integer of a pattern such as `a_`, then `False` is returned. See also `IndexQ`, `IndexAllTypesQ`.

■ **LowerIndexAllTypesQ(*)**

LowerIndexAllTypesQ[index] -> True if index is a lower index of any type
and False otherwise. See also LowerIndexQ, LowerIndexbQ, LowerIndexcQ,
LowerIndexAllTypesQ, UpperIndexQ, UpperIndexaQ, UpperIndexbQ,
UpperIndexcQ, UpperIndexAllTypesQ.

■ **LowerIndexaQ(*)**

LowerIndexaQ[index] -> True if index is a lower index of type-a and False
otherwise. See also LowerIndexQ, LowerIndexbQ, LowerIndexcQ,
LowerIndexAllTypesQ, UpperIndexQ, UpperIndexaQ, UpperIndexbQ,
UpperIndexcQ, UpperIndexAllTypesQ.

■ **LowerIndexbQ(*)**

LowerIndexbQ[index] -> True if index is a lower index of type-b and False
otherwise. See also LowerIndexQ, LowerIndexaQ, LowerIndexcQ,
LowerIndexAllTypesQ, UpperIndexQ, UpperIndexaQ, UpperIndexbQ,
UpperIndexcQ, UpperIndexAllTypesQ.

■ **LowerIndexcQ(*)**

LowerIndexcQ[index] -> True if index is a lower index of type-c and False
otherwise. See also LowerIndexQ, LowerIndexaQ, LowerIndexbQ,
LowerIndexAllTypesQ, UpperIndexQ, UpperIndexaQ, UpperIndexbQ,
UpperIndexcQ, UpperIndexAllTypesQ.

■ **LowerIndexQ**

LowerIndexQ[x] returns True if x is a possible lower tensor index and False
otherwise. If x is an integer of a pattern such as a_, then False is returned.
See also IndexQ, UpperIndexQ.

■ **LowerIndexQ(*)**

LowerIndexQ[index] -> True if index is a regular lower index and False oth-
erwise. See also LowerIndexa, LowerIndexbQ, LowerIndexcQ,
LowerIndexAllTypesQ, UpperIndexaQ, UpperIndexbQ, UpperIndexcQ,
UpperIndexAllTypesQ.

■ **MakeAllSymmetries**

MakeAllSymmetries[tensor[la,lb]], when applied to a tensor for that Symmetries[tensor[la,lb]] has a value, will produce a list of all symmetries of that tensor by closing the symmetry list, that is, by producing the list of permutations and weights that contains the list, Symmetries[tensor[la,lb]], and that forms a group closed under multiplication. See MakePermWeightGroup.

■ **MakeMetricFlat**

MakeMetricFlat[Euclid] produces a flat metric with diagonal values of 1 and off-diagonal values of 0. It also sets MetricgSign to 1, DetgSign to 1, and Detg to 1. It uses the value of Dimension, that should be an integer. MakeMetricFlat[Minkowski] produces a Minkowski metric with the first (Dimension - 1) diagonal values equal to MetricgSign and the last covariant diagonal value equal to (-MetricgSign) (Lightc)^2. This means that x[4] corresponds to t and not to (Lightc t). The off-diagonal values are 0. It also sets the value of Detg and DetgSign to -(Lightc)^2 (MetricgSign)^Dimension. In both cases, the components of AffineG are set to 0 and CD is made equivalent to OD.

■ **MakePermWeightGroup**

MakePermWeightGroup[symms], where symms is a list of permutations and weights such as {{2,1},-1}, produces the list of permutations and weights, that contains the original permutations and weights and forms a group closed under multiplication, such as {{1,2},1,{2,1},-1}. See MakeAllSymmetries.

■ **MakeSum**

MakeSum[expr] replaces symbolic summations of dummy indices by actual sums over concrete indices. Dimension should be an integer so that the Sum can be performed explicitly. MakeSum[expr,{la->lc,lb->ld}] will perform the summation with index la equal to lc and index lb equal to ld in each term. Each index appearing in the second argument must be a dummy index appearing in expr. For example,
MakeSum[RiemannR[la,ub,lc,ud] RiemannR[ua,lb,uc,ld],{la->lc,lb->ld}]
does the summation with the indicated dummy indices taking equal values in each term of the sum.

■ **MakeSumRange**

MakeSumRange[expr,{la,ala,bla,-4,-5},{cla,-6,-7}] means that the specific dummy index la appearing in expr will be summed over the values that follow it in the list, namely, ala, bla, -4, and -5. The complementary dummy index ua will be summed over the corresponding complementary indices. All values in each list should be permitted symbolic lower indices or negative integers. Similarly, the second list {cla,-6,-7} means that dummy index cla appearing in expr will be summed over the values -6 and -7 and its complementary dummy index cua will be summed on 6 and 7. All values to sum over must be listed, and only the indicated sums will be done. If more than regular indices appear, you should already have used AddIndexTypes to load the additional types of indices. Only recognized index-types and positive or negative integers should appear in the argument lists, and the first element of each list should be a lower dummy index in expr. See also AddIndexTypes, MakeSum.

■ **Matchlist**

Matchlist[list] returns a list of pairs of matching indices in the order in which they appear in list, but with the lower member of each pair first. Matching pair means paired lower and upper indices. The argument is an index list.

■ **Matchlist(*)**

Matchlist[list] returns a list of pairs of matching regular indices in the order in which they appear in list, but with the lower member of each pair first. Matching pair means paired lower and upper indices. See also Matchlista, Matchlistb, Matchlistc, MatchlistAllTypes.

■ **Matchlista**

Matchlista[list], after the command AddIndexTypes has been issued, returns a list of matching type-a indices.

■ **Matchlista(*)**

Matchlista[list] returns a list of pairs of matching type-a indices in the order in which they appear in list, but with the lower member of each pair first. Matching pair means paired lower and upper indices. See also Matchlistb, Matchlistc, MatchlistAllTypes, Matchlist.

■ **MatchlistAllTypes(*)**

`MatchlistAllTypes[list]` returns a list of pairs of matching indices in the order in which they appear in `list`, but with the lower member of each pair first. Matching pair means paired lower and upper indices of any type (regular, type-a, b, or c). See also `Matchlist, Matchlista, Matchlistb, Matchlistc`.

■ **Matchlistb**

`Matchlistb[list]`, after the command `AddIndexTypes` has been issued, returns a list of matching type-b indices.

■ **Matchlistb(*)**

`Matchlistb[list]` returns a list of pairs of matching type-b indices in the order in which they appear in `list`, but with the lower member of each pair first. Matching pair means paired lower and upper indices. See also `Matchlista, Matchlistc, MatchlistAllTypes, Matchlist`.

■ **Matchlistc**

`Matchlistc[list]`, after the command `AddIndexTypes` has been issued, returns a list of matching type-c indices.

■ **Matchlistc(*)**

`Matchlistc[list]` returns a list of pairs of matching type-c indices in the order in which they appear in `list`, but with the lower member of each pair first. Matching pair means paired lower and upper indices. See also `Matchlista, Matchlistb, MatchlistAllTypes, Matchlist`.

■ **MatchlistOrd**

`MatchlistOrd[list]` returns a list of pairs of matching indices in the order in which they appear in `list`, with the lower or upper member of each pair first, depending on original ordering. Matching pair means paired lower and upper indices. Internal function.

■ **$MathTensorVersionNumber**

`$MathTensorVersionNumber` is the version of *MathTensor* running in the current session.

■ **MatrixMap**

MatrixMap[op,matrix] applies the operator, op, to each element of a matrix.

■ **MatrixXP**

MatrixXP[mat1, mat2], where mat1 and mat2 are matrices having differential form elements, carries out matrix multiplication, but with the exterior product, XP, replacing the ordinary product in the multiplication of matrix elements.

■ **MaxwellA**

MaxwellA[la] is the electromagnetic vector potential.

■ **MaxwellCyclicEquation**

MaxwellCyclicEquation[la,lb,lc] is one of the Maxwell equations.

■ **MaxwellCyclicRule**

MaxwellCyclicRule[la,lb,lc] implements the Cyclic Rule on the covariant derivative of the Maxwell field tensor.

■ **MaxwellDivergenceEquation**

MaxwellDivergenceEquation is one of the Maxwell equations.

■ **MaxwellDivergenceRule**

oiMaxwellDivergenceRule replaces the divergence of the Maxwell field tensor by the current 4-vector.

■ **MaxwellF**

MaxwellF[la,lb] is the Maxwell field tensor.

■ **MaxwellJ**

MaxwellJ[la] is the electromagnetic current density.

- # Maxwellk1

  `Maxwellk1` is a constant that sets the system of units and is ordinarily assigned either by default or by the user in a file of conventions by putting in a single line with one of the following commands `esuUnits`, `emuUnits`, `GaussianUnits`, `HeavisideLorentzUnits`, `RationalizedGaussianUnits`, `RationalizedMKSUnits`, or `SIUnits`. See also `Maxwellk3`, `esuUnits`, `emuUnits`, `GaussianUnits`, `HeavisideLorentzUnits`, `RationalizedGaussianUnits`, `RationalizedMKSUnits`, `SIUnits`.

- # Maxwellk3

  `Maxwellk3` is a constant that sets the system of units and is ordinarily assigned either by default or by the user in a file of conventions by putting in a single line with one of the following commands `esuUnits`, `emuUnits`, `GaussianUnits`, `HeavisideLorentzUnits`, `RationalizedGaussianUnits`, `RationalizedMKSUnits`, or `SIUnits`. See also `Maxwellk3`, `esuUnits`, `emuUnits`, `GaussianUnits`, `HeavisideLorentzUnits`, `RationalizedGaussianUnits`, `RationalizedMKSUnits`, `SIUnits`.

- # Maxwellrho

  `Maxwellrho` is the electromagnetic charge density.

- # MaxwellT

  `MaxwellT[la,lb]` is the Maxwell stress tensor. See also `MaxwellTtoFrule`, `MaxwellTexpression`.

- # MaxwellTexpression

  `MaxwellTexpression[la,lb]` is the expression for the Maxwell stress tensor in terms of the Maxwell field tensor, `MaxwellF`. See `MaxwellT`, `MaxwellTtoFrule`.

- # MaxwellTtoFrule

  `MaxwellTtoFrule` can be used with `ApplyRules` to replace the electromagnetic stress tensor, `MaxwellT`, by the appropriate expression in terms of the electromagnetic field, `MaxwellF`. See also `MaxwellT`, `MaxwellTexpression`.

- ## MaxwellVectorPotentialRule

  MaxwellVectorPotentialRule replaces the Maxwell field tensor by its expression in terms of the vector potential.

- ## Metricg

  Metricg[a_,b_], where a,b are lower or upper indices, is the metric tensor. When MetricgFlag is True (default), the metric tensor will automatically be absorbed in raising or lowering indices whenever that is possible. When MetricgFlag is set to False, one can use Absorbg to raise and lower indices with Metricg. After resetting MetricgFlag to True, do Update[ ] so that previous expressions referred to will be reevaluated with the new flag setting.

- ## MetricgFlag

  When MetricgFlag is True (default), the metric tensor will automatically be absorbed in raising or lowering indices whenever that is possible. When MetricgFlag is set to False, one can use Absorbg to raise and lower indices with Metricg. After resetting MetricgFlag to True, do Update[ ] so that previous expressions referred to will be reevaluated with the new flag setting.

- ## MetricgFlagOn

  MetricgFlagOn sets MetricgFlag to True and does an Update[ ].

- ## MetricgFlagOff

  MetricgFlagOff sets MetricFlag to False and does an Update[ ].

- ## MetricgSign

  MetricSign is the sign of Metricg[-1,-1] in a local inertial coordinate system. See the file Conventions.m.

- ## Minkowski

  A possible argument of MakeMetricFlat.

- ## Mu0

  Mu0 is the permeability constant in MKS or SI units.

- **NaturalUnits**

  Entering the input line `NaturalUnits` will set up the system of units with the speed of light, `Lightc`, and the Planck constant divided by `2 Pi`, `hbar`, having the values `Lightc = 1` ; `hbar = 1`.

- **NegIntegerQ**

  `NegIntegerQ[x]` returns `True` if `x` is a negative integer (not 0) and otherwise returns `False`.

- **NewtonG**

  `NewtonG` is the Newtonian gravitational constant.

- **NoIntInArgQ**

  `NoIntInArgQ[expr]` is `False` if `expr` (that can be a sum of products of tensors) contains any integer indices and is `True` otherwise.

- **NonTensorPart**

  `NonTensorPart[expr]` returns the nontensorial factors in an expression. Here, `expr` should not be a sum of terms.

- **NotAllPatQ**

  `NotAllPatQ[symbol]` returns `True` if `symbol` is not one of the differential form operators. It is used internally.

- **OD**

  `OD[tensor expression,index1,index2,...]`. For example, `OD[f[la]*h[ua,lb]+j[lb],lc,ld]` is the second ordinary partial derivative, first with respect to `lc` and then `ld`. `OD` is symmetric in derivative indices.

- **Oddlist**

  `Oddlist[expr]` gives the odd-numbered elements of a list.

- ## OrderCD

  `OrderCD[CD[expr,list]]` will reorder the indices in the list of derivatives into alphabetical order (the same order as `Sort`) generating the extra Riemann tensor terms. All covariant derivatives in the generated terms are also re-ordered. This function does not work with numerical indices. If indices are already in the appropriate order, nothing is done.

- ## OrderedArgsQ

  `OrderedArgsQ[expr1,expr2]` returns `True` if the argument list of `expr1` is lexically before the argument list of `expr2` and `False` otherwise.

- ## Pair

  `Pair[index]` gives the lowered index if acting on an upper index or the raised index if acting on a lower index.

- ## PairAllTypes

  `PairAllTypes` works like `Pair`, except that it works on all index types that are present in memory.

- ## PairAllTypesInt

  `PairAllTypesInt[b]` gives the complementary index to `b` if `b` is an index of any of the possible types. If `b` is an integer, then it gives the integer `-b`. Otherwise, it returns `b` itself. `PairAllTypesInt` has the `Attribute Listable`. See also `Pair`, `Paira`, `Pairb`, `Pairc`, `PairAllTypes`.

- ## PairAllTypesQ

  `PairAllTypesQ` works like `PairQ`, except that after all index types are present in memory it recognizes pairs of any type of index. It is the same as `PairQ` until after `AddIndexTypes` has been entered.

- ## PairAllTypesQ(*)

  `PairAllTypesQ[a,b]` `->` `True` if `a` and `b` are a corresponding pair of lower and upper indices of any type. It gives `False` otherwise.
  `PairAllTypesQ[a,b,...,c,d,...]` `->`
  `PairAllTypesQ[a,c]` `&&` `PairAllTypesQ[b,d]` `&&` ... See also `PairaQ`, `PairbQ`, `PaircQ`, `PairQ`.

- ## PairAntisymmetrize

  `PairAntisymmetrize[expr,list]` takes a list of pairs of indices and symmetrizes over all the pairs.

- ## Paira(*)

  `Paira[index]` gives the corresponding raised index if acting on a lower index of type-a, and the corresponding lowered index if acting on a raised index of type-a. The action of `Paira` on other than type-a indices is undefined. See also `PairAllTypes`, `Pairb`, `Pairc`.

- ## PairaQ(*)

  `PairaQ[a,b] -> True` if a and b are a corresponding pair of type-a lower and upper indices. It gives `False` otherwise.
  `PairaQ[a,b,...,c,d,...]` -> `PairaQ[a,c] && PairaQ[b,d] && ...` See also `PairbQ`, `PaircQ`, `PairAllTypesQ`.

- ## Pairb(*)

  `Pairb[index]` gives the corresponding raised index if acting on a lower index of type-b, and the corresponding lowered index if acting on a raised index of type-b. The action of `Pairb` on other than type-b indices is undefined. See also `PairAllTypes`, `Paira`, `Pairc`.

- ## PairbQ(*)

  `PairbQ[a,b] -> True` if a and b are a corresponding pair of type-b lower and upper indices. It gives `False` otherwise.
  `PairbQ[a,b,...,c,d,...]` -> `PairbQ[a,c] && PairbQ[b,d] && ...` See also `PairaQ`, `PaircQ`, `PairAllTypesQ`.

- ## Pairc(*)

  `Pairc[index]` gives the corresponding raised index if acting on a lower index of type-c, and the corresponding lowered index if acting on a raised index of type-c. The action of `Pairc` on other than type-c indices is undefined. See also `PairAllTypes`, `Paira`, `Pairb`.

- ## PaircQ(*)

  PaircQ[a,b] -> True if a and b are a corresponding pair of type-c lower and upper indices. It gives False otherwise.
  PaircQ[a,b,...,c,d,...] -> PaircQ[a,ċ] && PaircQ[b,d] && ... See also PairaQ, PairbQ, PairAllTypesQ.

- ## Pairdum

  Pairdum[index] gives the lowered index if index is an upper program-generated dummy index or the raised index if index is a lower program-generated dummy index.

- ## PairQ

  PairQ[a,b] -> True if a and b are a corresponding pair of regular lower and upper indices. It gives False otherwise. PairQ[a,b,...,c,d,...] -> PairQ[a,c] && PairQ[b,d] && ... See also AddIndexTypes, PairaQ, PairbQ, PaircQ, PairAllTypesQ.

- ## PairQ(*)

  PairQ[a,b] -> True if a and b are a corresponding pair of regular lower and upper indices. It gives False otherwise.
  PairQ[a,b,...,c,d,...] -> PairQ[a,c] && PairQ[b,d] && ... See also PairaQ, PairbQ, PaircQ, PairAllTypesQ.

- ## PairSymmetrize

  PairSymmetrize[expr,list] takes a list of pairs of indices and symmetrizes over all the pairs.

- ## PermWeight

  PermWeight[name,list] assigns the symmetries specified in list to the tensor name. An example of list is {{2,1,3,4},-1,{1,2,4,3},1}, that indicates that under the permutation {2,1,3,4} of a 4-index tensor, the tensor is multiplied by the weight -1, while under the permutation {1,2,4,3} it is multiplied by 1. Thus PermWeight[f,{2,1,3,4},-1,{1,2,4,3},1] will make the tensor f[1a,1b,1c,1d] antisymmetric in the first pair of indices and symmetric in the second pair. If one then enters SymmetriesOfSymbol[f], the symmetry list is returned. If one enters ??SymmetriesOfSymbol, a list of tensors with their assigned symmetries is returned. You should be sure the list of permutations and weights entered is consistent and pertains to all the indices of the tensor, even if some are not affected. DefineTensor should be used to enter symmetries, since only then will Tsimplify work correctly. See also DefineTensor, SymmetriesOfSymbol, Symmetries, AllSymmetries.

■ **PIntegrate**

PIntegrate[expr,object] partially integrates one covariant derivative off of the object and takes the derivative of the other terms. PIntegrate[expr,object,n] will apply PIntegrate just to the nth term in expr.

■ **PosIntegerQ**

PosIntegerQ[x] returns True if x is a positive integer (not 0) and otherwise returns False.

■ **PrettyOff**

PrettyOff turns off automatic pretty printing.

■ **PrettyOn**

PrettyOn turns on automatic pretty printing. If you turn on global pretty printing, you will get tensors printed properly only if they have been defined using DefineTensor or loaded from a file.

■ **Raise**

Raise[index] gives the corresponding raised index if acting on a lower index. The action of Raise on other than regular indices is undefined.

■ **Raisea(*)**

Raisea[index] gives the corresponding raised index if acting on a lower index of type-a and returns index otherwise. The action of Raisea on other than type-a indices is undefined. See also RaiseAllTypes, Raiseb, Raisec.

■ **RaiseAllTypes**

RaiseAllTypes works like Raise, except on all index types that are present in memory.

■ **RaiseAllTypes(*)**

RaiseAllTypes[index] gives the corresponding raised index if acting on a lower index of any type and returns index otherwise. See also Raise, Raisea, Raiseb, Raisec.

- # Raiseb(*)

  `Raiseb[index]` gives the corresponding raised index if acting on a lower index of type-b and returns **index** otherwise. The action of **Raiseb** on other than type-b indices is undefined. See also `RaiseAllTypes, Raisea, Raisec`.

- # Raisec(*)

  `Raisec[index]` gives the corresponding raised index if acting on a lower index of type-c and returns **index** otherwise. The action of **Raisec** on other than type-c indices is undefined. See also `RaiseAllTypes, Raisea, Raiseb`.

- # RankForm

  `RankForm[expr]` gives the degree or rank of **expr**, where **expr** is a differential form expression. See also `FtoC, XP, XD, CoXD, HodgeStar, GenLap, Lap`.

- # RationalizedMKSUnits

  Entering the input line `RationalizedMKSUnits` will set up SI or rationalized MKS units in electromagnetism by setting the constants `Maxwellk1` and `Maxwellk3` to values `Maxwellk1 = (4*Pi*Eps0)^(-1) ; Maxwellk3 = 1`. See also `Maxwellk1, Maxwellk3, emuUnits, esuUnits, GaussianUnits, HeavisideLorentzUnits, RationalizedGaussianUnits, RationalizedMKSUnits, SIUnits`.

- # Rcsign

  See the file `Conventions.m`.

- # RegularIndices

  `RegularIndices` are always available and are input by typing `la, lb,..., lo` for lower indices and `ua, ub,..., uo` for the corresponding upper indices. Additional types of indices are available after the command `AddIndexTypes` is issued. In output lines, `le`, for example, appears as a subscripted e index and `ue` as a superscripted e index. See also `AddIndexTypes, aIndices, bIndices, cIndices`.

- # RicciR

  `RicciR[la,lb]` is the Ricci tensor.

- ## RicciToAffine

  `RicciToAffine[expr]` replaces any Ricci tensors in `expr` by their equivalents in terms of affine connections, `AffineG`. Dummy indices appear with standard system-generated names.

- ## RicciToAffineRule

  `ApplyRules[expr, RicciToAffineRule]` replaces any Ricci tensors in `expr` by their equivalents in terms of affine connections, `AffineG`. New dummy indices appear with `$` prefixes.

- ## RicciToTraceFreeRicciRule

  `RicciToTraceFreeRicciRule` converts expressions with Ricci tensors to expressions with trace-free Ricci tensors and `ScalarR`'s.

- ## RiemannCyclicFirstThreeRule

  `RiemannCyclicFirstThreeRule[la,lb,lc,ld]` performs the cyclic identity on `la`, `lb`, and `lc` in an expression using `expr/.RiemannCyclicFirstThreeRule[la,lb,lc,ld]`.

- ## RiemannCyclicSecondThreeRule

  `RiemannCyclicSecondThreeRule[la,lb,lc,ld]` performs the cyclic identity on `lb`, `lc`, and `ld` in an expression using `expr/.RiemannCyclicSecondThreeRule[la,lb,lc,ld]`.

- ## RiemannR

  `RiemannR[ua,lb,lc,ld]` is the Riemann tensor.

- ## RiemannRules

  The Riemann tensor properties. The normal symmetries of the `RiemannR`, `RicciR`, and `CD[ScalarR,la,lb]` tensors are applied automatically if their indices are canonical. If the `RiemannRules` are applied after a `Canonicalize` function, then all symmetries will be applied. The `RiemannRules` are built up from the 40 individual `RiemannRule[1-40]` documented in this book. `??RiemannRule[1-40]` will give the rule form for one of the rules 1–40. When the `RiemannRules` are applied, a message (or messages) is given indicating that one is used.

- ### RiemannRule*n*

  One of the `RiemannRules`, where *n* is an integer. For further information, type `??RiemannRule`*n*. To find out which `RiemannRules` exist in *MathTensor*, type `?RiemannRule*`. Then select the numbered rule you want to determine the value of *n* in `??RiemannRule`*n*.

- ### RiemannToAffine

  `RiemannToAffine[expr]` replaces any Riemann tensors in `expr` by their equivalents in terms of affine connections, `AffineG`. Dummy indices appear with standard system-generated names.

- ### RiemannToAffineRule

  `RiemannToAffineRule` is used by the command `RiemannToAffine`. The user should use the latter command instead. See `RiemannToAffine`.

- ### RiemannToWeylRule

  `RiemannToWeylRule` converts expressions with `RiemannR`'s to expressions with Weyl tensors, Ricci tensors, and `ScalarR`'s.

- ### Rmsign

  See the file `Conventions.m`.

- ### Rulelists

  `Rulelists` is defined in such a way that `Rulelists[a,b,c,d,e,f]` gives `{a->d, b->e, c->f}`.

- ### RuleUnique

  `RuleUnique[ruleName,lhs,rhs]`, where `ruleName` is the name for a new rule, `lhs` is the left-hand side of a transformation rule, and `rhs` is a tensor expression with dummy indices, uses `RuleDelayed (:>)` to produce a rule called `ruleName`, that transforms `lhs` into `rhs` in such a way that unique dummy indices are generated each time the transformation rule is called. For example, `RuleUnique[fTotRule,f[la_,lc_],t[la,lb] t[ub,lc]]` produces a transformation rule, `fTotRule`, such that typing `f[le,lf]/.fTotRule` will produce `t[le,ll1] t[uu1,lf]`. Here, `ll1,uu1` are a unique pair of dummy indices, that change each time that the transformation rule is applied in an expression. The print forms of `ll1`, `uu1` are as a subscript $1 and a superscript $1, respectively. `RuleUnique[ruleName,lhs,rhs,cond]` causes `ruleName` to transform `lhs` to `rhs` with unique dummy indices only if the conditional `cond` holds. A possible `cond` in the above example would be `PairQ[la,lc]`.

■ RuleUnique(*)

RuleUnique[ruleName,lhs,rhs], where ruleName is the name for a new rule, lhs is the left-hand side of a transformation rule, and rhs is a tensor expression with dummy indices, uses RuleDelayed (:>) to produce a rule called ruleName, that transforms lhs into rhs, in such a way that unique dummy indices are generated each time the transformation rule is called. For example, RuleUnique[fTotRule,f[la_,lc_],t[la,lb] t[ub,lc]] produces a transformation rule, fTotRule, such that typing f[le,lf]/.fTotRule will produce t[le,l11] t[uu1,lf]. Dummy indices of each available type can be used. The print forms of the dummy indices are $1, $a1, $b1, $c1 for regular and type-a, type-b, and type-c indices, respectively.

RuleUnique[ruleName,lhs,rhs,cond] causes ruleName to transform lhs to rhs with unique dummy indices only if the conditional cond holds. A possible cond in the above example would be PairQ[la,lc]. There are also PairaQ, PairbQ, PaircQ.

■ RuleUniqueAllTypes(*)

RuleUniqueAllTypes is an alternate name for RuleUnique when multiple index types are present. See the usage message for RuleUnique. See AddIndexTypes.

■ SAIsimp

SAIsimp and SAIsimpRules determines the form of simplification used by SetAllIndices. The default is

SAIsimp[a_] := Expand[Together[a/.SAIsimpRules];
SAIsimpRules = {}.

■ SAIsimpRules

SAIsimpRules gives a list of rules to be applied in SetAllIndices. See SAIsimp.

■ ScalarR

ScalarR is the Riemann scalar.

■ ScalarRtoAffine

ScalarRtoAffine[expr] replaces any appearance of ScalarR in expr by its equivalent in terms of affine connections, AffineG. Dummy indices appear with standard system-generated names.

- ## ScalarRtoAffineRule

  ApplyRules[expr], ScalarRtoAffineRule] replaces any appearances of ScalarR in expr by their equivalents in terms of affine connections, AffineG. New dummy indices appear with $ prefixes.

- ## SecondCubicRiemannRule

  SecondCubicRiemannRule relates the product of three Riemann tensors with certain cross sums to another product with pair-to-pair sums.

- ## SecondQuadraticRiemannRule

  SecondQuadraticRiemannRule is the inverse of FirstQuadraticRiemannRule.

- ## SetAllIndices

  SetAllIndices[t[la,lb]] assumes that all components with indices in the indicated position (lower in this case) are already assigned, and sets the appropriate values to all the other components. All components of Metricg should already be assigned since they are used to raise and lower indices as needed. All indices in the argument should be symbols, not integers, and should be of the same type, i.e., all lower or all upper. The components to be set should not already be assigned, since such assignments will not be changed. See also SetMovedIndices, SetEuclideanIndices.

- ## SetAntisymmetric

  SetAntisymmetric[tensor[la,lb,lc,ld,le]] will make tensor totally antisymmetric in all its indices. The names of the indices entered do not matter. To get proper formatting, first use DefineTensor to define the tensor of the desired rank with no symmetries, as in DefineTensor[tensor,t,{{1,2,3,4,5},1}].

- ## SetComponents

  SetComponents[tens[la,ub],Metricg[la,lc]*ta[uc,ld]*tb[ud,ub]] will sum dummy indices over concrete values and evaluate the expression in the second argument for all concrete values of the free indices (here la,ub), setting the result equal to the corresponding components of tens. Dimension should be set first to an integer. If components already have values, their values will not be changed by SetComponents. See also ClearComponents.

- ## SetEuclideanIndices

  SetEuclideanIndices[t[1a,1b]] assumes that the components of t with indices in the indicated positions are already assigned and assigns all other components of t, assuming the metric is Euclidean. The indices in the argument should be symbolic indices, not integers. All of the indices should be at the same level, upper or lower. Any number of indices up to four can appear in the tensor. See also SetMovedIndices, SetAllIndices.

- ## SetMovedIndices

  SetMovedIndices[t1[ua,ub],t2[1c,1d]] will take the components of t2[1c,1d], that are assumed to be known, and will apply Metricg to raise both indices, assigning the resulting values to the components of t1[ua,ub]. Conventionally, the tensor name t1 will be the same as t2, although that is not strictly required. In general, the second argument should indicate the positions of the components that are already assigned values, and the first argument should indicate the positions of the indices for that you wish to have components calculated by raising or lowering with the metric tensor. Another example is SetMovedIndices[s[1a,ub,uc],s[ud,ue,1f]], that would use Metricg to lower the first and raise the third index. Only symbolic indices, not integers, should appear in the arguments, and any two indices should not be either the same or the upper and lower versions of the same index. To save time, no simplification is done, so you may wish to simplify the results. See also SetAllIndices, SetEuclideanIndices.

- ## SetSymmetric

  SetSymmetric[tensor[1a,1b,1c,1d,1e]] will make tensor totally symmetric in all its indices. The names of the indices entered do not matter. To get proper formatting, first use DefineTensor to define the tensor of the desired rank with no symmetries, as in
  DefineTensor[tensor,"t",{{1,2,3,4,5},1}].

- ## ShowNumbers

  ShowNumbers[expr] splits up expr and numbers the terms so that a user can then find a particular term in expr.

■ ShowTime

On[ShowTime] turns timing information on. Off[ShowTime] turns it off again. The time taken for each command is printed just before the results (if any) of the command. ShowTime is not loaded automatically by *MathTensor*. You may turn it on with the On[ShowTime] command.

■ SIUnits

Entering the input line SIUnits will set up SI or rationalized MKS units in electromagnetism by setting the constants Maxwellk1 and Maxwellk3 to values Maxwellk1 = (4*Pi*Eps0)∧(-1) ; Maxwellk3 = 1. See also Maxwellk1, Maxwellk3, emuUnits, esuUnits, GaussianUnits, HeavisideLorentzUnits, RationalizedGaussianUnits, RationalizedMKSUnits, SIUnits.

■ SuperApplyRules

SuperApplyRules[expr,Rules] is a more powerful version of ApplyRulesRepeated. It may take much longer to give the most simplified expression but is guaranteed to apply all rules as many times as possible. Most users will not need this except in very large computations. SuperApplyRules[expr,Rules,n] will apply to the nth term in expr only. See ApplyRules, ApplyRulesRepeated, CanSuperApplyRules.

■ SwapDum

SwapDum[expr,a] raises and lowers the dummy indices in expr. The pairs are defined by each element of the list {a}. {a} has one element from each pair that the user wishes to swap up and down. This function is primarily used to put terms into some particular form that the user wants that is different from the canonicalizer's form.

■ Symmetries

Symmetries[tensor[la,lb,...]] returns a list of the permutations and weights entered using DefineTensor for the symmetries of tensor under permutations of the indices. Symmetries will also return a short list of symmetries of *MathTensor* system-defined tensors. For example, Symmetries[RicciR[la,lb]] gives {{2,1},1}. See also AllSymmetries, MakePermWeightGroup, MakeAllSymmetries.

■ **SymmetriesOfSymbol**

SymmetriesOfSymbol[name] returns a set of lists of symmetries assigned to tensors having the symbol name. For example, if r[la,lb] is symmetric and r[la,lb,lc] is symmetric only in the last two indices, then SymmetriesOfSymbol[r] returns {{{2,1},1},{{1,3,2},1}} with the permutations and weights listed in the order that the symmetries were assigned. Entering ??SymmetriesOfSymbol will return this message followed by a listing of tensors with their assigned symmetries.

■ **Symmetrize**

Symmetrize[expr,la,lb,...], where expr contains sums and products of tensors and la,lb,... are among the indices, will yield the tensor formed from expr, symmetrized with respect to indices a,b,.... Thus Symmetrize[f[la,lb,lc],la,lb] gives (1/2)(f[la,lb,lc]+f[lb,la,lc]). Factor and function names should not be the same as index names when applying Symmetrize.

■ **SyntaxCheck**

SyntaxCheck[expr] looks for unbalanced indices, duplicated indices, and bad dummy indices in a tensor equation. It can be applied explicitly or turned on or off using On[SyntaxCheck] and Off[SyntaxCheck]. It is designed to look for expressions with la or ub type indices and to not affect nontensorial input equations. See also SyntaxCheckOff, SyntaxCheckOn.

■ **SyntaxCheckOff**

SyntaxCheckOff turns off automatic use of the SyntaxCheck function.

■ **SyntaxCheckOn**

SyntaxCheckOn turns on automatic use of the SyntaxCheck function.

■ **TensorForm**

On[TensorForm] causes built-in and user-defined tensors to print to the screen in properly formatted tensor notation. This is the default setting. Off[TensorForm] causes tensors to print to the screen in the same form as the input. See also PrettyOn and PrettyOff.

- **TensorPart**

  `TensorPart[expr]` returns the tensorial factors in an expression. Here, `expr` should not be a sum of terms.

- **TensorPartSameQ**

  `TensorPartSameQ[expr1,expr2]` returns `True` if the tensor parts of `expr1` and `expr2` are identical and `False` otherwise. Here, `expr1` and `expr2` should not be sums of terms.

- **TensorQ**

  `TensorQ[expr]` returns `True` if `expr` contains tensors and `False` otherwise. Here, `expr` should not be a sum of terms.

- **TensorRankOfForm**

  `TensorRankOfForm[expr]`, when acting on a differential form expression, that may contain tensor-valued forms, gives the tensor rank of the expression, i.e., the number of tensor indices coming from tensor-valued forms in the expression. `TensorRankOfForm` does not recognize that contracted tensor indices do not contribute to the rank of a tensor. Thus it also counts contracted indices.

- **TensorSimp**

  `TensorSimp[expr]`, where `expr` is a sum of terms, will combine terms that are equal in `expr`. It will recognize trace and similar identities involving dummy indices. It will not recognize equality of terms under complicated symmetry transformation, as will `Tsimplify`. Sometimes it is advantageous to apply `TensorSimp` prior to canonicalization to reduce the number of terms or to find and simplify terms involving traces and internal summations. See also `Tsimplify`, `CanAll`, `Canonicalize`.

- **TensorSimpAfter**

  `TensorSimpAfter[expr,n]`, where `expr` is a sum of terms and `n` is an integer, will start at term `n` in the sum and combine terms that are equal in `expr`. It will leave unchanged the terms of the sum that come before term `n`. It will recognize trace and similar identities involving dummy indices. It will not recognize equality of terms under complicated symmetry transformation, as will `TsimplifyAfter`. See also `TensorSimp`, `Tsimplify`, `TsimplifyAfter`.

■ TraceFreeRicciR

TraceFreeRicciR[la,lb] is the trace-free part of the Ricci tensor. It is given in arbitrary dimensions.

■ TraceFreeRicciToRicciRule

TraceFreeRicciToRicciRule converts expressions with trace-free Ricci tensors to expressions with Ricci tensors and ScalarR's.

■ Tsimplify

Tsimplify simplifies tensor expressions, taking full account of symmetries. The expression should already be expanded using Expand. There are four basic forms. Tsimplify[expr,n,m], where expr is a sum of products of tensors, will compare terms n and m of expr and combine them if their tensor parts are equal. It will also recognize if they vanish by symmetry. Tsimplify[expr,n] will compare term n with all other terms in expr and combine terms with term n if that is possible. Tsimplify[expr] will combine all terms in expr that can be combined. Tsimplify[expr] is used also in the case in which expr consists of a single term that is a product of tensors. In that case, the term will be tested to see if it vanishes as a result of symmetry. Tsimplify should not be used on expressions having operators that do not commute with Metricg, such as OD. See also TsimplifyAfter, DefineTensor, Symmetries, AllSymmetries.

■ TsimplifyAfter

TsimplifyAfter[expr,n], where expr is a sum of products of tensors, will compare terms n with all terms following it in expr and combine them with term n if their tensor parts are equal. Symmetries are fully taken into account. It will also recognize if term n vanishes by symmetry (even if term n is the last term in expr). TsimplifyAfter should not be used on expressions having operators that do not commute with Metricg, such as OD. See also Tsimplify, DefineTensor, Symmetries, AllSymmetries.

■ **Ttransform**

Ttransform[t,s[la,ub],{x1,x2,x3},{rhs1,rhs2,rhs3},1or-1] transforms
the components of s to a new coordinate system and names the transformed
tensor t. The indices in s give positions of indices for that the components
are known. The indices in t will have the same positions and are therefore not
specified. The list {x1,x2,x3} gives the names of the old coordinates if the
last argument of Ttransform is 1 (for forward transformation) or the names
of the new coordinates if the last argument is -1 (for inverse transformation).
The value of Dimension should already be set to the number of coordinates.
The list {rhs1,rhs2,rhs3} gives the right-hand sides of the coordinate transformation equations and should involve the coordinates named in the previous
list. The coordinate names and components of the t should not already have
assignments.

■ **Units**

Units is a list of the unit systems that are being used. The choices of electromagnetic unit systems are emu, esu, Gaussian, Heaviside-Lorentz or rationalized
Gaussian, and Rationalized MKS or SI units. In addition, one may choose
natural units or gravitational units. See the file Conventions.m for definitions.
The choice of Rationalized MKS (or SI) units with natural or gravitational
units is inconsistent. The speed of light is Lightc, Planck's constant divided
by 2 Pi is hbar, and the Newtonian gravitational constant is NewtonG.

■ **Unlist**

Unlist[expr] is useful in forming a range of arguments of Do from a list of lists.
expr is a list.

■ **Updowndummylist**

Updowndummylist is the union of the Up and Down dummy lists.

■ **Updummylist**

Updummylist is the list of contravariant dummy indices.

■ **Uplist**

Uplist is the union of Updummylist and Upuserlist.

- ## UpLo

  UpLo[up1,lo1] sets the value of up1 to be a new unique contravariant index and lo1 to the corresponding covariant index. These indices are used in rules or definitions involving dummy indices that are not input by the user and that must not duplicate existing index names in an expression. UpLo generates the new indices at the time the rule or definition is called. When TensorForm is On, the new indices print as a raised or lowered $ followed by an integer, such as $1. UpLo[up1,up2,...,lo1,lo2,...] sets the values of up1, up2,... to be a set of unique contravariant indices and the values of lo1,lo2,... to be the corresponding set of covariant indices. See also ApplyRules.

- ## UpLo(*)

  UpLo[up1,lo1] sets up1 to a unique system-generated upper dummy index of the regular type and lo1 to the corresponding unique lower dummy index of regular type. See also UpLoa, UpLob, UpLoc.

- ## UpLoa(*)

  UpLoa[aup1,alo1] sets aup1 to a unique system-generated upper dummy index of type-a and alo1 to the corresponding unique lower dummy index of type-a.

- ## UpLob(*)

  UpLob[bup1,blo1] sets bup1 to a unique system-generated upper dummy index of type-b and blo1 to the corresponding unique lower dummy index of type-b.

- ## UpLoc(*)

  UpLoc[cup1,clo1] sets cup1 to a unique system-generated upper dummy index of type-c and clo1 to the corresponding unique lower dummy index of type-c.

- ## UpperIndexAllTypesQ(*)

  UpperIndexAllTypesQ[index] -> True if index is an upper index of any type and False otherwise. See also UpperIndexQ, UpperIndexbQ, UpperIndexcQ, UpperIndexAllTypesQ, LowerIndexQ, LowerIndexaQ, LowerIndexbQ, LowerIndexcQ, LowerIndexAllTypesQ.

- ## UpperIndexaQ(*)

  UpperIndexaQ[index] -> True if index is an upper index of type-a and False
    otherwise. See also UpperIndexQ, UpperIndexbQ, UpperIndexcQ,
    UpperIndexAllTypesQ, LowerIndexQ, LowerIndexaQ, LowerIndexbQ,
    LowerIndexcQ, LowerIndexAllTypesQ.

- ## UpperIndexbQ(*)

  UpperIndexbQ[index] -> True if index is an upper index of type-b and False
    otherwise. See also UpperIndexQ, UpperIndexaQ, UpperIndexcQ,
    UpperIndexAllTypesQ, LowerIndexQ, LowerIndexaQ, LowerIndexbQ,
    LowerIndexcQ, LowerIndexAllTypesQ.

- ## UpperIndexcQ(*)

  UpperIndexcQ[index] -> True if index is an upper index of type-c and False
    otherwise. See also UpperIndexQ, UpperIndexaQ, UpperIndexbQ,
    UpperIndexAllTypesQ, LowerIndexQ, LowerIndexaQ, LowerIndexbQ,
    LowerIndexcQ, LowerIndexAllTypesQ.

- ## UpperIndexQ

  UpperIndexQ[x] returns True if x is a possible tensor upper index and False
    otherwise. If x is an integer or a pattern such as a_, then False is returned.
    See also IndexQ, LowerIndexQ.

- ## UpperIndexQ(*)

  UpperIndexQ[index] -> True if index is a regular upper index and False
    otherwise. See also UpperIndexa, UpperIndexbQ, UpperIndexcQ,
    UpperIndexAllTypesQ, LowerIndexaQ, LowerIndexbQ, LowerIndexcQ,
    LowerIndexAllTypesQ.

- ## Upuserlist

  Upuserlist is the list of tensor indices for use as contravariant indices.

- ## Varg

  Varg[la,lb] is the variation of Metricg[la,lb].

■ **Variation**

Variation[expr,Metricg] takes the functional variation of the expression, that is a functional of the metric, with respect to **Metricg** and canonicalizes the resulting expression.

■ **VariationalDerivative**

VariationalDerivative[expr,Metricg,la,lb] factors off the Varg term from a functional derivative with respect to the metric. The resulting free indices ua and ub can be whatever the user wants.

■ **VectorA**

VectorA[la] = CD[Varg[la,lb],ub] is used as a shorthand notation in problems involving the variations of the metric.

■ **VectorAFlag**

When VectorAFlag is set to True, the object CD[Varg[la,lb],ub] is automatically set to VectorA[la].

■ **WeylC**

WeylC[ua,lb,lc,ld] is the Weyl tensor. It is given in arbitrary dimensions.

■ **WeylToRiemannRule**

WeylToRiemannRule converts expressions with WeylC's to expressions with Riemann tensors, Ricci tensors, and ScalarR's.

■ **XD**

XD[w] is the exterior derivative of a *p*-form w. XD[w] is a $(p+1)$-form. The flag XDtoCDflag controls whether the command FtoC acting on exterior derivatives will produce components involving covariant derivatives CD or ordinary partial derivatives OD. When exterior derivatives are converted to components, by default covariant derivatives CD will appear. If you want ordinary partial derivatives OD to appear instead, you must turn off XDtoCDflag by typing Off[XDtoCDflag]. When using tensor-valued *p*-forms, you should turn off XDtoCDflag before applying FtoC to produce components. The reason is that in the covariant derivative, there are affine connection terms associated with the tensor indices of the tensor-valued *p*-form, and those terms would not be taken into account if XDtoCDflag were True. See also FtoC, XDtoCDflag, XP, CoXD, HodgeStar, GenLap, Lap.

- **XDtoCDFlag**

  Same as `XDtoCDflag`.

- **XDtoCDflag**

  When `XDtoCDflag` is `True`, `FtoC` will replace exterior derivatives `XD` by expressions involving covariant derivatives `CD`. When `XDtoCDflag` is `False`, `FtoC` will replace exterior derivatives by expressions involving ordinary partial derivatives `OD`. The default setting is `XDtoCDflag = True` because covariant derivatives of the `Epsilon` tensor are zero, that simplifies expressions involving `XD` and `HodgeStar`, such as the codifferential and the generalized Laplacian. When using tensor-valued p-forms, the user should turn off `XDtoCDflag` by typing `Off[XDtoCDflag]`, that sets the flag to `False` and updates the system. The flag can be turned on again by typing `On[XDtoCDflag]`. See also `FtoC`, `DefineTensor`.

- **XP**

  `XP[expr1,expr2]` is the exterior product of `expr1` and `expr2`, where `expr1` and `expr2` are any differential form expressions. There can be up to four differential form arguments of `XP`. The infix form of `XP[f,g]` is `f~XP~g`, where `f` and `g` are forms. See also `FtoC`, `RankForm`, `XD`, `CoXD`, `HodgeStar`, `GenLap`, `Lap`.

- **ZeroDegreeQ**

  `ZeroDegreeQ[expr]` is `True` if `expr` is a 0-form or tensor-valued 0-form and `False` otherwise. `ZeroDegreeQ` differs from `ZeroFormQ` because the latter will not recognize that a component of a form or tensor-valued form is a scalar of degree zero.

- **ZeroFormQ**

  `ZeroFormQ[object]` returns `True` if the `object` is a 0-form and `False` otherwise.

Bibliography

This is an alphabetically ordered list of the books and articles referenced
in this book.

1. S. Chandrasekhar, *The Mathematical Theory of Black Holes* (Oxford University Press, Oxford, 1983).

2. M. Crampin and F. A. E. Pirani, *Applicable Differential Geometry* (Cambridge University Press, Cambridge, 1986).

3. T. Eguchi, P. B. Gilkey, and A. J. Hanson, Physics Reports **66**, 213–393 (1980).

4. A. Einstein, *The Meaning of Relativity* (Princeton University Press, Princeton, 1950).

5. H. Flanders, *Differential Forms* (Academic Press, New York, 1963).

6. A. E. Green and W. Zerna, *Theoretical Elasticity* (Oxford University Press, London, 1968).

7. J. D. Jackson, *Classical Electrodynamics* (John Wiley and Sons, New York, 1962)

8. C. W. Misner, K. S. Thorne, and J. A. Wheeler, *Gravitation* (W. H. Freeman and Company, San Francisco, 1973).

9. E. Schrödinger, *Space-Time Structure* (Cambridge University Press, London, 1963).

10. A. J. M. Spencer, *Continuum Mechanics* (Longman Group Ltd., London, 1980).

11. R. M. Wald, *Gravity* (University of Chicago Press, Chicago, 1984).

12. S. Weinberg, *Gravitation and Cosmology* (John Wiley & Sons, New York, 1972).

13. S. Wolfram, *Mathematica* (Addison-Wesley Publishing Company, Reading, Mass., 1991).

Index

MathTensor commands appear in boldface. If an entry for an object appears twice, the entry with an asterisk refers to the object after its definition has been altered during a *MathTensor* session by the user entering the command **AddIndexTypes** to increase the types of indices available.

369

The presentations in this book are based on *MathTensor* version 2.2. *MathTensor* is in academic, research, and commercial use worldwide. The *MathTensor* software requires *Mathematica* and is available for any computer that runs *Mathematica*.

MathTensor can be obtained by contacting your *Mathematica* dealer or from:

MathSolutions, Inc.   or   MathSolutions, Inc.
3049 N. Lake Drive   P.O. Box 16175
Milwaukee, WI 53211   Chapel Hill, NC 27516
USA   USA

Telephone: 414-964-6284 or 919-967-9853
Fax: 414-964-6284 or 919-967-9853
Email: mathtensor@wri.com

You may also fax or mail the following form to MathSolutions, Inc.

Please send information on *MathTensor* to:
(print or type carefully)

Name: _____

Institution: _____

Address: _____

_____

City: _____ State: _____

Zip/Postal Code: _____

Country: _____

Send information by:

☐ Regular Mail

☐ Fax: _____

☐ Email: (address) _____

Telephone: _____

Computer Type: _____

Mathematica Version: _____
(type $Version in a *Mathematica* session)

Potential Applications of *MathTensor*: _____

_____